PRAISE FOR *VALUES IN FO*ᵣₑᵢ*ɢN POLICY:*
INVESTIGATING IDEALS AND INTERESTS

What a rich harvest! With insight and verve, a constellation of esteemed
scholars appraises the charged and sometimes contradictory place national
(and transnational) values that can play to shape dispositions and decisions by key actors. Truly global in scope, the book reveals how specific,
situated patterns guide these discernments and determinations in a world
oriented to power, shaped by national particularities, and divided by sovereign boundaries.
            —**Ira Katznelson**, Ruggles Professor of Political Science
                              and History, Columbia University

At a time when rising populism, 'deal-making' and transactional diplomacy are
widely seen to be in the ascendant, this collection of essays could not be more
timely. It is never a simple question of either values or interests when it comes
to understanding to the conduct and drivers of foreign policy. What is needed
is a deeper appreciation of the complex relationship between the two. This is
precisely what this stimulating and thought-provoking book offers.
            —**Mats Berdal**, Professor of International Relations,
                              King's College London

With great intellectual verve the contributors to this volume engage with
the question of values in a world in which many old certainties about public
goods such as democracy and human rights are being questioned as never
before. The book provides a very worthy contribution to a critical and ongoing debate.
            —**Christopher Coker**, Professor of International Relations,
                      Director of IDEAS, London School of Economics

Many countries claim to conduct a foreign policy based on moral values or
ethical principles. In reality these claims have to compete with international
realities, power politics and the unforeseeable. This wide-ranging book
reflects the long and distinguished careers of its contributors in the clarity
and incisiveness with which it tackles this complex field and establishes the
essential elements in a major constituent of foreign policy as conducted in
Asia and the West.
            —**Sir Roger Hervey**, Former British Ambassador

Every country decides on its national interests and values and then pursues them pragmatically. You can read what these are in *Values in Foreign Policy*. You can then judge which countries are better prepared to accept the responsibilities for combating global problems such as accelerating climate change, religious and ethnic wars, poverty and mass migration.

—**Sir Colin Imray**, Former British Ambassador

The question of different countries' values and how, if at all, they are reflected in foreign policy is one of great importance for the future world order. Srinivasan, a distinguished Indian diplomat, and his co-editors have done us a great service in reaching beyond the usual Western academic suspects and bringing together perspectives on this crucial issue from different parts of the world.

—**Edward Mortimer**, Fellow of All Souls College,
University of Oxford

Values in Foreign Policy: Investigating Ideals and Interests discusses value systems lying behind foreign policies of major international players, often touching on their historical and cultural legacies, and compares them with their actual practices and pragmatic adjustments. It contains eighteen contributions of authors specialising in the foreign policies of important countries of Asia and the West. Written in very accessible language, this book is a must-read not only for policy makers and practitioners of foreign policy but for all interested in international relations.

—**Diwakar Acharya**, Spalding Professor of Eastern
Religion and Ethics, University of Oxford

As interest in foreign policy is being reignited and re-imagined to explore the values of multiple nations in an increasingly non-Western world, this is a very timely book. That it is written with an eye to context and fabric, and in language that makes sense to the world beyond the hallowed corridors of technical power, makes it not just timely but an important book for our time. Edited by Krishnan Srinivasan, this is a book that no one with an interest in foreign policy should miss.

—**Jeanne-Marie Gescher**, Senior Fellow,
SOAS China Institute

Values in Foreign Policy is about the relation of values to foreign policy. In a rather under-developed area of thinking, the studies in it are timely, clear and illuminating. The Introduction and inter alia, Krishnan Srinivasan's chapter on India, show a characteristic combination of objectivity, lucidity and mastery. It would be difficult to find a volume with a more subtle understanding of value systems.

—**Henry Mayr-Harting**, Former Regius Professor of
Ecclesiastical History, University of Oxford

At a time when the virtues of internationalisation and global citizenship are being challenged and borders seem to be narrowing, this is a timely book. In a series of lively essays, this book will be of interest to policy makers, NGOs and all interested in how pragmatism and idealism meet in diplomatic relations. It also contains a valuable critique of postcolonial legacies and how international relations are influenced by religion, culture and history.
—**Joanna Newman**, Secretary General, Association of Commonwealth Universities, London

At a time of great change and uncertainty in global affairs, the role of values and value systems in national foreign policies will be of crucial significance in moderating or exacerbating international tensions. In this book, a glittering array of scholars and former diplomats offer often startling insights into the nature, content and efficacy of values as they shape and affect the foreign policies of key countries in North America, Europe and, especially, Asia. Both individually and collectively they open up important new perspectives on the past, present and future of international relations.
—**Alex May**, Senior Research Editor, *Dictionary of National Biography*, University of Oxford

Values in Foreign Policy shows that, while the external activities of states are often analysed in terms of realpolitik, governments are guided by cultural parameters. This is evident when they claim to promote human rights – or alternatives to these values that are described as 'western'. But it is also true when rulers do not project any value-based discourse as then they comply unconsciously to some world view or *Weltanschauung*.
—**Christophe Jaffrelot**, Professor, Kings Institute London, Former Director CERI, Sciences Po, Paris

Values in Foreign Policy is a remarkable book with a truly global scope. It is an essential reading for anyone trying to understand the value systems in global politics in the twenty-first century.
—**Anders Andrén**, Professor, University of Stockholm

This book is a deep journey into the value systems shaping foreign policies around the world. An extremely important contribution today, when the connection between values and policy choices is increasingly confused and blurred.
—**Giorgio Barba Navaretti**, Professor of Economics, University of Milan

This book convincingly explores the interplay between theory and practice of different values in foreign policy, exemplified by expert studies on several countries in Asia, Europe and North America. The strength of this work lies, inter alia, in the fact that the detailed analyses of 'Asian' sets of values, especially when contrasted with 'the West', prove the great diversity of value systems in Asia based on their multi-religious background. The book also succeeds in illustrating that modern foreign policy cannot be fully comprehended without substantial historical knowledge of pre-modern Asian and European societies.

—**Annette Schmiedchen**, Humboldt University, Berlin

The book prompts a rethinking of many assumptions held about the role national values play in shaping a state's foreign policy. It explores how different countries can apply, export, exploit, ignore and sometimes wilfully controvert the values applied in their domestic policy in pursuit of international objectives. *Values in Foreign Policy* is an essential guide to both scholars and practitioners of diplomacy, as well as an informative and accessible read for anyone with even a passing interest in modern international history.

—**Anna Belkina**, Deputy Editor in Chief, Russia Today, Moscow

While reading the excellent chapter in *Values in Foreign Policy* by William J. Antholis on US foreign policy, key words caught my attention: multilateralism, engagement, democracy and intervention to protect these values. Antholis writes, 'While the president is the dominant player in setting US foreign policy, he cannot simply act alone'. This reinforces my faith in democracy and it is America which has to provide leadership.

—**Sushanta Duttagupta**, Professor and Former Vice Chancellor of Viswa Bharati University

The movement toward various forms of global convergence, even if fitful, with many areas fractious and contested, is now a reality for the world community. This pioneering book *Values in Foreign Policy* on the balance between values and the reality of foreign policy compulsions in different parts of the world is an essential and vital contribution to an understanding of the forces that will shape this evolution, which both the general reader and the expert will find gripping. You absolutely must buy this watershed publication, or at least make sure to read it.

—**Kamalesh Sharma**, Former Commonwealth Secretary General

While a good foreign policy should be based on a harmonious mix of national values and national interests, those who frame foreign policy usually know about their own value systems only, often misreading that of a neighbour or of more far-away countries. This has created a number of conflicts and even wars. Today the world has become a global village, but we still do not understand our neighbours and other nations. This book is important for those who believe that we can make the world better by understanding the values of the 'other'. Srinivasan and his colleagues should be congratulated on this compilation of the different value systems which lie at the heart of the foreign policies of all countries.

—**Claude Arpi**, Professor, United Service Institution of India

There is perhaps no riskier proposition in strategic discourse today than attempting to delineate values underlying decision-making in the realm of foreign policy. I commend Srinivasan, Mayall, Pulipaka and each author who has contributed to this seminal volume *Values in Foreign Policy* in providing valuable insights into, and seeking to make sense of, a complex set of variables. A state's values are not just part of its foreign policy; they are paramount to it. Asia's modern history is to a large extent about nations adapting their values to contemporaneous realities and attempting to fit the narrative to the circumstances.

—**M. K. Narayanan**, Former Indian Minister of State and National Security Adviser

In case of a conflict between pragmatism or national interest, and principles or values, the former invariably trumps the latter. Yet governments will try to convince their peoples that they are guided by principles. This book, edited by Srinivasan, Mayall and Pulipaka, will help readers understand how some countries genuinely want to abide by principles, but pressure from big powers, especially some permanent members of the UN Security Council, obliges them to deviate from their values. In the real world, there are no principles except hard power, military and economic.

—**Chinmaya Gharekhan**, Former Under Secretary General of the United Nations

The volume represents a timely and effective intervention to address the crucial issue of the relationship between value systems and the pursuit of foreign policy. Drawing upon case studies from all the main world power centres, the chapters reflect contemporary academic attempts to think beyond the age-old debate on the relative importance of ideology and realpolitik in international politics. The volume should be of interest to both practitioners of foreign policy and scholars in international relations.

—**Suranjan Das**, Professor and Vice Chancellor, Jadavpur University, Calcutta

Values in Foreign Policy brings together, in a garland of ideas, varied analyses by an impressive collection of foreign policy analysts. Foreign policy is necessarily an amalgam of idealism and realism, and the authors demonstrate how these interact with each other in policy formulation and implementation in the real world. A must-read for anyone with curiosity and interest in inter-state relations in the contemporary global matrix.

—**Iftekhar Ahmed Chowdhury**, Former Bangladesh Ambassador and Foreign Minister

Srinivasan, Mayall and Pulipaka have done great service by unpacking the dynamic tension between values and interests in the conduct of foreign policy by major nations. In doing so, they widen the terrain of a debate that has been traditionally framed in terms of a conflict between liberal international-ist and conservative conceptions of American/Western foreign policy or as a clash between 'Eastern' and 'Western' values. By taking a comparative perspective, the authors demonstrate the universal nature of the contradiction between high-minded ideals a nation proclaims and the pragmatic adaptation to the messy realities that its policy makers confront.

—**C. Raja Mohan**, Professor and Director, Institute of South Asian Studies, National University of Singapore

Values in Foreign Policy brilliantly captures the tensions between ideals and interests which have historically influenced policymaking across the globe. The work is particularly effective in tracking the progressive devaluation of value-based policymaking to a point where in the present world order relat-ing values to foreign policy appears almost an oxymoron. It is good to be reminded that there were moments in history where values did once play a role in some countries. The editors are to be commended for assembling such a wealth of expertise from across the world to give substance to their narrative.

—**Rehman Sobhan**, Professor and Founder Chairman of the Centre for Policy Dialogue, Dhaka

The editors of *Values in Foreign Policy* have compiled a set of incisive essays on the interplay of ethical aspirations and the practicalities of politics in the foreign policies of the world's most important players. I am convinced the book would be a tremendous contribution to an unexplored field of studies and invite keen attention. This book must find a place in the literature of international studies.

—**Takenori Horimoto**, Professor, Gifu University, Japan

Shared values define sovereignty, but, realistically, sovereign nations preach but rarely fully practise their values in totality. Srinivasan', Mayall and Pulip-aka's superb anthology of *Values in Foreign Policy* practised by key foreign policy countries is a first in comparative analysis of an increasingly vital area of foreign policy discourse, if not dispute. Its power rests on its realpolitik, yet penetrating insights, on an unending debate between Asian and Western values, thus a must-read and invaluable compass to all interested in what lies ahead in our rapidly changing global order.

—**Andrew Sheng**, Distinguished Fellow, Asia Global Institute, University of Hong Kong

Foreign policy is often understood to be driven above all by national interests. They do, indeed, matter greatly. Less well understood, but often equally important are national values colouring foreign policy preferences, for example, India's attachment to non-alignment between the superpowers during much of the Cold War. Krishnan Srinivasan, a former Indian foreign secretary and author on international relations, is ideally suited to exploring this proposition and to bringing together others who, in this volume, shed valuable light on it.

—**David M. Malone**, United Nations Under Secretary General, Chancellor of the United Nations University, Tokyo

A tremendously important work that explores the key values that drive the foreign policies of nations throughout the world. The book introduces the religions, cultures and historical experiences that define national values, and explicates how foreign policy decisions that otherwise seem difficult to understand make perfect sense once one understands the values undergirding the decisions.

—**Michael Puett**, Walter C. Klein Professor of Chinese History and Anthropology, Harvard University

Congratulations to the editors and their formidable range of contributors – *Values in Foreign Policy* is probably the first in-depth analysis of the relationship between values and foreign policy in different parts of the world, investigating the prospect of a consensus on a universal set of values to which all countries can subscribe. Looking at it from the perspective of academics and practitioners at values and rights – contrasting Western values with Asian values – is of crucial importance in looking to the future, with the rise of Asia in the decades to come.

—**Lord Karan Bilimoria**, House of Lords, UK

Authors from across the globe scrutinize foreign policies to reveal untidy, partially obscured mosaics of raw interests, professed ideals and assumed values. Taking perspective from east-west geography, history and political thought, this powerful collection of essays offers a range of views on when and how interests, values and power jostle to fill the foreground or seek to stay in the shadows. Combining incisive commentary with analytical depth, the book will appeal to practitioners and scholars of the diplomatic art.

—**Dame Sandra Dawson**, Professor Emerita of Management and former Master of Sidney Sussex College, Cambridge

Values in Foreign Policy

Values in Foreign Policy

Investigating Ideals and Interests

Edited by Krishnan Srinivasan,
James Mayall and Sanjay Pulipaka

ROWMAN & LITTLEFIELD
INTERNATIONAL
London • New York

Published by Rowman & Littlefield International Ltd
6 Tinworth Street, London SE11 5AL, United Kingdom
www.rowmaninternational.com
Rowman & Littlefield International Ltd.is an affiliate of Rowman & Littlefield
4501 Forbes Boulevard, Suite 200, Lanham, Maryland 20706, USA
With additional offices in Boulder, New York, Toronto (Canada), and Plymouth (UK)
www.rowman.com

British Library Cataloguing in Publication Data
A catalogue record for this book is available from the British Library

ISBN: HB 978-1-78660-749-2
          PB 978-1-78660-750-8

Library of Congress Cataloging-in-Publication Data

Names: Srinivasan, Krishnan, 1937– editor. | Mayall, James, editor. |
  Pulipaka, Sanjay, editor.
Title: Values in foreign policy : investigating ideals and interests /
  edited by Krishnan Srinivasan, James Mayall, and Sanjay Pulipaka.
Description: Lanham [Maryland] : Rowman & Littlefield International, 2019. |
  Includes bibliographical references and index.
Identifiers: LCCN 2018056382 (print) | LCCN 2019000337 (ebook) |
  ISBN 9781786607515 (electronic) | ISBN 9781786607492 |
  ISBN 9781786607492 (cloth ; alk. paper) | ISBN 9781786607508
  (pbk. ; alk. paper)
Subjects: LCSH: International relations and culture. | Values—Political
  aspects. | Values—Political aspects—Asia. | Asia—Foreign relations. |
  Political culture—Asia. | East and West.
Classification: LCC JZ1251 (ebook) | LCC JZ1251 .V35 2019 (print) |
  DDC 172/.4—dc23
LC record available at https://lccn.loc.gov/2018056382

Printed in the United States of America

The projection of attitudes, poses, and rhetoric that cause us to appear noble and altruistic in the mirror of our own vanity . . . lacks substance when related to the realities of international life.

—George F. Kennan, 1985

In the real world of politics, even in countries which claim to follow Jesus or Buddha, moral arguments do not carry weight.

—Parmeshwar Narayan Haksar, 1998

International politics is about values and principle, but first and foremost about what is possible. What matters is doing your job, not your principles. That the means match the ends can be maintained only by someone who has no notion of politics, let alone of a nation's fight for independence.

—Bernhard Jaumann, 2010

The problem comes in when moralistic impulses begin to intrude on the execution of a reasonable, responsible, and rational foreign policy, which is where we are today.

—James Carden, 2018

Acknowledgements

Our deep gratitude to Tata Trusts without whose support this book could not have been written; and to Rajat Kathuria and the Indian Council for Research on International Economic Relations for their invaluable support. We acknowledge the help in New Delhi of Shakti Sinha and the Nehru Memorial Museum and Library, and in Kolkata of the Azad Institute of Asian Studies.

Our thanks to Oliver Gadsby, Dhara Snowden and Rebecca Anastasi of Rowman & Littlefield International for their constant encouragement.

Contents

Abbreviations

ACP	African, Caribbean and Pacific Group
ADB	Asian Development Bank
AFC (US)	America First Committee
AIIB	Asian Infrastructure Investment Bank
AK Party	Adalet ve Kalkınma Partisi (Justice and Development Party)
ASEAN	Association of Southeast Asian Nations
BIMSTEC	Bay of Bengal Initiative for Multi-Sectoral Technical and Economic Cooperation
BREXIT	Britain's Exit from European Union
BRI	Belt and Road Initiative
BRICS	Brazil, Russia, India, China and South Africa
CCP	Common Commercial Policy
CIA	Central Intelligence Agency
CIS	Commonwealth of Independent States
CPSU	Communist Party of the Soviet Union
COMECON	Council for Mutual Economic Assistance
CTBT	Comprehensive Test Ban Treaty
Da'esh	Al-Dawla al-Islamiya fil Iraq wa al-Sham (Islamic State)
EAEU	Eurasian Economic Union
ECSC	European Coal and Steel Community
EEC	European Economic Community
EU	European Union
FBI	Federal Bureau of Investigation
FRG	Federal Republic of Germany
GATT	General Agreement on Tariffs and Trade
GDR	German Democratic Republic
GSP	Generalised System of Preferences

HAMAS	Ḥarakat al-Muqāwamah al-ʾIslāmiyyah Islamic Resistance Movement
IAEA	International Atomic Energy Agency
IFOR	Implementation Force
IMF	International Monetary Fund
IR	International Relations
JBIC	Japan Bank for International Cooperation
KGB	Komitet Gosudarstvennoy Bezopasnosti
KMT	Kuomintang
LDC	Less developed country
LDP	Liberal Democratic Party
LGBT	Lesbian, Gay, Bisexual and Transgender
LTTE	Liberation Tigers of Tamil Eelam
MEA	Ministry of External Affairs
MFN	Most favoured nation
NAFTA	North American Free Trade Agreement
NAM	Non-Aligned Movement
NATO	North Atlantic Treaty Organization
NGO	Non-governmental organization
NHK	Nippon Hōsō Kyōkai
NLD	National League for Democracy
NPT	Non-Proliferation Treaty
NSA	National Security Agency
NSS	National Security Strategy
ODA	Official Development Assistance
OECD	Organisation for Economic Co-operation and Development
OIC	Organisation of Islamic Cooperation
OSCE	Organisation for Security and Cooperation in Europe
PCP	Sekkyokuteki heiwa-shugi (Proactive Contribution to Peace)
PKI	Indonesian Communist Party
PRC	People's Republic of China
RIA	Russian Agency of International Information
RMB	Renminbi
ROC	Russian Orthodox Church
ROK	Republic of Korea
RSS	Rashtriya Swayamsevak Sangh
SCO	Shanghai Cooperation Organisation
SDF	Self-Defence Forces
SEATO	Southeast Asia Treaty Organisation
SFOR	Stabilization Force
SIPRI	Stockholm International Peace Research Institute
SPD	Social Democratic Party of Germany

SSBN	Ballistic-Missile Submarines
SSOD	Union of Soviet Friendship Societies
	(Soiuz Sovetskikh Obshchestv Druzhby)
THAAD	Terminal High Altitude Area Defense
TPP	Trans-Pacific Partnership
TTIP	Transatlantic Trade and Investment Partnership
UAE	United Arab Emirates
UK	United Kingdom
UN	United Nations
UNESCO	United Nations Educational, Scientific and Cultural Organization
UNGA	United Nations General Assembly
UNPKO	UN Peacekeeping Operations
US	United States
USA	United States of America
USNS	United States Naval Ship
USSR	Union of Soviet Socialist Republics
VOD	Value-oriented diplomacy
VOKS	All-Union Association for Cultural Relations
	(Vsesoiuznoe Obshchestvo Kul'turnoi Sviazi s zagranitse)
WTO	World Trade Organisation

Foreword

The Role of Values in Foreign Policy

Robert D. Kaplan

Foreign policy is ultimately the extension of a country's domestic condition: that is, the foreign extension of its domestic hopes and dreams and fears. When the domestic and economic circumstances of a country change, so too, must its foreign policy. And foremost among those domestic hopes and fears is an idea about the world that the state in question hopes to put forward. A state's values are not just part of its foreign policy, but they are paramount to it.

This is true not only of individual states but also of great empires. Indeed, small states must have survival itself as their core value. But a great state or empire can only operate as such with an equally grand conception, which, at least in its own mind, is idealistic to some degree. Usually, in the case of empires, from Rome to Great Britain, that conception, or value, has to do with its own culture: the more it spreads its own cultural values, the better off the world and the territories it conquers or influences will be.

Obviously, this can often be delusional, or self-serving, or cynical even, but it does not negate the fact that without such a belief in its own values, a foreign policy of any kind is nearly impossible to execute. Indeed, once a great state or empire loses such a belief in its own values, it must proceed into decline.

The subject of values of foreign policy is particularly acute in our own era. For the early twenty-first century, make no mistake, is a time of empire just like previous epochs, however much this phenomenon may be denied; and even if the European colonial systems of the modern age have vanished. The United States, for example, since the end of World War II, has been an empire in all but name, as scholars have said. This American Empire of sorts, as it loses its value system of encouraging free trade and democracy, is slipping into decline. Meanwhile, the United States and the world are faced with a rising Chinese Empire, again, in all but name. To be sure, China's Belt and Road Initiative across Eurasia recalls the Tang and Yuan dynasties, and across the Indian Ocean recalls the early Ming dynasty.

The American value system, which for decades motivated its foreign policy, was missionary in temperament: *adopt our belief system as your own and you shall be as happy as we are.* The Chinese value system is more elusive, yet just as real. The Chinese, encompassing a civilization thousands of years old, harbour no doubts about their own centrality, and therefore believe that a world, under a benign Chinese hegemony, will benefit just as much as East Asia once did under a Chinese tributary system.

India, too, encompasses a great world civilization. By pushing out its own sphere of influence it can serve as a balancer, helping to manage China's rise. There is intrinsic value in this for the peace of Eurasia and the world. The degree to which Indians can engage in an internal discussion about what their civilizational values are – and how they can help improve the world – will actually advance India's power and influence.

Japanese, German, French, Arab, Iranian and other values are also central to foreign policy as it is practised in these and other nations. Japanese and German values are partly tied to repentance over the crimes of World War II. French values are tied to the idea of French cultural and imperial greatness, as are, in a different but comparable way, Iranian values. Arab values are connected to pride in a language in which the Koran itself was written.

Because values are often spread through the projection of power, understanding a world of competing powers requires a discussion of values.

Introduction

Values and Foreign Policy

Krishnan Srinivasan, James Mayall, Sanjay Pulipaka

SETTING THE SCENE

Every generation has the task of engaging anew in the arduous search for the right way to order human affairs, said Pope Benedict XVI at the United Nations.[1] For several generations, governments have claimed that their foreign policy is based on a value system, and that they behave ethically in their dealings with foreign countries. Whatever the style of government, and however much the professed value system is shown to be a desirable rather than a practical guide to the conduct of foreign policy, the public over whom governments preside expects the enunciation of some values-based guidelines to justify their actions. This book examines the values professed by some major countries in three continents: America, Asia and Europe. This does not at all imply that countries of the Southern Hemisphere do not profess values in the pursuit of foreign policy, but the limitations of space and the need for some degree of coherence have circumscribed our examination. Of the countries examined, all are within the top seventeen in the International Monetary Fund 2017 world gross domestic product table,[2] which suggests they possess considerable weight in geopolitics, with outliers Iran at position 27 and Myanmar at 72.

Seventeen contributors to this volume attempt to identify the values that drive foreign policy in these locations. Two questions we have sought to answer are first, whether there is any discrete set of values that can be identified as Asian; and second, if indeed there are, whether those are congruent or in competition with values which originated and evolved in the West and are represented as a universal consensus.

Values are principles or standards of behaviour by which good and bad, right and wrong, may be assessed. Traditional values are a common feature

1

among individuals, and common behaviour derives from shared culture. Values can vary according to generation, class, education, origin, tradition and modernity, and provide the motivation to influence outcomes both in the minds of people and in governments. Although some are shared across cultures, it is the contrast of values in different cultures that accounts for many misunderstandings and misperceptions between countries. These distinctions are particularly marked between the West and Asia.

Values influence foreign policy especially when a country is strong enough to project power or influence. Where they have no foundation in power or cannot be supported by willing partners, they will not be taken seriously, as pointed out by Tadashi Anno in his chapter on Japan. Values that seem useful only for one country's particular interests could jeopardize its relations with other countries which do not share those interests. It is important therefore to recognize that values can lead to either agreement or discord with other countries.

There is no universal seedbed in which values germinate. Some countries derive them from foundational charters; others from inherited codes of behaviour, still others from religious sources, and most from an admixture of all these. Not all countries seek to propagate their values beyond their territorial boundaries, but every country believes that its values have moral standing.

Diplomatic engagement necessitates some knowledge of the values that originate in different national and local traditions because these are closely intertwined with global policies. This is an under-researched field of study even in foreign ministries across the world, where little importance is attached to the bedrocks of policy in other countries although sensitivity to this aspect should lead to more fruitful interactions. Another purpose of our project follows from this observation: it is to examine to what extent the values of certain axial countries have been successfully projected in the international arena and whether, despite differences between cultures, there is any prospect of arriving at a consensus on an universal set of values to which all countries can subscribe.

THE ANALYTICAL FRAMEWORK:
ACADEMICS AND PRACTITIONERS

The answer to this last question has long preoccupied theorists. In *The Anarchical Society* Hedley Bull[3] made the case for the existence of an international society which was simultaneously grounded in sovereignty but also embraced a set of common values and institutions that, however minimally, nonetheless transcended differences of ideology, culture and religion. These values are hotly contested from rival philosophical perspectives. Bull, who was a liberal realist, identified three, which, for our purposes, can be reduced to classical realism and rational liberalism. Within the limits set by an unchanging human nature and the quest for power, the former allows a role for human agency and hence values, while the essence of rationalism is the belief that human nature is malleable and that society can be improved through institutional cooperation. The Charter of the United Nations represents a compromise between these positions. Its underlying ideas are essentially Western, but only one state, Indonesia, ever tried to leave, and then not for very long.

For most practitioners and many academics, realism remains the default position in the study of international politics. Few realists have much time for international society and all believe in the primacy of interests over values. The difference between classical realism and neo-realism is the role allotted to human agency. Hans Morgenthau,[4] perhaps the most celebrated classicist, noted the need for 'distinguishing in politics between truth and opinion – between what is true objectively and rationally, supported by evidence and illuminated by reason, and what is only a subjective judgement, divorced from the facts as they are and informed by prejudice and wishful thinking'. He called on policymakers to distinguish 'between their "official duty" to advance the national interest, and their "personal wish", to see their own moral values and political principles realized throughout the world'. Neo-realists like Kenneth Waltz[5] discounted agency and argued that under conditions of anarchy what matters is the material capabilities of states, so that the unipolar/bipolar/multipolar structure of the international political system defines the responses of actors, rather than beliefs or values.

Both classical and neo-realism have limitations as explanatory frameworks. The former's principles do not explain how the policymaker rationally prioritizes the national interest; the latter does not explain how actors interpret the structure and, more importantly, how choices are made from among the available options.

The end of the Cold War in 1989 was greeted with enthusiasm by liberal thinkers and democratic governments. It was in this context that a new wave of liberal constructivists, like Alexander Wendt,[6] made an impact with their examination of the social identities of states and their shared ideas and values. Over the past decades three different kinds of constructivism have been put forward; systemic, unit-level and holistic.[7] The first focuses on the interaction between nation states, the second on domestic politics and national identities and the third on integrating the systemic and unit levels of analysis. The chapters in this book combine the second and third approaches to the interaction between values and foreign policy. In common usage the word 'values' refers to ethical principles that distinguish between binary opposites such as good and bad, but in this volume the word is defined as principles that influence political beliefs and action, and not deployed with an intention to pass judgement on political ideas or foreign policies.

VALUES AND RIGHTS

One of the unresolved debates about the nature of international society sketched in the previous section has been between those who hold that the shared value of respect for sovereignty confines cooperation strictly to the external relations of states and others who believe that sovereignty can and should be limited. These rival conceptions are termed, respectively, pluralist and solidarist. Pluralists believe that sovereignty trumps human rights and that international society can comprise radically different kinds of regime. To the extent that they acknowledge the existence of international society at all, it is the position adopted by classical realists. Solidarists believe in a community of mankind and in the convergence and deepening of its range of shared values.[8]

While both conceptions of values are of European origin, deriving from Aristotle, Judeo-Christianity, Magna Carta, the Enlightenment and the French Revolution, the first manifestation of solidarism appeared after the American War of Independence and, as far as the United States is concerned, has remained remarkably consistent since. It was re-exported to Europe and, through the conduit of European colonialism and imperialism, was arguably transformed into a universal yardstick. The pluralist conception had meanwhile developed in Europe from the middle of the seventeenth century and the fusion of pluralist and solidarist principles in the UN Charter was largely an Anglo-American construct.[9]

Most Western governments found the will to enshrine human rights into law, and their protection became the responsibility of the state. American President Woodrow Wilson was the first to propose a platform of universal values in 1918, but the League of Nations was unable to gain international acceptability for them. In the idealism that marked the end of World War II, values were transformed into rights when the UN General Assembly adopted the Universal Declaration of Human Rights. While not legally binding, member states were urged to abide by these commitments, and the normative language of the Declaration influenced the constitutions of several newly independent states, leading in 1966 and 1976 to the Covenants of Civil and Political Rights and Economic, Social and Cultural Rights. Along with the codification of the rights of women, children and the Convention against Torture, these documents are the foundational values professed most prominently by Western countries. After 1989 solidarist sentiment convinced liberal internationalists that these values should be promoted worldwide.

Priority was given in the Universal Declaration to individual rights, with the exception of the right to self-determination, and to civil and political over economic, social and cultural rights, with the recognition of the right to property as the first and for many subsequent years the sole economic right.[10] Human rights as both a moral ideal and pragmatic foreign policy tool can be frustrating for idealists but have maintained a grip on global politics when backed by the world's most powerful states. Normally the continuing power of sovereignty should itself signal the limits of universality, but besides the UN Charter itself, the Conventions on Human Rights have a sufficient number of formal endorsements to represent a high degree of acceptance because the non-Western world has signed up to the conventions at least as a token of intention. International human rights law thus has, if not the commitment, at least the acquiescence, of nearly all states. Even sceptics understood that without such notional compliance, their acceptance in the global community would be problematic.

The victory over Germany, Italy and Japan by the American-led allies and the Union of Soviet Socialist Republics in World War II brought about the initially slow, but later hastening, demise of colonialism and the resultant transformation of former colonies into independent states, a process that lasted towards the end of the twentieth century. For many newly independent states the outcome of the war was liberating, allowing them to craft an independent foreign policy that often renewed its links with the pre-colonial past. For others like Germany and Japan, as described in the chapters of Amit Das Gupta (Germany) and Anno (Japan), defeat and devastation resulted in a clean break with pre-war narratives and the shaping of new national values.

THEORIES AND TRADITIONS IN WESTERN VALUES

To juxtapose the indefinable West with an equally indeterminate Asia is to fabricate an 'orientalist' cultural context, but is impossible to avoid in this introduction. The Western value system places store on the individual and his or her rights to free speech and association, property and safeguards against the tyranny of the state, and has been successfully exported as standards in diverse fields like international law, biosafety, labour, environment, free and fair trade, the death penalty, LGBTQ rights and sustainable development. Multilateral institutions were created by the West after World War II with the purpose of promoting liberal ideas of world politics and economics. At the heart of Western values is the commitment to doctrines that can override national specificities and cultural legacies to invent identities that occasionally disrupt historical continuity – for example, in Europe the vision of federalists was to create a new beginning in 1945 to prevent the recurrence of destructive nationalism. The Europeans were the main beneficiaries of the

new international order underwritten by the Americans, though decolonization was a significant historical watershed.

The development of human rights law is linked with the West and its political project. Domestic public opinion in the West is important in stressing a
consensus on universal morality, and partly for expiating the forgettable past,
although as James Mayall and Bruno Macaes have adduced in their chapters,
the same public shows much less concern about enunciation of values in
domestic policy than in foreign affairs. Notwithstanding this paradox, and
repeated violations of values abroad, there remains a pervasive view that
Western liberal democracy is the final destination of human social evolution,
despite the underlying tension between individual rights and majoritarianism.
German chancellor Angela Merkel in 2016 iterated Euro-American values in
her first message to American President Donald Trump, offering cooperation
on the basis of 'democracy, freedom, respect for the rule of law and human
dignity, regardless of origin, skin colour, religion, gender, sexual orientation or political belief'.[11] This code of values is venerated in the West, and
Trump has come under criticism, as pointed out by William J. Antholis in his
chapter on America, for deviating from them, or rather, in a departure from
his six immediate predecessors, for not referencing the US value system for
his actions, an omission that angers the American liberal establishment. The
lapses on the part of previous presidents in upholding American values did
not provoke similar castigation because the rhetoric was considered sufficient
unto itself. Antholis points to the American conviction that values cannot be
separated from the US interests, though all presidents have faced opposition
from citizens who prefer to place national self-interest first. Anne-Marie
Slaughter, of the liberal wing of American society, urged the United States
to stand for its values in foreign policy, defining these as liberty, democracy,
equality, justice, tolerance, humility and faith. She suggests that these American standards are universal,[12] and she is not alone. Samuel Huntington wrote
the West's task 'is to preserve and renew the unique qualities of western civil-
isation'[13] and former President Clinton said that 'America's interests require
the US to lead an effort to build a world order shaped by the US values'.[14]

In Europe, with Euroscepticism rife in various parts of the European Union
(EU) due to fault lines created by inequalities between member states, terrorism and the refugee crisis, as Mayall points out in his chapter, the value
system is under strain. The recitation of values is more favoured in the
industrialized north, led by Brussels bureaucrats, the Nordic community and
the French presidency, than in the poorer agricultural south. In Britain, the
common values of the transatlantic alliance, despite the vagaries of Donald
Trump, have a stronger salience than Eurovalues after London's decision to
leave the EU.

THEORIES AND TRADITIONS IN ASIAN VALUES

If contrasting the West with Asia is necessarily orientalist, a focus on Asia is similarly occidentalist, if only because of the Western origins of modernity with which all Asian countries are preoccupied. Twentieth-century Asian nationalism was inspired by personalities like Rabindranath Tagore, Okakura Kuzuko and Sun Yat-sen, who called upon Asia to provide a political and cultural arena for resisting colonialism. 'Asia Is One' is the stirring opening sentence of Okakura's *Ideals of the East*,[15] but the reality was very different. Asia is characterized more by political, religious, economic, cultural and ethnic diversity than homogeneity, and the concept does not resonate politically in all parts of the continent.[16] Heterogeneity makes a collective identity impossible, and none of the Asians regarded themselves with fellow-feeling except in the context of anti-colonialism. There are no definable Asian values except by the broadest definition; nor do Asians hold that their values are unique. Given the differences between West Asia, India, China and Japan, there can be no 'Asian way' other than an emphasis on modernization and sovereignty, non-interference, top-down benevolent state philosophy and communitarian values, which posit that society is a collective value system, placing national above individual interests. There is scarce belief in separation of powers or checks and balances, though all countries command a high level of public political participation.

Jawaharlal Nehru's generation of Indian leaders saw themselves as the *avant-garde* in the implementation of human rights and claimed the same value-based platform for the colonized as for the colonizers, although some Asian nationalists insisted that order was more important than rights, a distinction that arose from the question whether priority should be given to individual rights over collective political stability and economic growth. The tension between negative and positive rights[17] divided the opposing camps during the Cold War and returned later as a clash of values, especially concerning the principle of non-intervention in other countries. Asian opinion is paradoxically anchored in an occidentalism, a Westphalian structure of government and power, making Asians allergic to any situation where others decide their policy preferences for them.

Yet the Asians are conflicted; there is pride in the development of an 'Asia-as-civilization' thesis, an assertiveness born of economic success, but with residual feelings of inferiority and resentment. Some feel like Ogura Kazuo that Asia should absorb what was offered by the West but develop a set of universal values in a new Asian model of political and economic development,[18] whereas others feel that Asia must first rid itself of feudalism, deference to authority, corruption and anti-materialism. There are various iterations of the Asian way, many of them contrived and misconceived, but some civilizational values remain valid.

Asian value systems flow from Buddhism, Confucianism, Hinduism, Islam, Legalism, Shintoism and other spiritual traditions that underscore social obligations over individual rights. These obligations include hard work, thrift, respect for ancestors, filial piety, harmony in society and family, duty to conscience, company loyalty, absence of confrontation, respect for conformity, reserve and restraint, age and status, consensus-based solutions and reluctance to extend blame or cause loss of face. Hierarchy and authority figures are widely accepted, especially after the Asian Tigers made rapid economic progress under authoritarian rule. Asian businesses are hierarchical; political parties are family-owned and stratified structures constitute the elite in both democratic and non-democratic states. The state has an obligation to secure basic material welfare, if necessary through restraints on the free market and property rights. Family is the basic unit of social organization; with the sense of obligation comes the presumption of benevolence from others, and an emotional bond has to be established to get anything done. Such sociological aspects can be located outside Asia, but they are prevalent in Asia, where savings and investment rates are high and a large proportion of family discretionary expenditure is spent on education.[19] The argument that economic progress will shatter family-based networks is negated by Hong Kong, the most capitalist Asian region, where family ties still hold sway.

Societal values have only a tenuous relationship with foreign policy, where sacral, civilizational and philosophical traditions count for more, but two points may be made; Asian traditional cultures do not prevent democratic transformations, as seen in Indonesia, Malaysia, all of South Asia, South Korea and Taiwan, though there are setbacks in Myanmar and Thailand; and the primacy given to caution and consensus is manifest in the Association of Southeast Asian Nations, where no summit gathering took place until 1976, nine years after the organization started, and there were only four summits during its first twenty-five years. Despite its dominating presence due to size and population, as Dewi Fortuna Anwar observes in her chapter, Indonesia exercises enormous discretion in its regional diplomacy. Other Asian organizations like the Organization of Islamic Cooperation and the South Asian Association for Regional Cooperation are not outcome-driven, and never openly criticize member states or hold them accountable.

THE ASIAN VALUES DEBATE OF THE 1990s

Liberal internationalism briefly captured the zeitgeist of the post–Cold War world, but the modern liberal state was not a finished product that could be delivered ready-made to another state, and relativism towards sovereignty as an organizing principle of international relations was anathema to Asian post-colonial countries. The conviction that the West was in decline and Asia on the rise reinforced the scepticism towards the concept of individual rights. Challenging supposedly neo-colonial 'imperial humanitarianism' and 'unilateral universalism', Western values were regarded with Asian cynicism due to their violation during the colonial era, but equally because of the arrogance with which they were promoted, whether in trade negotiations, periodical human rights assessments or social questions like the death penalty and discriminatory practices against the LGBTQ community, or in India, the caste system. Asians rejected the use of double standards, the imposition of Western versions of personhood and systems of government being projected as universal obligations. The values of free trade and open markets in the EU, as Fredrik Erixon points out in his chapter, do not apply to its restrictive and protectionist practices that raise non-tariff barriers. The EU, he writes, is a procedural power where process outweighs outcomes and confusion prevails on the relationship between economic interests and ideals – though there is no dispute as to what those ideals are.

Basic to the pushback against Western values is the Asian emphasis on national sovereignty and non-interference. China is the most strident in opposing the propagation of Western values as evidenced in its Document Number 9 issued in April 2013[20] which condemned Western values as an effort to 'westernize and disintegrate', and its annual ripostes on abuses of human rights in the United States, while Japan and South Korea, as formal American allies, are the most conformist. The remaining Asian countries take a nuanced position, raising no objections to Western values per se, but rejecting certain Western foreign policy actions and strenuously defending what they consider to be in their internal domain.

An overt Asian resistance to Western values was mounted in 1993 at the UN World Conference on Human Rights, and took the form of the Bangkok Declaration on which China, Malaysia and Singapore were the prime movers, though all the Asian nations covered in this book, other than Turkey, approved the final text, which stated

> while human rights are universal in nature they must be considered in the context of a dynamic and evolving process of international norm setting, bearing in mind the significance of national and regional peculiarities and various historical, cultural and religious backgrounds.

The Bangkok Declaration had an impact out of proportion to the restraint of the language used,[21] and the neologism of 'Asian Values' entered the international relations lexicon, though the same sentiments were echoed by the African group at the Conference when it affirmed that 'no ready-made model can be prescribed at the universal level since the historical and cultural realities . . . traditions, standards and values of each people cannot be disregarded'.[22]

Asians criticized what they saw as the West's belief in freedom over discipline, the individual over the community and the conviction that Western social practices were valid for all time and in all places. Asian values became a contested sphere in academic rather than political discourse, with supporters such as Daniel Bell[23] and Jack Donnelly[24] holding that particularist Asian – especially East Asian – value systems should be respected as valid by the West; and robust critics like Amartya Sen,[25] and Yash Ghei[26] – which vividly illustrated the universalist/parochial divide that cut across the Western/Asian one. Others like Alan Dupont[27] and Common Track 5[28] tried to moderate the discussion by seeking the middle ground. The universalists sought to foreclose discussion, assuming that Western liberal democracy met global aspirations without questioning the normative premise that the West should be propagating its values. The Asians for their part, seeking a role in norm-setting, held that the Western canon had a spurious universality deriving from its power over centuries to dictate what were delivered as global goals.

The universalist arguments were diminished by failing to investigate why Asian values influenced political behaviour, and no consideration was given to the growing spread of democratic practice in Asia or the economic progress that had lifted millions of people out of poverty since the last decades of the twentieth century. The entire idea of universality could be contestable: a clash not between universal and local values, but between different universalities. Islam, Buddhism and Confucianism, like Christianity, had sought to universalize in their known worlds, and there are legacies of Confucianism and Legalism (Han Feizi) in China, Japan, Korea, Singapore, Taiwan and Vietnam; Buddhism in Myanmar, Sri Lanka, Bhutan and Thailand; and Islam in Arabian Asia, Iran, Turkey, parts of Central, South and Southeast Asia.

Western repudiation of Asian values could stem from a failure to understand religious societies because in their secular societies, the religious roots of their own values are hidden below the surface. The debate on Asian values was a dialogue of the deaf since the arguments moved on parallel lines without mutual comprehension. Asian values were simplistically conflated by critics with human rights because the issue had arisen in the context of the UN Conference. Globalization and universality are Western cultural constructs, and it would have been appropriate to shift the debate to universal and cultural relativity. Notions of civilization are abstract and complex and lead to stereotyping and oversimplification, including by using terms like 'the West', 'the East' and the 'Asian way'. Asian values came to the fore when emerging economies in Asia led by the Asian Tigers were characterized by rapid growth and self-confidence. There was an unresolvable dilemma for the Asians; as long as Western values were used as standards of comparison, Western values were universalized. The Asian values debate of the 1990s proved to be a passing squall; the brouhaha died down after the Asian financial crisis of 1998, and no echoes are heard of it now. It is not our intention to dwell further on this debate: only to note its now-subdued presence.

It will be difficult for the West and Asia to arrive at a value consensus, though all can agree on tolerance, pluralism, equal rights and equal opportunities. There are inherent problems with dialogue when countries hold varying views on theology, epistemics and human nature. There should nevertheless be scope for cooperation through recognition that different value systems exist and have an influence on the reactions of nations to given situations. Keeping in view the culture of the West in emphasizing rights and that of Asia in giving priority to responsibilities, an international conference in 1997 drew up a Universal Declaration of Responsibilities,[29] which however never gained traction. Notwithstanding the obstacles, including the lack of authorized interlocutors and a suitable forum for such dialogue, the continents of America, Asia and Europe comprise a significant segment of human history, and can hopefully one day arrive at models of culture, human dignity and security that would command global consent.

RELIGION, SECULARISM AND MODERNITY

In the past, powerful countries sought to fashion international society in their image, and on the basis of their values, not always successfully. For example, Asian states resisted Western attempts to export secular and postmodern versions of their value system. Modernization has now arguably created the seedbed for the world's first global community, but urbanization and connectivity in Asia and the West have modified and hybridized values and norms. Self-image is important as a measure of the transition from medievalism, and with greater education and decline of the average age, Asian millennials, like their Western counterparts, stress the importance of sustainable development rather than modernization, as Ravi Velloor notes in his chapter. We cannot know where this process will end, but cultural patterns will not easily change, if only because social media can be used to celebrate difference as readily as commonality.

According to Partha Chatterjee,[30]

There cannot be just one modernity irrespective of geography, time, environment or social conditions. The forms of modernity will have to vary between different countries depending on specific circumstances and social practices. . . . The western philosophers of the Enlightenment wrote about a modernity that would bring in the era of universal reason and emancipation which belied the barbarities of colonialism that led to doubts about claims to modernity. . . [but Asians] would forever remain consumers of universal modernity, never would be taken seriously as its producers. . . . There is no promised land of modernity outside the network of power. . . . Ours is the modernity of the once-colonized.

Everyone has a different concept of modernity, and Macaes writes that we are all modern now. The Asian experience due to the lack, until recently, of any capacity for autonomous action largely accounts for its pre-modern status. The West is partly secularized, although more in Europe than in the United States, and religion plays a smaller part in its culture – though the roots of Western welfarism are in Protestant Christianity. The United States is not a post-religious society in the same way as Europe is so described, and the Westphalian system owes its origins to intra-Christian sectarian conflict. In Asia, religious sentiment is strongly bound to culture and tradition. As Mehmet Ozkan and Kingshuk Chatterjee state in their chapter, secular Turkey is largely conditioned by Islamic values and its foreign policy is Islam-sensitive, whereas Iranian foreign policy is *realpolitik* packaged in the language of political Islam because political discourse in Iran is Islamized despite a clear foreign policy continuity from before the 1979 revolution. Islam is used in both countries to legitimize and galvanize popular support. By contrast, as Anwar shows, Indonesia, as the biggest Muslim country, seeks to promote the healing touch of moderate Islam, but with little recordable success.

It is in the quest for identity that Asians have returned to the roots of their cultures based on religion and tradition. The causal connection between religion and foreign policy is not easy to establish, but cannot be ignored in Asia, being necessarily covered in several chapters: Christianity by Hari Vasudevan/Tatiana Shaumyan (Russia); Islam by Ozkan/Chatterjee (Turkey and Iran) and Anwar (Indonesia); Hinduism by Krishnan Srinivasan (India); Buddhism by Sanjay Pulipaka/Chaw Chaw Sein (Myanmar); and Confucianism by Zhang Lihua (China) and Lee Seong-hyon (South Korea). Daoism, Legalism and Shintoism also played their parts in the creation of Asian values.

VALUES AND PRACTICES

Power may be shifting from west to east, but the impact of Western ideas and values will not be easily dislodged. Liberalism, republicanism, capitalism, socialism, nationalism and communism were all bequeathed to the world by the West. Because of the dominance of Western civilization it is hard to conceive of a world where multiple civilizations, and the values inspired by them, can coexist. There is a teleological narrative of uninterrupted progress towards a global order that obfuscates and largely erases the colonized from the story. International law is West-centric; international institutions, norms, priorities and theories derive from the West; and the international knowledge system encapsulates values, experiences and perspectives crafted in European intellectual and cultural circles. Human rights law was largely their work, which presumed universal applicability, and the widespread acceptance of rights has given them the status of customary international law.

Since the rise of Europe from the sixteenth and seventeenth centuries, the world system has preserved much the same essential form, 'an ideology of enlightenment aimed straight at the heart of all traditional ways of thinking'[31] in Europe itself as well as elsewhere. Rights were inherent in all humans and flowed from a natural order of things which determined what was correct to do. The trend now is to recognize the values that underpin these rights, including dignity, liberty, autonomy of the individual and representative pluralist government, with law, tolerance and respect for diversity. Western values embody a belief system to which many Asians and others are willing to sign up, although alternative world views survive. Chinese, Russian and Islamic values are never likely to enjoy a comparable universality, but the future would probably be more transactional, bilateral, driven by power and national interests rather than values or sense of international community. This is already noticeable both in the West and in Asia, and as Macaes states, the world is regarded by some nations as an arena of contest for advantage, although weaker countries see benefit in a system that reduces competition.

The liberal democratic model was propagated sedulously as universally applicable by Western, especially American, policymakers, intellectuals and think tanks. Antholis comments that democratic intervention in other countries is considered in America's interests, though the non-Western world looked aghast at Angela Merkel bewailing that under Trump, the United States could not be relied upon to 'impose order'.[32] It could properly be asked – but whose order? Jurgen Habermas was prompted to write that "this pseudo-universalism is a kind of universalized ethnocentrism',[33] although no one would contest demands made of countries like China, India, Iran and many others in Asia to improve their human rights records.

In a Eurocentric world, legitimacy and leadership came naturally but after the Cold War the old certainties were increasingly questioned. Western quasi-imperial interventionism in Africa, Asia and Latin America was deeply controversial, although never without some local support. The West was accused of double standards and a messianic urge to export its values to unreceptive and resistant victims. The US-led coalitions of the willing were blamed for violations of the UN Charter and especially Article 2 in regard to the principle of non-interference and national sovereignty. Western values were therefore challenged or at least regarded with deep scepticism. Russia, like China, showed no inclination to compromise with Western values, described by Vasudevan/Shaumyan as a 'cocktail defined by US and European practices'. Russian values are parochial and lay stress on the evolution of an Eurasian Economic Union to support Russian autarchy, along with support for Russian communities in contested regions like Crimea, eastern Ukraine, trans-Dnistria, South Ossetia and Abkhazia.

Cultural relativity calls for radically non-judgemental analysis, but it is hard to define what is specifically Eastern or Western in a globalizing interconnected world. Universality relies on shared understandings, cultures, institutions: on countries thinking broadly similarly about social and political matters. The moral equality of all humans is endorsed in every continent, but universal claims are relative, and any discussion of cultures and religions presupposes differences and particularity.

Many contemporary Asian values are pre-modern and similar to the West's values of yesterday. In the search for identity, two paths are discernible – one forward looking, the other harking back to nostalgic ideas of purity and nationalism.[34] The more deep-rooted an idea, the further into the past it will look for its origins.[35] Some values have deep roots, as Antholis (the United States) and Zhang (China) have shown. Generally, the values of resurgent Western populism are backward-looking but others are freshly minted after 1945, arising from what Das Gupta refers to as a guilt complex in the case of Germany, and a desire to find a meaning in defeat as Anno explains for Japan. Germany embraced the concept of a civilian power and adopted the Western code of values enthusiastically to exorcize the trauma of aggressive nationalism, while Japan adopted pacifism as a new value to attain self-esteem and international status. In Myanmar's case, described by Pulipaka/Sein, Buddhism and the Sangha play an important role domestically in a similar fashion to that of Islam in Turkey, Iran and Indonesia, thereby impacting foreign affairs, and with Myanmar, inclining it towards neutralism. India's case is a paradox, as Srinivasan shows; the revival known as Hindutva by current ideologues is not from a hoary past that they seek to invoke, but the philosophies of twentieth-century nationalists. Engagement with religion also plays a role in Russia, seen in Vasudevan/Shaumyan's chapter, where 'official religion', especially the Russian Orthodox Church, is embraced to stress sovereignty and nationality.

The passage of time produces its own relativity. Confucianism exists but is no longer the same Confucianism; liberal democracy exported is never the same liberal democracy, and postmodern values such as the environment, LGBTQ and women's reproductive rights are controversial even in the West. What may lie ahead could be a very different modernism based on technologies used in ways that cannot be imagined today. Any new world system must run on universal values rather than the interests of any one group; meanwhile, there is a case to be made for coexistence of relativist claims before universal morality comes into being. Velloor concludes his chapter with the comment that universality without respect for diversity is a threat.

There is an inherent contradiction in foreign affairs between the pursuit of material goals and the application of moral and normative principles. Mayall and Velloor assert that few nations would allow a moral agenda to override national interests and priorities. The interests of any country must be consistent with its principles in a utilitarian logic, but interests play the critical role in decision making and supersede a principled approach. Srinivasan provides a narrative of India failing to live up to its stated values; what remains is its sense of exceptionalism and attachment to autonomy which makes it a difficult partner in bilateral and multilateral transactions. Zhang's chapter on China notes the value of harmony and seeking common ground while resolving differences, but China's departures from these values are not hard to find. It is axiomatic that any nation professing to uphold morality in its dealings with foreign countries will lay itself open to charges of hypocrisy. This is true for Asia no less than for the West.

It is clear from all the chapters that values in foreign policy are about positioning as much as subscribing. Most Asian nations have not shown the same consistency in pursuing a values system as the West has done, suggesting what Velloor implies are tactical considerations. Geography has determined, as Anno, Lee and Pulipaka/Sein explain, that proximity to a major civilization like China affects the evolution of values in Japan, South Korea and Myanmar. Japan and South Korea have to balance competing interests along with their alliance with the United States; Myanmar uses its status as a small country to eschew any larger role on the world stage. In making adjustments in its relations with dominant powers, South Korea concentrates on survival techniques rather than indigenous traditions; clichés like benefitting the human world and putting the national interest first are a consequence of the trauma of Japanese occupation and the Korean War, and the objective is to fashion a balancing role as a middle-level power while adjusting its relations with North Korea. Japan tweaks the formulations of values to adapt to the rise of China and, conscious of its separateness from the West, its unique status as the only country to endure nuclear attack and its search for a distinctive cultural identity, uses 'free world' and universal values at different times to show solidarity with the Western alliance.

Asian political and economic influence in regional and world affairs has increased, resulting in an unsettled relationship between rising and established world powers. The West initiated 80 percent of the norms that govern international trade and global markets, leading Erixon to state that Europe was the intellectual birthplace of protectionism, mercantilism and free trade, the three main paradigms – or systems of values – of how a country should design its foreign economic policy, and there are traces of all of them in current European practice.

The United States still claims its policies are invariably values-driven, and the EU remains an activist for human rights and democratic values. Asian countries have been subject to values-based conditionalities in contexts where rights issues have little relevance. China considers that human rights promotion by the West is designed to subvert its political system, while most of Asia adopts an uneasy middle position, endorsing the universality of human rights while defending their position on non-interference and non-intervention. The outcome is uncertain, but the West's ability to set the rules of global order is clearly diminishing with the lowered profile of US predominance being replaced by decentralization and atomization of power, along with a growing sense of empowerment in the global South.

CONCLUSION

Governments of different ideological and political persuasion draw legitimacy as the modern successors of the abiding community, religious or civilizational ethos. Interests are coloured by values, but since states practise self-interest as a definition of statehood, no state can avoid breaches of its own values, and the issue is the extent of deviation between principle and practice. It is clear from a study of foreign policy across continents that values give way to contingencies and circumstances, and above all, interests, and no government is able to chart a course by the compass of professed values alone. The more important the issue, the more national the policy, and bilateralism gains over multilateralism, as does power over idealism. That is why the saying that other nations had 'interests and no values, whereas the EU has values but no interests'[36] never stood up to examination.

No comparative study has yet been made on the relationship between values and foreign policy in various countries of the world. This book might be the first but will not be the last word. If it promotes further and fuller consideration of this fascinating and essential topic, its objective would be fully served.

NOTES

1. Address to the UN General Assembly, 12 April 2008. www.dstsisters.org/home/moment.

2. https://en.wikipedia.org/wiki/List_of_countries_by_GDP_(nominal).

3. Hedley Bull, *The Anarchical Society* (London: Macmillan, 1977).

4. Hans J. Morgenthau and Kenneth W. Thompson, *Politics among Nations: The Struggle for Power and Peace* (New York: McGraw-Hill, 1993).

5. Kenneth N. Waltz, *Theory of International Politics* (Reading, Mass: Addison-Wesley Pub. Co., 1979).

6. Alexander Wendt, *Social Theory of International Politics* (Cambridge: Cambridge University Press, 1999).

7. Scott Burchill and Andrew Linklater, *Theories of International Relations* (New York: St. Martin's Press, 1996).

8. This debate is discussed in James Mayall, 'Between Anarchy and Community in International Relations', in John Morrill (ed.). *The Promotion of Knowledge, Lectures to Mark the Centenary of the British Academy 1902–2002* (Oxford: Oxford University Press for the British Academy, 2004).

9. Mark Mazower, *No Enchanted Palace, The End of Empire and the Ideological Origins of the United Nations* (Princeton, NJ; Oxford: Princeton University Press, 2009).

10. Boaventura de Sousa Santos, 'Toward a Multicultural Conception of Human Rights', in *Moral Imperialism* (Berta Hernandez-Truyol: New York University Press, 2002): 45.

11. Carol Giacomo, 'Angela Merkel's Message to Trump', *New York Times* (9 November 2016). https://www.nytimes.com/interactive/projects/cp/opinion/election-night-2016/angela-merkels-warning-to-trump.

12. *New York Times*, Opinion Pages, (17 May 2007).

13. 'The West, Unique Not Universal', *Foreign Affairs* 75 (6 November/December 1996): 46.

14. Christopher Layne and Benjamin Schwarz, 'American Hegemony without an Enemy', *Foreign Policy* 92 (Fall 1993): 7.

15. Kakuzo Okakura, *Ideals of the East: The Spirit of Japanese Art* (New York: EP Dutton, 2005).

16. Rustom Bharucha, *Another Asia* (Oxford: Oxford University Press, 2006): xvi.

17. Isaiah Berlin, *Two Concepts of Liberty* (Oxford: Clarendon Press, 1958).

18. Ogura Kazuo, 'A Call for a New Concept of Asia', *Japan Echo* 20, no. 3 (Autumn 1993): 39.

19. Indian households spend considerable amounts on every level of education. See S Chandrasekhar, P. Geetha Rani and Soham Sahoo, 'Household Expenditure on Higher Education in India: What Do We Know & What Do Recent Data Have to Say?' Indira Gandhi Institute of Development Research, Mumbai (December 2016). http://www.igidr.ac.in/pdf/publication/WP-2016-030.pdf.

20. Leila Choukroune, 'The Language of Rights and the Politics of Law: Perspectives on China's Last Legal Ditch Struggle', *International Journal for the Semiotics of*

Law 29, no. 4 (December 2016): 779–803. https://link.springer.com/article/10.1007/s11196-015-9436-7.

21. 'Final Declaration of the Regional Meeting for Asia of the World Conference on Human Rights', Asia-Pacific Human Rights Information Center (HURIGHTS OSAKA). https://www.hurights.or.jp/archives/other_documents/section1/1993/04/final-declaration-of-the-regional-meeting-for-asia-of-the-world-conference-on-human-rights.html.

22. Jose Ayala Lasso, in Daniel Warner, *Human Rights and Humanitarian Law* (The Hague: M. Nijhoff, 1997), 88.

23. Daniel A. Bell, *East Meets West: Human Rights and Democracy in East Asia* (Princeton, NJ: Princeton University Press, 2000) and *Beyond Liberal Democracy* (Princeton, NJ: Princeton University Press, 2006).

24. Jack Donnelly, 'The Relative Universality of Human Rights', *John Hopkins Quarterly* 29, no. 2 (May 2007): 281–306.

25. Amartya Sen, 'Human Rights and Asian Values', *Sixteenth Morgenthau Memorial Lecture on Ethics & Foreign Policy, Carnegie Council on Ethics and International Affairs* (25 May 1997): 190. https://www.carnegiecouncil.org/publications/archive/morgenthau/254.

26. William Twining, 'Human Rights: Southern Voices – Francis Deng, Abdullahi An-Na'im, Yash Ghai and Upendra Baxi', *Review of Constitutional Studies* 11, no. 2 (2006): 203–279. https://www.researchgate.net/publication/32896769_Human_Rights_Southern_Voices_-_Frances_Deng_Abdullahi_An-Na'im_Yash_Ghai_and_Upendra_Baxi.

27. Alan Dupont, 'Is There an Asian way?' *Survival* 38, no. 2 (1996): 13–34.

28. 'Common Track 5: Asian Values, China and Human Rights', *The Rights' Future*. https://therightsfuture.com/common-tracks/asian-values.

29. 'A Universal Declaration of Human Responsibilities', *InterAction Council* (1 September 1997). https://www.interactioncouncil.org/sites/default/files/udhr.pdf.

30. Partha Chatterjee, *Our Modernity – All of Us Have a Different Kind of Modernity*. http://ccs.ukzn.ac.za/files/partha1.pdf, passim.

31. Bruno Macaes, *The Dawn of Eurasia* (London: Allen Lane, 2018), 119.

32. 'Merkel Says Europe Can't Rely on U.S. to Impose World Order', *Reuters* (20 July 2018). https://www.reuters.com/article/us-germany-merkel-usa/merkel-says-europe-cant-rely-on-u-s-to-impose-world-order-idUSKBN1KA1F9.

33. Jurgen Habermas, *The Divided West* (Cambridge: Polity, 2006), 103.

34. Andrew Sheng, 'Asia Needs Both Secular and Sacred', *The Statesman Kolkata* (8 April 2017).

35. Macaes, *The Dawn of Eurasia*, 19.

36. Mark Leonard, *Why Europe Will Run the 21st Century* (London: Fourth Estate, 2005), 119.

Chapter 1

Values in European Foreign Policies

Defending the Enlightenment in Troubled Times

James Mayall

The two questions I seek to answer in this chapter are, first, whether European foreign policies are grounded in values as well as interests, and second, whether as most European governments would claim, their values are universal rather than an expression of a particular, and as viewed from other parts of the world, parochial civilization. At first sight, these questions might seem distinctly odd to anyone not versed in the arcane debates of international political and legal theory and diplomatic practice. After all, no one would consider it worth asking if a country's education or health or pensions policy reflected its values. These values might be contested between political parties, but the fact that they are expressions of a government's fundamental beliefs about how the country should be governed would normally be regarded as self-evident. Why then should it be any different with foreign policy?

The answer is that foreign policy immediately comes up against the sovereignty of other states. In this respect, it is quite unlike education, health or any other domestic policy. In these areas the government has both legal authority and, in theory at least, the power to implement whatever policy it chooses. By contrast, in foreign policy while most governments could probably agree that their objective should be to provide both security and prosperity for the people, they have no legal authority to pursue these goals in other countries without the consent of those governments, established either by custom or in accordance with bilateral and/or multilateral treaties and agreements. In addition, if political or coercive pressure is employed in their pursuit, it runs the risk of being counter-productive, since it may well be interpreted as a blatant violation of the non-interference principle, a key entailment of sovereignty. This is a particular problem for Western states (i.e., European countries and those of European settlement in the Americas and elsewhere) because having dominated international society since the mid-seventeenth century until very recently, they tend to regard the twenty-first century iteration of their values – a belief in democracy, the rule of law, the protection of individual human rights and the maintenance of an open economy except when national security is deemed to require protection – as providing the standard to which all countries should aspire. Since the world is very diverse and involvement in global international relations necessarily involves them in doing business with countries that may not share these values, the assumption of universality immediately opens them to charges of hypocrisy and double standards.

RELATIONSHIP OF VALUES TO FOREIGN POLICY

Not only is the issue of foreign policy values unavoidable; it is also a peculiarly modern problem with its origins in the period in which the great powers have competed not merely militarily – as great powers have done throughout history – but ideologically, to establish a universal blueprint for modernity itself. When the world was largely run by dynastic or military empires plus a few oligarchic city states, everyone pursued his or her interests unashamedly and it has to be said often brutally, especially where the pursuit of power was closely allied with religious domination or economic exploitation. This did not prevent the Europeans eventually developing an international order based on sovereignty, the rule of law, diplomatic recognition and privilege, and the management of the central balance by the great powers. In a sense this earlier version of European foreign policy values – it is, after all, the one that most obviously underpins the United Nations (UN) Charter and most contemporary international organizations – causes less of a problem to the rest of the world than the more recent liberal internationalist version, which reaches far deeper inside the social and cultural organization of different societies.[1]

This more recent iteration has dominated European and European Union (EU) foreign policy debate since the end of the Cold War, although it too has a more venerable genealogy, and one which, as a result of its paradoxical links with European imperialism, is regarded with considerable suspicion in much of the former colonial world. Nonetheless, because its roots are sociological as much as political, it will be difficult to dislodge. Until well after the French and American Revolutions, only the political élite was seriously involved in politics, at home let alone abroad, so that while personal and even state honour may on occasions have been an important issue, ethics in an abstract sense was not. Once the consent of the governed is formally recognized as the source of political legitimacy, foreign policy has to be attached to the ethical foundations on which that consent has been built.[2] This requirement is even less discretionary in the case of the EU than its member states, since the organization is a hybrid entity, neither a state nor a conventional inter-governmental organization, constructed on the basis of treaties and identifying itself through legal cooperation among a group of democratic states.

Three other issues complicate the relationship of values to European foreign policies, although none is obviously merely a European problem. The first issue again revolves around the EU. To what extent are the values that European governments insist underlie their foreign policies those of the European great powers – France, Germany, Italy and Britain plus a group of smaller northern European countries with a similar political culture – rather than those of the member states that have joined more recently from the east and south?

The EU is the only multilateral organization with pretensions to a foreign policy and a diplomatic service of its own. It also insists that certain common standards should be met before membership can be negotiated. These include regular democratic elections, respect for individual human rights and the rule of law. Greece was kept out until the military government fell in 1974, and it took until 1981 for the government to negotiate entry. Similarly, after the collapse of communism, the Eastern European and Baltic states had to prove their democratic credentials before being allowed in. This was easier said than done. In the Baltic states, for example, where the population still tended to regard their Russian residents as representatives of an occupying power, it was difficult to persuade the people that they were nonetheless citizens and that discrimination against them was illegitimate. The determination of states that had escaped from the Soviet sphere of influence to join the affluent alliance of the EU was so strong that a way around these problems was found. But it did mean that for a time their foreign policy energies were almost totally exhausted by the effort required to meet the requirements of EU membership. Consequently, the question of whether the national values of these countries had any influence on their foreign policy did not seriously arise.

The second complicating issue is nationalism itself. More precisely it is the relationship of nationalism to the wider civilization out of which it grows and in which it is embedded. Nationalist ideology – broadly the proposition that each culture should have its own state – was a European invention, although it was quickly spread around the world, first in the saddle bags of Napoleon's armies and then by the worldwide spread of European imperialism.[3] Values – in the sense of ethical principles – are arguably more often associated with a civilization than with its component nations, but their influence on international relations is more likely to be filtered through a particular national culture. Since the separation of national cultures, rather than what they have in common, establishes their claim to statehood, national identities and national styles inevitably permeate approaches to foreign policy.

The final complicating factor is the contested basis of the nation. Within Europe there are two main contenders, which have very different implications for how values are projected on to foreign policy. Political nationalism in Europe starts with the French Revolution, when the nation was first defined as a community of citizens. While the British opposed the revolution, throughout the nineteenth century they too nationalized their constitution by progressively widening the franchise. In both cases – as also in the other centralized states of the North Atlantic seaboard – the form of nationalism was civic: what mattered was citizenship not ancestry. Civic nationalism did not mean that culture was unimportant – indeed in both Britain and France waves of immigrants were absorbed into and assimilated the respective national identities of the two countries – but the test of citizenship was a matter of territorial residence (*ius soli*), not a bloodline. Starting with Germany, which began to abandon providing automatic German citizenship to anyone of German ethnic descent only after the collapse of communism and the Soviet Union, many east and south European countries also viewed the world through the prism of *ius sanguinis* and struggled with the rival concept of *ius soli,* a modified version of which is favoured by European liberals. Indeed to the extent that ethnic nationalism is a stronger driving force for foreign policy in eastern and southern than in western Europe, the principal impact of the post–Cold War enlargement of the EU has been to weaken the liberal democratic value consensus on which its engagement with the rest of the world was based.

In the context of both the refugee crisis of recent years, which has been greatly intensified by the mass displacement of Syrians as a result of the civil war but has been building up since the early 1990s, and the upsurge of populist policies to which immigration pressures have contributed, the distinction between the two forms of European nationalism has blurred, and both have become more inward-looking and suspicious of the outside world. Nonetheless the legacy of the distinction between civic and ethnic nationalism inevitably introduces an element of incoherence and inconsistency into the values through which European states seek to engage the world beyond Europe. To those approaching the continent from outside it often seems a fortress, more concerned with self-preservation and cultural superiority than with the cosmopolitan and universal values to which their governments pay lip service. Across Europe, liberal internationalists, who had assumed they had a monopoly of official foreign policy pronouncements, are now on the back foot. This is not an old-fashioned debate between realists and idealists – all governments these days are determined to protect what they deem to be their core interests – but between liberal realists and exclusive nationalists.

Against this background what more can be said about the role of values in European foreign policies? Let us consider this question first in relation to the

EU and then to the two major European imperial powers, Britain and France, whose projection of power beyond Europe has left the deepest negative and positive legacies. An additional justification for singling out these two countries is that while their versions of liberal democracy were originally quite different, both were – even at the height of their nineteenth-century imperial expansion – democratic states, and it is arguably a hybrid fusion of their two liberal traditions which has dominated European debate on the nexus between foreign policy and values. The fact that both countries are permanent members of the UN Security Council and remain the leading European military powers also reinforces their role.

THE EUROPEAN UNION

The EU began to develop a foreign policy of its own only after the Cold War under a series of treaties starting with the Maastricht Treaty of 1993 creating the single market and ending with the Lisbon Treaty which came into force in 2009 and formally created the office of a Permanent High Representative for Foreign and Security policy.[4] Nonetheless, the prehistory of the EU starting with the establishment of the European Coal and Steel Community, which was then consolidated under the Treaty of Rome in 1957 into the European Economic Community (EEC), had already established the value base of the future Union. The founding fathers of the EEC were determined to use the positive values of the European enlightenment – scientific and legal rationality, humanitarianism and democratic freedom – to build a lasting peace in the continent and to prevent any retreat into the ferocious competition which had led the world into the two disastrous world wars of the twentieth century.

From this point of view, the technical aspects of the European project – the creation of a common framework for German and French industrial and energy resources – and the establishment of a Customs Union with a Common Commercial Policy as its centrepiece were the instruments but not the fundamental objectives of European integration. There has always been controversy about whether the functionalist (and neo-functionalist) approach to the building of Europe was a deliberate choice in an effort to break with the traditional pattern of power politics that had dominated European interstate relations for centuries, or was forced on the founding fathers by necessity following the collapse of the proposal for a Franco-German Defence Agreement in 1954 and the earlier establishment of the North Atlantic Treaty Organisation (NATO) in 1949. Either way, it established the platform for the subsequent development of the EU's foreign policy as that of a civilian power, a new kind of political actor whose international interests would be protected by commercial agreements and whose world role would rest on its reputational example. Since underpinning the commercial approach was the liberal belief that commerce is essentially peaceful – a proposition that has wide, if not universal, appeal – it is perhaps not surprising that Europeans seldom questioned the idea that their foreign policy values were universal rather than parochial. The tendency to regard functional integration as a universally applicable method of conflict resolution, regardless of the local political context and values, is less obviously a diplomatic asset, although, to be fair, as the enlarged EU has faced increasing centrifugal pressures of its own, it has become less strident in its attempts to export the European model.

The tension between the view that many non-Europeans have of the EU – of a fortress Europe excessively concerned with protecting its own standard of living, if necessary at the expense of third countries – and the view that the EU holds of itself – as an outward-looking political union built on universal liberal norms – was greatly reinforced first by the events surrounding the financial crisis of 2008 and second by the ongoing refugee crisis, primarily emanating from the Middle East and sub-Saharan Africa. But its origins lie further back than these events and have been constantly refreshed by changes in the international landscape. Three sources of the tension may help to explain why it has proved so difficult to resolve, particularly perhaps so far as Asia is concerned.

The first source of contradiction lies in the inherited pattern of post-imperial relationships. The British and French empires, both of which lingered on into the second half of the twentieth century, confusingly developed sharply contrasting views of the enlightenment legacy. Both were universalist, but while the French rooted their values in the republican tradition and tended to regard the political model created by the revolution – or at least the principles on which it was based – as applicable anywhere, the British, doubtless subconsciously, followed Edmund Burke in placing much more weight on local custom and tradition within a non-discriminatory economic and commercial framework. These differences in turn influenced the values that both countries imported into the reconstruction of Europe and its relations with the rest of the world after World War II. The French made their participation in the EEC dependent on the inclusion of Part IV of the Rome Treaty which provided very high levels of protection in the French market for their dependencies. This protection was maintained, but its cost was now to be shared by the other member states. The tension between French republican liberalism, which was openly discriminatory, and British classical liberalism was masked at the time because Britain was not a party to the Treaty of Rome. But it influenced how the fledgling European quasi-state was viewed by the outside world, particularly by Commonwealth countries whose products faced discrimination in European markets and whose governments were often inclined to describe the EEC as a neo-colonial project as a result.

When Britain finally joined the EEC in 1973, the British interpretation of liberal foreign policy values to some extent gained ascendancy over its French counterpart. This was partly because other members of the EEC believed that France was perpetuating its economic domination of its former African empire at their expense, and partly because neo-classical liberalism had become the dominant ideology in international trade negotiations, in which under American pressure, not only the French but also the British themselves were having to abandon special economic relationships. British membership did not, however, lead to a new international consensus that the EEC was based on universal values rather than particular European interests. The British had introduced a system of imperial preference in the 1930s when they finally abandoned free trade and introduced a general tariff, but with the establishment of the General Agreement on Tariffs and Trade (GATT) they had agreed to freeze these tariffs, and to negotiate them away under the most favoured nation principle (MFN) in successive rounds of multilateral trade negotiations. By the time the British gained entry into the EEC, developments at the UN and in the context of the Cold War had led to a North-South confrontation within which southern countries demanded special treatment as the price of participation in the liberal international economic order. Discrimination – so long as it was discrimination in favour of all developing countries – was now considered to be consistent with liberal principles. The trouble was that a special relationship had been established between the EEC and France's former colonies. With British entry, Commonwealth countries were unwilling to accept an arrangement that would leave them at a disadvantage with their natural competitors, regardless of the principle. A compromise which saw the creation of the African, Caribbean and Pacific Group (ACP) was reached, but since the major Commonwealth Asian countries were all excluded from the ACP – they would mostly not have wished to join anyway, but that was not the point – the first enlargement of the EEC did little to establish the claim that European values were universal, or that they took precedence when they were in conflict with European interests, for example in relation to trade in textiles.[5]

The second source of tension between the universal pretensions of EEC/ EU values and the priority accorded to European economic and security interests arises in its focus on its immediate neighbourhood. Liberal theory is based on the principle of non-discrimination. Admittedly, in economic policy the principle is normally interpreted in relation to third countries: MFN, for example, requires that all trading partners should be treated the same; it does not rule out preference being given to citizens. On the other hand, on humanitarian issues, including the protection of human rights and disaster relief, in theory, charity does not begin at home; it applies wherever the need is greatest. In practice, while EU foreign policy is clearly framed on the basis of liberal values, it has a distinctly regional bias towards the eastern Mediterranean, Middle East and North Africa. Countries in the region are encouraged to share the values of the EU and offered inducements to do so in the form of cooperative projects and financial loans. The daily online briefing *EU Neighbours Alert* provides a regular and vivid illustration of the policy. Thus, to take one day at random, on 10 October 2017, the EU 'welcomed the key role played by Algeria in the fight against the death penalty'; encouraged Lebanon to submit proposals for support under the Erasmus programme for Education, Training, Youth and Sport; launched an EU-Egypt Higher Education, Research and Innovation day 'to showcase existing cooperation and promote further cooperation' in these fields; announced a £200 million loan to Tunisia and launched a programme to publicize opportunities for cross-border cooperation 'from the Arctic to the Southern Mediterranean' within the European Neighbourhood Instrument for Cross-Border Cooperation.[6]

There is nothing in these policies to attract criticism from other countries, unless perhaps it is by congratulating Algeria on its attitude to the death penalty. This is the kind of pronouncement that is sometimes a source of diplomatic irritation since it implies that the EU itself embodies the best practice on the issue and, in this case, by no means all countries have signed up to the abolition. But many have, and the worldwide coalition against the death penalty is made up of many prominent non-governmental organizations and the topic is regularly debated at the UN. As a value-based organization which owes its origins to Europe's determination to resolve the major historical regional conflict, it is perhaps not surprising that the EU is proud of its achievement. Further, the fact that its liberal values are echoed throughout the UN system lends some weight to the idea of a global liberal consensus as the basis of the multilateral order. Nonetheless, such policies do not persuade other countries that European member states will allow their liberal and humanitarian values to trump their interests when their own security, welfare and political stability are perceived to be at stake.

The final source of tension in the EU between values and interests has been exposed by both the economic and security developments since the end of the Cold War. It has been said that the West won the Cold War by default: the triumphalism that briefly flowered in its aftermath in Europe as well as in North America was largely misplaced, since it was accompanied by a growth in political apathy when measured in terms of electoral turn-out at the state and even more at the European level. Even so, the self-confidence of the EU about the standing of its model of civilian power and liberal foreign policy was enormously enhanced by the enthusiasm that the Baltic and East European states showed in seeking to join an expanded Union. For the moment, the problems that would bring pressure on the priority given to European values lay over the horizon. The return of large numbers of ethnic Germans from Kazakhstan and the costs of German reunification, reinforcing the largest movement of people since the eighteenth century, the financial crisis, particularly in Greece, the fact that EU security was primarily guaranteed by NATO, the expansion of which was contested, as was the extension of its purpose to include expeditionary warfare 'out of area', and the vulnerability of European states to international terrorism – all these and more would soon expose the fault lines and contradictions in the European liberal consensus.

Writing towards the middle of 2018, it is difficult to avoid the conclusion that cumulatively these problems have led to an identity crisis in many European countries and within the EU itself, and contributed to a populist and exclusive nationalist backlash. This may not have destroyed but has certainly weakened European liberalism. The uneasy relationship between civic and ethnic nationalism had long been recognized as a potentially destabilizing feature of the European political and social landscape, although high levels of employment and general affluence until recently kept it in check. Increasingly after the Cold War the distinction between political asylum seekers and economic migrants had begun to blur, with the result that the EU and its member states found it difficult to defend their immigration policy on the grounds that they welcomed all genuine victims of political oppression who applied for asylum on a non-discriminatory basis. One British author has argued that the continent as a whole is in the process of committing collective suicide and that within a few years a distinctive European civilization and homeland will have disappeared.[7]

Unsurprisingly, the official European response was not so pessimistic. It amounted to an insurance policy for their value system, combining economic assistance to exporting countries to reduce the incentive for people to move abroad, and failing that, to establish efficient (and perhaps inevitably European look-alike) border posts and military deterrence. Well before the Syrian civil war led to a surge in illegal migration across the Mediterranean, the Spanish and Italian navies had been employed in trying to police the flow of migrants from north and sub-Saharan Africa and further afield. None of these stratagems was particularly successful, partly because the investment that migrant families had raised within their extended families in countries such as Afghanistan and Pakistan persuaded the migrants to take enormous risks, and partly because growing inequality between countries seems to have masked the fact that the same phenomenon was occurring within Europe itself.

In these circumstances, a flow of migrants – on which previously the EU had depended to fill gaps in the labour market caused by an ageing population – was transformed into a refugee crisis, which was in turn exploited by right-wing nationalist politicians. In Britain this led to demands for a referendum on the country's continued membership of the EU (Brexit), which the government lost, but the problem was Europe-wide. The deeper reasons for the political crisis were rarely, if ever, the migrants, and where a sudden surge of migrants from a particular country did cause social and or political problems, these were not always the groups that were targeted. The problem was the widening gap between the experience of the population at large, not merely the unskilled working class but increasingly the middle classes which had relatively suffered most during the years of austerity since 2008, and the political and technological élites. Former French President Hollande summed up Europe's plight in a speech to French ambassadors in 2016:

> Nothing will be possible in Europe unless trust is restored. Trust from the people of Europe, many of whom no longer understand the meaning of the European project, trust between the states, which see the EU either as having too much discipline or too much solidarity. Trust in European institutions, whose procedures – and this does not only apply to European institutions – are no longer suited to the urgent challenges currently facing us.[8]

By the middle of 2018 the credibility of the 'universal' liberal values on which European civilian power – and its nascent foreign policy – had been based, if not in tatters, had been seriously damaged.

BRITAIN AND FRANCE

Historically, Britain and France were rivals for hegemony in Europe and further afield. In the twenty-first century, although echoes of this rivalry surface from time to time, and although they were on opposite sides in supporting the US decision to invade Iraq in 2003, there is little to separate them in terms of the underlying values on which their foreign policies are based. Both insist that their foreign policy is grounded in liberal internationalism, which they similarly interpret as a belief in the rule of law, the protection of human rights, representative democracy and a recognition that the protection of national interests necessitates the maintenance of good relations with all manner of states. They are differentiated mostly by national style, reflecting two contrasting visions of national exceptionalism embedded in the republican and classical traditions of liberalism, respectively, which were discussed earlier in this chapter. The inescapable Gaullist legacy is well captured by another extract from Hollande's address to his ambassadors:[9]

> It is by remaining faithful to the message that France is sending – a message of respect, openness, solidarity, democracy and freedom – that France will continue to be listened to, respected and valued. At a time when extremism is feeding off people's fears, including among our major partners, at a time when others are seeking to make us doubt our shared destiny, I would like to

highlight an obvious fact. . . . The world knows – perhaps even more so than the French people themselves – what France represents. Not only because it is the nation of human rights, not only because it has always stood alongside countries fighting for their freedom, but because it is able to talk to all parties, and to take initiatives. Because it does not see its role as a permanent member of the Security Council as being to prevent or to block, even though this is sometimes necessary, but rather to take action, to find political solutions to crises. So compromising our values would not only be a step backwards for our rule of law, but would also endanger our national cohesion, even though we are aware of the extent of the threat. It would also undermine our international influence.

Allowing for the impact of time on public oratory there is little in this speech with which Lord Palmerston, the most famous architect of Britain's liberal foreign policy, would have disagreed. Speaking in 1848 he famously set out the framework within which most British governments have operated ever since:[10]

I hold that the real policy of England – apart from questions which involve her own particular interests, political or commercial – is to be the champion of justice and right; pursuing that course with moderation and prudence, not becoming the Quixote of the world, but giving the weight of her moral sanction and support wherever she thinks that justice is, and wherever she thinks that wrong has been done . . . as long as England keeps herself in the right, – as long as she wishes to permit no injustice . . . she never will find herself altogether alone. She is sure to find some other State, of sufficient power, influence and weight to support and aid her in the course that she may think fit to pursue. Therefore I say that it is a narrow policy to suppose that this country or that is marked out as the eternal ally or the perpetual enemy of England. We have no eternal allies, and we have no perpetual enemies. Our interests are eternal and perpetual, and those interests it is our duty to follow.

These sentiments have been repeated often by British leaders in the 160 years since Palmerston first voiced them. Although by 1999 Britain had moved down the pecking order, the same sentiments were resurrected by the then British Prime Minister Tony Blair when he framed his international doctrine on intervention in his Chicago speech, delivered in the wake of the NATO decision to 'liberate' Kosovo. Having outlined the five criteria that should govern decisions to intervene, Blair continued:[11]

Now our actions are guided by a more subtle blend of mutual self-interest and moral purpose in defending the values we cherish. . . . In the end, values and interests merge. . . . If we can establish and spread the values of liberty, the rule of law, human rights and an open society, then that is in our national interests too.

Britain's closeness with the United States has been viewed by some countries, more particularly perhaps by France under President de Gaulle, as breaching the balanced policy of accommodation between values and interests as classically portrayed by Palmerston. Winston Churchill, who had an almost mystical belief in the solidarity of the English-speaking world, might have secretly agreed, but most British governments would not. In any case, by the 1990s the French had reasserted their full membership of the Atlantic Alliance, including NATO. With the exception of the Iraq War, when their policies diverged sharply – a factor which may have benefitted France's diplomatic reputation in Asia at Britain's expense – the British and French have more often been on the same side of the debate on foreign policy. What separates them from most of the other major European powers, even including Germany, and leads to a similar world view, is that they retain, albeit on a greatly diminished scale, armed forces capable of being deployed in an expeditionary role within Europe but also beyond the continent.

This capacity, reinforced by the fact that both are nuclear powers and permanent members of the Security Council, has made them the major European voices in post–Cold War policymaking on international security. Both have taken a leading part in debates about international peacekeeping, and post-Iraq, their policies have converged again, first in their joint action in Libya in 2011 and second in solidarity on the priority to be given to national security in the wake of terrorist attacks in both countries. Both President Macron and Prime Minister Theresa May have abandoned the Blairite rhetoric of making over the rest of the world on the basis of liberal internationalist principles, in favour of giving priority to national security at the domestic level.[12] In the British case, the weakness of the government and the depth of its confusion over what to do about Brexit admittedly leaves little time for anything else, even if the government was disposed to cut a more dashing figure on the world stage. For the time being both Britain and France seem determined to nurture special partnerships with emerging Asia – and particularly with China and India – stressing the coincidence of their interests and avoiding as far as possible any conflict over values. The fact that China has emerged as a champion of the Paris climate accord and that all four countries have refused to follow President Trump in his attempt to withdraw the United States from it has no doubt helped to keep the prospect of a global value consensus alive. Whether this would survive another international humanitarian crisis in which domestic and/or regional pressure built up to demand intervention remains to be seen.

CONCLUSION

The Europeans are as varied a set of peoples as any other of the major regional civilizations on this planet. The cultural and ethical values that characterize their civilization similarly have deep roots, but they also have two features, both developed since the mid-seventeenth century when Western European states began to dominate world politics, that distinguish their values, for better or for worse, from those of other states and civilizations. The first is the claim that their values are not fundamentally a cultural, that is, the product of a specifically European set of social arrangements, beliefs and practices, but are universal: indeed, the essential prerequisites of a condition that apparently all desire and that is rather comically termed, 'modernity'. The second feature, which is not unique to Western civilization, is that the European values that underpin the foreign policies of European states are secular: the Europeans do not deny the validity of religious faith, but nor do they afford religion any political status. Freedom of religion is an inalienable human right, but belief in God has been consigned to the private sphere. There are, of course, specific historical reasons why religion was subordinated to politics in Europe and their public values stripped of any overt religious content. Sectarian violence is not confined to the three Abrahamic faiths, but Christian Europe nonetheless felt its full force over the centuries, both within states and between them. Domestically, the populations of several European countries were divided between Orthodox and Catholic (roughly Eastern and Western) versions of Christianity and/or between Protestants and Catholics. Internationally, Islam and Christianity were pitted against one another, first as the result of the Muslim conquest of the Iberian Peninsula and later the confrontation between the Ottoman Empire and Western Christianity. This conflict for dominion in Eastern and Central Europe lasted for over a hundred years and was not finally halted until the Battle of Vienna in 1683. Before that, the devastation caused by the Thirty Years War between Protestant and Catholic Europe was also finally ended.

The 1648 Treaty of Westphalia formalized the existing European states-system under the principle of *cuius regio eius religio*, roughly speaking 'to each prince his own religion'. The original Westphalian system was not based on religious toleration – and sectarian violence within states was always a possibility – but it did lay the foundation for an international system based on secular values, above all the idea that cooperation between sovereign states rested on the principle of non-interference in their domestic affairs. This system has been carried over, in a modified and updated version, into the multilateral global order which was established in its present form after World War II and is presided over by the UN Organization. It is probably fair to say that the values on which the Charter is based were understood by the majority of people in Europe as having derived from organized religion, which, despite the rapid secularization of society, continued to be the seedbed of public morality and national identities until after World War II. According to the Eurobarometer survey of 2012, approximately 70 percent of EU citizens still describe themselves as Christian, 48 percent of whom are Catholic.

But in terms of religiosity measured in terms of regular church attendance, there are significant differences between countries, with the largely Protestant countries of the Atlantic seaboard witnessing the most rapid decline in active religious belief, although the trend is not confined to these countries. The view of the EU as an organization of post-Christian Europe largely explains the prominence given to secular liberal values by all the leading European states. Nonetheless, it is becoming more difficult to sustain, partly because the expansion of the membership has brought in countries where religion remains an important marker of national identity, and partly because some of the most secular members of the Union, including Belgium, France, Britain and Spain, have sizeable Muslim minorities and have proved particularly vulnerable to attack by Muslim extremists. It is a paradox that, having more or less successfully domesticated religion and removed it as a source of violent conflict within Europe, religious toleration is again under threat as a result of the combined pressures of immigration and a rise in religious extremism, not all of which emanates from the Muslim community. As a foreign policy value system, secular liberalism – at least in its realist version which drew back from reaching too far into the social life and culture of other countries – had a reasonable prospect of being accepted as a universal political language. It is a sad fact that in present circumstances European states are likely to find it more and more difficult to sustain liberalism abroad while pulling up the drawbridge against the outside world and fending off political and discriminatory pressure on minorities at home.

NOTES

1. The classic account of the European model is Hedley Bull, *The Anarchical Society: A Study of Order in World Politics* (London: Macmillan, 1977). For its evolution on the basis of the values of medieval Christendom see Maurice Keens-Soper, 'The Practice of a States-System', in Michael Donelan (ed.) *The Reason of States* (London; New York: Routledge Library Edition, 2016), 25–44.

2. The presumption of universality of European values, and the way they became embedded in European consciousness, is brilliantly explained by Ortega Gasset, Minister of Culture in the Spanish Republican government before the Civil War. See his *Revolt of the Masses* (London: Allen and Unwin, 1932), 224–25.

3. I have discussed this definition and its global dissemination in James Mayall, *Nationalism and International Society* (Cambridge: Cambridge University Press, 1990).

4. S. Kekeleire and J. MacNaughtan, *The Foreign Policy of the European Union* (Basingstoke: Palgrave Macmillan, 2008).

5. These issues are discussed in James Mayall (ed.), *The Contemporary Commonwealth, An Assessment 1965–2009* (Abingdon: Routledge, 2010). See in

particular, 'Introduction', 8–11; Nicholas Bayne, 'Managing Globalisation: The Commonwealth in the Global Economy', 103–21; and Paul Taylor, 'The Commonwealth and the European Union', 139–56.

6. Euneighbours.euinfo@euneighbours.eu, 10 October 2017.

7. Douglas Murray, *The Strange Death of Europe* (London: Bloomsbury, 2017).

8. Francois Hollande, President of the French Republic, Paris. 30 October 2016. http://ae.ambafrance.org.

9. Ibid.

10. Viscount Palmerston, House of Commons, 1 March 1848.

11. Economic Club of Chicago 23 April 1999. http://webarchive:nationalarchives. gov.uk/+/www.number10.gov.uk/Page 1297.

12. Jonathan Gilmore, 'The Uncertain Merger of Values and Interests in UK Foreign Policy', *International Affairs* 90, no. 3 (May 2014): 541–48.

BIBLIOGRAPHY

Bull, Hedley. *The Anarchical Society, A Study of Order in World Politics*. London: Macmillan, 1977.

Gilmore, Jonathan. 'The Uncertain Merger of Values and Interests in UK Foreign Policy'. *International Affairs* 90, no. 3 (May 2014): 541–57.

Gasset, Ortega. *The Revolt of the Masses*. London: Allen and Unwin, 1932.

Hill, Christopher. *The National Interest in Question, Foreign Policy in Multilateral Societies*. Oxford: Oxford University Press, 2013.

Hill, Christopher and Michael Smith (eds.). *International Relations and the European Union*. Oxford: Oxford University Press, 2nd edition, 2011.

Keens-Soper, Maurice. 'The Practice of a States-System', in Michael Donelan (ed.). *The Reason of States, A Study in International Political Theory*. London: George Allen and Unwin, 1978, London; New York: Routledge, Library Edition, 2016.

Kekeleire, S. and J. MacNaughtan. *The Foreign Policy of the European Union*. Basingstoke: Palgrave Macmillan, 2008.

Mayall, James (ed.). *The Contemporary Commonwealth: An Assessment 1965–2009*. Abingdon: Routledge, 2010.

Mayall, James. *Nationalism and International Society*. Cambridge: Cambridge University Press, 1990.

Murray, Douglas. *The Strange Death of Europe*. London: Bloomsbury, 2016.

Poli, Sara (ed.). *The European Neighbourhood Policy – Values and Principles*. Abingdon: Routledge, 2016.

Chapter 2

Values and European Foreign Economic Policy

Ideas, Institutions and Interests

Fredrik Erixon

Europe's foreign economic policy is defined by the pursuit of prosperity and power.[1] That does not make the European Union (EU) unique, however: neither in a historic analysis nor in modern world affairs. Just like other economies of size, the EU aspires to raise the welfare of its population and shape the world around it through its external economic policy or the use of its economic statecraft. And the values that it wants to promote conform to the basic elements of a 'liberal word order', such as human rights, civil liberties, democratic governance, protection of the environment and solidarity. It believes in universalism and broadly defines its own role in world affairs to carry rights and liberties to other parts of the world.

However, the declaration of values in European policy only takes us so far in understanding the role and significance they have in actual policy, and for the purpose of this chapter, which is limited to foreign economic policy, how they stand up to the protection and promotion of economic interests. It is the argument of this chapter that Europe's own experience defines both the actual substance and form of its foreign economic policy, and that happens in a way that is different from other powers like China, Japan and the United States. While Europe is similar to other powers in that economic interests play a critical role for shaping its international economic policy, Europe's own experience complicates the pursuit of both power and plenty. What ends up as policy in Europe is as much a reflection of internal political and institutional factors as it is defined by exogenous events and conditions, and it is these internal factors that continue to set the tone for what Europe aspires to achieve with its foreign economic policy and how Europe defines what values that this policy reflects. In other words, Europe's foreign economic policy grows inside-out: it is as much about itself as it is about any particular outcome that Europe wants to see abroad.

Obviously, there is a historical explanation for it: the EU is the product of centuries of war in Europe, and its chief purpose is to build stability on the continent. When countries in Western Europe started to construct a new form of European cooperation after World War II, the aim was to build a stronger economic basis for peace by means of foreign economic policy, especially trade and investment across the border. Later, foreign economic policy in Europe was key to chart the new course for how former countries in the Soviet bloc would integrate with the EU – indeed, even join the EU – and move to become democratic market economies. These are two signature achievements in Europe for foreign economic and other policies, and what is revealing is that they are about the EU itself and its extension.

Beyond that, however, Europe's use of foreign economic policy for non-economic objectives remains something of an experiment, or work in progress. Generally, the promotion of economic development and welfare in other parts of the world, especially in countries that formerly were European colonies, has been part and parcel of EU trade policy for some time and is often supported by programmes of development assistance. It is more recently that the EU has started to condition the signing of trade agreements on compliance with non-trade or non-economic policies. The EU has established some standards that gradually have become non-controversial, at least in Europe, such as including in its free trade agreements chapters on sustainable development and commitments to international agreements in that area.[2] In newer free trade agreements, the EU has sought to widen the scope of sustainable development to include areas like gender rights, but the approach remains the same: reference in trade agreements to the participation in international conventions such as the International Labour Organization's convention governing workers' rights and the Rio Convention. Some developing economies without free trade agreements with the EU can qualify for additional tariff preferences in Europe if they sign up to the same conventions.

However, policies like these are often aimed at procedural or declaratory rather than substantive outcomes. For instance, countries can be signatories to an international convention without following its rules and recommendations, and Europe has not generally been policing compliance (or sanctioning non-compliance) with international conventions referenced in its trade agreements. Other countries have protested against EU ambitions of including policies on sustainable development in trade agreements. For some, the habit of forcing some policies upon other countries reflects old imperial instincts. For others, the inclusion of non-economic conditions rather amounts to protectionism: it is a policy that can limit their potential export gains because the policies they are asked to adopt can raise the cost of production. Even if both objections carry some truth, the plain fact is that the inclusion of these provisions in trade agreements has little capacity to change outcomes. Few governments have been willing to press through substantial changes in their non-trade or non-economic regulations because of a trade agreement with Europe.

The contribution of EU trade policy to economic progress in developing countries is an area for discussion – not a point of fact – for the simple reason that Europe for a long time has maintained high market access barriers for typical agricultural export products from these countries. While it is obvious that trade with Europe (and the rest of the world) has helped many economies to expand welfare, it is equally obvious that high barriers on products like sugar and coffee have reduced trade opportunities for other economies.

Importantly, the closer the EU gets to a 'hard' use of its economic power, the more its policy becomes one about itself. There are few cases to point to when Europe has wielded its economic power in order to promote its declared values outside its own neighbourhood. And that is not because of an absence of opportunities for Europe to put power behind the demonstration of its values; it is rather because there is no agreed policy in Europe for when a 'hard' use of economic power is motivated. There is no common understanding in Europe about what type of behaviour in other countries would constitute such a breach of values that sanctions or other economic measures are justified. Both the injurious action and Europe's response to it are subjects for internal negotiation.

In part, this is because European countries are motivated by different economic ideas. Europe was the intellectual birthplace of protectionism, mercantilism as well as free trade, the three main paradigms – or systems of values – of how a country should design its economic policy vis-à-vis other countries. There are traces of all of them in current policy and debates, and they tend to follow national lines. Europe has also been a continent of economic sanctions and trade boycotts, not to mention the use of military confrontation as a means to settle disputes over commerce. Combined with other experiences of war, key European powers like Germany have been uneasy about the concept of power and the use of it for political objectives.

These and other historic experiences have been critical for how the pursuit of both power and plenty has been embodied in European foreign economic policy. Europe has economic interests that it defends by its foreign economic policy, but it considers itself as a 'soft power' and one that puts dialogue, diplomacy and international agreements in the front seat, as a procedural power. While it upholds the principles and norms of the global economic order emerging after 1945, based on trade and investment freedom, and restrictions on state distortions of the market economy, it is uncomfortable deploying its foreign economic power and to speak its language. The EU is often constrained by substantial differences between European governments, which limit the range of available options and place a lot of emphasis on procedure rather than outcome. Europe increasingly finds itself in the position that its economic authority does not get the attention that most European leaders think it deserves.

EUROPE'S FOREIGN ECONOMIC POLICY
AND THE CASE OF RUSSIA

Europe's response to Russian aggression in Georgia and Ukraine is a revealing example of Europe's foreign economic policy. Russia's wars in these countries have been critical events for stability and security in Europe, and both aggressions prompted Europe to make decisions about using its economic statecraft to promote its values and to sanction behaviour that violate them. After Russia's invasion of Georgia in 2008, the EU was uncertain about the degree to which its response should involve the use of economic power. The EU wanted, at the least, to support Georgia's economy which had been damaged by the Russian attacks. But it was equally clear that EU countries were divided about the response, and how to weigh own economic interests against non-economic objectives. After a period with increasingly charged policy discussions, it became clear that the EU could not move beyond the status quo and, from the perspective of foreign economic policy, decided only to prolong Georgia's preferential trade status under the Generalised System of Preferences.

The response signalled internal divisions, and many observers were quick to point out Europe's ineffectiveness in aiding Georgia. The EU refrained, for instance, from offering Georgian exporters much better, let alone full, access to the EU market for its products, which would have given Georgian exports a boost. Nor did the EU direct the attention of its trade policy towards Russia's exports to Europe. Trade sanctions against Russia were proposed but ran up against heavy opposition from both commercial interests and member states.

The then newly elected French President Nicolas Sarkozy, whose country held the rotating presidency of the EU, helped to broker a peace agreement between Russia and Georgia. Although the deal later failed, it was initially heralded as Sarkozy's moment in global politics, and showed that the pursuit of peace can be more successful when diplomatic efforts are not disturbed by sanctions and value demonstration. In reality, however, efforts to broker peace were only one part of the equation. In a subsequent speech to EU ambassadors, Sarkozy offered to put France's 'friendship with Russia at the service of the whole of the European Union',[3] but it was clear that, for France, the relations it had built up with Russia were to a great extent about its own commercial interests. At the time of the war, a French company, partly owned by the government, was negotiating a contract to sell Mistral-class warships to Russia – ships that, according to the Russian Navy Chief Admiral Vladimir Vysotsky, would have enabled Russia to win the war against Georgia 'in 40 minutes instead of 26 hours' had they been in Russia's possession.[4] Other countries had similar economic interests to protect.

Russia's 2014 annexation of Crimea and its war in Eastern Ukraine was a more important event for Europe's foreign economic policy, partly because it was motivated by the prospect of deeper trade and political relations between Ukraine and the EU. Moreover, Europe's collective policy vis-à-vis Russia can be understood only in light of their commercial interactions. Europe was yet again torn about using economic sanctions against Russia, and member states were openly haggling about whether the economic consequences for Europe of sanctions against Russia were a reasonable price to pay for demonstrating its values. When the decision about the imposition of sanctions finally came, it was clear that Europe could not agree on a deployment of its economic power that would have strong economic consequences.

Sanctions are not necessarily an effective response to events; nor are they necessary in order to demonstrate opposition to, or deep concerns about, a chosen policy by a foreign government. But for sanctions to stand any chance of changing the behaviour of another country, they need to hit 'thick and fast'. Europe, however, did not respond fast. In reality, it was only after the United States moved towards sanctions that most governments in Europe felt compelled to proceed in the same direction. Nor were sanctions 'thick' in the sense that the economic consequences of them would be immediately strong; they were rather designed to avoid forceful economic consequences for Russia and the EU, partly because the dominant exports of Russia to the EU – hydrocarbons – were exempted from the sanctions. Once the prospect of economic sanctions against Russia emerged in March 2014, the process of political and economic log-rolling in Europe reached extraordinary levels. The EU decided against using sanctions that were far more likely to be effective because commercial actors had the economic power to stop them. In the second round of sanctions, Europe decided also to use selected financial sanctions, partly because of their effectiveness, and partly and importantly, because the financial sector had been given time to protect itself from the consequences of the sanctions.

STATE, POWER AND FOREIGN ECONOMIC POLICY

Europe's economic responses to Russia's wars in Georgia and Ukraine exhibit the role of economic interests when the EU formulates a foreign economic policy for specific and critical events. However, just as declaration of values may be of little use for understanding the actual conduct of foreign economic policy in Europe, it is equally easy to oversimplify the role of economic interests. What makes the role of values and norms different in the embodiment of Europe's foreign economic policy is not that it is pragmatic in the choice between idealism and interests, but derives rather from how Europe's own experiences have created a different class of perceptions and loyalties that other countries do not share.

First, the alliance with the United States is an important part of EU foreign economic policy, and until the 2016 presidential election in the United States, Europe had been broadly accepting America's leadership in that field of international affairs. There are historical roots as to why Europe has accepted to play a junior role in the transatlantic firm, and they still guide the substance and form of its foreign economic policy. While the United States has both been a partner and a competitor to Europe in the field of the international economy, it is impossible to understand Europe's foreign economic policy without the history of American leadership.

In the first place, the United States played a critical role in pushing Europe towards policies of regional economic integration after World War II. The acute economic distress and, at the macro level, the dollar shortage in Europe after the war prompted the US government to craft a plan for aid that, by today's economic standards, was remarkably generous. But part of the US aid to Europe, known as the Marshall Plan, was conditioned on renewed efforts in Europe to open up its economies towards each other and build more cooperation for peace and economic development. The United States also kept itself part of that ambition by helping to set up organizations like the Organisation for Economic Co-operation and Development, a Paris-based organization to promote economic integration. Moreover, US leaders were also determined to anchor Europe's own regional efforts to lower barriers to trade and investment in international trade agreements. As Europe recovered, that ambition became increasingly important: if Europe only had liberalized internally and not reduced tariffs with other countries, American firms would have been disadvantaged in European markets. Together with the provision of security in Europe, America's economic policy for integration in Europe made the old continent conform to American leadership for global economic policy. While individual European countries chose different paths than the United States in critical world affairs, they never really departed from the global economic institutions that America powered. One consequence of this development is that Europe has a strong belief in the role of institutions and international agreements for the provision of a rules-based international economic policy. Europe is skilled at managing institutions and agreements and forging the compromises that are necessary for them to stay relevant. However, Europe feels uncomfortable to step outside this world of international economic rules, even when values would prompt governments to do so.

Second, Europe's own mix of ideas for foreign economic policy – protectionism, mercantilism and free trade – is complex and a source of friction that routinely makes it difficult for Europe to pursue a proactive foreign economic policy and command authority through its sheer economic power. Foreign economic policy in the EU is a mix between countries with different economic capabilities, levels of economic development and culture of economic ideas. And lately, the sum of these differences has begun to change. While the EU was a reluctant liberalizer for many decades, the gradually declining role of US leadership and the growing role for new economic powers have made it more difficult for European countries to agree on the adequate course of action in many areas of international economic policy.

The European compact of trade and an open world economic order still stands, but it has been fraying at the edges. The economic crisis hardened the spirit of mercantilism in Europe's foreign economic policy, and the perceived threat of economic competition from abroad has strengthened Europe's resolve to condition access to the European market on compliance with EU regulation. Just as in America, there is an increasing suspicion that open trade does not benefit Europe as much as it has done in the past. And part of the anxiety over trade and globalization rests on domestic economic problems and a disbelief in Europe's industry-led model for trade and growth.

Structural economic change in the Western European economies has been slow. Growth in output and employment in service-based and innovative sectors has not been high enough to foster a smooth transition from an industry-based economy to a knowledge-based economy. Global trade speeds up structural change and is a vector for dissemination of technology, the greatest factor behind structural change. But policies in Europe have made this change more difficult, and governments have been unwilling to pursue substantial economic reforms. For instance, inflexibilities in European labour markets have prevented Europe from reaping the full benefits of trade and digitalization, and with new prospects for rapid innovation across the economy, Europe is increasingly preoccupied by the protection of jobs.

Third, Europe's foreign economic policy is often an image of its own post-war project to reduce the significance of national borders and territorial integrity. European post-war cooperation has arguably been a success, but it has deceived many in Europe into believing that the world, especially after the end of the Cold War, desired to follow the same playbook. While the economic interdependence that follows on the heels of cross-border trade and investment has been accepted in most parts of the world, few other countries are involved in postmodern enterprises to diminish the 'classic' or Westphalian role of the state. Arguably, Europe's own experience in creating a new form of political cooperation, distanced from the core concept of territorial protection and the formulation of a national interest, is today more important than any other source of guidance for the conduct of foreign economy policy. Therefore, we need to discuss it at greater length.

EUROPE: A POSTMODERN STATE CONSTRUCTION

The EU is a complex political structure. Europe is a continent of nation states that at the centre has the EU and common institutions for its twenty-eight members – twenty-seven after the United Kingdom has left the EU. But the jurisdictional competence of these institutions is limited. Typically, policy in Europe does not gravitate from Brussels. Many policies are not decided by Brussels and remain within the confines of its member states. Over the past decades an increasing number of policy issues have been centralized to the EU, and there are few issues without a Brussels dimension.

The EU, however, is not the only pan-European institution for policy considerations. There is a European Court of Justice which is institutionally unrelated to the EU. There are economic cooperations that have nothing to do with Brussels. Some EU countries share a common currency, but only nineteen of EU's members use it as legal tender. Some EU countries are members of NATO; others are not. The varieties of European cooperation are significant and also affect the effectiveness of European cooperation at large. Consequently, European policymaking is a cumbersome, bureaucratic and time-consuming process, and often, its main goal is to bridge internal differences between member states rather to achieve the stated ambitions with Europe-wide policy cooperation: for instance, in enabling European countries to exercise greater influence in world affairs by sharing policy and pooling resources. Hence any understanding of Europe must start in its institutional complexities. Its foreign economic policy offers a good example.

Foreign economic policy is the power centre of Europe's global ambitions. With the size of its common market, Europe could exercise considerable influence on foreign governments by allowing or denying access to its market. From a policy perspective, commercial policy is the backbone of the EU. It is a Customs Union and runs a Common Commercial Policy – a trade policy, in normal language. But this does not mean unlimited power for the EU. EU's trade policy is constitutionally limited. Issues related to services often do not fall under the power structure of Brussels – these are issues belonging to the jurisdictional sphere of the member states, and many of them have offered fierce resistance against moves towards centralizing policies in the services sectors. Thus Brussels is constrained in negotiating reduced barriers to trade in services with third countries, a constraint which presents real difficulties in modern trade negotiations, and limits Europe's capability of using its economic statecraft internationally.

This list of limits on European internal cooperation could be made longer and comprise key areas in foreign economic policy such as energy. The overall pattern, however, is that Europe can be influential internationally only if it has opened its own markets internally and formed joint policies and institutions to exercise it. The fragmentation of power undermines the effectiveness of its foreign economic policy and economic statecraft, but it shows that European countries have not been ready to discard national sovereignty for the purpose of Europe's international power.

Nor are European member states convinced about the case for centralizing more foreign economic policy in the EU. Take the International Monetary Fund (IMF) as an example. Europe is vastly over-represented in this organization as the quota of votes is based on the relative economic size of countries as was the case far back in time. A common European approach in a reformed membership structure would lead to lower aggregate formal influence in the IMF for European members, but its effective power would increase as the bloc could exercise an influence that is not possible today. However, almost all EU countries have so far rejected reforms that would seriously dilute their own formal status in the IMF and other similar bodies.

European cooperation is increasingly becoming postmodern. In recent decades, economic globalization has tied European countries so close to each other that it is difficult to separate states from each other. In some economic aspects, but far from all, borders have been rendered meaningless: it is a fruitless exercise to distinguish the national identity of a particular type of goods when the supply and value chains are based on the contributions of many entities spread out over Europe. Yet there is arguably something more to the term postmodern than the mere economics. In philosophy, the term 'postmodern' not only represents a chronological position – after the modern – but it also sets out a discourse with its own conceptual views, often defined in opposition to views underpinning the era of the modern state. And it is that conception which increasingly has been guiding Europe's perception of itself and the purpose of economic statecraft.

A first aspect of the postmodern state conception is its fluid political personality. Despite its gradually expanding role, there is no fundamental concept of the state and state institutions in the EU. There are treaties, but no constitution. There is an assembly, but it does not control the execution of power. European courts are more important than European elections for determining the substance and conduct of policy. The postmodern state is one in which territory, the core theme in the political personality of the modern state, is secondary to a more fundamental guide for policy. In the case of the EU, it is transnational cooperation between European nation states and the attendant move of autonomous authority away from nation state institutions. This transfer of power is done to gain something else, for instance, greater international power. Yet the postmodern construction sometimes prevents the pursuit of power: it does not rest on the perception of a common strategic and national/regional interest or a shared understanding about when common ideals should trump specific interests. The classic idea of the state has its own weaknesses, but the quest of the political personality, and attendant state institutions, of the new postmodern construction has become a central character in the way Europe presents itself to the rest of the world.

It follows that the concept of power gets transformed in a political and institutional atmosphere of postmodernism. Europe today largely embodies a postmodern concept of power. Process takes primacy over outcome also in Europe's international relations, because at the core of the postmodern concept of foreign economic policy is the alienation of the classic concept of power. In that old view, power is not hard or soft; it is neither smart nor dumb. Power is power. It is the capacity to get other countries to do what they do not wish to do. The postmodern concept of power does not accept this view – and that is increasingly true also for Europe. Europe's central idea is, for obvious historic reasons, to weaken national power and interests. While eroding past concepts about national interest and power has been a survival necessity, the move of authority from nation states to pan-European institutions has not enabled Europe to become the international power that commands authority corresponding with its economic size and wealth. European foreign economic policy is now located somewhere between the old concept of national interest, and visions of a pan-European political personality with a shared understanding in Europe about both interests and values in its international affairs.

CONCLUSION: THE FUTURE OF ECONOMIC STATECRAFT IN EUROPE

Europe's foreign economic policy is a reflection of Europe's experiences and can be understood only in light of the variations of interests that exist between EU member states and the way the quest for internal unity in Europe takes primacy over any outcome it wants to achieve. The complex structure of governance makes it difficult to define a common interest and to pursue non-economic values in foreign economic policy, even if there is not much of a dispute in Europe as to what those values are. Europe's own history makes the continent hesitant to accept hard concepts of power and use them in its foreign economy policy. In essence, Europe's foreign economic policy is at work only when it proceeds with long-term objectives anchored in international agreements and institutions. Its prime role has been to foment peace and stability in Europe, first between those in Western Europe, and then with countries in the former Soviet bloc.

There are new pressures in Europe that may come to disturb foreign economic policy. Some European governments are at loggerheads with the EU institutions, either because of differing opinions over migration or because they no longer are willing to conform to all the liberal values and norms of the EU. While these countries may want to distance themselves even more from areas of EU policy in the future, economic and security policy interests still pull them close to the EU and leave them with few other options.

Pressure is also coming from other countries, but it is a different kind of change that they would like to advance. Some Eurozone countries have charted a new discourse for economic policy cooperation that entails more cooperation and shared responsibilities in new areas of policy. It is unclear, however, how far these countries are willing to go and if they have domestic support for it. For all their federalist pretences, governments in countries such as France, Germany and the Netherlands have, over time, become less convinced by Europe's ideology of 'ever closer union' and grown more attentive to opinions that are sceptical, if not hostile, to the EU.

Even if governments in Central and Eastern Europe would yet again conform to the values and norms of the EU, and the Eurozone core would accelerate reforms to make the European Monetary Union fiscally and financially more stable, Europe remains a long way from having a full new political personality that entitles the EU to build the institutions necessary to command power in the world. It will remain a halfway house for the foreseeable future and the confusion over what constitutes a common European economic interest – and how that interest should be balanced by ideals – is unlikely to be settled. In fact, a strong case can be made for accentuated uncertainty over the conduct of foreign economic policy in Europe. Without American leadership, Europe is not easily pulled into a certain direction by the sheer economic and political force of an ally. The declining relevance of international economic institutions and the rules-based economic order deprives Europe of a key anchor for building internal unity and an accepted form for advancing long-term objectives. With growing economic dependence on new regions and countries, there are more commercial interests that can use the absence of a common economic interest and a shared understanding of when a values-driven foreign economic policy is legitimate, for their own purposes.

NOTES

1. This chapter is predominantly concerned with values in the foreign economic policy of the European Union. While all foreign economic policies in Europe are not in the domain of the EU, central areas like trade and investment policies – including economic sanctions – are part of EU policy. When this chapter talks about Europe, it means the EU.

2. European Commission, *Trade for All: Towards a More Responsible Trade and Investment Policy*, 2015. http://trade.ec.europa.eu/doclib/docs/2015/october/tradoc_153846.pdf.

3. Par Tita Aver, 'Russia – France Relations: The Fools of the Georgia War', *Nouvelle-Europe.eu* (18 January 2011). http://www.nouvelle-europe.eu/node/998.

4. 'Mistral Blows', *The Economist* (17 May 2014). https://www.economist.com/news/europe/21602291-why-france-insists-going-ahead-selling-warships-russia-mistral-blows.

Chapter 3

Values in German Foreign Policy

*How Changes of Course
Created Lasting Values*

Amit Das Gupta

Debates on values in foreign policy tend to end with a most trivial conclusion. A truly value-based foreign policy is near-impossibility given the multiple pragmatic needs in international relations. There seem to be two extremes between regularly failing idealism as most prominently proposed by the United States and mere pragmatists like German Chancellor Otto von Bismarck's understanding of policy as the art of managing practical possibilities. Such reduction indicates a black-and-white view, ignoring that values can and do work well as hermeneutic ideals or general guidelines in practical politics, even with pragmatists like Bismarck. As the German case shows, they do have an impact, playing a much more prominent role than forcing politicians or officials to pay lip service to them in order to justify a policy which is actually determined by other considerations. Values can be based on, or establish, attitudes and taboos and predispose decision makers.

This chapter is not going to provide a general definition of the term 'value', as it would occupy much space without providing satisfactory results. Only naturally, values in the pursuit of foreign affairs of a state are understood as something positive and idealistic. At least today, no government or people would confess to pursue a foreign policy without values or with unacceptable aims such as aggressive expansionism. Nevertheless, values can have a problematic side as well; they can, for example, be considered a hindrance in times when reshaping foreign affairs seems necessary. In this chapter values will be understood as long-term determinants, which do not belong to a certain party, government or narrowly limited time frame. They correspond with the self-image of a political entity and its people, and have developed from historical experiences and certain attitudes. Whereas the French due to the revolution in 1789 see themselves committed to the ideals of freedom, equality and brotherhood, and the United States to democratic rule, it is often said that Adolf Hitler, as a most negative experience, stands at the beginning of all modern German policy. This is only partly true. There are indeed values based on older experiences and insights playing a crucial role in modern German foreign policy. Certain features in the political apparatus relevant over decades have step by step transformed into what today are understood as values. The chapter will focus on four values, often closely interrelated – modesty, belonging to the Western world, the rejection of the use of force and multilateralism.

To understand values in German foreign policy today, it is worth investigating four crucial debates which were based on values, or which have created new ones. The first is the never-ending discussion about Germany's role in Europe, as answered differently by Bismarck and his immediate successors, taken up once again by Chancellors Konrad Adenauer, Willy Brandt and Helmut Kohl. Second, Adenauer's decision from 1949 onwards to join the Western camp in the Cold War was not only massively challenged over the years, among others by the Social Democrats, but has also resulted in a reorientation of the German self-image. The third is actually a belated debate; Brandt's rejection of any use of force in the pursuit of national interests in 1969, making possible the treaties with the Soviet Union and its satellites, was based on a broad consensus. The true debate took place, but in 1998/1999, around the decision to join the North Atlantic Treaty Organization (NATO) forces in the Kosovo War. Finally, Kohl's confession from 1990 that a united Germany must be part of a united Europe and play a constructive role in a multipolar world instead of pursuing national interests, which finally cemented the credo in favour of multilateralism.

MODESTY – STRATEGY GROWN INTO VALUE

Helmuth Plessner coined the term of Germany as a 'late nation' – the last of the European great powers to gain national unity in 1871.[1] The birth of the Prussian-dominated Reich was the outcome of three successive wars against Denmark, Austria and France waged by Bismarck. United Germany, with its large territory and booming economy, its modern army and the largest population in Europe after Russia, had reached what Ludwig Dehio termed a 'half-hegemonic position'.[2] Though Prussia was the smallest of the five great European powers, the Reich was the strongest on the continent, but not strong enough to enforce its policy on others. Bismarck learned this lesson in a major crisis with France in 1875, understanding that the German newcomer was considered a threat by the established powers. Germany's half-hegemonic position was prone to destabilize the continent and cause anti-German alliances. His response was to declare the Reich 'saturated', to deviate tensions in Europe towards the periphery and to play the role of honest broker in conflicts among other great powers. Bismarck and his successors, however, proved unable to stabilize Germany's fragile position between domination and encirclement, one of many reasons contributing to the German decision of July 1914 to take the risk of a major European war, transforming into the Great War.

Ironically, notwithstanding its defeat, by late 1918 a now-democratic Germany seemed to be its actual winner, having saved its industrial potential and looking forward to unification with Austria; and due to the October Revolution, free from the Russian threat. The ban on unification, demilitarized zones in the West and heavy reparations did not prevent Germany soon rising again. Gustav Stresemann's policy of reconciliation was replaced by another military attempt to establish German rule over Europe and the world. The partition of Germany in 1949 in the eyes of contemporaries seemed to settle the problem of German dominance once and for all. Small East Germany, not being able to provide any nationalist agenda, was more of a satellite than any other part of the Soviet bloc, and Austria, glad to have escaped the German imbroglio, made its peace with a separate existence in neutrality. Only the Federal Republic (FRG) exercised great influence in Europe and global politics. It soon transformed into a leading industrial power and maintained the largest military forces among the European members of NATO. Not only for contractual restrictions, however, it could not play any dominant role. Its security depended on NATO and particularly the United States. Within the European Economic Community (EEC), FRG was the key economic player, but left leadership in political issues to its partner France. German acceptance of playing second fiddle is visible even over a minor European issue. Though by the number of native speakers German is by far the most widely used language in Europe, it is not an official language of the European Union (EU). When in September 2009 Foreign Minister Guido Westerwelle during a press conference in Berlin refused to answer a question asked in English – 'we are in Germany' – in the resulting domestic debate this was considered a symptom of a return of nationalist hubris.[3]

Fears of German domination resurfaced with the collapse of the Soviet Empire and the prospect of reunification, both in European capitals and within Germany. Chancellor Kohl, however, had learned the lessons of forty years of partition. Notwithstanding the gains in population, territory and industrial potential, united Germany willingly retained its low profile. Against regular demands for German leadership in global and particularly European crises, Berlin has mostly lain low. The few cases of unilateral initiatives – most prominently the recognition of Croatian independence in January 1992 or the refusal to join the 'Coalition of the Willing' in the Second Gulf War – were criticized by Germany's partners and allies, but even caused domestic protests. The latter hardly focused on the decisions itself – the clear majority of Germans was strongly opposed to the Gulf War. The key problem was considered decision making without consulting foreign governments. Typically, the stillborn German initiative for a reform of the United Nations (UN) Security Council, undertaken with Brazil, India and Japan, did not trigger any enthusiasm in Germany, and its main protagonist, Foreign Minister Klaus Kinkel, was considered a political lightweight.

The warning against returning to the 'bad old ways' is never distant as soon as the Federal Government takes any initiative before securing the consent of its partners. What had once been adopted as a political concept to allow Germany to live in peace and friendship with its smaller European neighbours has transformed into a value. Its existence is reassuring both foreign governments and the domestic public that German foreign policy is calculable and hardly ever unilateral. Furthermore, it is binding on all Federal Governments who can afford to leave this path only occasionally and in special circumstances.

INTEGRATION INTO THE WESTERN WORLD – ESCAPING THE PAST

In 1949, Adenauer opted for close cooperation with the Western powers. This was a renunciation of a 'third way' in international affairs, which under earlier governments often had resulted in a seesaw policy, as evident in the 1922 Rapallo Treaty with the Soviet Union followed by the October 1925 Locarno Treaties with the Western powers. For his siding with one Cold War bloc, opposition leader Kurt Schumacher from the Social Democrats (SPD) rebuked Adenauer as 'chancellor of the western allies',[4] or a leader selling out German interests. Schumacher held that only neutrality or non-alignment would keep the door open for unification, to which he gave top priority. For the chancellor, however, security stood first, which he saw guaranteed only by those able to block a Soviet attack, namely the United States. Adenauer also deeply distrusted his own people, fearing they might easily be deceived by another demagogue. He had grown up in imperial Germany, when many politicians and intellectuals had despised what they considered degenerate Western democracies, and started his political career during the Weimar Republic of the interwar period, aptly described as democracy without democrats. Defining the FRG as part of the West, therefore, served both purposes, securing the survival of the newborn democracy against both external and internal enemies. When in 1952 Stalin indicated that he might agree to unification if united Germany stayed out of military alliances – whether this was meant seriously or not is still an open debate[5] – Adenauer immediately turned down the offer. Apart from deeply distrusting the Soviets, he considered it a litmus test for his trustworthiness as future part of the Western alliance.

With both Germanies formally joining antagonistic military blocs in 1955, unification became a remote prospect. In 1960, the SPD made its peace with integration into the Western camp with the Godesberg Programme. European integration played its part as well. What in 1957 with the Treaties of Rome began mostly as an economic undertaking, soon transformed into a political project in the narrower sense. When the partners in 1969/1970 decided to coordinate their foreign policies in the framework of European Political Cooperation, the FRG in many ways had become an essential part of Western Europe, and the close cooperation with France, manifested in the Élysée Treaty in 1963, resulting in large-scale exchange programmes in the educational and cultural sector, had made its mark. The impact of Westernization and Americanization could be seen first in domestic developments; American living standards and lifestyle – or at least what was perceived as such – became a model for Germans. To what extent they felt part of the Western world could be seen in 1968, when the nearly worldwide students' revolt affected FRG as much as France or the United States, though the German focus was more on the fight of the young against their parents' generation deeply involved with National Socialism. The German protests contributed to a change of government, bringing the SPD back to power after four decades in 1969. The party had maintained channels with East European governments and, after Adenauer had made friends with the West, came to terms with them. Brandt's *New Eastern Policy* is renowned for rapprochement with the Soviet bloc: in a series of treaties Bonn renounced the use of force to re-establish the borders of 1937, which legally were considered valid until 1990. Brandt, however, knew very well that the opening towards the Socialist bloc was possible only with the consent of the Western partners, who kept a distrustful eye on the rapid change. They had urged Bonn to come to terms with its Eastern neighbours, but conducting secret talks via backchannels with Moscow and later its satellites, nevertheless, was a different story.[6] The FRG's reputation as a totally reliable camp follower in NATO did not suffer, because the Federal Government made it a point to keep its partners updated on all relevant points and notwithstanding coming to terms with its socialist neighbours, FRG remained firmly in the Western camp. When, surprisingly, the collapse of the German Democratic Republic (GDR) in November 1989 opened the door to reunification, neither Bonn nor its allies left any doubt that this was conceivable only with Germany fulfilling its obligations in NATO and the European community. This was more than political wisdom. Voices suggesting that united Germany might pursue a more independent course in foreign affairs, let alone leave NATO or EEC, found no echo at all. What had been a deliberate political decision in 1949 had become a value long before 1990. Germans and German politics have kept a soft corner towards Russia, claiming the existence of a special bond of friendship and understanding between the people of both countries, and at least until the Russian annexation of Crimea in 2014, they saw themselves in the role of those more capable than others in interpreting Russian views to Germany's Western partners, though this has never come along with any dreams for a return to the old seesaw policy. For this reason, the fact that the United States after the end of the Cold War gave less importance to NATO and, therefore, among others, loosened the bond with Germany, is still viewed with great concern, whereas other European governments took it with relief that they won more room to manoeuvre.

In the process, Germany has also made Western values German values. The idea of a 'peace dividend' after the end of the Cold War was strongly supported. After the Germans themselves achieved reunification in a democratic system, the wish to set an example to others played a strong role in German foreign affairs in the 1990s. The right to self-determination had become a sacred cow as early as 1918 when the Reich capitulated, expecting that Woodrow Wilson's 14 Points, including the right to self-determination,[7] would be valid for the Germans as well. Throughout the four decades of German partition, it remained fundamental to the claim for reunification. In the 1990s, especially in the Balkans, but also in the Commonwealth of Independent States, the Federal Government soon learned its lesson that claims for self-determination can be a destructive force as well. The same was true for humanitarian interventions closely linked with the American missionary approach to bring freedom and human rights to people all over the world. With the Kosovo War, for once the fight for humanitarian issues overrode another sacred principle of German foreign affairs, namely, never to go to war, let alone without a UN mandate. The wisdom of this war from a realist perspective was and is much under debate.[8] In Germany, it was marketed less as a pragmatic decision – showing solidarity within NATO and stopping the flood of refugees – but an imperative if Germany did not want to betray its own values. Being a part of the Western world comes with certain treaty obligations and, more so, sharing a set of values, and the Germans, shameful of their own past, have adopted them possibly more enthusiastically than others. Being a part of the Western world means to be with the righteous ones. On the contrary, pursuing a foreign policy in the name of national interest not closely connected with Western values is most difficult to justify.

NO FORCE – AN OUTDATED CONCEPT?

On 7 December 1970, Chancellor Willy Brandt fell on his knees in front of the memorial of the murdered Jews of the Warsaw Ghetto. The photograph became iconic. Brandt, who was among the very few West German politicians who had actively fought the Third Reich, and stood for a new Germany, reflecting on and confessing its historic guilt. For long, humility had not been considered a German virtue. On the contrary, since the 1860s Germans had been considered Europe's proud and arrogant warrior race, ready to use the combination of advanced technologies, a perfectly drilled army and expansionist thinking to subdue their neighbours. This image was even valid throughout the Cold War. Though the Federal army due to protocol no. II of the Western European Union in 1954 was denied weapons of mass destruction, bombers or large warships, both the United States and the Soviet Union considered it a relevant part in calculations for all war scenarios. A paradigm shift in the German attitude to warfare, nevertheless, had begun with the defeat in 1945. After two lost wars and the country destructively bombed, the clear majority of Germans wanted to be left alone without any military aspirations. When rearmament in the FRG began in 1955, it was restricted not only by certain treaty obligations; there were also massive public protestations against the reestablishment of German armed forces. Accordingly, paragraph 87a of the Basic Law, the constitution of the FRG, ruled that the Federal army must be used for defence purposes only unless the Basic Law explicitly ruled otherwise. According to paragraphs 24 and 115a, this included defence against any outside attack on the European or North American territories of any member of NATO, the alliance being a mutual assistance pact, mostly to the benefit of FRG as the main frontier state in Europe.

With half a million Germans under arms, the Federal Government soon had by numbers the second-largest army in Europe. German politicians and public, however, remained distrustful. The draft was not only considered a necessity to fill the ranks but was also combined with the concept of 'inner guidance'.[9] The permanent influx of young conscripts was meant to ensure that the army could not again become a 'state above the state',[10] as it had been in the imperial and the interwar period. When Defence Minster Franz Josef Strauss between 1956 and 1958 considered acquiring nuclear weapons in order to enhance both FRG's defence capacities and its status within the Western alliance – a step undertaken by France and the United Kingdom at roughly the same time and for the same reasons – in Germany he was considered an irresponsible warmonger.[11] Portrayed as pursuing great power ambitions, he finally met his downfall in 1962.[12]

FRG was spared any use of military force as the Cold War never turned into a hot one. Furthermore, after having joined the United Nations in 1972, there were no requests for German blue helmets. The decision of the Federal Cabinet to join a NATO force for peacekeeping in Cyprus in 1964 remained inconsequential and was completely forgotten thereafter.[13] The German self-image became that of Brandt falling on his knees. The Federal Government did not renounce its territorial claims against the Czechoslovak Socialist Republic, Poland and the Soviet Union, but in a series of treaties it committed itself never to use force to implement them. Brandt with his unusual biography had managed to win the trust of Leonid Brezhnev and personified the image of a peaceful Germany, enthusiastically embraced by German liberals and leftists. The paradigm shift became even more pronounced with massive protests against the implementation of the NATO Double-Resolution in December 1979, which foresaw the stationing of new mid-range nuclear missiles if the Soviets did not stop their own ongoing arms build-up with the same weapon systems. Over the controversial issue, SPD de facto toppled its own chancellor Helmut Schmidt. Although a new coalition of conservatives and liberals supported and implemented the Double-Resolution, the German peace movement, on both sides of the Iron Curtain, remained influential for the next decade.

The Two-Plus-Four Agreement in September 1990 resulted in a reduction of the armed forces from around 600,000 to 370,000. The two Germanies had been the frontier states of the European theatre in the Cold War, and demands for a massive reduction of the defence budget were very popular. Now that Germany was surrounded by friends, the public wanted a focus on inner unification with massive investments in East Germany, combined with support for the transformation processes in the former Soviet satellite states. Furthermore, East and West Germans agreed on the idea of Germany as a peace power. The GDR leadership, having survived the Third Reich in concentration camps or in exile, held that it had nothing to do with German militarism and expansionism. GDR claims to be part of Soviet peace policy were as credible as the latter itself, but – against common belief – the National People's Army was never deployed for any military operation of the Warsaw Pact, not even the violent repression of the Prague Spring in 1968. German soldiers had not issued a single shot in any interstate military conflict since 1945, and both Germanies were somewhat proud of that.

After unification, Germany was asked to shoulder more responsibility and actively support peacekeeping missions with own units. Federal Government and Parliament followed suit, though with great reluctance. Minesweepers, air defence personnel or medical professionals – all not involved in immediate combat – were sent to the Gulf, Turkey, Cambodia and Somalia, complemented by those supporting the Implementation Force and Stabilisation Force in the Balkans. The 'Out of Area-Debate',[14] the last relevant one on values in foreign affairs, reached its peak during 1998/1999 when NATO requested German support in the Kosovo War. There had been a broad consensus in Germany, too, that the Federal Army must not be deployed to areas which had been under Nazi occupation. Yugoslavia with its strong partisan movement had witnessed great bloodshed due to German militarism. Furthermore, in October 1998, a new coalition government under SPD Chancellor Gerhard Schröder had been formed. For the first time ever, the Greens joined a coalition in the centre, having their roots in the environmental and peace movements in both Germanies, and peacekeeping missions had always been a difficult issue with them. A combat mission in Yugoslavia without UN mandate appeared totally out of the question.

The general mood in Germany, however, pointed rather in the opposite direction. The brutal wars among the successor states of nearby Yugoslavia, especially in Bosnia-Herzegovina, had been covered in much detail in the German media. Here the Serb leadership of Slobodan Milošević, Radovan Karadžić and Ratko Mladić was attributed the main responsibility for crimes against humanity, including mass executions, mass rapes and torture. The steady influx of refugees into Germany and even more the helplessness of the international community passively watching the bombardment of Sarajevo or the massacre at Srebrenica had triggered demands for intervention, though legitimated by a UN mandate and without discussing German participation. When news reports came of Serb attempts at ethnic cleansing in Kosovo, German patience came to the end of its tether. As Russia vetoed any UN intervention, the United States pushed forward, asking NATO allies to join a war on Serbia.

It was Foreign Minister Joschka Fischer who convinced his own Green Party that in certain cases keeping still was the opposite of a moral stand. On the contrary, the Germans having committed genocide against European Jews, were obliged to prevent any further genocides. 'No more war', therefore, transformed into 'no more genocide'.[15] Warfare was no longer considered a crime if it undoubtedly and exclusively served humanitarian purposes. The German Air Force supported the aerial attacks with reconnaissance flights and again did not fire a single shot. Nevertheless, the Kosovo War was and is viewed with uneasiness, in particular when later on it turned out that the news about Serb atrocities was partly fake. Observers agree that the concept of 'civilian power' remains valid,[16] whereas 'no more genocide' has lost weight and has never been used again as an argument for participation in a combat mission. Accordingly, when Chancellor Schröder refused to join George W. Bush's 'Alliance of the Willing' against Iraq, the decision enjoyed broad popular support as a return to normality. To the surprise of the United States, the allegedly worst warmongers of the world had transformed into one of the most pacifist nations within half a century.

Most characteristic for the predominant German attitude towards military deployment out of area was the engagement in Afghanistan between 2002 and 2014. After the conclusion of the actual war, the FRG sent a large contingent of troops. Initially, it was rather popular, for the naïve believed that the conflict had ended, and the Federal Army would be used mostly for helping and protecting the reconstruction of infrastructure. The popular illusion that the United States wins wars, whereas Europeans and especially Germans would win peace, was deeply shaken when the Taliban started attacking German forces in Kunduz Province in 2007. After 2009 the German commander in Kunduz, wrongly informed, ordered an aerial attack on what turned out to be civilians; this caused a political crisis in Germany. The end of the German military presence in Afghanistan, though nothing like stability had been achieved there, was wholeheartedly welcomed by all sections of public opinion and politics. A considerable number of German forces remain abroad, mostly in the Balkans. Those missions, however, are considered unproblematic, being part of peacekeeping missions and not creating any headlines.

Today, the only party demanding an end of all foreign assignments is the post-communist Left. Its predominantly East German voters define peace policy as the Federal Army having no business abroad at all. Accordingly, the party opposes all arms exports, an issue closely watched and coming under criticism regularly. Germany regularly ranks among the top five of the world's arms exporters, with its main customers in recent years being Middle Eastern nations. Whether it is morally acceptable to export weapons is discussed intensely in some European countries, for example the Netherlands, with an equally strong moral approach.[17] The obvious link between affordable arms production as a safeguard against complete dependence on others, and arms exports, nevertheless, is widely ignored. This is particularly true in Germany, where the debate is inevitably linked with the crimes of the *Wehrmacht*. The War Weapons Control Act was introduced in 1961 and since has been modified several times. It foresees the necessity for an export permit by the Federal Government, which is not meant to be granted if the buyer is located in what is considered an area of tension. Repeatedly, critics complain about too much flexibility and exceptions against the spirit of the Act, recent cases being NATO-ally Turkey, Saudi Arabia or the Kurdish Peshmerga. The general German aversion against anything military is reflected in the absence of uniforms in public and the generally low image of the armed forces. Germany does not hold any military parades on national days. When military resistance against Hitler is remembered, 20 July is only a minor affair with little public. The fashionable uniforms of the *Wehrmacht*, so often seen in films, have been replaced by less impressive ones. Going out in uniform apart from official duty is a sort of taboo.

The general attitude towards anything military goes hand in hand with the one in German foreign affairs. Hanns W. Maull in the cases of Germany and Japan has evolved the term 'civilian power', exercising influence via soft power and resorting to force only when attacked. Civilian powers instead of pursuing politics along the guideline that might is right, aim at the peaceful resolution of conflicts through accepted norms.[18] The fact that more and more states do not follow norms anymore and violent interstate conflicts like those in Ukraine or in the Middle East take place not too far from German borders causes uneasiness. Germans had hoped to be left alone from all wars in Francis Fukuyama's post-historical world,[19] which might turn out to be an illusion. Though such discussion is strictly avoided by all quarters, German politics might one day be forced to consider a more proactive line in the deployment of troops.

MULTILATERALISM – MEANS OR VALUE?

On 1 October 1990, two days before reunification, Kohl in a speech at a party convention coined the phrase that a united Germany should merge into a united Europe.[20] The ideal that Germany should become part of a larger political body was not new. In 1951, with the establishment of the European Coal and Steel Community, FRG transferred sovereign rights to a supranational institution. It placed its security interests with NATO four years later and was a founding member of the EEC in 1957. And though the two Germanies became members of the UN only in 1972, both were highly active in New York with their permanent observers before that.

One could discuss whether the German dedication to multilateralism is a value or a means. After Germany, because of the crimes committed in the Nazi period, had become a pariah in the international community, joining European and transatlantic organizations opened the door for a West German comeback as a respected and more or less equal partner. Furthermore, it secured physical survival against a possible attack by the Red Army, for which German forces alone would not have been a match. Emancipation and security, though, came with a price. Bonn not only surrendered its sovereignty over national steel production. It also accepted NATO Secretary-General Lord Ismay's famous saying that NATO was created to 'keep the Soviet Union out, the Americans in, and the Germans down'.[21] The alliance was certainly not merely made for, but also against, the FRG. Both cases helped to assuage fears of a return to German militarism both in and outside Germany. Adenauer, together with many of his contemporaries, did not trust the German capacity to control its own ambition.

One could view those steps as *realpolitik*. In a system of five great powers in Europe, Bismarck's dictum had been to be always with three, the majority. The experience of isolation and encirclement before the outbreak of the Great War and defeat against a superior coalition in 1945 made joining the most powerful Western military alliance the only logical conclusion in a world with two nuclear superpowers. That FRG also ran the danger of getting involved in conflicts which were not of its choice became obvious only after the end of the Cold War, especially with the Second Gulf War. European integration, too, with its common market seemed to be a project mostly benefitting one of the world's strongest exporters. This also explains German support of the General Agreement on Tariffs and Trade or the World Trade Organization.

All this appears to be a brilliant realist calculation if one does not take into account the German trauma with nationalism and the German national state. In 1871, Germans were the last major ethnic group in Europe to establish a national state, and they immediately realized that its mere existence tended to destabilize the continent. Combined with the atrocities of the Third Reich, this transformed into a formidable guilt complex. Unlike in most other countries, until 1990 showing the German colours by private citizens was considered nearly a taboo. When during 1989/1990, with reunification and the football world championships, the flag became a common feature, this was declared an exception and regarded with uneasiness. Only with the football world championships of 2006, hosted by Germany, did harmless national enthusiasm under the German colours in the context of sports events become acceptable.

Germany adopting a higher profile is considered a necessity when economic and financial stability in Europe appears to be threatened. Otherwise, the prospect of a post-national state has quite a number of supporters, as indicated by Kohl in 1990. At times, when reunification seemed impossible, being European rather than German offered a way out of the guilt complex. Multilateralism ensures that responsibility in case of difficult or unpopular decisions rests on many shoulders; the post-1945 Germans were always with the good people. This alone, however, would draw a too negative picture. German experience over the past century shows that major tasks can best be achieved not through confrontation, but in cooperation with others. European integration has brought unknown prosperity and permanent peace to a continent war ridden for centuries. Today, Germany is surrounded by friends. While the EU has created a win-win situation for all participants, Germany was particularly successful in pursuing its own national interests through multilateral cooperation. The Conference for Security and Cooperation in Europe in 1975 crowned Brandt's New Eastern Policy, bringing together the hostile Cold War blocs. Bonn was the main winner, prompting humanitarian improvements in the GDR and other satellite states which finally contributed to the collapse of the Soviet Union. The Two-Plus-Four Treaty in 1990 achieved what had been unimaginable only a year earlier, namely peaceful unification with the consent of the victorious powers of World War II and its partners. The Maastricht Treaty ensured the consent of the rest of Europe as well.

Berlin's active role at the UN fits into the picture. Be it development policy or climate protection, the Germans are willing to take a prominent role for the benefit of the greater good. Unilateralism, in German eyes mostly associated with the United States, appears bad in itself; and resulting failures like the

American disaster in Iraq are taken as proof. On the contrary, multilateralism is considered as providing those checks and balances necessary for a sustainable policy including in foreign affairs. The concept of civilian power is based on the rule of international law. Playing by such rules makes German foreign policy transparent for everyone and acceptable to critics at home and abroad. Furthermore, German diplomacy is especially well prepared when judicial issues are debated. Between 1949 and 1990, the German question was related to an endless number of legal issues requiring expert knowledge of restricted sovereignty, territorial claims and reparations, to name only the most relevant ones. To no surprise, the German Foreign Service is traditionally dominated by jurists. Their skills come in handy, too, when dealing with EU issues, the *acquis communautaire*. The same is true for multilateral negotiations on agreements like the former Transatlantic Trade and Investment Partnership.

CONCLUSION

The German case shows values in foreign affairs as historically grown. The starting point is not necessarily the Hitler years, but also German experiences with a national state not fitting into a European framework. Nevertheless, the guilt complex from 1945 has an ongoing impact, visible with the near-taboo on the use of force and the concept of civilian power. Crucial political decisions, which were not necessarily popular with contemporaries, pushed German society and politics in certain directions. The results were considered acceptable and beneficial in the long run, achieving a broad political and societal consensus. In today's Germany there are hardly any voices to be taken seriously against membership in NATO, EU or the commitment to multilateralism. Not only for unification but also for hitherto unknown wealth and stability, German foreign policy since 1949 in sum must be considered a tremendous success. Accordingly, though there is no lack of debate between former West and former East Germany, this is never about foreign affairs. The GDR did not provide any inheritance in that field, and East Germans, a sort of internal migrants into an extended FRG, are not known for decidedly different views, and they are mostly focusing on domestic issues anyway.

There is a broad, value-based consensus in German society. The change is the newcomer to German politics, the Alternative for Germany, which provides evidence of how deep rooted those values are. Initially openly against the euro, and implicitly the EU, the party soon found that an alternate course in foreign affairs does not attract voters. Likewise, although German citizens are divided on sanctions against Russia imposed after the annexation of

Crimea, the party quickly gave up championing a more pro-Russian policy. Though the current debate on immigration is influencing foreign affairs, it is essentially a domestic debate aiming at mobilizing fears and xenophobia for party purposes. Furthermore, like earlier in German post-Hitler history, radical voices are likely to disappear soon.

Nevertheless, since the end of the Cold War and unification, policymakers are confronted with new tasks. Given the ongoing weakening of NATO and signs of erosion in the EU, consent-building in larger groups of states might become more difficult in future and Berlin's multilateralism lacking partners. Apart from the stable German-French axis, there is hardly any partnership without doubt. A recalibration of German foreign affairs might become inevitable, and this, once again, might lead to modifications of current values. Those who are in favour of a more assertive foreign policy approach complain about certain values as a hindrance, such as modesty. They claim that the decade-long success story has created self-complacency and inertia, whereas rapid changes in the immediate neighbourhood as well as globally need a response beyond managing and carefully modifying the established course. As long as Berlin needs to justify its performance on the international stage to a critical public, however, a major turn-around is most unlikely. What has grown over generations can be replaced only over the long term. Whatever options lie ahead, there are no plausible alternatives to a further deepening of European integration with Germany as its economic, but not political, motor – whether combined with a transatlantic partnership revitalized after the Trump presidency or not. Therefore, modesty, the Western identity, the concept of a civilian power and multilateralism are most unlikely to be cast overboard.

NOTES

1. Helmuth Plessner, *Die verspätete Nation. Über die politische Verführbarkeit bürgerlichen Geistes* (Stuttgart: Kohlhammer, 1959).

2. Ludwig Dehio, 'Deutschland und die Epoche der Weltkriege', *Historische Zeitschrift* 173 (1952): 80.

3. 'Westerwelle lässt BBC-Reporter abblitzen', *Der Spiegel* (28 September 2009). http://www.spiegel.de/politik/deutschland/frage-auf-englisch-westerwelle-laesst-bbc-reporter-abblitzen-a-651842.html.

4. Debate in Federal Parliament, 24/25 November 1949. *Stenographische Berichte*, 1. Deutscher Bundestag, vol. 1, 524–26.

5. Most recently Gerhard Wettig, *Die Stalin-Note. Historische Kontroversen im Spiegel der Quellen* (Berlin: be.bra verlag, 2015).

6. Peter Bender, *Neue Ostpolitik. Vom Mauerbau bis zum Moskauer Vertrag* (München: dtv, 1986), 182–85.

7. Speech by U.S. President Woodrow Wilson, 8 January 1918.

8. Günter Joetze, *Der letzte Krieg in Europa? Das Kosovo und die deutsche Politik* (Stuttgart: Deutsche Verlags-Anstalt, 2001), 192.

9. Donald Abenheim, 'The Citizen in Uniform. Reform and Its Critics in the Bundeswehr', in Stephen F. Szabo (ed.). *The Bundeswehr and Western Security* (Basingstoke: Macmillan, 1990), 31–51.

10. Karl Liebknecht, *Militarismus und Antimilitarismus unter besonderer Berücksichtigung der internationalen Jugendbewegung* (Zürich: Verlag der Buchhandlung des Schweiz. Grütlivereins, 2nd edition, 1907), 16.

11. Peter Siebenmorgen, *Franz Josef Strauß. Ein Leben im Übermaß* (München: Siedler Verlag, 2015), 125–47.

12. Ibid., 259.

13. Alexander Troche, ' "Ich habe nur die Hoffnung, dass der Kelch an uns vorübergeht. . . " Der Zypernkonflikt und die erste deutsche Out-of-area-Entscheidung', *Historisch-Politische Mitteilungen* (2000): 183–95.

14. Rainer Baumann and Gunther Hellmann, 'Germany and the Use of military Force: "Total War", the "Culture of Restraint" and the Quest for Normality', *German Politics* 10, no. 1 (2001): 61–82.

15. Sebastian Harnisch, 'Change and Continuity in Post-Unification German Foreign Policy', *German Politics* 10, no. 1 (2001): 35–60.

16. Adrian Hyde-Price, 'Germany and the Kosovo War: Still a Civilian Power?', *German Politics* 10, no. 1 (2001): 19–34.

17. See for example Martin Broek and Frank Slijper, *Explosieve Materie. Nederlandse Wapenhandel blootgelegd* (Breda: Papieren Tijger, 2003).

18. Hanns W. Maull, 'Deutschland als Zivilmacht', in Siegmar Schmidt et. al. (eds.). *Handbuch zur deutschen Außenpolitik* (Wiesbaden: VS Verlag für Sozialwissenschaften, 2007), 73–84.

19. Francis Fukuyama, 'The End of History?' *The National Interest* no. 16 (Summer 1989): 3–18.

20. Speech at the Party Convention of CDU, 1 October 1990, Hamburg. Bundesgeschäftsstelle der CDU (ed.), *Parteitagsprotokoll*, Bonn: 22–37.

21. Quoted after Joseph S. Nye Jr., *The Paradox of American Power: Why the World's Only Superpower Can't Go It Alone* (London: Oxford University Press, 2002), 33.

BIBLIOGRAPHY

Abenheim, Donald. 'The Citizen in Uniform. Reform and Its Critics in the Bundeswehr', in Stephen F. Szabo (ed.). *The Bundeswehr and Western Security*. Basingstoke: Macmillan, 1990.

Baumann, Rainer and Gunther Hellmann. 'Germany and the Use of Military Force: "Total War", the "Culture of Restraint" and the "Quest for Normality" '. *German Politics* 10, no. 1 (2001).

Bender, Peter. *Neue Ostpolitik. Vom Mauerbau bis zum Moskauer Vertrag*. München: dtv, 1986.

Broek, Martin and Frank Slijper. *Explosieve Materie. NederlandseWapenhandel-blootgelegd*. Breda: Papieren Tijger, 2003.

Dehio, Ludwig. 'Deutschland und die Epoche der Weltkriege'. *Historische Zeitschrift* 173 (1952).

Fukuyama, Francis, 'The End of History?' *The National Interest* 16 (Summer 1989).

Harnisch, Sebastian. 'Change and Continuity in Post-Unification German Foreign Policy'. *German Politics* 10, no. 1 (2001).

Hyde-Price, Adrian. 'Germany and the Kosovo War: Still a Civilian Power?' *German Politics* 10, no. 1 (2001).

Joetze, Günter. *Der letzte Krieg in Europa? Das Kosovo und die deutsche Politik*. Stuttgart: Deutsche Verlags-Anstalt, 2001.

Liebknecht, Karl. *Militarismus und Antimilitarismus unter besonderer Berücksichtigung der internationalen Jugendbewegung*. Zürich: Verlag der Buchhandlung des Schweiz. Grütlivereins, 2nd edition, 1907.

Maull, Hanns W. 'Deutschland als Zivilmacht', in Siegmar Schmidt et al. (eds.). *Handbuch zur deutschen Außenpolitik*. Wiesbaden: VS Verlag für Sozialwissenschaften, 2007.

Nye, Joseph S. Jr. *The Paradox of American Power: Why the World's Only Superpower Can't Go It Alone*. London: Oxford University Press, 2002.

Plessner, Helmuth. *Die verspätete Nation. Über die politische Verführbarkeit bürgerlichen Geistes*. Stuttgart: Kohlhammer, 1959.

Siebenmorgen, Peter. *Franz Josef Strauß. Ein Leben im Übermaß*. München: Siedler Verlag, 2015.

Troche, Alexander. 'Ich habe nur die Hoffnung, dass der Kelch an uns vorübergeht . . . Der Zypernkonflikt und die erste deutsche Out-of-area-Entscheidung'. *Historisch-Politische Mitteilungen* (2000).

Wettig, Gerhard. *Die Stalin-Note. Historische Kontroversen im Spiegel der Quellen*. Berlin: be.braverlag, 2015.

Chapter 4

Values in US Foreign Policy

'America First' Meets the Pro-Democracy State

William J. Antholis

President Donald J. Trump's 'America First' doctrine has helped to revive a series of related concepts in US foreign policy: isolationism, unilateralism, regional hegemony, protectionism, ethnocentrism and non-intervention. They stand in opposition to a set of values, spanning both major political parties, that have dominated since World War II, emphasizing engagement, multilateralism, integration, rules-based arrangements, trade liberalization and (often) intervention to protect those values and interests.

PARTICULARISM AND UNIVERSALISM IN US FOREIGN POLICY

Indeed, debates between particularists and universalists stretch back to the founding of the republic.[1] For roughly the first half of the 250-year history of the United States – from the Declaration of Independence in 1776 from England through the early twentieth century – US foreign policy leaned towards the particularist end of the spectrum. Then, beginning with its entry into World War I in 1917 until the present, Americans leaned more towards multilateralism, free trade and democracy. Since foreign policy is a braided strand of issues, however, each of these periods involved a blending of universalism and particularism.

What appears striking about the past two years is that President Trump's America First doctrine swings towards the farthest end away from universalism across *all* strands of values and interests. The president is giving voice to those in American politics who reject democratic enlargement, multilateral engagement, trade integration and open borders. The reality of US foreign policy in practice, however, continues to contain a commitment to universalist tendencies. While the president is the dominant player in setting US policy, he cannot simply act alone. Long-standing policies embedded in the American system and in the human resources of the US foreign policy community remain far more universalist in orientation than the current president.

This chapter traces those contending traditions. It places emphasis on the extent to which each tradition – and policy strands that embody those traditions – has been embraced not just by presidents but also by the people who actually conduct and implement policy and by the broader public.

Founding Principles

From the beginning of the republic, there was a push to keep the business of the United States separate from that of Europe, to act first for America. In President George Washington's farewell address, he warned against the danger of foreign entanglements. Still, that was connected to a belief that the principles of a self-governing republic, based on democratic ideals, were inspired by universal values. That included the importance of open trade. The president wrote in 1796

> The great rule of conduct for us in regard to foreign nations is, in extending our commercial relations to have with them as little political connection as possible. So far as we have already formed engagements let them be fulfilled with perfect good faith. Here let us stop. . . . There can be no greater error than to expect or calculate upon real favours from nation to nation. It is an illusion which experience must cure, which a just pride ought to discard.[2]

President Thomas Jefferson had his own brand of America First. His Louisiana Purchase in 1803 was in part driven by a desire to run away from Europe's wars, to build an exceptional place at home where universal values would take root. 'We had not been unaware of the danger to which our peace would be perpetually exposed while so important a key to the commerce of the western country remained under foreign power', Jefferson told Congress in 1803.[3] Nevertheless, Jefferson also was the leading voice for some American commitment to universal values. As author of the young republic's most important document, Jefferson pointed to universal human rights in an international context. The Declaration of Independence was, in fact, a diplomatic document, addressed to 'the powers of the earth' and 'the opinions of mankind'. It begins with a clarion statement of self-evident truths that all men are created equal. A decade later, those values guided the federal Constitution, which stated the will of the people as its basis; it required an extensive popular ratification process and incorporated the protection of basic rights of free speech, religion, assembly and protest.[4]

America's universal values gained international notice. A series of democratic revolutions swept Europe – first in France and then across the continent. Yet by 1848, almost two decades after Jefferson had died, the United States was the only democracy left in the world that believed (at any level) in universal values.[5] And within the United States, the debate over the exact meaning of those values raged.[6] Less than a century into its existence, America itself was convulsed in a horrific civil war, with the definition and meaning of those values at its core. The debates in that war extended beyond slavery; they included disputes about protectionism, non-intervention and the role of entangling alliances. Each side in the war subscribed to a hybrid of universalism and protectionism. The South denied that *all* men were created equal, but it did believe that the right to property should be unfettered – and that included opposition to tariffs and other trade protections. The North believed in the universal value of human freedom and the right to free labour, but it also favoured trade protectionism and non-intervention. The North's victory meant that trade protectionism, isolation and non-intervention would dominate for decades.

The American Century and a
Universal Vision of Democratic Capitalism

One of the great truisms of the twentieth century is that America grew to global pre-eminence while embracing universal values and ignoring the ideology of America First. The reality is rather more complicated, as the general drive towards universalism was seen by Woodrow Wilson and other internationalist presidents as consistent with US interests. Despite that, it still met regular resistance from those who believed that approach was not self-interested enough. President Wilson was the first to make the universalist turn, bringing the country into World War I. He was not initially inclined to do so. When war erupted in Europe in 1914, Wilson at first made the case for non-intervention with a 'Proclamation of Neutrality'. In fact, Wilson was among the first to invoke the phrase 'America First', using it as part of his re-election campaign slogan in 1916.

By 1917, after Germany's sinking of RMS *Lusitania* and defeat of Belgium, fear spread of both German militarism and threats to democracy, and American public opinion had swung dramatically. 'The world must be made safe for democracy', Wilson said during a speech in which he implored Congress to enact a Declaration of War against Germany and bring the United States, finally, into the Great War.[7] The country reacted with a swell of patriotism and wide public support for the war. But over time, the American people became disillusioned. Despite Wilson's strong campaign in favour of the post-war League of Nations – including especially the collective security arrangement – the Senate failed to ratify the treaty. Wilson gave way to a trio of Republican presidents – Warren Harding, Calvin Coolidge and Herbert Hoover – who 'trimmed their sails to this isolationist sentiment and avoided entangling alliances with European nations'.[8]

Even with Franklin Roosevelt's election, and a growing fear of German and Italian aggression in Europe, an increasingly popular America First movement emerged to limit further commitments to multilateralism and defence of democracy and human rights around the world. The America First campaign would flourish in the decades between World Wars I and II, as the country was faced yet again with the possibility of entering a European war.

As Hitler's Germany began its march across Europe in 1939, Americans embraced both unilateralism and isolationism. Between 1940 and 1941, the America First Committee (AFC) established hundreds of chapters across the United States, counting almost a million members as its faithful, including its most famous leader, aviation pioneer Charles Lindbergh. Supporters were not just Far Right; they came from across the political spectrum. The AFC argued for US neutrality, painting globalism and interventionism as a bigger threat than Germany or Japan.[9] In its original 1940 policy statement, the AFC asserted that the United States should 'concentrate all energies on building a strong defence for this hemisphere', a throwback to the Monroe Doctrine. President Franklin D. Roosevelt pushed back against the isolationist tide to make the case for intervention in his radio broadcast *Fireside Chats*, appealing to Americans' self-interest and sense of civic duty.[10] Nonetheless, polls as late as November 1941 showed that most Americans were against military action. But the Japanese strike on Pearl Harbour the very next month eliminated all doubts about the war. The AFC disbanded four days later.[11]

Since then, administrations have based American foreign policy on four connected strands of universalism, viewing them as consistent with US national interests. The first is a belief in the superiority of democratic capitalism, with an open rules-based trading system. The second is multilateral action, particularly among democracies. The third is a broad commitment to human rights. The fourth is intervention in the affairs of other nations, particularly on behalf of democratic government or – more selfishly – US national interests.

For the second half of the twentieth century, this was tied up in a global battle with another universalist power, the Soviet Union, fuelled by an internationalist communist ideology. Between 1945 and 1969 in particular, debates within US foreign policy circles were about whether containing the Soviet Union meant keeping it in its place, or rolling it back to pre–World War II status.

Isolationism, protectionism and unilateralism did not disappear, however; they were merely marginalized. In the 1950s, Ohio Republican Senator Robert Taft led the resistance movement, arguing that the Soviet threat was exaggerated and doubting the efficacy of multilateralism. Taft emphasized mercantilism over international trade[12] and, in January 1951, spoke before the Senate: 'The principal purpose of the foreign policy of the United States is to maintain the liberty of the American people. It is not to reform the entire world or spread sweetness and light and economic prosperity'.[13] Thus, while the United States led in negotiating the Bretton Woods global trade and economic system that followed World War II, it had a difficult time gaining Senate approval for the International Trade Organization in 1947 – settling instead for a General Agreement on Tariffs and Trade (GATT), which allowed a higher degree of national autonomy.

Combatting the more isolationist, unilateralist and protectionist wing of his own party, General Dwight D. Eisenhower sought the Republican nomination with a more internationalist vision. In a speech in Detroit, Michigan, he argued for universal values: 'The vast majority of Americans of both parties know that to keep their own nation free they bear a majestic responsibility for freedom through all the world'.[14] Eisenhower saw that responsibility as consistent with American security and economic interests. He advanced trade negotiations and strengthened America's commitment to the United Nations, World Bank, International Monetary Fund (IMF) and collective decision making. He also thought America's global responsibility justified intervening in the affairs of other nations. In both Iran and Guatemala, for example, Eisenhower authorized the Central Intelligence Agency (CIA) to depose governments, replacing them with officials more inclined to protect democratic capitalism. In these instances, American officials used the fight against Soviet communism as a cover for crass American pursuits. Nevertheless, most policy professionals believed that universal democratic values and American national interests were consistent and reinforcing, even if they debated where and how to apply them.

John Kennedy largely followed his predecessor's global commitments – and contradictions. That included intervening to protect West Berlin after the Soviet blockade, the failed Bay of Pigs invasion in Cuba and the tacit approval of the assassination of President Ngo Dinh Diem in South Vietnam. Kennedy's commitment to human rights abroad reinforced the movement towards equality for African Americans at home. After Kennedy's death, Lyndon Johnson signed major laws on civil rights in 1964 and 1965 – advancing America's domestic commitment to its founding values. But the Vietnam War proved the application of universal values in foreign affairs could be disastrous.

In the shadow of the Vietnam quagmire, America's first explicit post–World War II retreat from universalism came under President Richard Nixon and his national security advisor, Henry Kissinger. There was some irony in this. Nixon had been a Cold War hawk as Eisenhower's vice president. Across the Kennedy and Johnson administrations, he had generally accepted a more proactive, internationalist approach and, once in office, escalated the war in Vietnam. Yet as president – and with Kissinger's coaching – he strategically retreated from global universalism. Nixon's new *realpolitik* approach toned down the moralism embedded in Cold War liberal internationalist ideology. He accepted Russia and China where they were and tried to negotiate directly with them as equals. But Nixon's realism was not zero-sum. It was consistent with scholars of international affairs who regard it possible for a nation to pursue its narrow self-interest while still finding other countries who share common interests. At this point, however, Nixon was coming up against a foreign policy establishment that had internalized liberal internationalism. The twenty-five years of policies from 1945 to 1969 promoting democratic capitalism – including human rights, open political institutions, rule of law and economic integration – had taken root. During the Truman, Eisenhower, Kennedy and Johnson presidencies, career professionals had embraced the view that policy must be consistent with American values. That view extended from State to Defence to the CIA, Federal Bureau of Investigation (FBI) and National Security Agency.

Amid the Watergate crisis, the White House ignored State Department advice in Cyprus, failing to prevent a coup attempt against the island's democratically elected government. The coup prompted an invasion by Turkey, forcing a brutal division of Cyprus into a Turkish army–controlled north and a Greek Cypriot south. Turkey's invasion nearly led to war with Greece – two countries that were (and remain) members of the North Atlantic Treaty Organization (NATO) alliance. Kissinger seemed to care little about democracy on Cyprus and viewed the State Department as an unwelcome voice. Here, Nixon and Kissinger ignored democratic norms. They had come to see the Johnson administration's exuberant belief in democracy as the reason for the Vietnam disaster. After Nixon's resignation, President Gerald Ford also ignored norms when – during the 1976 presidential election – he suggested that the leaders of Soviet-bloc Poland were freely elected. The Nixon-Ford-Kissinger flirtations with realism turned out to be a diversion. The next six presidents – Jimmy Carter, Ronald Reagan, George H. W. Bush, Bill Clinton, George W. Bush and Barack Obama – each sustained the post-war consensus that American values cannot be separated from American interests.

In 1978, a young Madeleine Albright served on Jimmy Carter's National Security Council under Zbigniew Brzezinski. In the aftermath of the Nixon presidency, she touted 'democratic enlargement' – an idea that as democratic states grow in quantity and strength, democracies around the world benefit with increased prosperity and security. That concept would remain a part of US foreign policy through the Carter and Reagan administrations. The return to universalist values did not get in the way of nuclear arms negotiations with the Soviets or normalization of relations with Communist China. But it did restore a rhetorical commitment to NATO, to democratic partners in Asia and to trade liberalization. From Carter's boycott of the 1980 Moscow Olympics – in protest of Russia's invasion of Afghanistan – to Ronald Reagan's Cold War rhetoric, both administrations embraced a universalism of democratic ideals.

The end of the Cold War brought a series of efforts to more deeply integrate the political and economic fates of market-based democracies. After the fall of the Berlin Wall, Bush spoke of 'a new world order', where open political and economic systems would coordinate and collaborate with one another. That extended from Bush's UN-sanctioned mission to counter Iraqi President Saddam Hussein's invasion of Kuwait to both North American Free Trade Agreement (NAFTA) and GATT trade negotiations.

Clinton continued in the same vein. As war erupted in the former Yugoslavia, he initially vacillated about collective security. He eventually announced his endorsement of Albright's democratic enlargement strategy in a speech at the United Nations. For his administration, that commitment led to the enlargement of NATO and to efforts to bring Russia into liberal arrangements such as NATO, the G-7 and the World Trade Organization (WTO). Similarly, Clinton began to reach out to a democratic India, promoted trade and political engagement with liberal elements in China and deepened US commitment to market democracies in Latin America and Africa. Clinton matched these national security and political arrangements with deepened economic ties, through the WTO, NAFTA and Asia-Pacific Economic Cooperation summits. These efforts were not entirely successful. They were resisted by political opponents at home – from economic nationalists and protectionists on the Right and Left, including Ross Perot, who opposed NAFTA, and trade union officials, who opposed the WTO and other trade liberalization efforts. During the 1980s and 1990s, many on the Right and Left felt that NAFTA deepened the damage to the American worker through globalization of the labour market. To its detractors, NAFTA was viewed as capitulation to the transnational order.[15]

Despite those lingering protectionists, George W. Bush similarly pursued a policy that embraced universalism – both on trade and on national security issues. While first somewhat reluctant on international affairs, Bush embraced an expansive view of democracy after the attacks of September 11. Sometimes the Bush administration acted in a collaborative fashion, as in the efforts to defeat the Taliban and Al Qaeda in Afghanistan. At other times, it acted unilaterally in pursuing that vision, such as in the invasion of Iraq. As the Bush presidency evolved – particularly into his second term – the championing of democracy became the core of its foreign policy vision. But that commitment was not limited to just the Middle East. Like Clinton, Bush believed it extended to security and economic ties in Europe, Asia, Latin America and Africa. The administration negotiated a breakthrough with democratic India, recognizing it as a responsible nuclear power. It also recommitted to NATO allies, particularly in Bush's second term, and adopted a global economic vision through both trade and investment (the launch of the WTO's Doha Round trade negotiations) and even humanitarian engagement (efforts in sub-Saharan Africa to combat AIDS, malaria and tuberculosis).

Similarly, the Obama administration continued to embrace a commitment to the institutions and practices of liberal democracy. While the president and his national security team had won office by challenging the Bush administration's choice and conduct of the Iraq War, they reinforced relationships with European allies and continued to emphasize ties to NATO, Japan and India. They also pursued considerable continuity in Africa and Latin America. The administration showed ambivalence, however, to intervene in the domestic affairs of other nations – including on humanitarian disasters and civil wars – with a mixed record, in particular, in the Middle East and North Africa. In some instances, such as Libya and Egypt, the Obama administration sought to stand up for democratic movements and vulnerable political minorities. In others – in particular, Syria – the administration stood back and chose not to intervene.

In economic affairs, the Obama administration also moved increasingly in the direction of deepening economic engagement. Having inherited the greatest global recession since the Great Depression, it worked pragmatically with a newly enhanced G-20 to manage the crisis. It saw the European Union as a critical partner in fighting global contagion, and elevated trade and finance relations with China as essential to managing the global economy – despite lingering and growing concerns about that country's domestic governance. Once the global recession eased, the Obama team emphasized global trade – seeking to negotiate a Trans-Pacific Partnership (TPP) and a Transatlantic Trade and Investment Partnership (TTIP). Both agreements sought to build a high-standards approach, based on best practices among developed market democracies.

Of course, the apparent consensus that runs across these last six democratic administrations has not been without domestic controversies, intense resistance and international missteps. Even if particular applications have been vigorously debated since World War II, the bipartisan centrist view among political leaders has been that universal liberal democratic values are at least consistent with definitions of interests – if not essential to them. And each of these presidents battled opponents in both parties who felt this strategy was not self-interested enough.

President Trump's 'America First' and the Return of Particularism

'From this moment on, it's going to be America First', President Donald J. Trump told the crowd gathered at his inauguration on 20 January 2017. With those words, the new president returned America to a more particularist view of both values and interests. Before Trump, no post-war US president had consistently challenged the core democratic values underlying American foreign policy, nor challenged the idea that the United States had a natural alliance with other democracies. Even Nixon's more realist approach did not have the explicit, dramatic distancing from universal values and interests. Trump's America First is actually a series of breaks with the universal values that underlie a liberal international order. The slogan explicitly emphasizes unilateralism over multilateralism. It emphasizes protectionism over economic integration. It emphasizes direct relations with national governments regardless of their domestic institutions, rather than giving priority to democratically elected leaders. And it emphasizes maintaining American national identity over global or humanitarian concerns.

Trump's realist policy views have been pronounced across a spectrum of issues. He has downgraded the status of the NATO alliance and the G-7, as well as multilateralism in general. He has elevated negotiations with North Korea, despite concerns from democratic allies in Japan and South Korea. He has walked away from – or threatened to walk away from – a wide range of international trade agreements, from the concluded negotiations over the TPP to trade obligations under the WTO or NAFTA. The president has insisted that the European Union (EU) was designed in opposition to American interests and has sought to directly undermine it. And he has walked away from G-7 negotiations – and even the EU itself – indicating that these multilateral arrangements were aimed to constrain American interests. Still – at least in the Trump administration's formal statement – America First is not entirely divorced from American democracy. On 18 December 2017 (eleven months into Trump's first year), his team issued its National Security Strategy document, which forges a tense compromise between its insurgent realism, 'America First', and a national security establishment that remains committed to those values. The document begins with a clear statement: 'This National Security Strategy puts America first'. Surprisingly, the democratic foundations of American government are placed early in the document as well: 'All political power is ultimately delegated from, and accountable to, the people'. It then expands on that principle, on how it should guide US policy:

> We protect American sovereignty by defending these institutions, traditions, and principles that have allowed us to live in freedom, to build the nation that we love. And we prize our national heritage, for the rare and fragile institutions of republican government can only endure if they are sustained by a culture that cherishes those institutions.[16]

Other nations that share those views 'form the foundation of our most enduring alliances, and the United States will continue to champion them'. Moreover, democracies are different and better. 'Governments that respect the rights of their citizens remain the best vehicle for prosperity, human happiness, and peace. In contrast, governments that routinely abuse the rights of their citizens do not play constructive roles in the world'.

Yet, throughout the document, there is a countervailing tension. Trump's National Security Strategy reads like a Nixonian response to democratic exuberance. Just as an excessive belief in democracy in the 1950s and 1960s led to disastrous interventions in Korea and Vietnam, it also led to recent interventions in Iraq and Afghanistan that have not ended well for the United States. Even worse, from the president's perspective, democratic alliances have not blunted or moderated China's rise. They have not ended North Korea's or Iran's nuclear programmes. And they have not produced a trading system that helps American workers. 'We will stand up for ourselves and we will stand up for our country like we have never stood up before', Trump said in a speech coinciding with the release of his strategy.

In Trump's view of the world, nation states are unitary, narrowly self-interested actors. They are 'unitary' in that they act with one mind, preferably that of a strong leader, focused solely on what is good for that country. And they are narrowly self-interested in that they single-mindedly pursue economic and security interests without any regard for domestic dissent or democratic norms within other countries. For Trump, some of the hostility towards these norms is conveyed in tone, and some of it is in the actual substance. Trump's dismissive attitude towards traditional democratic norms has been a central feature of his presidency, including his vigorous challenge of the law enforcement and intelligence agencies that were investigating Russia's interference in the 2016 American election. Indeed, most of Trump's National Security Strategy document, between its democratic opening and its democratic conclusion, focuses on direct threats to American interests. While the United States stands behind regional arrangements such as NATO, including the commitment to defend other countries if attacked, the National Security Strategy emphasizes the importance of burden-sharing: 'The NATO alliance will become stronger when all members assume greater responsibility for and pay their fair share to protect our mutual interests, sovereignty, and values'. The same applies to economic relations. For America's free market democratic partners in both Europe and Asia, the document indicates that economic priorities require free *and fair* trade. It emphasizes bilateral trade agreements with all countries and fails to mention the multilateral pacts that were negotiated with a network of market democracies in the previous administration, namely, the TPP and the TTIP.

As Miller Center academic Melvyn Leffler described recently:

> Trump's international order is anarchic, characterized by scheming and aggressive rival powers and ruthless non-state actors. Struggle is the name of the game; only the most fit survive. There is confidence, but no optimism.[17]

Those challenges are from non-democracies and democracies alike. The National Security Strategy highlights four major competitors, all of which are non-democracies: China, Russia, Iran and North Korea. The last two have been regularly leading exhibits in America's rogue-state gallery. Both pose existential threats because of nuclear capabilities. In Trump's National Security Strategy, both China and Russia are labelled disruptive actors. And in the language of the document, China's interests present a direct challenge: 'China is using economic inducements and penalties, influence operations and implied military threats to persuade other states to heed its political and security agenda'. Likewise, Russia regularly seeks to 'interfere in the domestic political affairs of countries around the world'. For these four major challengers, the document builds on previous national security assessments but leans in the direction of enduring conflict and discord.

> These competitions require the United States to rethink the policies of the past two decades – policies based on the assumption that engagement with rivals and their inclusion in international institutions and global commerce would turn them into benign actors and trustworthy partners.

There should be little doubt that Trump has personally chosen this particularist course. However, attributing this solely to the president misses the deeper and resilient particularism in the American people. Trump's lack of trust in democratic values and institutions reflects a fundamental public scepticism re-emerging after disastrous wars in the Middle East and accelerating globalization – much in the same way Johnson's involvement in Vietnam led to Nixon's realism. Indeed, that scepticism has never left American politics, but rather receded to the wings of both political parties for most of the past seven decades. Trumpian realism is still coming into focus. At its most jarring, it means seeing the world as an intrinsically hostile place, with little difference between democracies and non-democracies. When asked about Vladimir Putin, who was described to him as a killer, Trump responded, 'We got a lot of killers. What, you think our country's so innocent?' Still, Trump's dramatic move back in the direction of particularism is meeting resistance – just as a century of movement towards universalism had by his America First predecessors. That resistance is not just political but is coming from the national security establishment within the US government that still is animated by a universalist, pro-democracy world view – a view embraced by the career officials and the bipartisan collection of professionals who actually shape policy. Trump and his supporters view these establishment officials as part of the swamp that needs to be drained – and as part of a 'deep state' whose mission is to thwart his administration and the people who elected him.

That tension became apparent in the first week of the new administration's term. After the new president signed an executive order halting the admission of all refugees and temporarily banning people from seven Muslim-majority countries, he was met with a bureaucratic backlash. A State Department dissent cable made its way around American embassies across the globe, and then back to Washington. Approximately 1,000 foreign service officers and civil servants signed on to a letter expressing their dissatisfaction with Trump's executive order. Among other criticisms, the dissent cable stated that 'such a policy runs counter to core American values of non-discrimination, fair play and extending a warm welcome to foreign visitors and immigrants'.

Similarly, in May 2017, Trump's newly installed Secretary of State, Rex Tillerson, spoke to State Department officials. He tossed aside nearly seven decades of US foreign policy to argue that the United States should not let values like human rights become 'obstacles' to pursuing its interests. At that point, it was Tillerson against an entire bureaucracy. Following the speech, his top advisor (and one of the few political appointees in the department) tried to frame – and dial-back – his radical departure from standing policy and practice: 'Your remarks . . . revived the debate over how far to emphasize human rights, democracy promotion and liberal values in American foreign policy'.[18] In a striking display of realism, the same memorandum goes on to say that the United States should use human rights as leverage with adversaries such as China, Iran and North Korea, while not interfering with authoritarian allies such as Turkey, the Philippines and Saudi Arabia.

On 25 May 2017, Trump made his first speech in front of NATO leaders during his first trip overseas. What was remarkable was not what he said, but what he did not say. For weeks, the president's top national security officials, National Security Adviser H. R. McMaster, Defence Secretary James Mattis and Secretary of State Rex Tillerson, had worked to make sure that their boss reaffirmed America's seven-decade commitment to collective self-defence for Europe's democracies. Article 5 of the NATO charter assured that an attack against any ally (all of whom are democracies) would be considered an attack against all. The reference had been included in early drafts of the speech, yet when it came time to deliver the speech, Trump (or possibly a junior advisor) had removed it. McMaster, Mattis and Tillerson were aghast, and by the following month, at a joint news conference with Romanian President Klaus Iohannis, Trump had reaffirmed his commitment to Article 5. Just over a year later, at the 2018 NATO Summit, a similar dynamic played out. The president began the summit blasting NATO allies but was met with a 97–2 vote in the Senate reaffirming the commitment to the alliance. The president himself echoed this as he left the summit.

America's pro-democracy establishment was working to resist change. While President Trump was trying to chart a clearly particularist course on security and trade, both his national security establishment and Congress were pulling in the opposite direction. Former Deputy Secretary of State Strobe Talbott summed up the situation best: 'The president has hobbled his own executive branch, and the executive branch has hobbled its own president. . . . It's a three-legged race with the contestants going in opposite directions'.[19]

During 11 and 12 August 2017, a group of neo-Nazis invaded Charlottesville, Virginia, home state of US Founding Fathers Thomas Jefferson, James Madison and James Monroe (and the city from which this chapter has been written). The neo-Nazis and other white supremacist protesters violently clashed with counter-protesters. Rather than condemning the anti-democratic and bigoted marchers who began the encounter, Trump equivocated, saying that there were 'some very fine people on both sides'. Many members of Congress from the president's own party saw it differently, as did some in his inner circle. In an appearance on *Fox News Sunday*, Tillerson was pressed about what values the president's comments on Charlottesville suggested. His answer was powerfully succinct: 'The president speaks for himself'.[20] Here, the pro-democracy establishment seemed to win over the president's secretary of state. Of course, the president had the last word, and Tillerson was replaced six months later.

Moreover, the administration's actions against free trade are also beginning to engender a globalist resistance. As the president has imposed tariffs on hundreds of products – aimed at trading partners both in the democratic G-7 and in authoritarian China – a coalition that extends from farmers to pharmaceuticals to automobile manufacturers has emerged. That coalition has champions within the government itself – from the US Trade Representative's office to Treasury, Commerce, and Agriculture, which see a rules-based global trading system as being in American interests.

It should be no surprise that much of the American system is now constraining its particularist president. Trump, after all, is intentionally challenging a seven-decade status quo. This particular strain of Trumpism even has a name, as coined by former advisor Steve Bannon at the February 2017 Conservative Political Action Conference: 'deconstruction of the administrative state'. What Bannon's phrase seems to either miss or ignore is that the administrative state is filled with democratic norms, as well as generations of public servants who embrace those norms. That includes not only the career government officials that the Trump administration inherited, but even some of the officials whom he has appointed.

Trump's approach echoes a democratic recession around the world, under way for about a decade. 'With a decline of political rights globally, along with a decreasing number of democracies, autocrats have become more aggressive and sophisticated in stifling the voices of civil society and political opponents', said Kenneth Wollack, president of the National Democratic Institute (NDI), as he testified before the House Committee on Foreign Affairs on 14 June 2018.[21] Still, the past decade is a snapshot in a longer history. As Wollack explained, 'Four years after President Reagan delivered his landmark democracy speech before the British parliament in 1982... Freedom House scored only 52 countries as "free" as compared to 88 in 2018'.[22] This would support the notion that a president who promotes universal values sees results around the globe.

CONCLUSION: UNDERSTANDING THE PRO-DEMOCRACY ESTABLISHMENT

The president has often referred to bureaucratic resistance as the deep state, a concept most often associated with Turkey, Pakistan and Egypt, and other countries where career officials embrace an ideology of bureaucratic self-preservation against the whims of elected governments. It is not a coincidence that Turkey, Pakistan and Egypt generally have been governed by secular governments with a strong military. Each of these countries has kept up the appearance of democracy, but fears of Islamist factions, in particular, are deeply embedded in all their governing establishments. While President Trump is certainly meeting bureaucratic resistance – similar to deep state tactics elsewhere – the comparison misses a key point: much of the resistance is in defence of universalist pro-democracy values and institutions. Precise technical definitions of deep states are elusive. But generally speaking, they tend to be anti-democratic because they prioritize protecting government officials against populist forces, which in many cases would unleash religious-based extremists. 'Be careful playing with the deep-state idea', warns Turkish political scientist Soner Cagaptay. 'It can so easily get out of control that it becomes a monster that helps whoever's in charge curb freedom and intimidate dissidents'.[23]

One deep state tool that Trump has seized upon is the leaking of classified information about private individuals for political ends. In American politics, leaking information for political ends is as old as the republic itself. Thomas Jefferson let his disagreements with President Washington be well known – mostly through pamphleteers and a growing opposition press – despite the fact that Jefferson served as the first secretary of state. Two centuries later, when Richard Nixon succeeded Lyndon Johnson as president, he began ramping up military engagement in Vietnam. Military officials leaked an internal review of Johnson's conduct of the war, namely the Pentagon Papers, to reporters at the *New York Times* and the *Washington Post*. Though the Pentagon Papers were mostly damaging about Johnson's policies, and especially about Johnson-administration doubts that the war could be won, Nixon feared that their release would undermine both his authority and public support for the war.

Leaks have continued ever since. In the Obama administration, military officials leaked information to force an increase in troop numbers in Afghanistan causing the president to lose trust in the career officials who worked for him. As a result, any particular individual leak by a career official threatens all other career government officials and the essential role they play in the policy process. With this in mind, the US national security establishment has sought to find ways to allow career officials to speak their minds without fear. Airing dissent has been deemed not only important for effectiveness but also essential to democratic values. But if career officials are regularly overruled, and if their only outlet for dissent is leaks, then the system does not operate effectively. During the early days of the Nixon administration, the Department of State established a Dissent Channel – essentially a formalized process of expressing opposition to a standing policy. This was in the aftermath of Vietnam, where Johnson administration group-think led the country into war over the warnings of lower-level officials. A comprehensive study of the Dissent Channel by historian Hannah Gurman showed that some of its greatest uses have been in settings where the policy process lacked input from officials who were needed for implementation, and also where policy broke with democratic principles.[24]

Early in Trump's first year, the leaks began to multiply as his war with the intelligence community went public. This brought the concept of the deep state from conspiratorial fringe to mainstream. Indeed, most Americans view it to be credible: 48 percent believe it exists, according to an April 2017 ABC/*Washington Post* poll.[25] In his first year, Trump found it difficult to change the pro-democratic establishment, as many in the FBI, CIA and State and Defence Departments felt as if they were fighting for the integrity of the political system, especially when attacked by a non-democratic adversary such as Russia. The pushback from bureaucrats should not have been surprising. Given the hostility towards the US system from this White House, career public servants were speaking out. This 'rebellion' in turn fuelled White House suspicions that the deep state conspiracy is at work. And thus, a loop of distrust has been established. What is astounding is how many of those agencies are lining up against Trump. For the president to ultimately succeed in establishing a new US foreign policy philosophy, he will have to change minds or replace policymakers. That will require challenging the pro-democracy ethos and tenures of generations of public servants, replacing them with a cadre of national security officials that share Trump's realist view – both in the career bureaucracy and through political appointments. Those political appointees must be confirmed by the US Senate, which currently includes a bipartisan commitment to pro-democracy values. Generating an even larger wave of career officials committed to Trump's vision will require vetting by a pro-Trump wave of political appointees that has yet to be found.

However, the pro-democracy bias among today's foreign policy professionals by itself will not change the growing public ambivalence about pro-democracy policy. Democratic institutions will need to deliver if they are to withstand a populist-realist challenge. Internationally, democratic allies and partners will need to continue to educate the president on why multilateral institutions already are paying off in terms of greater security cooperation and economic prosperity. At home, majorities at the local, state and federal levels will need to regularly impress upon the president and his team that democratic values and institutions matter.

So the real question then is not just whether a pro-democracy establishment can withstand Trump's initial challenge to their role in the system, but also whether they have the support of democratic publics at home and abroad. That conflict is as old as the republic.

NOTES

1. For a good overview of the resilient power of isolationist thinking, see Christopher Nichols, 'The Enduring Power of Isolationism: An Historical Perspective', *Orbis* 57, no. 3 (11 May 2013).

2. George Washington, 'Farewell Address, 19 September 1796'. https://founders.archives.gov/documents/Washington/99-01-02-00963.

3. Thomas Jefferson, 'To the Senate and House of Representatives of the United States'. 17 October 1803, National Archives.

4. Louis Hartz, *The Liberal Tradition in America* (New York: Harcourt, Brace and Company, 1955); Bernard Bailyn, *The Ideological Origins of the American Revolution* (Cambridge: Harvard University Press, 1967).

5. Gordon Wood, address to the Miller Center, 3 May 2018.

6. Rogers Smith, *Civic Ideals* (New Haven, CT: Yale University Press, 1997).

7. Woodrow Wilson, 'War Message to Congress, 1917'. Address delivered at Joint Session of the Two Houses of Congress, 2 April 1917; US 65th Congress, 1st Session, Senate Document 5.

8. William Hitchcock, 'How the GOP Embraced the World and Then Turned Away', *Politico* (13 July 2018).

9. Christopher Nichols, 'America First, American Isolationism, and the Coming of World War'. The 2018 Stevenson Conference: America First: The Past and Future of an Idea (April 2018).

10. Franklin D. Roosevelt, Press Conference, 7 December, 1940.

11. Nichols, 'America First, American Isolationism, and the Coming of World War'.

12. David Farber, ' "America First" and International Trade Policy in the Cold War Era'. The 2018 Stevenson Conference: America First: The Past and Future of an Idea (April 2018).

13. Bill Kauffman, *Ain't My America: The Long, Noble History of Antiwar Conservatism and Middle-American Anti-Imperialism* (New York: Metropolitan Books, 2008).

14. Martin J. Medhurst, 'Text and Context in the 1952 Presidential Campaign: Eisenhower's "I Shall Go to Korea" Speech'. *Presidential Studies Quarterly* 30, no. 3 (September 2000).

15. Jefferson Cowie, 'American Workers First? The Politics of Blue Collar Nationalism in an Age of Decline'. The 2018 Stevenson Conference: America First: The Past and Future of an Idea (April 2018).

16. Donald J. Trump, *National Security Strategy of the United States of America* (Washington: The White House, 2017).

17. Melvyn P. Leffler, 'Trump's Delusional National Security Strategy: How the Trump Administration Ignores What Made America Great'. *Foreign Affairs* (21 December 2017).

18. Brian Hook, 'Balancing Interests and Values' (17 May 2017). https://www.politico.com/f/?id=00000160-6c37-da3c-a371-ec3f13380001 (accessed online 24 August, 2018).

19. As quoted in Mark Landler and Julie Hirshfeld Davis, 'Trump Opens His Arms to Russia. His Administration Closes Its Fist', *New York Times* (14 July 2018).

20. *Fox News Sunday* (27 August 2017).

21. Kenneth Wollack, 'Democracy Promotion in a Challenging World'. House Committee on Foreign Affairs. 14 June 2018.

22. Ibid.

23. David A. Graham, 'There Is No American "Deep State" ', *The Atlantic* (20 February 2017).

24. Hannah Gurman, *The Dissent Papers: The Voices of Diplomats in the Cold War and Beyond* (New York: Columbia University Press, 2012).

25. *Washington Post* – ABC News, poll 17–20 April 2017.

BIBLIOGRAPHY

Bailyn, Bernard. *The Ideological Origins of the American Revolution*. Cambridge, MA: Harvard University Press, 1967.

Barnes, Melody. 'A Republic If You Can Keep It', *The Miller Center University of Virginia*, 28 September 2017.

Bush, George H. W. and Brent Scowcroft. *A World Transformed*. New York: Vintage Books, 1999.

'Dissent Channel: Alternatives to Closing Doors in Order to Secure Our Borders'. Washington: US State Department, 2017.

Doyle, Michael W. 'Kant, Liberal Legacies, and Foreign Affairs', *Philosophy and Public Affairs* 12, no. 3 (Summer 1983): 205–35.

'Gary Cohn Urges Trump Team to Do More to Condemn Neo-Nazis', *Financial Times* (August 2017). *Fox News Sunday,* 27 August 2017.

Graham, David A. 'There Is No American "Deep State"', *The Atlantic*, 20 February 2017.

Gurman, Hannah. *The Dissent Papers: The Voices of Diplomats in the Cold War and Beyond.* New York: Columbia University Press, 2012.

Hartz, Louis. *The Liberal Tradition in America.* New York: Harcourt, Brace and Company, 1955.

Hook, Brian. 'Balancing Interests and Values', *Politico*, 17 May 2017. https://www.politico.com/f/?id=00000160-6c37-da3c-a371-ec3f13380001.

Huntington, Samuel P. *American Politics: The Promise of Disharmony.* Cambridge, MA: Harvard University Press, 1981.

Kagan, Robert. *Of Paradise and Power: America and Europe in the New World Order.* New York: Vintage Books, 2004.

Kagan, Robert. 'The Twilight of the Liberal World Order'. *Brookings Institution*, 24 January 2017.

Kagan, Robert. *The World America Made.* New York: Alfred A. Knopf, 2012.

Keohane, Robert O. *International Institutions and State Power: Essays in International Relations Theory.* Boulder, CO: Westview Press, 1989.

Keohane Robert O. and Joseph S. Nye. *Power and Independence: World Politics in Transition.* Boston: Little, Brown and Company, 1977.

Kissinger, Henry. *A World Restored: Metternich, Castlereagh, and the Problems of Peace, 1812–22.* Wilmington, DE: Mariner Books, 1957.

Leffler, Melvyn P. *Safeguarding Democratic Capitalism: US Foreign Policy and National Security, 1920–2015.* Princeton, NJ: Princeton University Press, 2017.

Leffler, Melvyn P. 'Trump's Delusional National Security Strategy: How the Trump Administration Ignores What Made America Great'. *Foreign Affairs*, 21 December 2017.

McMaster, H. R. *Dereliction of Duty: Lyndon Johnson, Robert McNamara, the Joint Chiefs of Staff, and the Lies That Led to Vietnam.* New York: HarperCollins, 1997.

Morgenthau, Hans Joachim and Kenneth W. Thompson. *Politics among Nations: The Struggle for Power and Peace.* New York: Knopf, 1985.

Nichols, Christopher McNight. 'The Enduring Power of Isolationism: An Historical Perspective'. *Orbis* 57, no. 3 (11 May 2013).

Ruggie, John Gerard. 'International Regimes, Transactions and Change: Embedded Liberalism in the Postwar Economic Order'. *International Regimes*. Ithaca, NY: Cornell University Press, 1983.

Smith, Rogers M. *Civic Ideals.* New Haven, CT: Yale University Press, 1997.

Sparrow, Andrew. 'Theresa May Says Trump Retweeting Britain First Was "Wrong Thing to Do" – As It Happened'. *The Guardian*, 30 November 2017.

Trump, Donald J. *National Security Strategy of the United States of America.* Washington: The White House, 2017.

'Washington Post – ABC News Poll April 17–20, 2017'. *Washington Post*, 27 April 2017.

Chapter 5

Reflections on Values in Western Foreign Policy

From the Liberal World Order to Antithetical Values

Bruno Maçães

The topic of values in foreign policy is at first glance puzzling. What are values, and what are they opposed to? How can they be pursued by individual states while preserving a claim to universality? Why is the concept and even the word so prevalent in discussions of foreign policy, while remaining of secondary importance in discussions of domestic policy?

Writing forty years ago, Nathan Glazer argued that one of the elements of American exceptionalism was the way values seemed to be central to American foreign policy. Other countries seemed much less convinced that they could define a specific variety of national values and then proceed to claim that they should be applied everywhere. He then qualifies his initial thesis somewhat by noting that a similar drive could be found in Soviet statements on foreign policy:

> Only the great Communist powers make a similar one. They too say they represent the interests of humanity, and of democracy – a 'truer' democracy than our own. Countries like England, West Germany, and Japan put forward much more modest claims. They limit themselves to defending their national interests, and if they also say they are pursuing the values of democracy and liberty, it is only by way of following the lead of the United States.[1]

Both the United States and the Soviet Union were then struggling for global primacy. They both hoped to define the shape of the global order. The concept of values was meant to support and promote that desideratum.

Today we face a different situation. Countries like Norway and Sweden deliberately link their foreign policy to a set of values. No one would argue that they have any ambitions to global primacy, but they still believe that their national interests are intimately connected to the global order. Now it is not superpower status that determines a vital concern with global rules, principles and institutions, but rather the opposite, the sense that a chaotic global system cannot serve the interests of small and open countries and economies. While some have moved from interests to values, others seem to have refocused on interests. In an early attempt to explain the basis of Trump's foreign policy, two of his most senior advisers argued that the world should not be seen as a global community but rather as an arena where nations and other actors engage and compete for advantage. It was a clarifying distinction. If one takes the view that world politics is no more than an arena, a physical space, then the only perspective available is that of each individual nation, fighting to defend and promote its interests. These, incidentally, may well be non-economic and have to do with security or a certain favoured way of life or, as always happens in politics, the increase in influence and power. What marks them as interests is the fact that they exist only for those who attempt to promote them. By contrast, we speak of values when it is a question of giving a thicker content to world politics and making it resemble a political regime, a global regime embodying principles and rules and having some measure of normative power – some claim on what ought to be or what ought to happen.

VALUES AND INTERESTS

How does it happen that a country tries to refocus on its national interests while growing sceptical of the role of values in foreign policy? The history of American foreign policy over the past century is one of the gradual construction of a global system of rules and institutions. This system was always intended to be one suited to American interests. In other words, it was meant to be the system which the United States would like to see governing relations between states. There was an initial contradiction in this project, of course. The system promoted by the world's most powerful democracy was not to be a democracy in the sense that its structures benefitted from equal and weighted input from all mankind. Is this the contradiction responsible for our current predicament?

In a way, the answer is *yes*. Countries such as Russia and China are quick to point out that the international system is tilted in favour of American interests. It calls for the maintenance of order by the only state capable of fighting two or three simultaneous wars anywhere on the planet. It is based on economic competition between major multinational companies, which are predominantly based in the United States, while capital flows to the dollar, which only one actor can print at will. When calling for a multipolar world, China and Russia fall into a contradiction of their own: their call for democracy in the global community is not met by democratization at home. But they have been successful to a considerable extent in challenging American power, so much so that, faced with the choice between a global democracy – no one can say at present what this means and how it could be built – and the return to the state of nature, the United States may well choose the latter.

China is a signal case of all the ambiguities behind the concept of a global community. The Chinese state and Chinese companies are able to benefit from the rewards of open trade and investment, but many of the reciprocal obligations are never delivered because Chinese authorities have no intention of applying those principles to their domestic sphere and may even attempt to convince other countries to break away from the existing world order. World politics will tend to become increasingly fractured between different constellations of interests, and as a result the very notion of a global community may approach the breaking point. The role of the United States is, of course, critical: If the global system no longer works as intended, if more and more countries act autonomously from it, then Washington will be tempted to dismantle it and avoid paying its share of the costs and obligations.

Interests and values, thus, can indeed be distinguished, but they are concepts that remain meaningful only within a complex web of connections and superimpositions. As we have seen, what underpins a global order of values and institutions for the past century was its strong connection to the interests of the most powerful state in the system. Once these two variables are weakened – if and when the pivotal state sees its power decrease and the connection between global rules and national interest dilute – we can expect those values to weaken as well. Authors such as John Ikenberry have argued that nothing in principle stops us from envisioning a world where China has become the dominant actor in the global system while supporting the same fundamental values and institutions existing today. That seems implausible to me for the obvious reason that those values and institutions were never meant to be neutral or to exist above the fray of interstate conflict.[2]

If values are often underpinned by national interests, the reverse is no less true. One international actor that understands this very well is the European Union (EU). Its way of doing politics is uniquely suited to an international system based on rules and common institutions. Officials in Brussels will readily concede that the EU would struggle to defend its interests in a world where the naked defence of the national interest was the only game in town. This fact goes a long way towards explaining why the EU has taken over the mantle of a values-based foreign policy from the United States. It feels the connection between values and interests as strongly as the United States once did.

That in itself signals an important change. The EU may perhaps have in the past thought too generously of itself as a global legislator of values. Recent developments such as the Eurozone crisis have forced it to look more closely at its own interests, while reinforcing a sense that in a multipolar world neither the EU institutions nor the member states are in a position to impose their will on a recalcitrant world. The result is a new kind of balance. The realism of national interests has been strengthened, but then the EU quickly discovered that its interests were better pursued through a global system that reduced competition between states – the EU after all, being an incomplete state, lacks many of the tools of state power needed for such competition – and kept the threat of armed conflict at bay. Richard Youngs writes that a feeling has taken root in European foreign policy circles that the EU will benefit by replacing its liberal ardour with a more pragmatic approach where the promotion of liberal values is closely connected to a hard-edged realization that European interests are thereby also promoted. The EU is more likely to get what it wants the less it is seen as a normative power and the more it helps promote a liberal world order for the sake of its own interests and in a less obtrusive manner. 'The post crisis trend is toward a more unsentimental multilateralism and a more selective and rationalized form of cosmopolitan liberalism'.[3] In practice, European foreign policy has become more selective, seeking to distinguish between those values and those value issues that really matter and those seen as more of a luxury. Obviously, the standard used to implement the distinction must be that of its collective interest.

Perhaps paradoxically, the discovery that what the EU used to take as universal values are after all not universally shared could lead to a more activist foreign policy, as these values now need to be defended and promoted in a hostile environment, rather than absorbed more or less automatically by other world actors.

The final question we must address in this section is whether a world where different blocs compete for power and influence is a world where one can still speak of values in foreign policy. I would argue that at first the trend will be to desacralize those values and present them as more naked and particularistic state goals – state or national interests, in the terminology adopted here. In time, however, the language of values will tend to reassert itself. The foreign policy goals defended by different actors may regain their claim to universality. If they clash, it is just because they all have universalist ambitions – and values, by definition, have such ambitions. We have learned from Isaiah Berlin that values are not necessarily single.[4] We may have different constellations of values. They may conflict, they may be incompatible, without thereby becoming mere expressions of particular interests.

In order to better address these conundrums, we now turn to a brief discussion of how values have been approached in international relations theory and how those approaches need to be revised in light of the current situation.

WORLD ORDER

The question of values in foreign policy is inescapable because the question of the global order is inescapable. The theorists who have taken the notion of a global order to its logical conclusion form part of a vaguely defined liberal school, but they ultimately share a certain intellectual assumption: the idea that states are not the only sources of order but that some important normative and institutional content also exists at the global level. When Michael Doyle argues that democracies deal with each other in a way different from relations with or between other regimes, he is defending the view that the global order can be shaped in different ways depending on which values prevail.[5] In similar tones, just war theorists argue that an objective set of principles and rules applies universally and governs conflict or war between nations. Hobbes was wrong when he thought that what he defined as the state of nature still exists in the international sphere. There is no world state, to be sure, but there is a world order, a way of doing international politics, which has some normative and even coercive force.

Liberals are usually contrasted to realists. In the crudest terms, realists would argue that the only consideration governing relations between states – in the absence of an agent or a set of values existing above them – is power and its distribution. World politics need not necessarily be chaotic or destructive, but whatever stability may be found is the contingent result of the power balance. Critically, the only level at which one can speak of principles and rules, of hierarchy and process, is the level of the state. One must always adopt the perspective of a specific state actor. A view from above remains a view from nowhere. Principles are no more than general rules of conduct by which a given country chooses to abide in the conduct of its relations with other countries. A consistent realist would be careful to avoid using the term values in this context.

Systemic realists do not question the critique of the view from above. To take but one example, when Kenneth Waltz suggested that state behaviour can be explained by the structure of the international system, he did not mean that the international system can be used to judge or evaluate state action.[6] On the contrary, his intuition was that states act in a world where only other states matter. His improvement on previous realist theories was to explain that states must consider their relative power and how the whole gamut of power equations has been determined. The game becomes more complex, but it is still a game and the international system no more than an arena. Again, this does mean that material resources are all that matters. Such a committed realist as Stephen Walt is interested in balances of threat – the element of threat appeals to the role of perception and identity and may be particularly at home in the world of political emotions and narratives.[7]

On the question that interests us here, the so-called English or international society school may turn out to be more illuminating. Hedley Bull starts his famous *The Anarchical Society* by noting that, while being interested in the question of order in world politics, he means by that not, as realists would have it, the totality of relationships between states, but rather something approaching a normative quality: order as opposed to disorder. At the same time, he recognizes that other values may conflict with the desire for order. He goes only so far as to claim that these values and the inevitable clash between them presuppose a certain political structure and this is what the question of order is about. In other words, Bull is interested in the constitutive moment of the international society, where something like a system of world politics and effective institutions are already in place, awaiting to be given content by different and conflicting values. When we speak of order as opposed to disorder what we have in mind is not simply the pattern of behaviour, but an arrangement of social life promoting certain goals or values. Sovereign states, even in circumstances of war and crisis, may behave in regular ways, but these are examples not of order in social life but of disorder.[8]

Now, as Bull explains, an international society exists only when states – it certainly does not have to include all states – regard themselves as bound by common rules, values or claims in their dealings with each other. Which word we use in this context seems to me decisively less important than the qualifier 'common'. In order to underline the distinction between an international system and an international society, Bull refers to the case of Turkey. Since the sixteenth century, the Ottoman Empire formed part of a system of relations including European states, taking part in wars and alliances as a member of that system, but agreements to which it entered were not binding and the notion that a constellation of values, interests and institutions were shared between Turkey and its neighbours to the West did not make its appearance until the nineteenth century. European states were seen as bound by a code of conduct that did not apply to their relations with other societies. At the same time, the exclusiveness of the idea of a European order was mitigated by the very universalist aspirations which so appealed to Europeans, and by the nineteenth century the orthodox doctrine was that international society was a European creation to which other states might be admitted if and when they met a standard of civilization laid down by the Europeans – the test which Turkey was the first to pass. 'In the twentieth century international society ceased to be regarded as specifically European and came to be considered as global or world wide'. Presciently, Bull goes on to ask a fundamental question, one whose importance has become clearer only after he wrote:

> If the Christian and later European international system that existed from sixteenth century to the nineteenth was also an international society, were not the bonds of this society stretched and ultimately broken as the system expanded and became world-wide? Is not the international politics of the present time best viewed as an international system that is not an international society?[9]

JUSTICE IN THE WORLD

Taken to its logical conclusion, the notion of a world society would mean that its constituent elements are individuals rather than states and that these individuals are endowed with rights, which they can claim even against their own state. In certain circumstances, an intervention from a power outside the state in order to protect these rights would be considered legitimate.

The concept and practice of humanitarian intervention are relatively recent. In its common designation, it requires the existence of a framework of universal human rights against which to define the existence of serious harm and the means to remove it, including the punishment of those responsible. Its historical moment now looks limited to a very particular set of circumstances. With the end of the Cold War, it suddenly seemed that the world would now be united around one set of political values. Practically, it was now possible to use the overwhelming military superiority of the victorious side to make sure that those values could at last be shared everywhere. Even the fact that the Soviet Union had not been defeated militarily seemed to suggest that its population had revolted against an oppressive state much in the same way that Europeans and Americans had in past built their own liberal democracies. All that remained to be done was to smoothen the curve of historical development, which to all evidence remained uneven. In some parts of the world, populations were already fully on the side of liberal democracy on a Western model, but their ability to impose their wishes on a corrupt state apparatus was doubtful. The concept of humanitarian intervention was meant to bridge the gap. Limited in time and scope, a military intervention from the outside could help remove the contradiction. It was felt that a foreign government or group of governments could claim to be more representative than the national government in an extreme case, because at least it shared the values of those populations whose rights were being violated.

The flaws with the theory and practice of humanitarian intervention were quickly exposed. On the one hand, there was an unbridgeable distance between the theory and the practice. Defined as universal and predicated on a strong theory of equality, intervention would have to be universally and equally applied. In practice, it could not. Intervention fatigue was bound to set in, while some of the most blatant human rights violations were ignored because the offending party was too powerful or influential. On the other hand, even in those cases where humanitarian interventions were carried out, as in Somalia or the former Yugoslavia, its results were mixed. Often they tended to deal with the symptoms rather than the causes of human rights violations, while creating a sense of grievance in those countries carrying out the intervention and resentment in those which it targeted. The Iraq invasion of 2003 – while not strictly a humanitarian intervention – convinced most observers that military force would never be able to push a country on the path of liberal democracy.

In recent years, the trend has been towards recovering an older principle of non-intervention. While often couched in political cynicism and used to further a naked approach to national interest, it does have a moral basis which can be convincingly elaborated and whose impact can sometimes be useful. Non-intervention can mean a rule of respect for different societies with their own cultures and histories. Even someone committed to a strong theory of human rights may feel that the best way to promote them is to allow every society to feel fully responsible for its fate and to chart its own path of political development. Finally, non-intervention can work as a brake on the temptation to use humanitarian concerns as a mask for geopolitical ambitions, while being better suited to a world where political societies no longer seem to be converging to the same set of values.[10] Unsurprisingly, countries less able to project their power abroad will be more inclined to defend a principle of non-intervention.

When discussing world politics today, we often revert to one of two models. The first, popularized by Francis Fukuyama, sees the whole world converging to a European or Western political framework, after which no further historical development is possible.[11] Every country or region is measured by the time it will still take to reach this final destination, but all doubts and debates about where we are heading have been fundamentally resolved. The other model, defended by Samuel Huntington, is sceptical of such irreversible movement.[12] The world it depicts is that of a clash between different civilizations having little or nothing in common, particularly since Western political culture will remain geographically limited. But there is a third way. I agree with Fukuyama that the whole world is on the path to modern society, but there are numerous paths and, naturally, different visions of what a modern society looks like.

Everyone is modern now, but there are different models of modern society. From this fact the essential terms of the new world order follow more or less directly. The hard distinction between modern and traditional has broken down, giving way to a deeply integrated world, but its most distinctive trait is the incessant competition between different ideas of how worldwide networks should be organized.[13]

ANTITHETICAL VALUES

The strategic issue today is which paradigm of international relations will ultimately prevail. On the one hand, we see a return to a vision of global politics as marked by a renewed competition for spheres of influence. This is the paradigm of national interests, and its defining characteristic is the absence of common or overlapping perspectives. On the other hand, however their force has been weakened, it is still the case that common institutions and cooperative relations dominate most relations between states. Interdependence has intensified and states still find it necessary to engage in multiple cooperative endeavours. The struggle to find common perspectives and ways to manage common challenges and problems continues unabated. It is perhaps less formalized, more chaotic and, as a result, its outcomes have become correspondingly uncertain or even unpredictable. Above all, integration projects are now multiple and contradictory. Globalization has not retreated, it has multiplied and we now have different globalization projects superimposed upon each other.

China's Belt and Road goes so far as to advocate innovative forms of economic policy coordination, an area where, for example, the EU has made limited progress. China also plans to set up a new international court for settling disputes among companies participating in the Belt and Road. The new Belt and Road dispute settlement mechanism is aimed at protecting both Chinese and foreign parties' legal rights and interests, and creating a stable, fair, transparent business environment with rule of law. It will be comprised of three international commercial courts. The court in Xian will deal with commercial disputes along the Silk Road Economic Belt. The Shenzhen court will cover cases arising along the twenty-first-century Maritime Silk Road. The headquarters of the Belt and Road court will be based in Beijing.

The belief in universal values is a fair description of how the EU sees world politics, but this vision is increasingly difficult to sustain. On its periphery, the conviction – once taken for a truism – that countries would converge to European norms has become something of a Kantian ideal, something that helps one determine the direction of movement but impossible to reach or attain. In recent years countries such as Ukraine, Georgia and Moldova have oscillated more or less wildly between different models. Setbacks and recursions now abound. If in the past the complaint was that progress was slow, now the very notion of progress has become doubtful.

In the case of Russia, the rejection of European values is complete and definitive. In a first stage, Russian leaders still spoke approvingly of adopting modern European norms and standards, even if this was always combined with the assertion that a 'common European home' would be multipolar and could not simply absorb Russia into existing structures. After the Ukraine crisis, the break was much deeper, and the Kremlin has even flirted with the notion that Russia is now much more interested in its relations with China than in its old and halting movement towards Europe.

In China, the EU and the US face an even greater challenge. While Russian revisionism may still be shrugged off as incapable of durable consequences for the global order – Russia might after all become an increasingly marginal state, incapable of solving its modernization problems – China now offers an alternative model with an increasingly global appeal. In the past, the belief that China would ultimately follow the adoption of a capitalist market economy with the corresponding conversion to liberal democracy helped define Western foreign policy.

That particular illusion has long been abandoned. We realize much better now that even countries on the same modernization path may end up in very different places. On the one hand, the very idea of a modern society now appears to us as much more capacious than before. Its basic elements – abstract social relations and the widespread use of technology – are compatible with a myriad of different ways of life. Even the path taken by Western societies could easily reveal junctures where different alternatives could have been pursued.

On the other hand, the choices made in the West – Western values but also technical solutions only loosely related to those values – have lost their immediacy and appeal. The 2008 financial crisis, the rise of populism, the growing inability to deal with the consequences of a diminished global status – all these moments have awakened Western self-doubt where before only missionary zeal could be found.

Chinese élites – and broader tendencies in Chinese public opinion tend to follow – implicitly believe that to move closer to Western values or to attempt to imitate the West in different areas would be tantamount to abdicating China's edge, opting to compete on territory defined by the West and therefore on terms clearly tilted in its favour. As a recent report puts it, if in the eighteenth century a Chinese emperor famously explained to a British embassy that he had no need for Western goods, the view in China today is that the country has no need for Western culture, ideas and values.[14]

Two issues stand out and will have critical consequences for relations between China and the West. First, on the question of reciprocity, the West now recognizes that China is unlikely to accept at home those norms of economic openness and market governance from which it benefits when its companies operate in the American and European markets. The difficulty here is that full reciprocity can be established only if the West renounces all pretences to the universality of its own values and starts to exclude China from the purview of a system of norms once intended for all. Closing the borders to Chinese investment or applying new tariffs and regulatory barriers to Chinese exports on the grounds that China does the same may serve different purposes: it could be an attempt to influence China to change its ways or, on the contrary, a measure meant to protect Western markets from Chinese interests. In practice we are likely to end up with some combination of these two goals. A multipolar world system would be based on different spheres of influence, as different actors pursue independent paths, even if they are also able – in limited areas – to influence and shape each other's system of norms.

The second major issue is directly related to security and the role of international law. As China pushes its own national interest in such conflict areas as the South China Sea and its disputed border with India, the West – in this case the EU more than the United States – has an important stake in defending the status of international law and rules-based methods for conflict resolution, but the challenge in this case is that those positions will increasingly be impossible to defend if the EU continues lagging behind China and the United States in hard power. Conversely, if Europeans come to a common understanding that their values now need to be supported with better tools of power projection, might that conclusion not raise doubts whether the EU is sacrificing its own values in response to a new world of cut-throat competition?

In his 2002 report to the National Congress, General Secretary Jiang Zemin foresaw a '20 years period of strategic opportunity', during which China would benefit from good relations with the United States, allowing it to concentrate on economic growth and full-scale modernization. During this period, Deng's teaching of *tao guang yang hui*, or keeping a low profile, would retain its validity, but no one among China's leadership ever entertained any illusions that such a favourable environment could last forever. China was growing too big and too powerful to avoid raising new suspicions among the major global powers, zealous of their position and naturally unhappy to see a new rival arriving on the scene. Nor could it expect the international political and economic system to continue to satisfy its domestic needs, now that these were becoming increasingly more demanding.

Chinese authorities are obviously right that a win-win solution is always possible in the sense that cooperation between two or more states can leave them all better off. Where the model breaks down is at the level of different political concepts because these are always defined in opposition to one another. The ideological question – as opposed to the economic one – is inevitably zero-sum because to accept a certain way to organize social relations is to discard different concepts and principles. What changed in the past two or three years is that China is no longer satisfied with waging an ideological war at home – staving off Western challenges to party rule – but wants to take that war to the world stage. It can no longer be said that the Chinese are indifferent to how other peoples govern themselves. In his opening speech to the Communist Party's 19th Congress in October 2017, Xi Jinping spoke loudly and openly about posing an ideological challenge to Western liberal democracy. China is 'blazing a new trail for other developing countries to achieve modernization', providing 'a new option for other countries and nations who want to speed up their development'.

The National Security Strategy approved by President Trump in December 2017 claims:

> The United States helped expand the liberal economic trading system to countries that did not share our values, in the hope that these states would liberalize their economic and political practices and provide commensurate benefits to the United States. Experience shows that these countries distorted and undermined key economic institutions without undertaking significant reform of their economies or politics. They espouse free trade rhetoric and exploit its benefits, but only adhere selectively to the rules and agreements.[15]

The document advocates that the United States distinguishes between those countries that adhere to the same values and those that do not. With like-minded states competition should happen in the 'economic domain', but with other states competition is taken to the political level, where it should be conducted through 'enforcement measures'. Every year, it argues, countries such as China steal intellectual property valued at hundreds of billions of dollars, an economic and security risk to which the United States will respond with counterintelligence and law enforcement activities to curtail intellectual property theft by all sources, while exploring new legal and regulatory mechanisms to prevent and prosecute violations. This is a world where competition, not cooperation, is the predominant reality. Values are less the common perspective of all nations than a specific way of life targeted by one's enemies and adversaries. They are antithetical. As the strategy puts it in a crucial passage, 'China and Russia want to shape a world antithetical to US values and interests'.[16]

CONCLUSION

We are thus at a critical juncture when the language of values may enter a period of crisis. Antithetical values are a difficult concept to defend. It may be seen as internally contradictory: if each state actor defends its own set of values, it can no longer endow them with universal significance. Valid only for the agent asserting them, they may become too dependent on the logic of state power and conflict. In order to rebuild the concept of values on a new plane, the effort to bridge differences and find common ground will have to begin anew. At the current moment, that effort still seems to lie far in the future.

NOTES

1. Nathan Glazer, 'American Values and American Foreign Policy', *Commentary* (July 1976).
2. G. John Ikenberry, 'The Future of the Liberal Order: Internationalism after America', *Foreign Affairs* 90, no. 3 (May/June 2011): 56–68.
3. Richard Youngs, *The Uncertain Legacy of Crisis: European Foreign Policy Faces the Future* (Washington, DC: Carnegie Endowment, 2014), 128.
4. Isaiah Berlin and Henry Hardy, *The Crooked Timber of Humanity: Chapters in the History of Ideas* (New York: Fontana Press, 1991).
5. Michael Doyle, 'Liberalism and World Politics', *American Political Science Review* 80, no. 4 (December 1986): 1151–69.
6. Kenneth N. Waltz, *Theory of International Politics* (Reading, MA: Addison-Wesley, 1979).
7. Stephen Walt, 'Alliance Formation and the Balance of World Power', *International Security* 9, no. 4 (Spring 1985): 3–43.
8. Hedley Bull, *The Anarchical Society* (London: Palgrave, 1977).
9. Ibid., 32–39.
10. R. J. Vincent, *Nonintervention and International Order* (Princeton, NJ: Princeton University Press, 2015).
11. Francis Fukuyama, *The Origins of Political Order: From Prehuman Times to the French Revolution* (New York: Farrar, Straus and Giroux, 2011).
12. Samuel P. Huntington, *The Clash of Civilizations and the Remaking of World Order* (New York: Touchstone, 1997).
13. See Bruno Maçães, *The Dawn of Eurasia: On the Trail of the New World Order* (London: Allen Lane, 2018), 35.
14. François Godement and Abigael Vasselier, *China at the Gates: A New Power Audito of EU-China Relations* (European Council on Foreign Relations, 2017).
15. National Security Strategy of the United States of America (December 2017), 17.
16. Ibid., 25.

BIBLIOGRAPHY

Berlin, Isaiah and Henry Hardy. *The Crooked Timber of Humanity: Chapters in the History of Ideas*. New York: Fontana Press, 1991.
Bull, Hedley. *The Anarchical Society*. London: Palgrave, 1977.
Doyle, Michael. 'Liberalism and World Politics'. *American Political Science Review* 80, no. 4 (December 1986): 1151–69.
Fukuyama, Francis. *The Origins of Political Order: From Prehuman Times to the French Revolution*. New York: Farrar, Straus and Giroux, 2011.
Huntington, Samuel P. *The Clash of Civilizations and the Remaking of World Order*. New York: Touchstone, 1997.

Ikenberry, G. John. 'The Future of the Liberal Order: Internationalism after America'. *Foreign Affairs* 90, no. 3 (May/June 2011): 56–62.

Maçães, Bruno. *The Dawn of Eurasia: On the Trail of the New World Order*. London: Allen Lane, 2018.

Vincent, R. J. *Nonintervention and International Order*. Princeton, NJ: Princeton University Press, 2015.

Walt, Stephen. 'Alliance Formation and the Balance of World Power'. *International Security* 9, no. 4 (Spring 1985).

Waltz, Kenneth N. *Theory of International Politics*. Reading, MA: Addison-Wesley, 1979.

Chapter 6

Values in Russian Foreign Policy

Soviet Values, Revisionism and President Putin

Hari Vasudevan and Tatiana Shaumyan

Revisionist features that have marked Russian foreign policy in the first two decades of this century have coincided with projection of the significance of values (*tsennosti*) by administrations associated with President Vladimir Putin. The process has not involved acknowledgement of a discernible value system comparable to Soviet communism. The latter was a catch-all of ideology, behavioural maxims and ethics intertwined with the Soviet experience of Communist rule and the planned economy; closely linked was a perspective on international relations based on interpretations of class, the exploitative functions of capitalism globally and a commitment to build world communism. To the contrary, although the position is under review,[1] post–Soviet Russia still adheres to Article 13 of the 1993 constitution, which disavows commitment to any single ideology.

Nevertheless, for over a decade, Russian official pronouncements involve a revisionist approach to terms such as 'sovereignty', 'democracy' and 'market economics' as articulated by the European Union (EU), the United States and their allies. Here and in foreign policy, stress falls on the strengthening of values as a means to achieve better levels of security where 'values' are conceived as formulations generated as much by reference points of Eurasian practice as any universal ethical code. Strong condemnation is expressed of 'illegal' and 'neo-fascist' initiatives across the world, applying official Russian standards to do so. Assertion of common interests with the EU and the US coexists with a strong critique of their policies. These points of focus are outlined in the Foreign Policy Concept of Russia of 2016.[2]

Much of this is at variance with post–Soviet Russia's initial lack of clarity in priority-building, and an early assumption that the West was a model. That model was associated with pluralist electoral democracy, private enterprise and property and cultivation of civil liberties – all in a cocktail defined by

US and Western European practices. The Russian position was a reverse of long-standing Soviet critique of Euro-American practice around such values. But the extent and rate of assimilation of EU/US paradigms post-1991 was uneven. The application of terms such as 'Atlanticist' and 'Eurasianist' to swings in Russian foreign policy was a reflection of this unevenness and marked the Yeltsin era (1992–1999) in Russian politics. At that time, overarching commitment to the Organization for Security and Co-operation in Europe (OSCE) more than any other cooperative framework outside the Commonwealth of Independent States (CIS) demonstrated the importance given by all actors to the Helsinki Act and the Paris Charter (1990).

Post-2004, Russian revisionism has been shaped with this in mind, but also a deep focus on the cooperative formation of the Eurasian Economic Union (EAEU). Crude authoritarianism and Russian self-aggrandizement in the Soviet space under Putin, rather than well-conceived values, are held to be responsible for change in policy. But the subject has been thinly explored analytically.[3]

This chapter provides a narrative that draws out values orientation in Russian foreign policy through Soviet and post-Soviet times to show a chequered phenomenon in the present. An argument evolves that values bind Russia to the West more than in Soviet times; but they are also a source and expression of conflict with the West. Following scattered interest in values in the Yeltsin era, exceptional initiatives focused on values have been generated under Putin after 2000. These initiatives have reflected firmly on foreign policy and have persisted through Putin's tenures as president/prime minister. The initiatives are not directly linked to ministers or policymakers, but they coincide with the projection of Russian positions internationally. The trend consolidates as a cultural force which draws from construction of official history, negotiates with religion in Russia and ranges broadly through a substantial presence in the digital media inside Russia and outside, in the space of the former Union of Soviet Socialist Republics (USSR). The development has been subject to state direction, but it has social depth because it overlaps with attributes of education, school upwards.

This outcome coexists with the engagement with countries outside the former Soviet sphere on terms that involve respect for alternative national perspectives: a position considered more respectful of sovereignty and democracy than Euro-American approaches. The duality compares with pre-1991 Soviet treatment of non-Communist developing states. Here, the approach to India is the best example of adaptation of past relationships to a thin post-1991 'values fabric' in policy. The engagement is not exceptional in range and may be compared with Russia's relations with China. But since there are neighbourhood perspectives involved in the latter, it is the relationship with India that is the best example of the flexibility of the complex matrix of Russia-centric initiatives in the developing world. Strikingly, the development shows the formative influence of the Indian engagement in the past on Russian foreign policymaking.

BACKGROUND: THE USSR'S FOREIGN POLICY VALUES AND INSTITUTIONS

Russian foreign policy evolved from a critique of Soviet foreign policy. That critique touched on pre-1991 practices and values where the Soviet state vaunted its real achievements to guarantee social attributes valued in Western Europe and the United States (democracy, civil liberties, etc.).

Rejecting such Soviet claims in memoirs of his early years as minister of external affairs of the Soviet Russian Republic, Andrei Kozyrev pithily described foreign policy in the USSR as the concern of a few and a matter rarely discussed with knowledge among the general public. Confidentiality surrounded the conduct of foreign affairs.[4] Practitioners of policy were made up of recruits from institutions held to be appropriate such as the Moscow Institute of International Relations,[5] their ranks supplemented from the Communist Party of the Soviet Union (CPSU), the Komitet Gosudarstvennoy Bezopasnosti (KGB) and the armed forces. Appointment was decided by bureaucratic format, awareness or skill, but as much by the rules of advancement set by the party's *nomenklatura* system. Such rules prioritized obedience to the party and the different 'lines' of ideas that it evolved.

In this snapshot of the poor democratic credentials of Soviet policymaking, Kozyrev indicated the consequences of the guiding influence in Soviet policy of Bolshevik or Soviet 'civilization'. That civilization was meant to express the best of European progressive values, including commitment to representative and democratic government, the rule of law, personal liberty, social equality, social justice and tolerance of religious and national difference, but with a focus on institutionalized social engineering rather than constitutional or legal provision. Here, 'socialist legality' required law to be guided by CPSU priorities.

A reading of history underpinned this civilization: where the USSR stood in advance of other countries as a state that had passed from feudalism to capitalism to a stage of socialist and communist construction. The codes and behavioural practices of Soviet institutions acquired the status of values. Stress fell on eschewing private property, and the utilization of public enterprise and planning as instruments, justification being provided by CPSU Marxist-Leninist perspective.

Internationally, Soviet foreign policy argued for a meaningful peace agenda, and work with appropriate trades union, peasant and youth bodies committed to opposition to imperialism and reduction of inequalities between nations. This was counterposed to commitments, articulated in bodies such as the League of Nations/United Nations that were said to lack substance.

Soviet Values and External Relations: The Cold War

During 1945–1991, practitioners of foreign policy were moulded by such a 'Second World' civilization and developed a global perspective which framed their view of the Cold War and divided the world into three zones. The zones were the Soviet state itself and allied states of eastern Europe, Vietnam and Cuba; a more distant range of friendly countries, Iraq, Syria and India among them, and the more hostile capitalist world led by the North Atlantic Treaty Organization (NATO). In the four decades of Cold War before 1991, the USSR was sustained by the alliances and interactions among the first two zones, and competed for global hegemony with the third. International relations theory common among Euro-American communities of specialists was often appropriated to guide policy, but seldom in any systematic manner. This led to a sense that Soviet and non-Soviet practitioners of policy did not mean the same thing when they used the same terms.

Soviet Values and Bilateral Relations

Significantly, in African and Asian countries with friendly ties to the USSR, projection of the values of 'Soviet man' was important,[6] but engagement went beyond this. Economic policy sought a new international division of labour to decentre manufacturing away from the West with Soviet assistance. Soviet enterprises for technology transfer were state enterprises working for the notion of such enterprise in principle. But equally Soviet spokesmen argued for the consolidation of nation-building in partners on terms preferred by such partners, working with the private sector as much as the public sector when required. This was a feature of the Khrushchev era (1956–1964) and was partly led by the special engagement with Egypt. It was more firmly shaped thereafter by the links with India which were to be more sustained in the long term.[7]

Soviet self-projection as the bulwark of nationalism was accompanied by the complex role played in relations with the developing world by the All-Union Association for Cultural Relations (1925–1958) (VOKS) and its successor in 1958, the Union of Soviet Societies of Friendship with Foreign Countries (SSOD).[8] These organizations projected Soviet ideas in individual countries; they also united activists of Soviet science, literature, art, education and sport with the aim of acquainting Soviet society with the achievements of foreign countries. VOKS ran friendship societies in the USSR, studied the world and arranged visits of foreign writers, artists and film-makers to the USSR. In 1941, VOKS appeared in Libya, Syria, New Zealand, Australia, Chile and India. Many other countries came into the picture post-war, encouraging respect in the Soviet Union for national aspects of culture among individual emerging nations.

The case of India increasingly stood out as the largest single area of state-to-state collaboration in the non-Communist world. Here, the activities of VOKS and SSOD and the visits of dignitaries and technical personnel between the countries led to relationships that did not take, as given, the healthy nature of Soviet values. In the circumstances, the engagement with India, flanked by economic and military technical collaboration and its overall justification, nuanced Soviet communism itself. The lessons of the relationship shaped Soviet connections with West Asia and Africa during the Brezhnev era.[9]

SOVIET DISINTEGRATION, REJECTION OF SOVIET PERSPECTIVES AND 'VALUES'

It was in Eastern Europe and within the USSR itself that the notion of Soviet values as an enhancement of progressive Western values was most questioned. The Soviet Communist Party was accused of tyranny; Soviet practice was criticized for failure to satisfy national aspirations in the Baltic, Ukraine and the Caucasus as well as Eastern Europe. Nationalists in Russia expressed such opinions.

The disintegration of the Soviet Union led to the decisive control of the Russian government by votaries of the anti-Soviet critique during the creation of the Russian Federation as the successor state. The new state did not have the population, territory or resources of the USSR. However, Russia inherited the USSR's international responsibilities and nuclear arsenal; and Moscow continued to be the pivot of Soviet-era economic networks, statesmen retaining a sense of their world importance.

To give a post-Communist meaning to this profile, in the early months of its existence Russia witnessed the banning of the Communist Party and abolition of the planning system. The new state committed itself to no ideology. The Constitution of 1993 was clear in Article 13 that '(1) Ideological diversity shall be recognized in the Russian Federation and (2) No ideology shall be proclaimed as State ideology or as obligatory'.

Structural features of politics, though, prevented priority-building in foreign policy or substantial values construction. In government, institutional chaos marked 1992–1999, where the presidential establishment was the

pivot of the post-1991 Russian economic reforms and, under Boris Yeltsin, emerged as the centre of Russian government with exceptional powers
accorded it during 1992. In the faction-ridden parliamentary framework the
Ministry of External Affairs revolved around the president. The situation generated only limited equilibrium to decision making, since the politics internal
to the presidential establishment did not make for coherent policy.[10]

During the post-1991 Russian reforms, commitment to a transition to capitalism led to the formation of 'oligarchic' empires and public corporations in
an unstable economy. Such entities possessed networks throughout former
Soviet areas of influence and financial holdings positioned in offshore locations and had 'mafia' operators to guide them. Public corporations worked
closely with the presidency, which shaped many of the new Federal State
Unitary Enterprises and the combines (*obedinenia*) that they fed into.

Post-Soviet Russian Foreign Policy: Values in the Doldrums

Foreign policy came to be influenced by these centres of power – even as
earlier Soviet connections were a bond between senior members of the Russian government and leadership elsewhere in the erstwhile Soviet space –
poorly structured by the CIS. Social links through communities that straddled
boundaries made this 'near abroad' a crucial area of foreign policy. Former
members of the Soviet Communist Party, now situated in high office in
Russia, used their erstwhile connections to shape policy for personal and
institutional benefit, often without reference to the ministries, which had yet
to form fully equipped embassies and develop specialists. The residue of
Soviet values – loyalties and preferences generated by common training and
personal networks – guided interactions.

Russia evolved bilateral and multilateral relationships in this framework,
a path followed by other CIS members.[11] Inconsistency of purpose was to be
seen in the countervailing forces that worked against Atlanticist approaches that
were tilted to favourable engagement with the United States and the EU and
symbolized by Russia's first Minister of External Affairs Kozyrev. The countervailing forces were represented by Eurasianist approaches and were symbolized
by Russia's second Minister of External Affairs Yevgenii Primakov. Euro-
American neglect of Russian minority rights in the former USSR and hostility
to allied states such as Serbia shaped the influence in policy of Eurasianism.

Attempts to evolve appropriate theoretical apparatus for geopolitics of
the former USSR added a layer of complication. The overall ideological
framework of Soviet socialism ceased to be of value in the new situation,
and foreign agencies, such as the Carnegie Foundation and the Soros

Foundation, along with think tanks and universities in the Euro-American world, stepped in to 'train' a new Russian cohort. No clear 'values' were discernible – although held to be necessary.

Poor professionalism along new lines in the domain of foreign policy added to institutional incoherence. Entrants into the Ministry of External Affairs and Russian think tanks dealt with the vicissitudes of Russian everyday life and attempted to emigrate when opportunities arose. Educational and research institutions faced severe funding problems and variations in personnel. Clusters of Russian specialists oriented themselves around Euro-American, Chinese, Japanese and Korean institutions, spending long periods outside the country. The OSCE was a point of reference through all this, giving shape to adjustments over the dismemberment of the COMECON and the Warsaw Pact and providing Russia with a foundation for partnership with the EU. However, Russia's aspirations for exceptional status were an indication of unease with the offer.

Bilateral Relations in the Developing World

Bilateral relations between the developing world and Russia were shaped on an ad hoc basis. Neighbourhood was significant in the case of Iran and Turkey, but policy drew little from graduation from developmental concerns of the past to liberalization concerns of the present to form common ground in values. Elsewhere, demand for Russian military hardware underpinned relations with countries in West and Southeast Asia and Africa and Latin America.

Projecting the new Russia and its priorities, meanwhile, SSOD was recast into the organization Roszarubezhtsentr, continuing to be headed by Valentina Tereshkova. Initial attempts were made to generate an agenda. But much of the inputs into this became hampered under the Russian reforms. Initially, in all cases, the importance attached to ideas, values and culture as part of bilateral exchange tailed off. During the last months of *perestroika*, the commitment to projection of Soviet culture and its use as a bridge with partners outside the 'socialist world' had decreased precipitately. Post-1991, this trend continued.

The spectacular improvement in cultural relations with China has been discussed by M. L. Titarenko. Poor contact during years of Sino-Soviet hostility and persistence of a Communist idiom in Chinese policy led to a slow start to enunciation of common values. Language learning and commercial arrangements made up most of the new activity, to support trade and military-technical cooperation.

In construction of bilateral relations elsewhere in the developing world, India was significant. Trading relations developed with debt settlement beneficial to Russia, and military-technical cooperation was crucial to the relationship. But unlike erstwhile partnerships of the USSR in the developing world which oriented towards globalization ad hoc, the connections with India projected common values that came from a commitment to post-1991 economic reform and multi-ethnic state formation. India was required to accept economic liberalization after 1992. Structures and processes based on public enterprise and autarchic trade regimes were altered to accommodate the International Monetary Fund requirements to deal with a prevailing financial crisis. In this process of adaptation, India and Russia found common ground in a language centred on new precepts. An entente of sorts existed between the two countries in international affairs based on these issues during 1995–1998, though the depth of the entente thinned due to poor Russian support for Indian nuclearization in 1998.

Debates that took place in the Russian Federation were projected in India by the country's journalists and scholars based in Russia. Exchanges of ideas persisted under the aegis of the Indo-Russian Joint Commission and the Russian Academy of Sciences, and seminars or projects.[12] The incoherent values of the new Russia included a respect for Indian culture.

VLADIMIR PUTIN'S CHANGE OF COURSE AFTER THE 'COLOUR' REVOLUTIONS

Values Initiatives as a Strategy of Foreign Policy

Vladimir Putin's emergence as president of the Russian Federation in 2000 hardly affected this situation, even if a clear coherence came to characterize politics (a trend often viewed critically)[13] and this affected foreign policymaking as other aspects of government. The apparatus centred on the presidency, and the Ministry of External Affairs was not altered, but the sub-systems associated with neighbourhood policy and the energy complex[14] were brought more firmly under presidential control.

In policy, the Afghan crisis of 2001 and Russia's collaboration with the United States was a clear indicator that engagements with the West remained important and Igor Ivanov's presence at the Ministry of External Affairs until 2004 was a marker of this. Mention in a National Security Concept document of 2000 of spiritual challenges that Russia faced did not find follow-up in other statements or policies. Putin and Medvedev administrations participated actively in a variant of the European Neighbourhood Program; after 2005, four 'common spaces' were defined for cooperation between the EU and Russia: on trade, freedom and justice, security and education.

However, in 2003, following the 'colour revolutions' (Rose Revolution in Georgia and Orange Revolution of 2004 in Ukraine) and the expansion eastward of the EU, a hard edge increasingly marked Russian foreign policy; sui generis interpretations of market economics[15] and parliamentarism were on view.[16] During the second Putin presidential term (2004–2008) and the decade that followed, taking up strands in a National Security Concept document (2000) and ideas in the Russian foreign policy concept document of 2016, views critical of Euro-Atlantic policies figure prominently. Euro-American support for regime change outside NATO was regarded as breach of sovereignty. Full support was expressed for contested political regimes, like trans-Dnistria, South Ossetia and Abkhazia, of the former Soviet space that rejected an EU orientation. These developments have coincided with the tenure of Sergei Lavrov as minister of external affairs.

The turn came at a time of confidence in the Russian economy under the regulatory regime established by Putin, and Russia's settlement of foreign debts. The confidence overcame any sense of inadequacy in official circles that remained from the Yeltsin years.

The departure had much in common with Eurasianist positions expressed in the 1990s but had broader dimensions. In presidential circles the stress in pronouncements fell on necessity for international respect to sovereignty and nationality according to history and religion. 'Official History', engagement with the Orthodox Church and engagement with 'official' religion in the case of Buddhism and Islam (religions that accept the diktats of the state) were integral to the approach. In foreign policymaking, focus fell on a larger domain of media initiatives linked to Russia's global positions. Institutions evolved under Putin that were designed to inspire values centred on this approach.

The Putin Values Initiatives

Foundations

In the Putin initiatives, echoes exist of pre-1991 motifs and ideas and trends post-disintegration. Pre-1991, patriotism was tapped to provide emotional ballast to the creation of 'Soviet man'. Toleration in a low key of the Ortho-dox Church, Islam and Buddhism was the hallmark of this pre-*perestroika* era. Focus on Russian nationalism was shaped around societies for the pres-ervation of monuments.[17]

Those involved were active publicly during *perestroika* and after Soviet disintegration, generating debate about Russia's global position. Such discussion was not focused purely on foreign policy, but broadly on Russia's identity. Persons of differing opinions like Alexander Dugin, Gleb Pavlovsky,

A. S. Panarin and Andrannik Migranyan were concerned.[18] The discussions took place in magazines such as the *Russkii Zhurnal*. In the Yeltsin era, the Orthodox Church had fetters removed from it, as did Islam and Buddhism. Links with government developed on an ad hoc basis, and public presence in debate evolved with the diversification of the press.

The use of digital media by nationalist organizations fixed on the consolidation of Russian identity dates from this time. In the 1990s, the nationalist agenda was taken up by scattered media organizations; the most prominent was lenta.ru who obtained subvention from the Foundation for Effective Policy established by Maxim Mayer and the ex-dissident Gleb Pavlovsky, who had close links with the Yeltsin administration. Comparable information agencies circulated Internet information in Russia and abroad, using equipment and methods that were an advance of older organizations associated with the print media, such as Pravda.ru, which were burdened with ideas and technological know-how that failed to gain momentum during *perestroika*.

However, pre-2000, the ramshackle economy made the stability of new organizations limited, and they survived on a mixture of state subsidy and handouts of businessmen working across post-Soviet borders. In the case of lenta.ru, the US head of the media organization SUP provided funding. Again, there was no specific target for the initiatives except an undifferentiated public, distinguished by the specific range of the ventures concerned.

In the circumstances, how far Putin's policies since 2003 may be deemed part of a larger project centred on generation of values for Russia may be a matter for justifiable speculation.[19] In so far as they fit into trends in the past in Russia's development of nationhood, they have foundations. However, as an interrelated format, they centre on institutions and individuals that cannot always be firmly traced to older phenomena. Most prominent among the initiatives are cultivation of the Russkii Mir and Regnum foundations and a special closeness to religious bodies. The values involve a firm reference to Russian historical precedent and practice defined by the institutions concerned, a form of official history.

Official History

Generation of official history became a feature of the presidential establishment in Vladimir Putin's second term, and continued during the Medvedev presidency and the third Putin term. The Russkiy Mir Foundation has been pivotal. This was established in 2007, and its chairman is Soviet Foreign Minister V. M. Molotov's grandson Vyacheslav Nikonov. The foundation operates inside and outside Russia; has staged events in Europe, United States, Australasia and Latin America; and covers China and India. It provides forums for discussions of Russian history and Russia's global links. Many of the topics are taken up in the foundation's flagship journal circulated in Russian missions abroad. Articles discuss subjects that vary from the status of the Russian language in countries ranging from UK and Peru to India and the Russian experience of interpretation and translation and the lives of major writers and their work (Ivan Bunin and Leo Tolstoy among the classics). The journal projects the complexity of the Russian civilizational experience: the Buddhist legacy of Buriatia and Kalmykia featuring in an early number of the journal.[20]

Nikonov is clear that the foundation wishes to go beyond philosophical speculation on what Russia is and what its future should be and that the need of the moment is a practical support to those aware of Russian legacies for consolidation and development of this awareness. Russkii Mir articles draw out implications of the agenda for Russian speakers who are citizens of the Russian Federation, or spread through the CIS and beyond. But the foundation's goals touch non-Russian language speakers too: for those who see in their own history a serious Russian connection. The foundation stresses that Russia is globally engaged, and that many in the world are, and have been, engaged with Russia.

Nikonov has drawn attention to the writing of V. N. Molotov, considering Soviet legacies appropriate for the creation of centripetal forces around Russia and Russian practices as a paradigm. Nikonov's projection is modern and takes into account the increase and scattering of Russian-speaking populations during the twentieth century as well as global sympathies inspired by Soviet Russia, which made writing in Russian, sourced from Russia, a part of global engagements during the Cold War.

Since 2015, the Nikonov project for generation of official history has been supplemented by Putin's restoration of the Tsarist-origin Russian Historical Society. This has been given important tasks, including appropriate celebration of the Russian Revolution of 1917.

Official Religion

The state's engagement with history has coincided with a similar engagement with religion. The establishment has projected itself as protector of faiths that claim a Russian mooring. Such a role vis-à-vis the Russian Orthodox Church (ROC) takes the lead. Close relations have existed between the ROC and the presidential establishment: relations that have been reflected in the formal document relating to Social Concept of the Church. Presidential and ministerial pronouncements have associated Russian culture and Russian values closely with the Church. But a similar closeness has been evinced with Islam and Buddhism as practised within Russia, where the relationships attract emphasis in public.

The situation does not reflect any assertive role the ROC plays in Russian society. Reduced to a minor force under Communist rule, religion generally ceased to be associated with public ritual and practice and was deeply personal. Post-1991 the Orthodox Church registers only 6 percent of the population as formal practitioners attending Church regularly. Under Patriarch Alexei (until 2008) and Patriarch Kirill thereafter, though the claim of the Church to the monopoly of Christian presence in the former Soviet Union has been assertive, the social significance of this is not clear. Nevertheless, the Church has received firm support from the presidential establishment. Symbolically its acceptability was stressed through formal support for church construction and restoration. Since 2000, firm attempts have been made to exclude churches that have non-Russian provenance from actively pursuing evangelical goals in the country, even if they have some record of having been present in the region earlier.[21]

Meanwhile, looking beyond the ROC, Putin has made it clear that 'Islam has always been one of the foundations of Russian statehood and of course the state authority in Russia will always support our traditional Islam'.[22] Regular interactions take place between the presidential establishment and the muftiates that exist in cis-Ural Russia, the North Caucasus and Siberia: the conflicting apex organizations of various Muslim spiritual boards (*Dukhovne Upravlenie Musalman*) are the *Tsentral'noe Dukhovnoe Upravlenie Musalman* and the Soviet *Muftiev Rossii*.[23] This level of interaction with the presidency is also true of the Buddhist establishments in the Buryat, Tuva and Kalmyk republics.

Targeted Media Offensives

Projects such as Russkii Mir and the engagement with the ROC, Islam and Buddhism have generated dynamic media projection specific to the organizations themselves. But the presidential establishment has steered media focus in its own right through agencies loyal to it, which work among a general public and are outside the standard 'soft' material put out by the Kremlin's websites.

In Russia's scattered family of media bodies, late in the first Putin administration a focus emerged, supported by the president, and funded by a more stable economy and better revenues. In the course of the fifteen years during and after Putin's first term, Internet users in Russia rose to over 60 million. The information agencies figured the giants, RIA Novosti, Interfax and Prime, with agreements with China and Europe and US-based agencies.

In this framework, the president evolved a focus that was centred on the historian-publicist Modest Kolerov,[24] who developed the information agency Regnum, with the assistance of Vigen Akopyan, an information specialist, in

2002. In Russia itself, indicating its domestic range, the agency had offices in Moscow and St. Petersburg, with regional bases at Voronezh, for Central Russia, the Volga regions, the Far East and the Urals. Abroad, it has offices in Kazakhstan and Kyrgyzstan but also covers the Baltic and the Balkans.

Kolerov became a leading figure in the presidential administration during Putin's second term as head of the Department for Interregional and Cultural Relations with Foreign Countries (2005–2007). He took up propaganda exercises in the Baltic states on behalf of the Russian minority. Subsequently he was declared *persona non grata* in Lithuania, Latvia and Estonia by the end of the 2000s. Finding his hands tied by his official position, Kolerov left it, but heads Regnum, which supports presidential policies, and has formed a subsidiary that deals with economic affairs. Regnum is sceptical of the appropriateness of Euro-American institutions for Russia. The project represents the EU as an 'empire' whose expansion is funded and directed by the United States. Whether within government or out of it, Kolerov has been associated with Putin's stress on close attention to the welfare of Russian communities outside the Federation, and the projection in Russia of their plight.

The Putin Initiatives as Support for Foreign Policy

The preceding Putin initiatives have as an agenda the promotion of values and cannot be equated with the 'soft power' initiatives taken by the president (for instance, the Institute of Democracy and Cooperation or the Russia Today television channel). In the ill-defined context of post-Soviet institutionalization, such distinctions are not spelt out, but a variety in range and content is clear. Unlike soft power initiatives, the values initiatives establish a focus on the legacies of Russian history and language and practices of the past as interpreted by the establishment. They derive their tenor and content heavily from 'cultural education' – which stresses Russia's uniqueness and has replaced Marxism-Leninism as a compulsory subject in Russian higher education since 1995. This is a subject whose content is influenced by the state, and the values initiatives reinforce the impact of the subject and take that impact in new directions. Consequently, they possess relevance both outside Russia's borders and domestically.

Soft power activity is rhetorical and seeks to legitimize Russian global positions against challengers, without elaboration. Its target is external; and engagement is firmly with positions articulated outside the country.

Presidential engagement with Russkii Mir and the other bodies has distinct import for foreign policy without a formal link. While foreign policy documents claim commitment to universal values, they also speak of commitment to obligations to the protection of Russian-speaking peoples, the advancement of the Russian language and those states of the neighbourhood that have claimed Russia as protector (Abkhazia, South Ossetia, trans-Dnistria).

Putin's foreign policy initiatives have almost direct implications for the operations and output of the bodies concerned. Following the Ukraine crisis of 2014, for instance, V. Nikonov discussed Russia's readiness for a 'strategic break' in the pages of the journal which has featured other articles on policy.

In the case of religious bodies, the link with foreign policy shapes in a different manner. The first visit of Patriarch Alexei to the Ministry of External Affairs in 2003 was followed by regular meetings of a working group between the Ministry and the Church.[25] In its claims to primacy as a Christian organization in the former Soviet space, and not merely in Russia, the ROC looks to the Russian government for support; and in turn, it supports the capacity of the Russian state for strong action in the CIS. Among its congregations, the ROC rhetorically asserts its regard for the range and authority of that state. The ROC's External Affairs department monitors its status outside Russia as its Patriarch conducts negotiations. In the case of Islam, Russia's participation in the Organization of Islamic Countries has not been formal and is tied to the 'spiritual boards' that interact with the presidential establishment. In the case of Buddhism, although Russian foreign policy seeks to maintain accord in Sino-Russian relations, the establishment has allowed regular interactions between the Buddhist communities in Buriatia, Tuva and Kalmykia and the Dalai Lama and Buddhism in Mongolia and Japan. This has occurred at the behest of the Lamaic establishments in Russia.

All bodies of the Putin initiatives seek to draw support to the evolution of the EAEU,[26] a key concern of Putin. On 1 January 2017, the Union included Russia, Belarus, Kazakhstan, Armenia and Kyrgyzstan. The Union centres on a Free Trade Area that was established in October 2007 by members of the Eurasian Economic Community founded in 2000, but the Union also involves coordination of legal regulations and a developmental edge.

Values in the Putin Initiatives:
Institutions as a Challenge for Foreign Policy

Ironically, the values sponsored under the Putin initiatives generate challenges for foreign policy. Initiatives work at cross purposes; Russian official history is at variance with the official history generated in states of the EAEU. The promotion of the Russian language militates against the support for Tatar among Muslim groups that straddle CIS borders and look to the Russian state for support. In the ROC, proselytization and conversion come from confidence generated by the initiatives, but the process accentuates intra-religious tensions and affects relations with Muslim countries. In turn, foreign policy generates challenges to the initiatives. In post-2014 Crimea, Russian policy is at odds with Muslim Crimean Tatars; the latter, through links in Russia, undermine the support of official Muslim bodies for the Russian state and increase support for non-official Muslim groups.

As the list of Kolerov's contact points and the range of the ROC indicates, the institutions based on the Putin initiatives are focused heavily on the CIS, former Warsaw Pact countries and former Yugoslavia. In the developing world, the work of the Putin initiatives has figured marginally in foreign policy success in Syria and Iran, countries that are at variance with Russia in terms of development models and political institutions. Ethnic links are minimal. Presidential connections to official Islam in Russia have seldom been a factor in building links. Elsewhere, the initiatives dovetail with the main agency that deals with the projection of Russian values Rossotrudnichestvo, the heir in 2008 of Roszarubezhtsentr, which Kolerov has sharply criticized for inadequacies. Rossotrudnichestvo has been the pivot of various initiatives in China to promote the Russian language. This has been popular, given the country's trading interests in the CIS.

Foreign Policy and Values within a Larger Matrix

In engagements with China and India, which figure strongly in Putin's strategic perception as counterpodes to the West, projection of values initiatives indicates a degree of multivocality in the way values are read, understood and applied. Common ground on necessity to protect sovereignty from Western expansion was on display after the colour revolutions, China being strongly assertive at the China-Russia-India Trilateral meetings in 2005.

Multidimensional trans-border interactions in China, though, have not always provided the best terrain for development of the Putin initiatives. This includes the various areas of interaction: trade, cooperation in energy production, military technology and the consequences of Chinese migration into the Far East. Contention has been regular: dispute has been coloured by the Chinese negative reaction to the achievement motif in official accounts of Russia's Far Eastern presence.

Rather than press the aims of the values initiatives, Russian policy has bought into Chinese cultural initiative that projects the People's Republic of China. This has included gala occasions and a round of spectacles to support for the One Belt One Road project since 2015.

In India, the complex manner in which Rossotrudnichestvo works – projecting a Russian interest in local cultures rather than purely Russian history, practice and language per se – has been important for a relationship in drift. At the time of Vladimir Putin's election as president, Russia's relations with India stood 'thinned' by the cool Russian response to the Pokhran nuclear tests of 1998. Negotiations with the United States formed the umbrella of a special relationship that matured in the Indo-US nuclear deal of 2009. Despite this, a cordial bilateral relationship has been sustained through major Russian projects of energy and military technology collaboration. Brazil-Russia-India-China-South Africa (BRICS) and the Shanghai Cooperation Organization have been important points of interaction.

Putin's initiatives have seldom been given importance in the sustenance of the bilateral relationship. True, Rossotrudnichestvo in India has set an agenda in keeping with values initiatives. This includes action as the information-propaganda corollary of Russian foreign policy: Russia itself, promotion of Russian language, culture, science and education and support to Russians in India.[27] Rossotrudnichestvo has been active in sponsoring projection of Russian work on India and Russian interest in Indian culture. Russian Indology and its achievements have been on display, and meetings have been arranged on 'India in Russian publications', while local cultural centres have sponsored Indian themes.

CONCLUSION

The example of Rossotrudnichestvo's activities in India, developments in the Russia-China relationship and the pre-2000 background of the Putin initiatives indicate a complex context and character to those initiatives. The complexity raises questions regarding Timothy Snyder's argument that Russian perspectives are invariably tantamount to 'a proposition that everyone should be a nation-state and we should all compete to see who is stronger and who is weaker'.[28] Russian acknowledgement of the authority of other nationalisms is understated in this contention. This is important, since the Putin initiatives have acquired accentuation during further reorientation of Russian foreign policy in the direction of autarky and national focus. The reorientation follows estrangement of Russia from Western partners after the Ukrainian crisis of 2014, the EU-US sanctions regime on Russia and the downturn in the Russian economy. Self-awareness in terms of 'civilization' is even more than before a motif of officially sponsored public discourse in Russia.

It remains moot whether values promoted by such strategy can be meaningful except tentatively. Contradictions between the initiatives make the strategy problematic; the exclusive features of the values that are promoted pose problems in engagements with long-standing international partners such as China or India.

As a binding force between Soviet and post-Soviet, and communities inside and outside Russia, the Putin initiatives may serve a purpose. It may be likely that in promoting them, this is the prime objective of the Russian establishment, rather than to use the values generated as a guide to foreign policy. This may come of an impasse regarding a decision about what values are Russian or the desirability to enshrine them: an impasse reflected in the state's inability to reframe constitutional positions regarding ideology during 2015–2017.

NOTES

1. 'В Госдуму внесен законопроект о новой идеологии в России' in *NezavisimaiaGazeta* (9 November 2016).

2. Foreign Policy Concept of the Russian Federation (approved by President of the Russian Federation Vladimir Putin on 30 November 2016), *The Ministry of Foreign Affairs of the Russian Federation* (1 December 2016). http://www.mid.ru/en/foreign_policy/official_documents/-/asset_publisher/cptickb6bz29/content/id/2542248.

3. It has not been wholly unexplored. See Sinikukka Saari, 'The Persistence of Putin's Russia', *Finnish Institute of International Affairs* 92 (November 2011); 'Putin's Eurasian Union Initiative: Are the Premises of Russia's Post-Soviet Policy Changing?' *Swedish Institute for International Affairs, Stockholm Ul Brief* no. 9 (1 November 2011) [Hereafter Saari, *Eurasia*]. Also Marcel van Herpen, *Putin's Propaganda Machine: Soft Power in Russia* (London: Rowman & Littlefield, 2015).

4. Andrei Kozyrev, *Preobrazheniia MezhdunarodyeOtnosheniia* (Moscow, 1994), 275–76.

5. Iu. V. Dubinin, *DiplomaticheskaiaByl'* (Moscow: Rosspen, 1997).

6. A good example is the tone of V. V. Zagladin (ed.). *Mezhdunarodnoekommunisticheskoedvizhnie. Ocherkstrategii is taktiki* (Moscow: Politizdat, 1970).

7. For a modern review, see Vojtech Mastny, 'The Soviet Union's Partnership with India', *Journal of Cold War Studies* 12, no. 3 (2010).

8. T. N. Zagorodnikova, V. P. Kashin and T. L. Shaumian, *ObrazRossii v obshchestvennomsoznaniiIndii: Proshloe I Nastoiashchee* (Moscow: Centre for Indian Studies, RAN, 2011): 194–95. [Hereafter *Obraz*]. 194–95.

9. Hari Vasudevan, 'Communism in India', in Silvio Pons, Norman Naimark and Sophie Quinn Judge (eds.). *Cambridge History of Communism* 2 (Cambridge: Cambridge University Press, 2017).

10. A memoir that indicates as much is Alexander Korzhakov, *Otrssveta do zakata* (Moscow: Interbook, 1997).

11. This trend in the CIS was looked upon as natural in Russian debate. See *Vostok I Rossiianarubezhe XXI veka* (Institute of Oriental Studies, RAN, 1998); the same is true of responses to developments in sensitive areas such as Central Asia and the Caucasus, as indicated in *Zapadnaiaaziia, Tsesntral'naiaAziia I Zakavkaz'e. Integratiia I konflikty* (ibid., 1995).

12. *Induizm I sovremennost' (Materialynauchnoikonferentsii* (Moscow: Centre for Indian Studies, 1994); *ProvozvestieVivekanda (Materialynauchnoikonferentsii)* (Moscow: Centre for Indian Studies, 1993); Rossiia I *Indiia v sovremennom mire. Voprosysotrudnichestva I vzaimodeistviia v sveteikhnational'no-gosudarstvennykhinteresov*

(Materialynauchnoikonferentsii) (Moscow: Centre for Indian Studies, 1995); *Rossiia I Indiia. Na porogetret'egotysiacheletiia* (Materialynauchnoikonferentsii) (Moscow: Centre for Indian Studies, 1998). In cases such as the latter, the articles by B. I. Kliuev (56–60), E. F. Mizhenskaia (61–66) and F. N. Iurlov (67–71) compared the reform processes in India and Russia and attempted to generate a debate of sorts.

13. Joel Ostrow, Georgii Satarov and Irina Khakameida, *The Consolidation of Dictatorship in Russia* (Westport: Greenwood Publishing House, 2007).

14. A. M. Salmin, 'Iznankavneshneipolitiki', in *RossiiskaiaPolitiianarubezhevekov* (Moscow: Politiia, 1997).

15. A statist approach to private enterprise was initiated in proceedings against the oligarch Khodorkovskii in 2004–2005.

16. 'Sovereign Democracy' as a concept gained ground, initially touted by Putin's aide Vladislav Surkov in 2006. Ya. Iu. Matvienko, *Институционально-правовыем оделилегитимацииисуверенной демократииисовременнойРоссии* (aftoreferat of the Kandidate Dissertation for the Juridical University of the Ministry of Internal Affairs, Rostov on the Don, 2008).

17. John Dunlop, *The Faces of Contemporary Russian Nationalism* (Princeton, NJ: Princeton University Press, 1983).

18. V. Agafonov, V. Rokitianskii, *Rossiia v poiskakhbudushchego* (Progress, 1993) for examples of this kind of speculation, interview with Iu. Iu Boldyrev, pp. 38–55, who argued that the changes indicated the end of one 'civilization', and the beginning of another, but also looked for continuity; A. V. Sobolev, the philosopher, spoke of Russia as a cultural heritage, as a personality and argued for a large view of Russia's future. 'Russia will be saved only as Great Russia, Russia with a Great Culture'. This was a time for far-ranging discussions of different aspects of Russian identity. See S. B. Chernyshev, *Inoe. Khrestomatiianovagorossiiskogosamosoznaniia* (Moscow: Argus, 1995). 4 vols.

19. Ben Smith, 'Russian Foreign and Security Policy', *House of Commons Library – Briefing Paper* 7646 (5 July 2016).

20. For all issues of the journal see www.russkiimir.ru. VyacheslavNikonov reflections on Russian identity are in 'Ne vospominaniia o proshlom a mechta o budushchem' in V. Nikonnov (ed.). *Smysli I TsennostiRusskago Mira* (Moscow: Russkii Mir, 2010).

21. Kathy Rousselet, 'L'eglise orthodoxerusse et le territoire', in *Revue d'etudes comparatives est-ouest* 35, no. 4 (2007): 149–71.

22. Rinat Mukhametov, 'Russian Muslims and Foreign Policy Russia', *Global Affairs* (7 October 2012).

23. Gordon M. Hahn, in a critique of Putin in *Russia's Islamic Threat* (New Haven, CT: Yale University Press, 2007), 26–27, is not able to ignore this interaction. Tatarstan being a case in point, 185–86.

24. See Saari, *Eurasia* for Kolerov. Material on Regnum is from its website, www.regnum.ru.

25. Robert C. Blitt, 'Russia's Orthodox Foreign Policy', *University of Pennsylvania Journal of International Law* 33, no. 2 (2011): 364–458.

26. Eurasian Economic Union (www.eaeunion.org) for the basic information on the entity.

27. Zagorodnikova et al., *Obraz,* 196–97.
28. 'Timothy Snyder: "History Is Always Plural"', *Radio Free Europe/Radio Liberty* (20 June 2015). https://www.rferl.org/a/russia-ukraine-interview-bloodlands-timothy-snyder-history/27082683.html.

BIBLIOGRAPHY

Agafonov, V. V. Rokitianskii. *Rossiia v poiskakh budushchego.* Moscow: Progress, 1993.

Blitt, Robert C. 'Russia's Orthodox Foreign Policy'. *University of Pennsylvania Journal of International Law* 33, no. 2 (2011).

Chernyshev, S. B. *Inoe. Khrestomatiia novago rossiiskogo samosoznaniia.* Moscow: Argus, 1995.

Donaldson, R. H. and J. Nogee. *The Foreign Policy of Russia.* Armonk: M.E. Sharpe, 2014.

Dubinin, Iu. V. *Diplomaticheskaia Byl'.* Moscow: Rosspen 1997.

Dunlop, John. *The Faces of Contemporary Russian Nationalism.* Princeton, NJ: Princeton University Press, 1983.

Evrard, John T. 'Human Rights in the Soviet Union: The Politics of Dissimulation'. *De Paul Law Review* 29, no. 3 (1980).

Foreign Policy Concept of the Russian Federation (approved by President of the Russian Federation Vladimir Putin on 30 November 2016). *Ministry of Foreign Affairs of the Russian Federation* (1 December 2016). http://www.mid.ru/en/foreign_policy/official_documents/-/asset_publisher/CptICkB6BZ29/content/id/2542248.

Foreign Policy Concept of the Russian Federation (approved by President of the Russian Federation Vladimir Putin on 12 February, 2013). *Ministry of Foreign Affairs of the Russian Federation,* 18 February 2013. http://www.mid.ru/en/foreign_policy/official_documents/-/asset_publisher/CptICkB6BZ29/content/id/122186.

Hahn, Gordon M. *Russia's Islamic Threat.* New Haven, CT: Yale University Press, 2007.

Korzhakov, Alexander. *Ot rssveta do zakata.* Moscow: Interbook, 1997.

Kozyrev, Andrei. *Preobrazheniia.* Moscow: Mezhdunarodye Otnosheniia, 1994.

Laruelle, Marlène (ed.). *Russian Nationalism and the National Reassertion of Russia.* New York: Routledge, 2009.

Litman, A.D. *Induizm I sovremennost' Materialy nauchnoi konferentsii.* Moscow: Centre for Indian Studies, 1994.

Mastny, Vojtech. 'The Soviet Union's Partnership with India'. *Journal of Cold War Studies* 12, no. 3 (2010).

Matvienko Ya. Iu. *Institutsial'no-pravovye modeli legitimatsii suvrennoi demokratii sovremennoi Rossii* (aftoreferat of the Kandidate Dissertation for the Juridical University of the Ministry of Internal Affairs, Rostov on the Don, 2008).

Mukhametov, Rinat. 'Russian Muslims and Foreign Policy of Russia'. *Global Affairs,* 7 October 2012.

National Security Concept of the Russian Federation (approved by Presidential Decree). *Ministry of Foreign Affairs of the Russian Federation,* 10 January 2000.

http://www.mid.ru/en/foreign_policy/official_documents/-/asset_publisher/ CptICkB6BZ29/content/id/589768.

Nikonov, V. (ed.). *Smysli I Tsennosti Russkago Mira.* Moscow: Russkii Mir, 2010.

Nizameddin, Talal. *Putin's New Order in the Middle East.* London: Hurst, 2013.

Ostrow, Joel, Georgii Satarov and Irina Khakameida. *The Consolidation of Dictatorship in Russia.* Westport, CT: Greenwood Publishing House, 2007.

Provozvestie Vivekanda (Materialy nauchnoi konferentsii). Moscow: Centre for Indian Studies, 1993.

Rossiia I Indiia. Na poroge tret'ego tysiacheletiia (Materialy nauchnoi konferentsii). Moscow: Centre for Indian Studies, 1998.

Rossiia I Indiia v sovremennom mire. Voprosy sotrudnichestva I vzaimodeistviia v svete ikh national'no-gosudarstvennykh interesov (Materialy nauchnoi konferentsii). Moscow: Centre for Indian Studies, 1995.

Rousselet, Kathy. 'L'eglise orthodoxe russe et le territoire'. *Revue d'etudes comparatives est-ouest* 35, no. 4 (2007).

Salmin, A. M. 'Iznanka vneshnei politiki'. *Rossiiskaia Politiia na rubezhe vekov.* Moscow: Politiia, 1997.

Scherer, Jutta. 'The Cultural Civilizational Turn in P-Soviet Identity Building', in Per Arne Bodin, Stefan Hedlund and Elena Namli (eds.). *Power and Legitimacy Challenges from Russia.* London: Routledge 2013.

Saari, Sinikukka. 'The Persistence of Putin's Russia'. *Finnish Institute of International Affairs* 92 (November 2011).

Saari, Sinikukka. 'Putin's Eurasian Union Initiative. Are the Premises of Russia's Post-Soviet Policy Changing?' *Swedish Institute for International Affairs, Stockholm Ul Brief* no. 9 (1 November 2011).

Smith, Ben. 'Russian Foreign and Security Policy'. *House of Commons Library – Briefing Paper* 7646 (5 July 2016).

Titarenko, M. L. and Petrovskii V. E. Rossiia. *Kitai I Novyi Mirovoi Poriadok. Teoriia I Prakika.* Moscow: Ves' Mir, 2016.

Towe, Thomas E. 'Fundamental Rights in the Soviet Union: A Comparative Approach'. *University of Pennsylvania Law Review* 115 (1967).

Van Herpen, Marcel. *Putin's Propaganda Machine: Soft Power in Russia.* London: Rowman & Littlefield, 2015.

'V Gosdumu vnesen zakonoproekt o novoi ideologii Rossii'. *Nezavisimaia Gazeta,* 9 November 2016.

Vostok I Rossiia na rubezhe XXI veka. Institute of Oriental Studies, RAN, 1998.

Zagladin, V. V. (ed.). *Mezhdunarodnoe kommunisticheskoe dvizhnie. Ocherk strategii is taktiki.* Moscow: Politizdat, 1970.

Zagorodnikova, T. N., V. P. Kashin and T. L. Shaumian. *Obraz Rossii v obshchestvennom soznanii Indii: Proshloe I Nastoiashchee.* Moscow: Centre for Indian Studies, RAN, 2011.

Zapadnaia aziia, Tsesntral'naia Aziia I Zakavkaz'e. Integratiia I konflikty. Institut Vostokovedenia, RAN, 1995.

Chapter 7

Islamic Values in Foreign Policy

Perspectives on 'Secular' Turkey and 'Islamic' Iran

Mehmet Ozkan and Kingshuk Chatterjee

The search for values, of one sort or the other, in foreign policy is an approach fraught with the usual consequences of 'looking for something', for you are likely to find only what you are looking for. To look for Islamic values in foreign policy could well be a case in point. Among scholars of Muslim/ Islamic politics, there are those who would subscribe to the position that any action that is professedly inspired by considerations of the faith must ipso facto be accepted as such, unless contrary evidence can be produced – thus all the violent and outrageous actions of Da'ish (or the Islamic State) in the name of Islam should be understood to be 'Islamic'. There are yet others who seem to think actions need not necessarily be professedly Islamic; it is quite enough that they address considerations that are generally associated with the faith or practice of Muslims – hence any expression of solidarity of any predominantly Muslim country for the Palestinian cause has been often read as axiomatic on account of the fact that a majority of Palestinians happen to be Muslims. Still others would choose to shop between these positions, without being beholden to any one argument.

While the literature on the interface between Islamic values and international relations is still sketchy, the question of the role played by religion in international relations has been steadily growing over the past decade and a half. Some have argued that religious phenomena should be investigated at all three levels of independent, intervening (link between cause and effect) and dependent variables (product of non-religious causes) in international politics[1] – that is to say, religious values may condition foreign policy behaviour by causing, facilitating or justifying the course of action undertaken. Others have argued that religious values can be both prescriptive and proscriptive in their effect on foreign policymaking – they might impel a course of action in some direction in accordance with the faith and preclude or make difficult certain other options.[2] A third approach suggests that political behaviour is socially conditioned (for foreign policy actors are not individuals insulated from the society they live in); thus policy is formulated and played out necessarily within a larger social context in which religion frequently has a definitive role.[3]

In the light of these approaches, how does one identify or decode the Islamic element in a country's foreign policy? Does a foreign policy choice qualify automatically as Islamic if it is merely claimed to be so, since every speech is also reflective of the deliberation behind it?[4] Do all foreign policy choices of an Islamic state tend to be ipso facto Islamic, since the language of politics is heavily laced with Islamic terms of reference? Can a predominantly Muslim state that is not professedly Islamic in its dispensation be motivated by Islamic values in its foreign policy choices, because the societal context within which such policy is framed is heavily influenced by Islamic values, even if the political system is not? Also, whether Shi'i values are different from Sunni values, and, if so, should both qualify as Islamic?

It is useful to understand that it is not possible to essentialize any single set of values (except in very general terms) that can be identified as exclusively Islamic (i.e. found in no other belief system), or even generally understood as such across the Muslim world. The faith and practice of Islam have tended to vary across time and space, much like any other religion or body of ideas, and has tended to acquire distinctive characteristics that make the Muslim world nearly as diverse as any other group of countries in the world. Thus far from all predominantly Muslim countries following similar tropes of political behaviour in the international arena, it is difficult to find any two Muslim countries pursuing similar policies motivated by similar considerations of the faith in exclusion of other factors. Geostrategic, economic and political factors, inter alia, make any exclusively Islamic consideration in foreign policy formulation virtually impossible. And yet quite a number of predominantly Muslim countries tend to claim their policies and actions as being motivated by Islamic values. This could be either because such policies are actually guided by a particular understanding of what Islam is taken to *signify* in a particular situation (i.e., Islamic values are contextual and semiotic in character), or because it is expected/useful to deploy Islamic terms of reference to legitimize any policy or action which may actually have little or no consideration of Islam behind it (i.e., Islamic values are instrumental in character).

In this chapter, the authors propose to deal with these questions for a better understanding of the role Islamic values may or may not play in international politics. It is presented in three sections. The first section deals with a case study of Turkey in the past four decades to explore how the foreign policy of a professedly secular state can nevertheless be argued to be heavily conditioned by Islamic values. The second section deals with a case study of the Islamic

Republic of Iran for nearly the same period in order to contend how despite its professedly Islamic orientation, Iranian foreign policy can be argued to be motivated predominantly by *realpolitik* packaged in the language of political Islam. In the last section an attempt is made to tease out the polyvalence of Islamic values which tend to be signified by different *signifiers* (in this case, policies) using a common set of *signs* (Islamic terms of reference) in the arena of international relations.

TURKEY:
Policymaking in a 'Secular' State

Constitutionally, Turkey is a secular state. However, its population happens to be predominantly Sunni Muslim. Since the secular reforms of Ataturk in the 1920s, the state has had a difficult relationship with religion itself and its repercussions in the society. Top-down secularization approach and the policies followed afterwards have not made Turkey more secular (i.e., getting rid of religion from social and political life), but Turkey has become more modern (i.e., opening to the world and following the developments in the world). Turkish society, though, consists of a large number of pious Muslims who have always had a broader perspective. Islam is so embedded in Turkish society and culture that even the most secular Turks continue to derive their sustenance from it.

During the Cold War, Turkish leaders followed a strictly Western orientation in foreign policy, leaving almost no space for religion. Security concerns, the Soviet threat, economic reasons and a state policy to create a secular Turkish identity based on Westernization have denied religion any space, even in cultural terms. The implication of this for foreign policy was that Ankara saw the Middle East as a region not to get involved in actively even though all the Western (i.e., secular) countries had an active Middle East policy. Strangely, talking about the Middle East and speaking Arabic were enough to be considered as following an Islamic perspective on foreign affairs.

Developments following the military coup in 1980 changed the dynamics in Turkey. Coupled with the need to create a 'moderate Islam' urged by the United States in the 1980s, Turkish military coup leaders (such as then President Kenan Evren) began to refer openly to Islam. These references to Islam were no more than paying political lip service to protect Turks from falling prey to the leftists, which seemed a possibility late into the 1970s. Then prime Minister Turgut Ozal (who had a conservative background with a secular leaning) popularized the cultural heritage of Turkey with references to the Ottoman State and liberalized the Turkish economy. Economic liberalization has opened Turkish society to the world and strengthened Turkey's periphery, which is predominantly conservative and pious Muslim in its orientation. Economic well-being of the periphery later on had repercussions on the political level, and more conservative, more Islamic parties started to rise steadily. The rise of Refah Party in Turkish politics and the premiership of Necmettin Erbakan during 1996–1997 was a shock to the secular establishment in Turkey. Erbakan was removed in a postmodern military coup in 1997; however, Turkish society has never shied away from its desire to live and act in accordance with its deep-seated cultural and religious values. After a turbulent period during 1997–2002, Turkey elected the Justice and Development Party (AK Party) of Recep Tayyip Erdogan to office in Ankara. For many, Erdogan himself and his party are seen as a fusion of traditional (Islam, Ottoman legacy, etc.) and Western values (democracy, human rights, etc.). Since then, Turkey has started to create a balanced foreign policy approach without neglecting religion as an element in foreign policy.

Since AK Party came to power in 2002, there has been a huge transformation in Turkish foreign policy. Until the early 2000s, Turkey had largely followed a one-dimensional foreign policy based on Western orientation despite different push factors coming from society to reach out to different parts of the world such as the Middle East, Africa, Asia and the Balkans. In those years, the state elite mostly acted upon the need to satisfy social pressure whenever a crisis emerged, such as during the Bosnia War, but these shifts were neither deep-rooted nor comprehensive, based rather on ad hoc policies. Since 2002, one can talk about a period of openings to previously neglected regions of the world in Turkish foreign policy to widen Turkey's options in international politics. However, these openings have occurred not only in economic and political terms but also have strong social and religious dimensions. This is a novel phenomenon in Turkey's conventional/traditional approach to foreign and security policy because Turkey is constitutionally a secular state.

The dimension of religious diplomacy has always been underestimated and neglected by the scholars of Turkish politics.[5] Perhaps many considered it only as a natural repercussion and part of a soft power approach,[6] but the time has come for a comprehensive understanding of, and locating religious diplomacy within, the overall structure of Turkish foreign policy. Although until recently this religious diplomacy has not been used much in foreign policy discourse for a variety of reasons, its influence and significance for Turkey's foreign relations during almost the whole of the past decade are worth considering.

While it is not possible to separate the rise, nature and involvement of religious elements from the general tendencies of Turkey's foreign policy, it is possible to evaluate the economic, political and intellectual foundations of this necessity in three basic points. First, Turkey is today looking at its region and the world with a new and different perspective, and as a consequence there have been radical changes in its approach to Africa, the Middle East, Latin America, Balkans and Asia. According to this new perspective, these regions are not regarded as distant and troubled regions but as possible partners with which relations in political and economic areas ought to be established and developed, and where coordination of action should be undertaken when necessary. For that reason, invoking cultural ties that can be traced back to history and religion wherever possible has become one of the key elements of Turkey's foreign policy normalization.

Second, economic openings are central to Turkey's efforts to reposition itself in a changing global economy. The struggle to redefine a world view, which concentrated on economics, has led the way and laid the foundations for the definitions of a new national role and foreign policy orientation, which have manifested themselves even more during the AK Party era. Under Erdogan's leadership, Turkey now has been trying to develop a new regional and global perspective based especially on historical and cultural components. Ankara's proactive and dynamic openings towards different regions of the world have been systematic and important initiatives rather than being appendages to its relations with the West.[7]

Third, the political foundations of Turkey's openings, which are parallel to the two approaches just mentioned earlier, are to increase Ankara's activities in all regions, international organizations and international relations, and to increase Turkey's activities to contribute to regional and global peace. In that sense, Turkey wants to display an active presence in all international and regional organizations and has determined its foreign policy inclinations within this framework.[8] Turkey's observer status in the African Union, dialogue partnership in the Association of Southeast Asian Nations, its active stance in the G-20 and its non-permanent member status in the United Nations Security Council during 2008–2010 have to be evaluated within this framework.

Similarly, Ankara's serious interest in the Organization of Islamic Cooperation (OIC) since 2003 has indicated the intention to utilize religious diplomacy at institutional level as well. Because of this, then Turkish Foreign Minister Abdullah Gul announced before the thirty-first meeting of the Islamic Foreign Ministers Conference in May 2004 that Turkey attaches special importance to its relations with the Islamic world, and aimed to get the OIC its deserved place in international arena and transform into a more effective and dynamic structure. With the election of Ekmeleddin Ihsanoglu as the OIC secretary-general in 2004, Turkey upgraded its role within the OIC structure to the highest level.[9]

In this new foreign policy framework, the role of religion can be analysed only as a legitimizing or supportive element in Ankara's relations with the world. One should emphasize that Turkey does not follow a religion-based foreign policy, nor can it do so for constitutional obstacles. However, as long as Turkish society continues to be Muslim, Islam will always have a place. Since 2002, Erdogan has incorporated religion into foreign policy in two forms. First, the Directorate for Religious Affairs (*Diyanet*), a state institution established in 1924 to observe and control the Muslims by managing mosques and shaping a discourse suitable to the state, has transformed itself into an international actor, facilitating and contributing to Turkish foreign policy.

Diyanet has organized religious leaders' meetings with Africa, Latin America, Eurasia and Balkans as part of Turkey's opening in those regions.[10] *Diyanet*, for the first time, organized a Summit of Latin American Religious Leaders in Istanbul in November 2014 with a total of seventy-one people from forty countries in attendance. Not only had community leaders participated from key countries like Brazil, Argentina, Venezuela and Colombia, but there had also been representatives from small countries like Belize and Barbados among the invitees. One of the main aims of the summit was to establish links and share experiences. Because of this, most of the topics discussed had been related to the understanding and identification of problems that Latin American Muslims face. *Diyanet*'s summit cannot be understood without contextualizing the political opening of Turkey to Latin America in the past decade. Since the announcement of 2006 as 'the Year of Latin America' in Turkey, Turkish foreign policymakers have placed a special emphasis on Latin America. Ankara has opened new embassies, and mutual visits have intensified.[11]

Similarly, *Diyanet* organized the first Religious Leaders Meeting of African Continent Muslim Countries and Societies in Istanbul in November 2006 in which representatives from twenty-one countries participated. The second meeting took place in Istanbul and Ankara between 21 and 25 November 2011. In this meeting, Muslim religious authorities from Africa had called on Turkey to take a greater role in Islamic education in African communities. In a joint declaration, they urged that educational institutions similar to the Imam-Hatip schools[12] in Turkey should be used 'as an example for schools in Africa and backed with faculties providing higher religious education like [Turkey's] theology faculties'.[13] These meetings have been part of Turkey's opening to Africa policy since 2005. Turkey has now thirty-nine embassies in Africa (it had only twelve in 2002), and trade between Turkey and Africa has tripled since 2002.[14]

Diyanet continues to play a similar role in Balkans and Eurasia by educating, financing and bringing religious leaders together. In Turkey, *Diyanet* is no longer seen as a simple state institution; rather it holds now more respect and credibility than ever historically among Turkish society.

The second way in which Turkey incorporated religion into foreign policy is by taking demands of Turkish society into consideration with regard to developments in the world. One can call this an Islam-sensitive foreign policy, but not an Islamic one per se. Whatever happens to Muslims in Palestine, Myanmar, Balkans or Africa, the Turkish government has acted fast and in most cases is leading the process. This has expanded Turkey's and Erdogan's popularity as Muslim statesman among the broader Islamic world. If Turkey today commands respect and admiration among the general public in Muslim countries, it cannot be explained only by the economic success of a Muslim country blending modernization with Islam successfully; it is also related directly to Turkey's Islam-sensitive approach to developments.

Despite the increasing role of *Diyanet* as an actor in foreign policy and existence of Ankara's Islamic-sensitive policies, it is difficult to argue that Turkey follows an Islamic foreign policy. Indeed, there is no definition of what qualifies a policy as 'Islamic' in the world today. The Turkish case, based on the past two decades, suggests that rather than looking for Islamic components in the foreign policy of any country, it is better to search for how sensitivity towards Islam and its values get reflected in a state's foreign policy. The Turkish case suggests that any exaggerated discourse on Islam and Muslims as an imminent danger/threat in international politics should now be put to an end. A predominantly Muslim country can create an 'Islamic' foreign policy by taking into account religious and cultural values with modern diplomatic rationality and the economic and political needs of its citizens without jeopardizing the global order.

IRAN:
Policymaking in a 'Religious' State

Unlike Turkey, Iran is professedly an Islamic state. The Islamic Republic of Iran came into being as a result of the Iranian Revolution of 1979. In the three decades and a half that have elapsed since then, it has often been claimed that Tehran's foreign policy manifests a deep ideological commitment to Ithna 'Ashari Shi'i Islam, the official ideology of the Islamic Republic. At a pinch, Iranian foreign policy could be taken to indicate a fascinating convergence between Islamic and strategic considerations.[15] While it is difficult to make the case that all policy formulations are necessarily guided by Islamic considerations, most of them are articulated in terms of these. In other cases, Islamic considerations are believed to have imposed limitations on the courses of action to be pursued. Thus, Iranian foreign policy exhibits attributes of Islamic values both in an instrumental sense and in terms of sensibilities to be (or appearing to be) addressed.

The impact of Tehran's Islamic orientation is argued to have been most readily discernible in the Levantine region of Syria, Lebanon and Palestine, as also in its apparently implacable hostility to United States and Israel. Iran's Arab neighbours, in particular the Saudi kingdom and the United Arab Emirates (UAE), have contended that Tehran aims at establishing a Shi'i axis of influence in the region. Since 1983, Tehran has provided the militant Hizballah movement with financial, military, logistic and political support.[16] After the end of the Lebanese civil war, Iran has continued to provide Hizballah with logistical support to emerge as the principal force of opposition in Lebanon, and Hizballah's television and propaganda network, Al-Manar, was set up with support from Iran.[17] Iran has also been involved in the Israeli-Palestine conflict since the latter part of the 1980s. Tehran has financed and possibly also trained the Hamas since the late 1980s, and definitely since the mid-1990s.[18] Since 2012, Tehran, along with Russia, has effectively salvaged the embattled Syrian regime of Bashar al-Assad, locked into a civil war with a myriad group of his own countrymen disgruntled with the regime. Additionally, Tehran's role in the Shi'i-dominated Iraqi government's successful struggle with the Da'ish has given it a degree of leverage in Baghdad that is second to none. All these are considered to be part of a steady programme for regional domination by the Islamic Republic, which is believed to be flourishing at the expense of the traditional Sunni orientation of almost all countries of the region. Of late, Iran is believed to have supported the Houthi rebels, with both money and arms, in the civil war in Yemen.

However, any observer of the political dynamics of the Middle East would discern major continuities between the foreign policy of the Islamic Republic and the Pahlavi regime it had overthrown. The suspicion of an agenda for regional domination that Riyadh, Amman, Baghdad, Cairo, Manama and Abu Dhabi harbour against the Islamic Republic today echoes similar suspicions about the rulers of the Pahlavi dynasty (1925–1979). In terms of its territorial ambition, the Islamic Republic is every bit as much a status quo power as its predecessor used to be – be it regarding the contested claims over the Caspian Sea (with first the Union of Soviet Socialist Republics and then the successor states), the frontier with Iraq along the Shatt al-Arab waterways (which caused frictions for the whole of the twentieth century and war in the 1980s) or the possession of the Abu Musa and Tunb islands (which Tehran holds and UAE claims).[19] All through the 1930s, and then from the 1950s to the 1970s, Iran vied for regional domination with Cairo, Ankara and (from the 1970s) Riyadh – much as it is now suspected of doing for the past decade or so.

In fact, much of Iran's 'revolutionary' adventurism in its neighbourhood is susceptible of a geopolitical explanation. The war with Iraq (1980–1987) saw Tehran completely isolated in the neighbourhood with Saudi Arabia, Kuwait, UAE and the United States actively supporting Iraq at various stages of its war effort in various ways. Tehran broke out of this diplomatic isolation by turning to Damascus at a time when Syria's intervention in the Lebanese civil war had isolated Damascus from the West and its Arab neighbours. Tehran began supporting Syria and then the Hizballah, after they began fighting Israel in Lebanon, principally in order to open a second front that could distract American interest and therefore concentrate less on Iraq.[20] Iran's interest in the Hamas also was presumably driven by similar concerns of keeping the second front open after the Lebanese civil war was over; US preoccupation with the Arab-Israeli dispute would serve to reduce the heat on Iran. Additionally, in the light of the funding of Iraq during the Iran-Iraq War by Arab governments in the name of Arab solidarity, Tehran's espousal of the Palestinian cause was meant to send a powerful message to the Arab streets, that on the crucial question of Palestine, Tehran remained more true to the Arab cause than all the Arab regimes. This also explains the relentless hostility (albeit muted, except during the presidency of Ahmedinejad) that the Islamic Republic has been showing to Israel over the past three decades. Tehran clearly targets Israel in order to hurt the United States, by keeping the option of opening a second front at hand. This is why military support for Hamas and Hizballah from Iran escalated whenever Tehran came under international (read US) pressure on any issue (as in the 1980s, between 1994 and 1996, during 2003, and 2006–2008).[21]

Geopolitics can also explain Iran's interest in creating a series of Shi'i centres of power in the Arab heartland by propping up various Shi'i forces in Iraq, Lebanon, Bahrain and Yemen.[22] Indeed, Tehran appears to believe that its best chances of success in regional politics would come with strengthening the Shi'i ('Alavid, Ithna 'Ashari or Zaidi) elements in regional politics that have been hitherto repressed by the Sunni ruling classes. Even if such Shi'i opposition does not come to power, their mere existence weakens Tehran's neighbouring Sunni states somewhat.[23] Iran would prefer a weak neighbour to a strong neighbour, and a stable neighbour to an unstable one.

In large measure, the urge to seek an ideological rationale behind the Islamic Republic's foreign policy stems from its own pronouncements right from 1979. In a major departure from the Pahlavi regime, the revolutionary order identified early on the United States and Israel as the *mustakbirun* (literally, arrogant ones, implying oppressors),[24] referred to as the Greater and Lesser Evils (*Shaitan-e Bozorg, Shaitan-e Kochak*), respectively, using semi-Islamic terminology, occasioning a running undercurrent of hostility and tension. The moves towards Syria and Lebanon were justified as keenness of the revolutionary regime to support the *mazlum-ha* or *mustadhafun* (the oppressed) in their struggle against the *mustakbirun* with the 'Alawite Shi'i rulers of Syria and the Shi'i organization of Hizballah in Lebanon being natural constituencies for Tehran. Tehran's support for the predominantly Sunni Palestinians (and later, specifically, the Hamas movement) in Israel was justified by saying that Zionism was an offshoot of Western imperialism; hence it was incumbent upon the Islamic Republic to support the Palestinians till they were free.[25]

One of the most distinctive features of the 1979 revolution, which is seldom discussed any longer, was that revolutionary order was *Islamized* in course of the months after the toppling of the previous regime.[26] In the chaos that followed the abdication of the Shah and the return of Ayatollah Khomeini from exile, protagonists of constitutional democratic order were progressively marginalized by more radical revolutionaries who captured in the name of Islam the various institutional structures left standing. By October 1979, the initial (and more liberal democratic) constitution was replaced by a more Islamic constitution, deriving its rationale from Ayatollah Khomeini's own views on the matter. However, this process of Islamization was thoroughly contested by other stakeholders in the revolution. The Islamic radicals used first the bogey of the US-Israel axis and later the Iraq War as a smokescreen to eliminate much of this political dissent in the months and years that followed. One of the major instruments in this regard was the progressive Islamization of the language of politics and legitimacy in the Islamic Republic – to the extent that policies and measures could be proposed or opposed as long as Islamic terms of reference were deployed.[27] With the opposition to the Islamist forces eliminated, driven into exile, rehabilitated in or marginalized by the revolutionary dispensation, by the time the Iraq War came to an end and normal politics resumed, the terms of reference in Iranian political discourse were virtually completely Islamized, with foreign policy being no exception.

During the revolution, apprehensions abounded about the role of the United States and Israel, allies of the previous regime, who were therefore identified as the *mustakbirun*.[28] The more radical elements among the revolutionaries were at odds with the efforts of the provisional government led by Mehdi Bazargan to negotiate an understanding of sorts with the United States. The resultant seizure of the US embassy in Tehran by the radical elements, and the US response to it, pushed Tehran down a belligerent path that has now become a rut. At least two Iranian presidents (Khatami and Rouhani) have tried to break out of this rut, and each time their opponents decried such efforts as a betrayal of the Islamic Revolution.[29]

Much of the revolutionary ranting about the United States, the United Kingdom and Israel was formulated in terms of Western conspiracies to retain their stranglehold on the lives of Muslims and the need to wage *jihad* against these – an argument that was sold easily to Iranians brought up with stories of Western penetration of the Iranian economy in the nineteenth century. When Muslim-ruled Iraq invaded Iran, Ayatollah Khomeini responded by identifying the Baʻathist ideology of Iraq as (a hypocrite who pretends to adhere to Islam), and hence the war against it as a *jihad-e defai* (a struggle waged in defence of Islam) or *jihad fi sabil Allah* (Jihad in the Path of God) to reclaim territory belonging to the Islamic Republic.[30] By 1983, as Iran successfully drove the Iraqis out of Iranian territory, the question was whether Iran should press home its advantage at the expense of the suffering of the Muslims of Iraq. Those who argued for pushing on called for a *jihad-e ibtedaʻi* (an initiatory or pre-emptive struggle) – a category that had no previous currency.[31]

To a large extent, values discernible in the realm of the foreign policy of the Islamic Republic are products of Islamization of the language of politics. The Islamic character of the dispensation requires the regime to voice solidarity with Muslims elsewhere.[32] Hence when the Soviet Union collapsed, Tehran provided crucial support for the Central Asian Republics to find their feet on the ground. The Islamic Republic takes exception to violence perpetrated against Muslims around the world, expressing solidarity for Palestinians and Lebanese, Kashmiris and Rohingyas.[33] Tehran also works to promote well-being in Muslim countries, for instance by promoting polio-inoculation in Bangladesh through the state-owned broadcasting agency, and has sent aid to Myanmar to help rehabilitate the Rohingyas in that country.[34]

However, it is difficult to argue that Islamic principles in foreign policy trump *realpolitik*. A good illustration is the Kashmir question. During the Iran-Iraq War, New Delhi remained closer to Baghdad, which occasioned Tehran to extend diplomatic support to Islamabad on the Kashmir issue in forums like the OIC. However, from the days of Rafsanjani, as Tehran's relationship with Delhi improved, the Islamic Republic persistently refrained from criticizing Delhi in international forums at a time when Kashmiri insurgency and the Indian response were under international scrutiny.[35] Tehran briefly resumed its support of Pakistan's attempts to internationalize the Kashmir issue after India voted against Iran at the International Atomic Energy Agency in 2008,[36] and has of late raised the issue, wary of India's increasing affinity with Iran's Arab Gulf neighbours. Clearly, an Islamic argument is stronger once the decision is already arrived at for non-Islamic considerations.

It is, thus, difficult to make the case that Islamic values weigh effectively in the making of foreign policy in the Islamic Republic, but more often Islamic terms of references are deployed for the instrumental value they possess within the context of an Islamized political discourse. The regime rationalizes its measures in Islamic terms either in conforming to the expectations that the people of a Muslim society are believed to have from an Islamic regime, as in supporting the oppressed Muslim people of Palestine, or from the urge to be *adequately* Islamic.[37] It is thus moot whether a Muslim country necessarily resorts to Islamic values, or whether it appears to do so because the political discourse has been Islamized.

State and Islam in Foreign Policy

In looking for religious values in foreign policy, one should look at least from two perspectives: first, whether the country itself considers, uses or resorts to religion as an element in foreign policy; second, how others perceive the element of religion operating in that country's policymaking.

The two case studies of Turkey and Iran show that being a constitutionally secular state (Turkey) or a professedly religious state (Iran) does not make much difference for religion as a factor in foreign policy. Both cases show that in formulating foreign policy, geopolitical considerations, *realpolitik* and political/economic gains continue to have greater weightage. Religion shows itself as an element to legitimize, support, and in some cases a discourse to be utilized, to galvanize domestic support. By and large, both Turkey and Iran have resorted to the language of Islam, albeit differently in differing circumstances since the early 1980s. Depending on regional and international conditions, the role of religion in foreign policy discourse has tended to fluctuate. Turkey, especially since Erdogan came to power in 2002, has added religion as yet another element in shaping its foreign relations. Public sensitivity about being Muslim has begun to be reflected in political language and discourse. Iran, despite being a religious state, is known for its *realpolitik* approach to regional and global politics. As indicated, there is a noticeable continuity in the foreign policy goals of Iran. National issues unite all segments of Iranians irrespective of their religious or secular orientation. For example, the nuclear issue is known to have the elicited support of a large section of both the secular and religious segments of Iranian society.[38]

It is interesting to see how the religious element is believed to influence the foreign policies of Turkey and Iran. Many of the observers maintain, and many people in the Muslim world expect, that the Islamic Republic of Iran prioritizes considerations of Muslims as an important element in foreign policy. Similarly many hold that Turkey, a secular country aspiring to join the European Union, should not use religion at all in foreign affairs, even though secular Turkey's President Erdogan is considered the most powerful Muslim leader from whom Muslims in distress may seek help. Ironically, thus, from a comparative perspective on Iran and Turkey, many in the Muslim world see constitutionally secular Turkey as more religious in its approach to foreign policy towards Muslims than Iran, that is often seen as more sectarian.

There are still others who simply see in the Islamic or religious terms of reference nothing more than a legitimizing instrument within the larger rubric of the prevalent political discourse. Both Turkey and Iran happen to routinely engage in diplomatic relations with other countries, both Muslim (Shiʻi and Sunni) and non-Muslim. When they deal with non-Muslim countries, policies are seldom marketed as of Islamic vintage, except to the domestic audience where such labelling is believed to have some traction. Hence both Turkey (since the late 1990s) and Iran (since 1979) have publicly chosen to thunder against Israel on the question of Palestine where many, but not all, happen to be Muslims. Such assertion of solidarity does not either necessarily or readily translate into material support for Muslim brethren. Turkey has proven wary of actively involving itself with such causes unless they are affected directly. Hence Ankara initially tacitly supported the (Sunni Islamist) opposition to Assad but chose to reverse its policy when the Kurdish regions of Syria began to pose an irredentist challenge and appears to have reconciled with Assad remaining in power.[39] Similarly, Ankara stayed away from the Iraqi quagmire even at the height of the threat posed by the Daʻish till the prospect emerged of Syria unravelling altogether, which raised the prospect of Kurdish irredentism, and Ankara resorted to unilateral military action inside Iraq in March 2018.[40] On conflict situations away from its neighbourhood, Turkey has refrained from venturing out in the name of Islam. Ankara's only such military involvement outside its immediate neighbourhood in recent times (viz. Afghanistan) was as a part of NATO obligations. Despite Ankara's best efforts there to project itself as a key Muslim interlocutor, its investments are yet to pay off noticeably.[41]

Similar considerations of *realpolitik* in Iran's policy towards Iraq and Palestine have previously been discussed. It needs to be spelt out that the apparently sectarian character of the Islamic Republic also is a kind of optical illusion or window-dressing. In Iraq, Tehran tried to strengthen the Shiʻi forces at the expense of the Sunnis because the latter were integral to the Baʻathist regime that had been hostile to the Islamic Republic. The alleged Shiʻi connection in Syria and Yemen also appears somewhat puerile because from the standpoint of Ithna ʻAshari Shiʻi theology prevalent in Iran, both the ʻAlavi Shiʻi (from which comes Bashar al-Assad) and the Zaidi Shiʻi (who make up most of Yemen's Shiʻi population) are situated at different levels of *bidʻa* (heresy). Besides, unlike Syria, Tehran's support for the Shiʻi of Yemen is of recent vintage. There were no noticeable intimacies between Tehran and the Shiʻi during the days of ʻAli Abdullah Saleh, which should not have been the case if the idea of a Shiʻi axis was actually religious/sectarian in character.

That said, it is equally facile to deny the role played by Islam in the realm of diplomacy in the Muslim world. Periodic scholarly conferences and increasing academic exchanges on Islamic themes have gained substantial currency over the past several decades – both Ankara and Tehran use these *carpe diem* situations to engage with those parts of the world where Muslims are not in a majority. Tehran's role in organizing annual musical performances of the works of Amir Khusrau in India, or scholarships to Muslim students from South, Central and Southeast Asia, such as those provided by the Al-Mustafa International University of Qom or the Ministry of Islamic Culture and Guidance, has a major value in the realm of Track-II diplomatic engagement with these parts of the Muslim world. Turkey has similarly developed such networks over the past two decades in Africa and South and Central Asia – this explains why the schools associated with the Gülen network have been taken over by the Turkish state after the coup attempt in July 2016, rather than being shut down.[42] Whether these networks would allow Ankara and Tehran the same kind of mileage in the future that the United States has with Fulbright and the UK with the British Council, or even China with its Confucius scholarships, would depend on the total volume of money pumped in over a period of time.

CONCLUSION

This chapter suggests that deep-seated cultural and religious elements often produce certain strategic perspectives that inform state action, in particular historical conjunctures, subsumed within the broader rubric of values. Such factors derived from the intellectual and cultural tradition of Islam, varying across time and space, influence the grand strategy of countries of the Muslim world as profoundly as they do in other cultural spaces. They influence how governments employ domestic and international resources of a state towards the accomplishment of overarching national and global goals. This in turn may result in defining what will be the priorities of foreign policy tenets in terms of issue or region/area of focus, which becomes pivotal to foreign policy decision making.

In terms of analysing a country's foreign policy, this chapter argued that the religious element in foreign policymaking can be neglected only to weaken the analysis. Foreign policy analysis has often concentrated only on what has come to occur, rather than the intellectual parameters within which the policies were formulated. By bringing cultural and religious elements into the analysis, and understanding the boundaries of thinking within which political actors operate, one can explain developments better and project a range of possible outcomes.

Important contributions have already been made in terms of arguing that the global resurgence of religion challenges hegemonic concepts and thought patterns of the study of international relations (IR). Beyond observing the religious challenge to the secular foundations of IR as a discipline, one needs to illuminate paths to integrate non-biased concepts of religion into analyses carried out within IR.[43] In that sense, Eva Bellin argues, 'understanding the role of religion in international politics requires grasping its *meaning* for believers' and '*understanding* precludes *explanation*'.[44] She recommends, first, that 'students of religion in IR should aim for interpretive narratives, not for predictive sciences',[45] and, second, they 'need to focus more on developing empirically grounded middle-range theory'.[46]

As in the cases of Turkey and Iran, in today's world the role of religion is not considered by many of its practitioners as incongruous to foreign policy. There are now increasing calls for an inclusion of religions and religious diplomacy for peace processes, problem solving and other areas of foreign policy.[47] Turkey has already considered and followed this line and included religious diplomacy as part and parcel of foreign policy since the early 2000s. Today with the change towards a multidimensional approach to foreign policy, religion has become one of Turkey's new tools in implementing its vision and policies. Iran, in its own way, has been doing so since the Islamic Revolution in 1979.

Today, unlike in the past, religious diplomacy has acquired a much more sophisticated and comprehensive form. Given the political success of forces deploying a language of politics derived from Islam, institutions that implement and develop religious diplomacy in Turkey and Iran have begun to evolve. *Diyanet* is no longer a state body to cater to religious needs of Turkish citizens alone; rather it is one of the flagbearers of Turkey abroad. Similarly for Iran, the Ministry for Islamic Culture and Guidance and several other such instruments, institutions and channels are deployed by Tehran to exert religious influence in different parts of the world. In coming years, it is extremely likely that the use of Islam and the political language of Islam in diplomatic activities of both Iran and Turkey will continue to expand in scope as both a source of inspiration for policy formulation and the language of legitimacy.

NOTES

1. Nukhet A. Sandal and Patrick James, 'Religion and International Relations Theory: Towards a Mutual Understanding', *European Journal of International Relations* 17, no. 1 (March 2011): 6.

2. Jonathan Fox and Shmuel Sandler, *Bringing Religion into International Relations* (New York: Palgrave Macmillan, 2004), 58.

3. See Mehmet Ozkan, *Religion, Historical Legacy and Weltanschauungs: The Cases of Turkey, India and South Africa* (Unpublished Ph. D. Dissertation, University of Seville, 2013): 48–50; See also Michael Barnett, 'Another Great Awakening? International Relations Theory and Religion', in Jack Snyder (ed.). *Religion and International Relations Theory* (New York: Columbia University Press, 2011), 91–114.

4. For a discussion on how every speech is also an 'act' in itself, see John Searle, 'How Performatives Work', *Linguistics and Philosophy* 12, no. 5 (October, 1989): 535–58. http://www.jstor.org/stable/25001359.

5. Mehmet Aydın, *'Diyanet's* Global Vision', *The Muslim World* 98, no. 2–3, (2008): 164–72.

6. Ibrahim Kalın, 'Soft Power and Public Diplomacy in Turkey', *Perceptions* XVI, no. 3 (2011): 5–23.

7. Ahmet Davutoğlu, 'Turkey's New Foreign Policy Vision: An Assessment of 2007', *Insight Turkey* 10, no. 1 (2008): 77–96.

8. Ahmet Davutoğlu, 'Principles of Turkish Foreign Policy'. Address by foreign minister of Republic of Turkey at the SETA Foundation's Washington, DC Branch (8 December 2009). http://www.setadc.org/images/stories/food/FM%20of%20Turkey%20A.Davutoglu%20Address%20at%20SETA-DC%2012-08-2009.pdf.

9. Mehmet Ozkan, 'Turkey in the Islamic World: An Institutional Perspective', *Turkish Review of Middle East Studies* 18 (2007): 159–93.

10. This section on the rise of *Diyanet* in Turkey's foreing policy is summarized from Mehmet Ozkan, 'Turkey's Religious Diplomacy', *The Arab World Geographer* 17, no. 3 (2014): 223–37.

11. Ariel Levaggi, 'Turkey and Latin America: A New Horizon for a Strategic Relationship', *Perceptions* XVIII, no. 4 (2013): 99–116.

12. Imam-Hatip Schools are public vocational schools with a curriculum of both Islamic education and modern sciences. Originally established to cater to the need of producing religious leaders (*imams*) in the mosques by the secular establishment, they have come to provide exposure to Western education without neglecting Islamic/cultural values. See Irem Ozgur, *Islamic Schools in Modern Turkey: Faith, Politics, and Education* (Cambridge: Cambridge University Press, 2012).

13. Quoted in 'Africa Seeks Turkish Islamic Education', *Hurriyet Daily* (24 November 2011).

14. For more on this, see Mehmet Ozkan, 'Turkey's Political-Economic Engagement with Africa', in Justin van der Merwe, Ian Taylor and Alexandra Arkhangelskaya (eds.). *Emerging Powers in Africa: A New Wave in the Relationship?* (London: Palgrave Macmillan, 2016), 217–31.

15. R. K. Ramazani, 'Iran's Foreign Policy: Independence, Freedom and the Islamic Republic', in Anoushiravan Ehtesami and Mahjoob Zweiri (eds.). *Iranian Foreign Policy: From Khatami to Ahmedinejad* (Reading, MA: Ithaca Press, 2008), 1–16.

16. See, Anthony H. Cordesman, 'Iran's Support for the Hezbollah in Lebanon', *Center for Strategic and International Studies* (15 July 2006). http://csis.org/files/media/csis/pubs/060715_hezbollah.pdf.

17. Ibrahim Mousawi, Director, Political Programmes, Al-Manar Television, in conversation with one of the authors, Beirut, May 2005.

18. US sources have estimated Iranian support to Hamas has ranged between $30 million and $50 million during the 1990s; Canadian intelligence estimates the transfer for the same period to have been between $3 million and $18 million. Matthew Levitt, *HAMAS: Politics, Charity and Terrorism in the Service of Jihad* (New Haven, CT; London: Yale University Press, 2006), 172.

19. Kingshuk Chatterjee, 'The "Tehran" Factor: Doomed to Destabilise?' in Priya Singh and Sushmita Bhattacharya (eds.). *Perspectives on West Asia: The Evolving Geopolitical Discourses* (Kolkata and New Delhi: Makaias and Shipra Publications, 2012), 116–20.

20. For a detailed argument along these lines, see Anoushiravan Ehteshami and Raymond Hinnebusch, *Syria and Iran: Middle Powers in a Penetrated Regional System* (London; New York: Routledge, 1997).

21. Chatterjee, 'the "Tehran" Factor'. 122–23.

22. Anoushiravan Ehteshami, 'Iran's Regional Policies since the End of the Cold War', in Ali Gheissari (ed.). *Contemporary Iran: Economy, Society, Politics* (Oxford; New York: Oxford University Press, 2009), 345

23. For instance, see Mohsen M. Milani, 'Iran's Persian Gulf Policy in the Post-Saddam Era', in Ali Gheissari (ed.). *Contemporary Iran: Economy, Society, Politics* (Oxford; New York: Oxford University Press, 2009), 359–63; See also, Kayhan Barzegar, 'Iran's Foreign Policy Strategy after Saddam', *The Washington Quarterly* 33, no. 1 (January 2010): 173–89.

24. In Islamic theology, the *mustakbirun* were those like Iblis or the Pharaohs who were too arrogant to accept the Revelation, God and His Prophet. Khomeini used this term to depict the Shah and all who had supported him, implying a lack of political legitimacy being equivalent to infidelity.

25. A. H. Rafsanjani, in *Dar Maktab-i Jum'a*: *Muajmu'a Khutbaha-ye Namaz-i Juma'a-ye Tehran*, 6 (Tehran: Ministry of Islamic Culture and Guidance, 1990), 10, cited in Saskia Gieling, *Religion and War in Revolutionary Iran* (London: I.B. Tauris, 1999), 143.

26. Shaul Bakhash. *The Reign of the Ayatollahs*: *Iran and the Islamic Revolution* (New York: Basic Books, 1984).

27. Kingshuk Chatterjee, 'Of Islam and Other Things: The Drivers and Rhetoric in Iranian Politics', in Priya Singh (ed.). *Re-envisaging West Asia: Looking beyond the Arab Uprisings* (Kolkata and New Delhi: Makaias and Shipra Publications, 2016), 56–84.

28. Gieling, *Religion and War in Revolutionary Iran*, 88

29. Rouhani's efforts during the closing months of the Obama era resulted in the nuclear deal. For a discussion of Khatami's efforts to normalize relations, see Kingshuk Chatterjee, *A Spilt in the Middle: The Making of the Political Centre in Iran 1987–2004*, IFPS/CPWAS Occasional Paper, no. 2 (New Delhi: KW Publishers, 2012): 43–45.

30. *Ettela'at*, 21st Esfand 1360/ 3 March, 1983.

31. Gieling, *Religion and War in Revolutionary Iran*, 84–86.

32. Ibid., 143–44.

33. See, Ayatollah Khamenei's 'Id speech 'Why Is the World Silent towards Massacre of Muslims in Myanmar, Kashmir and Palestine', *Khamenei.ir* (29 August 2017). http://english.khamenei.ir/news/5088/Ayatollah-Khamenei-Why-is-world-silent-towards-massacre-of-Muslims.

34. 'Iran Distributes Humanitarian Aid to Rohingya Refugees', *Mehr News Agency* (17 September 2017). https://en.mehrnews.com/news/127871/Iran-distributes-humanitarian-aid-to-Rohingya-refugees.

35. Muhammad Faysal, 'How Rafsanjani Sabotaged the Kashmir Cause to Save India', *With Kashmir* (9 January 2017). http://withkashmir.org/2017/01/09/rafsanjani-sabotaged-kashmir-cause-save-india-1994-updated/.

36. Iftikhar Gilani, 'How Iran Saved India in 1994', *Milli Gazette* (19 January 2011). http://www.milligazette.com/news/333-how-iran-saved-india-in-1994-kashmir-UN-voting.

37. The best example is the case of the *fatwa* on Salman Rushdie, on account of his book *the Satanic Verses*, which Ayatollah Khomeini is believed to have initially suggested should be ignored. It is argued that coming under attack from the right-wing conservative elements of the revolutionary elite on domestic issues, Khomeini changed his mind and issued the *fatwa* on Rushdie and his book largely to pre-empt any challenge to his position within the Islamic Republic, unmindful of the consequences Tehran had to face for years to follow. See Baqer Moin, *Khomeini: Life of the Ayatollah* (London; New York: I.B. Tauris, 1999), 282–85.

38. See Saideh Lotfian, 'Nuclear Policy and International Relations', in Homa Katouzian and Hossein Shahidi. *Iran in the 21st Century: Politics, Economics and Conflict* (London: Routledge, 2008), 158–80.

39. Alexander Christie-Miller, 'Turkey's Policy Shift in Syria Reflects New Priorities', *The National* (16 April 2018). https://www.thenational.ae/world/mena/turkey-s-policy-shift-in-syria-reflects-new-priorities-1.722147.

40. Mohamed Mostafa, 'Iraq Denounces Turkish Strikes on Kurdistan That Left Civilians Dead', *Iraqi News* (22 March 2018). https://www.iraqinews.com/features/iraq-denounces-turkish-strikes-on-kurdistan-that-left-civilians-dead/.

41. Masood Saifullah, 'Is Turkey's Erdogan Seeking a Leading Role in Afghanistan?' *Deutschewelle* (6 July 2017). https://www.dw.com/en/is-turkeys-erdogan-seeking-a-leading-role-in-afghanistan/a-39575830.

42. 'Turkish Foundation Takes Over 108 Gülen-Linked Schools Abroad', *Hurriyet Daily News* (24 April 2018). http://www.hurriyetdailynews.com/turkish-foundation-takes-over-108-gulen-linked-schools-abroad-130823.

43. Mona Kanwal Sheikh, 'How Does Religion Matter? Pathways to Religion in International Relations', *Review of International Studies* 38, no. 2 (2012): 366.

44. Eva Bellin, 'Faith in Politics: New Trends in the Study of Religion and Politics', *World Politics* 60, no. 2 (2008): 343.

45. Ibid., 343.

46. Ibid., 346.

47. Peter Mandaville and Sara Silvestri, *Integrating Religious Engagement into Diplomacy: Challenges and Opportunities* (Brookings Papers No. 67: 2015).

BIBLIOGRAPHY

Aydın, Mehmet. '*Diyanet's* Global Vision'. *The Muslim World* 98, no. 2–3 (2008): 164–72.

Bakhash, Shau. *The Reign of the Ayatollahs: Iran and the Islamic Revolution*. New York: Basic Books, 1984.

Barnett, Michael. 'Another Great Awakening? International Relations Theory and Religion', in Jack Snyder (ed.). *Religion and International Relations Theory.* New York: Columbia University Press, 2011: 91–114.

Barzegar, Kayhan. 'Iran's Foreign Policy Strategy after Saddam'. *The Washington Quarterly* 33, no. 1 (January 2010): 173–89.

Bellin, Eva. 'Faith in Politics: New Trends in the Study of Religion and Politics'. *World Politics* 60, no. 2 (2008): 315–47.

Chatterjee, Kingshuk. 'Of Islam and Other Things: The Drivers and Rhetoric in Iranian Politics', in Priya Singh (ed.). *Re-envisaging West Asia: Looking beyond the Arab Uprisings.* Kolkata; New Delhi: Makaias and Shipra Publications, 2016: 56–84.

Chatterjee, Kingshuk. *A Spilt in the Middle: The Making of the Political Centre in Iran 1987–2004.* IFPS/CPWAS Occasional Paper, no. 2. New Delhi: KW Publishers, 2012.

Chatterjee, Kingshuk. 'The "Tehran" Factor: Doomed to Destabilise?' in Priya Singh and Sushmita Bhattacharya (eds.). *Perspectives on West Asia: The Evolving Geopolitical Discourses.* Kolkata; New Delhi: Makaias and Shipra Publications, 2012: 115–40.

Cordesman, Anthony H. 'Iran's Support for the Hezbollah in Lebanon'. *Center for Strategic and International Studies* (15 July 2006) http://csis.org/files/media/csis/pubs/060715_hezbollah.pdf.

Davutoğlu, Ahmet. 'Turkey's New Foreign Policy Vision: An Assessment of 2007'. *Insight Turkey* 10, no. 1 (2008): 77–96.

Ehteshami, Anoushiravan. 'Iran's Regional Policies since the End of the Cold War', in Ali Gheissari (ed.). *Contemporary Iran: Economy, Society, Politics.* Oxford; New York: Oxford University Press, 2009: 324–48.

Ehteshami, Anoushiravan and Raymond Hinnebusch. *Syria and Iran: Middle Powers in a Penetrated Regional System.* London; New York: Routledge, 1997.

Fox, Jonathan and Shmuel Sandler. *Bringing Religion into International Relations.* New York: Palgrave Macmillan, 2004.

Gieling, Saskia. *Religion and War in Revolutionary Iran.* London: I.B. Tauris, 1999.

Kalın, Ibrahim. 'Soft Power and Public Diplomacy in Turkey'. *Perceptions* XVI, no. 3 (2011): 5–23.

Levaggi, Ariel. 'Turkey and Latin America: A New Horizon for a Strategic Relationship'. *Perceptions* XVIII, no. 4 (2013): 99–116.

Levitt, Matthew. *Hamas: Politics, Charity and Terrorism in the Service of Jihad.* New Haven, CT; London: Yale University Press, 2006.

Lotfian, Saideh. 'Nuclear Policy and International Relations', in Homa Katouzian and Hossein Shahidi. *Iran in the 21st Century: Politics, Economics and Conflict.* London: Routledge, 2008: 158–80.

Mandeville, Peter and Sara Silvestri. *Integrating Religious Engagement into Diplomacy: Challenges and Opportunities.* Brookings Papers no. 67 (2015).

Milani, Mohsen M. 'Iran's Persian Gulf Policy in the Post-Saddam Era', in Ali Gheissari (ed.). *Contemporary Iran: Economy, Society, Politics.* Oxford; New York: Oxford University Press, 2009: 349–66.

Moin, Baqer. *Khomeini: Life of the Ayatollah.* London; New York: I.B. Tauris, 1999.

Ozgur, Irem. *Islamic Schools in Modern Turkey: Faith, Politics, and Education.* Cambridge: Cambridge University Press, 2012.

Ozkan, Mehmet. *Religion, Historical Legacy and Weltanschauungs: The Cases of Turkey, India and South Africa.* [Unpublished PhD Dissertation] University of Seville, 2013.

Ozkan, Mehmet. 'Turkey in the Islamic World: An Institutional Perspective'. *Turkish Review of Middle East Studies* 18 (2007): 159–93.

Ozkan, Mehmet. 'Turkey's Political-Economic Engagement with Africa', in Justin van der Merwe, Ian Taylor and Alexandra Arkhangelskaya (eds.). *Emerging Powers in Africa: A New Wave in the Relationship?* London: Palgrave Macmillan, 2016: 217–31.

Ozkan, Mehmet. 'Turkey's Religious Diplomacy'. *The Arab World Geographer* 17, no. 3, (2014): 223–37.

Ramazani, R. K. 'Iran's Foreign Policy: Independence, Freedom and the Islamic Republic', in Anoushiravan Ehtesami and Mahjoob Zweiri (eds.). *Iranian Foreign Policy: From Khatami to Ahmedinejad.* Reading, MA: Ithaca Press, 2008: 1–16.

Sandal, Nukhet A. and Patrick James. 'Religion and International Relations Theory: Towards a Mutual Understanding'. *European Journal of International Relations* 17, no. 1 (March 2011): 3–25.

Searle, John. 'How Performatives Work'. *Linguistics and Philosophy* 12: no. 5 (October, 1989): 535–58.

Sheikh, Mona Kanwal. 'How Does Religion Matter? Pathways to Religion in International Relations'. *Review of International Studies* 38, no. 2 (2012): 365–92.

Chapter 8

Values in Indian Foreign Policy

*Lofty Ideals Give Way
to Parochial Pragmatism*

Krishnan Srinivasan

At the time of independence, Indian foreign policy directed by Prime Minister Jawaharlal Nehru was firmly anchored to values-based principles derived from religious traditions, the struggle by colonized countries against imperialism and racialism and the legacy of Mahatma Gandhi's non-violent freedom movement. These principles, advanced in a hortatory manner that presumed Indian moral superiority and unique universalism, quickly foundered against the harsh realities of government responsibilities and international politics. After Nehru's death, only some rhetorical flourishes of an ethical foreign policy survived, though repeatedly belied by his successors' policies of realism and opportunism. However, an ingrained self-belief in Indian exceptionalism, particularly in respect of the pursuit of peace, continues to be regularly invoked as an example to the international community. This claim to the moral high ground, together with the exclusivist nature of *Hindutva* now prevalent in governing circles, renders India's closer integration in a globalizing world more problematic.

FOUNDATIONAL VALUES

Early Foreign Connections

India was unique among newly independent countries in respect of diplomatic experience and could therefore act on the world stage quickly and forcefully. Besides participation at the League of Nations and Imperial Commonwealth conferences, overseas connections were important for the Indian National Congress throughout the freedom struggle. Information centres among Indian expatriates were established, and a foreign department was organized from

135

1936 to 1938. From its early days the Congress had opined on foreign affairs, criticizing the British Empire's use of Indian troops abroad and the treatment of overseas Indians. Pioneer nationalists like Rammohun Roy and Swami Vivekananda were also internationalists; the Vedanta Society in 1894 in New York could be considered the first Indian resident representation overseas.

Congress joined the League against Imperialism and the International Peace Campaign with Jawaharlal Nehru as its foreign affairs specialist, but he was one among many, such as Rabindranath Tagore, Mohandas Gandhi, Subhas Bose and Sarvepalli Radhakrishnan, who all promoted the cause of Indian independence overseas. Senior bureaucrats were also trained; at independence India had diplomatic missions in important world capitals. In Nehru's words, 'The Congress gradually developed a foreign policy which was based on the elimination of political and economic imperialism everywhere and the cooperation of free countries. This fitted in with the demand for Indian independence'.[1]

Nehru was influenced by Lenin's ideas that capitalism, imperialism and war were interrelated, and European socialism was attractive to most Indian intelligentsia. Nehru was also attracted to Wendell Willkie's ideas of One World, and by the inspiration of Gandhi, reflecting that 'in those long years of struggle we were taught by our great leader never to forget not only the objectives we had but also the methods whereby we should achieve those objectives. Out of hatred you will not build peace'.[2] Gandhi's stretcher-bearers of the Boer War foreshadowed the Congress dispatching a medical mission to China in 1938, and later a medical team during the Korean War.

Ancient Traditions

It is hard to separate Indian civilization, philosophy and nationality. All contributed to the evolution of foreign policy, as did Hinduism, professed, if not practised, by 80 percent of Indians, Gandhi who emerged into politics from the masses and the non-violent means he deployed for independence, and Nehru's unquestioned authority from 1927 to 1964.

Hinduism, the world's oldest living faith, without founder or prescribed text, has at its core *dharma* or righteous conduct; that rights follow the performance of duties and obligations discharged. Accommodating many theological perspectives, Hinduism is civilizational rather than doctrinal. During the nineteenth century and the period of Arya Samaj, Brahmo Samaj and Swami Ramakrishna, Hindus began to discard their self-belittlement. Vivekananda declared he was proud to call himself a Hindu, and Gandhi gave India an ideal that emphasized universal truth and non-violence. If India was free, he said, it would make 'the largest contribution yet to world peace[3] . . . the very right to live accrues to us only when we do the duty of citizenship to the world'.[4]

Indophile John Holwell's view in the eighteenth century that Hinduism was a combination of religion, philosophy and nationality found later echoes in writers like Vinayak Savarkar and Madhav Golwalkar, who emphasized Indian religious, territorial and cultural identity. Hindus were a nation, *Bharatvarsha*, which was a cultural concept, and Hinduism was a derivative of *Hindutva* or Hindu-ness. They propounded the theory that all Hindus were united in the common inheritance of race, land, festivals, rituals and literature, an idea reiterated in 2017 by Mohan Bhagwat, leader of the Rashtriya Swayamsevak Sangh (RSS): 'We believe that our forefathers, no matter which community we represent today, were Hindus'.[5] This aspect of nationalism was also to play its part in moulding foreign policy over the decades.

Savarkar described Buddhism as the first and greatest attempt to propagate the law of righteousness as a universal religion, which accorded with Nehru's ideas of internationalism. Nehru called Buddha 'the greatest of the sons of India',[6] and independent India adopted Ashoka's Lion Pillar as the state emblem, Ashoka's *Dharma Chakra* as the centrepiece of the national flag and the nomenclature of the new Indian calendar as the Saka Era.[7] Buddhism represented the golden mean, the middle way, and Nehru said of the *Dharma Chakra*, 'We took that symbol . . . because we do wish to continue as far as possible the old cultural outlook, the philosophic outlook, the peaceful outlook, with the dynamism of today'.[8]

Nehru was not religious. His will declared, 'My desire to have a handful of my ashes thrown into the Ganga at Allahabad has no religious significance as far as I am concerned. I have no religious sentiment in the matter'.[9] Nevertheless, he felt drawn to the cultural importance of Hinduism and Buddhism:

> I have no doubt that the policy of speaking out and pursuit of peace that India has been following is the right and logical policy. . . . It is derived from the great principles laid down by Emperor Ashoka several centuries ago. I do not see how any government in India in the next ten or hundred or thousand years can basically change the policy . . . any deviation from the path would make India untrue to itself.[10]

When it came to the name of the country, he wrote, 'The next argument [in the Constituent Assembly] is going to be the name of this unhappy country. Bharat is suggested. I have no objection to Bharat but I hate to give up Hindustan. Anyway, India will remain officially and for foreign purposes and that is one good thing'.[11]

Much is written about the diplomatic legacy of Chanakya's *Arthashastra* of the third century B.C. and Kamandaki's fourth- or fifth-century text *Nitisara*, but there is no evidence that such precepts were ever practised at any time in history. Nehru and his successors rarely referred to either author and never as a guide to practical policy.

Non-Violence

The non-violence concept in the Upanishads, Mahabharata, Jainism and Buddhism was invoked by early Indian leaders, drawing from Ashokan edicts such as 'Here in my domain no living beings are to be slaughtered or offered in sacrifice'.[12] *Ahimsa* is Sanskrit for 'non-violence' or 'non-injury', appearing as an essential virtue in the *Chandogya Upanishad* along with truth, charity and eschewing theft and anger. The invocation of such qualities – though there is no evidence they were ever practised in India – was fundamental to Gandhi's non-cooperation movement for independence. *Ahimsa* to him represented love, compassion and the absence of hostility to adversaries. In 1930 at the League of Nations the Maharaja of Bikaner asserted that India would forever be inspired by peace – 'should anyone doubt it, let him read her philosophy, with its embodiment of the most complete and consistent code of pacifism in the world',[13] and in 1938 Nehru wrote:

> India stands significantly as a country which has deliberately based its policy on peace and non-violence. How far it is possible to apply these methods in the international sphere today it is difficult to say. But it must be remembered that non-violence of the Indian struggle is not a weak, passive and ineffective pacifism . . . if the world is to progress in its culture and civilization, it will have to adopt peaceful methods of solving its problems.[14]

Gandhi nominated Nehru his political heir in 1942, saying 'when I am gone, he will speak my language'.[15] Nehru was acutely conscious of this inheritance and attempted to adapt Gandhi's moral standards to foreign policy: 'We were bred up in a high tradition under a great man. That tradition was an ethical tradition . . . a technique of action which was unique to the world. We have to keep in mind those very ideals[16] . . . the world's sickness today can be cured only by his methods of love and non-violence'.[17] Nehru told the chief of army staff in 1947, 'We don't need any defence plan. Our policy is non-violence. We foresee no military threats. You can scrap the army'.[18] Because of the presence of Gandhi, India felt no animosity towards any country, which contributed to the policy of non-alignment that became India's seminal contribution to international relations. But the attempt at non-violence rapidly fell apart under the compulsions of government. As early as 1949, Nehru admitted:

> Logically and practically speaking, the theory of non-violence carried to its extreme would mean no police or army. I cannot say if any country can be brave enough to do so[19] . . . I feel we may adopt the principle of non-violence but everything depends on our strength to adhere to it[20]. . . . I regret I am no pacifist. I should like to be one but I am no pacifist in the circumstances of today and because of the responsibility I have.[21]

Universality and Exceptionalism

The Hindu viewpoint starts with the cosmic unity of the whole world, animate and inanimate, and all humans possessing certain attributes as a result of their common humanity. The *Atharva Veda* said, 'The yoke of the chariot is placed equally on the shoulders of all, who should live in harmony supporting one another like the spokes of a wheel'.[22] Since God exists in every human, there is universal brotherhood, equality in diversity and all humanity as one family. Many countries pretend to exceptionalism, but Indians alone lay claim to the eternal uncontestable spiritual truth. Vivekananda asserted that 'no religion on earth preaches the dignity of humanity in such a lofty strain as Hinduism[23] . . . this must be our eternal foreign policy, preaching the truths of our *shastras* to the nations',[24] while Tagore considered India as ordained to convey universal principles to the world: 'we are the custodians of this light which burns for all time and for all men'.[25] This became a recurrent theme; Sarojini Naidu in 1929 exclaimed, 'Give us our flag and then India will be the deliverer of the whole world!'[26] Indian spokespersons were not slow to chide others for their ethical shortcomings and became 'merchants of the high-minded phrase'[27] – failings that would become liabilities later.

The conviction that India's unique civilization was an overarching cultural space remains basic to India's self-image. India commands respect as a new kind of power, a paradigm of autonomous and influential morality and peaceful persuasion, an alternative spiritual and intellectual universality. Independence was the start of an Asian renaissance with proactive India as its natural leader, with special obligations in the management of international society. As always, Nehru gave the clearest expression to this belief, informing the US Congress in 1949, 'India's voice is somewhat different; it is the voice of an ancient civilization, distinctive, vital'.[28] Back in India, Nehru said:

> Whatever the present position of India might be, she is potentially a great power. . . .[29] We talk of world government and one world. As long as we do not recognize the supremacy of the moral law in . . . international relations we shall have no enduring peace[30] . . . we are placed in such a position that we are destined to be the nerve centre of Asia. . . .[31] India by virtue of her past genius . . . culture if you like, has got perhaps a special role to play. . . .[32] We perform a service . . . which no other country in the world can perform . . . the policy that we have pursued is . . . the natural and inevitable policy which any government which represents India can pursue. . . .[33] Ours is a country of high ideals and high thinking, an ancient culture and civilization.[34]

In India a durable consensus formed around this sense of exceptionalism and superiority. Foreign Minister Inder Gujral in 1990 warned his interlocutor, 'Do not forget that every Indian carries on his shoulders the burden of a thousand years of history',[35] and former President Pranab Mukherjee claimed that 'we taught the entire world that we have to live in peace'.[36]

Anti-Colonialism and Anti-Racialism

Hindus were under minority rule from approximately AD 1200 to 1947. The attainment of majority rule therefore acquired peculiar significance. The extended period of minority rule resulted in intense fears of foreign interference and the return of colonialism, which led to a policy of self-reliance with Nehru pronouncing, 'we would rather delay our development . . . than submit to any kind of economic domination'.[37] Before independence, Indian nationalists were anxious to develop contacts with other independence movements with the goal of anti-imperial unity. Indian subjugation was regarded as part of the world problem of imperial rule. 'The strongest urge in Asia . . . is the anti-colonial urge',[38] said Nehru, 'you cannot have a world half-free and half-slave[39] . . . we believe that peace and freedom are indivisible and the denial of freedom anywhere must endanger freedom everywhere. . . .'[40] We repudiate utterly the . . . doctrine of racialism wheresoever and in whatever form. . . .'[41] we want to fit in our nationhood and national freedom with internationalism and international freedom'.[42]

Related to the anti-racial stance was the status of Indians overseas. In 1936 there were 2.48 million Indians abroad, of whom 2.35 million were in British colonies and dominions. The Indian Diaspora generated both anxieties to Congress and an involvement in foreign affairs, since discrimination against overseas Indians was a concern that united all Indians. Although Congress's advice to Indian emigrants was to identify with their country of residence, it was also concerned 'both directly and indirectly with the problem of racial equality. In view of the fact that large numbers of Indians live abroad, it becomes our duty to take interest in them'.[43] Representatives of British India attempted to alleviate the conditions of Indians overseas, and in South Africa, Burma (now Myanmar) and Malaysia in particular, representations were made, and many future Indian diplomats received practical training as agents abroad of the Department of Education, Health and Lands of the British Raj.

In 1946, with independence looming, India took the cause against racial discrimination in South Africa to the United Nations (UN) General Assembly and succeeded by a two-thirds majority. India's resolution preventing South Africa annexing South West Africa was also passed. For the Nehru government there was a broader context: this was 'a struggle for equality of opportunity for all races. The struggle in South Africa is not merely an Indian issue . . . our cause thus becomes a world cause'.[44]

Afro-Asian Solidarity

An Asian federation was mooted by Congressman Chittaranjan Das in 1922, but Nehru was wary; he thought the idea premature though cooperation between Asian nations was necessary for decolonization and the growth of trade. 'Asia is a huge continent', he said, 'and when we talk about an Asian feeling, I do not quite know what it means, because we differ too much amongst ourselves. . . . And yet I think it is true that . . . there is such a thing as an Asian sentiment'.[45] His scepticism was justified at an Asian Relations Conference in New Delhi in 1947 where he and Gandhi spoke of the unity of Asia and its spiritual enlightenment which was 'of enormous value for humanity'.[46] But the conference led to no institutional continuity. The postulate that Asians had something special to contribute was an ingredient in foreign policy for some while after independence, but it was never clear what this contribution should be. The Congress's contacts with others oppressed by imperialism and racism led to the conviction that India was the natural leader of the African-Asian world, free from motives of expansionism or imperialism, but the presumption of moral leadership gave rise to an unrealistic assessment of India's weight in world affairs, and lack of preparedness for the setbacks that were to come. Initially, non-alignment, anti-racialism and anti-imperialism gave India a platform attractive to African-Asian countries; Nehru in 1948 declared, 'Asia counts in world affairs. Tomorrow it will count more than today',[47] and the Geneva agreements on Indo-China of 1954 were regarded as a triumph for Asian leadership, but the Bandung Conference in 1955 failed to create any continuing mechanism, let alone an Afro-Asian bloc.

THE INFLUENCE OF NEHRU

Nehru's Foreign Policy

Nehru's words dominate the quotations in this chapter because the guiding values in Indian foreign policy are based on his philosophy and practices. 'In no other state', wrote Michael Brecher, 'does one man dominate foreign policy as does Nehru of India. Indeed, so overwhelming is his influence that India's policy has come to mean . . . the personal policy of Pandit Nehru. . . . Nehru is the philosopher, the architect, the engineer and the voice of his country's policy toward the outside world'.[48] Nehru was the colossus; he fashioned a policy that was 'the continuity of the idea that is India from long ages past to the present day'.[49] Nehru clothed realism in the rhetoric of idealism, but like most natural politicians, he was unaware of the distinction. As Willard

Range said: 'We do not know and cannot know . . . whether Nehru is a naïve utopian, a super realist, or something in between'.[50]

Foreign policy was an important plank in Nehru's nation-building. Congress, before and at independence, was a big tent of several contradictory ideologies and influential individuals. Though he was party president for only four of his eighteen years of premiership, Nehru remained unchallenged and understood that only a policy that did not lean towards West or East could enjoy a consensus. A weak country could not withstand either bloc but might be able to maintain its independence due to big power rivalry. 'Mutual rivalry', Nehru said, 'would in itself be the surest guarantee against an attack on India'.[51] He disclaimed the attribution of being the founder of Indian foreign policy.

> I have not originated it. It is a policy inherent in the circumstances of India, inherent in the past thinking of India, inherent in the whole mental outlook of India, inherent in the conditioning of the Indian mind during our struggle for freedom . . . India's policy has not been some sudden bright inspiration of an individual but a gradual growth evolving from even before independence.[52]

Yet Nehru was prone to use the first person in elaborating the nation's viewpoint. 'My simple policy – and it is not a negative policy, it is not a passive policy – is . . . as far as possible doing our utmost for the avoidance of world war or any war; secondly of judging issues on the merits. . . .'[53] I hope and try to follow a policy which might lead to a better world'.[54]

Nehru believed that India had a special capacity to promote international cooperation, and his first Independence Day address included the following: 'We take the pledge of dedication to the service of India and her people and to the still larger cause of humanity. And so we have to . . . give reality to our dreams. Those dreams are for India, but they are also for the world, for all the nations and peoples are too closely knit together today for anyone of them to imagine that it can live apart'.[55]

Non-Alignment

Non-alignment, which became the signature policy in Indian diplomacy, was foreshadowed prior to independence when the freedom movement promoted religion as a rallying point and source of national pride. An observer remarked that 'Hindus are always elated when they hear that a problem is going to be solved all by itself',[56] reflecting the trait of agnosticism in Hinduism – 'There the eye goes not, speech goes not, nor mind, we know not, we understand not how one would teach it'.[57] Non-alignment was the shifting middle ground between two extremes while taking the extremes into account, an attitude dear to Jainism and Buddhism.

Peaceful coexistence was urged by officials like Girija Shankar Bajpai: 'Only the Great Powers can hope to be completely sovereign and even their sovereignty may dwell in the perilous shadow of war unless they learn to live in enmity based on understanding and compromise'.[58] In 1946 Nehru said, 'We propose as far as possible to keep away from power politics of groups aligned against one another which have led in the past to world wars . . . we believe that peace and freedom are indivisible'.[59] Non-alignment was practical for a newly independent country lacking resources but under the influence of Gandhi and Nehru, was framed in morality and idealism. For pragmatic reasons, a national consensus and its connection with non-violence, non-alignment was the only policy a follower of Gandhi could adopt. 'I once heard Nehru say', writes Yezdi Gundevia, 'that Indian foreign policy was so simple that even an *ekkawala* [driver of a horse-drawn two-wheel cart] in Lucknow could understand it'.[60] It comprised anti-imperialism, anti-racialism and the creation of an area of peace despite the existence of two opposing power blocs. Nehru was naturally the main exponent of non-alignment's virtues, though he rarely used the term, preferring peaceful coexistence or independent foreign policy.

> Neither of these big blocs looks with favour on us . . . to some extent we have to plough a lonely furrow. One cannot rely merely on idealistic principles . . . whatever policy you may lay down, the main feature has to be to find out what is the most advantageous. . . .[61] We have repeatedly said that India should not ally herself with any of the power blocs. This policy fits in with our basic principles and is . . . beneficial even from the narrow opportunistic point of view.[62]

Nehru drew a distinction between non-alignment and neutrality. 'It is sometimes said that our foreign policy is one of neutrality or impartiality; that is not correct. These words can be used only when two countries are at war and a third remains aloof . . . our policy is merely to do what we think is right and not give in to pressure . . . I shall merely call it an independent foreign policy'.[63]

Nehru initially opposed any non-aligned conference and explained his misgivings: 'Non-alignment did not mean standing aloof only from the Soviet Union or the Western Powers; it means non-alignment with other countries as well'.[64] He realized that joining a movement would detract from the autonomous unilateral policy he favoured. He also decried any 'third force', saying, 'There has been mention of what is called a third force. I have not been able to understand exactly what it means'.[65] The 1961 Belgrade Conference eventually led to the creation of a formal movement, though this took place long after his death.

Highest and Lowest Points of Indian Non-Alignment

During the Korean War, India's role as an independent facilitator was disliked by every protagonist at one time or other, but established India's credentials. Nehru's finest moment was when Chinese Premier Zhou Enlai summoned Indian Ambassador K. M. Panikkar on 3 October 1950 to inform him that China was going to invade North Korea, with the unspoken request that India should communicate his warning to the West.

The peculiar mixture of internationalism and isolationalism which was non-alignment was viewed with suspicion by the West but generated moral influence for India and sustained Nehru's view that to ally with either super-power would mortgage India's emergence. The policy was neither isolationist nor neutral, since India criticized the big powers over Korea, Congo, Suez and Vietnam, but such criticism targeted expansionism rather than ideology.

American assistance to India after the 1962 China war meant that non-alignment required a fresh definition. Nehru fell back on the argument that the essence of the policy was refusal to join any military alliance in the context of the Cold War. The same argument, with diminishing credibility, was used for the Indo-Soviet Treaty of 1971 by Prime Minister Indira Gandhi, who sought regional pre-eminence and saw the Non-Aligned Movement as a means to project influence. Prime Minister Morarji Desai was unhappy with the Indo-Soviet Treaty but did not abrogate it. He professed 'genuine non-alignment' to introduce greater flexibility in foreign relations, but this change brought no benefits from the West or India's neighbours.

DEVIATIONS AND DEROGATIONS

Setbacks to an Ethical Foreign Policy

Gandhi's legacy encouraged India to play the moral teacher and resort to declaration of values rather than exercising diplomacy; India professed qualities not present in the policies of other states. The consequence was widespread criticism when India fell short of its own rhetoric. As Bajpai had warned before independence, 'Moral strength is not enough to prevent a clash between blocs or to protect neutrality. Armed power is the only safeguard for independence. Politics cannot be divorced from power'.[66] Deviations from pre-independence values were not caused by an apprehension that policies based on values would inhibit India's ambitions in a world of power politics; rather that Nehru soon realized that protecting Indian interests would result in departures from values, confessing, 'I am not strong enough even morally . . . to advise the world. . . .'[67] Not a crusading policy or a seer-like policy, we are too humble for that. We know our limitations'.[68]

The majority rule argument was used to justify military action against Junagadh and Hyderabad when persuasion failed to integrate these states. Force was also necessary to protect Kashmir from Pakistan-sponsored invasion, and Nehru conceded that 'New India has been forced to depart from the principles of Mahatma Gandhi in certain recent actions'.[69] At the UN in 1946 India denounced racial discrimination in South Africa but played it down in the United States despite sympathy for black people, and did not raise it in the British Commonwealth due to the desire not to make Commonwealth summits a forum for bilateral disputes such as Kashmir. Inconsistency also occurred when liberating the Portuguese colonies in India. Nehru repeatedly stressed the desirability of a peaceful solution:

> It has become necessary for these possessions to be politically incorporated in India . . . the Congress trusts this change will be brought about soon by peaceful means and the friendly cooperation of the governments concerned[70] . . . we stick to our policy [of non-violence] and shall continue to do so. . . .[71] Let me tell you once again today that we have no intention of taking military action in Goa but will solve it by peaceful means.[72]

But India resorted to economic blockade of Goa when the peaceful non-resistance movement failed, and in 1961 Goa was integrated with the Indian Union by force.

Early features of foreign policy were modified because it became clear that aggression and imperialism were not confined to Western capitalist nations. A moral stance was valid only through total impartiality between power blocs, which disappeared with different criteria for Russia and the West. Nehru pleaded a lack of information about the Soviet invasion of Hungary in 1956, which departed from India's values, irrespective of the merits or otherwise of communism. Nehru was anxious to avoid any impression that India was pro-West, but alienating the West, on which India was dependent economically, had clear limits, and whatever the faults of Western democracies, India was more in tune with them than with communist ideology. Nehru experienced the non-moral security, strategic and political complexities of the real world during the UN Security Council debates on Kashmir, the Hungarian crisis and the 1962 China war, which destroyed the ideological bases of his foreign policy.

Panchsheel: Five Principles of Peaceful Coexistence

Addressing Parliament on 15 May 1954, Nehru narrated with satisfaction the *Panchsheel* values of mutual respect for territorial integrity and sovereignty, mutual non-aggression, non-interference in each other's internal affairs, equality and mutual benefit and peaceful coexistence. Contrary to Indian belief, Nehru was not the coiner of these principles, nor were they drawn from ancient Indian, or specifically Buddhist, philosophy. Several had been enunciated in different previous contexts, like the 1949 Chinese Common Programme, the 1950 China-Soviet treaty and Zhou's letter to Nehru in 1950. Zhou gave shape to the composite package in 1954 for the Sino-Indian Agreement on Tibet, adding mutual non-aggression and peaceful coexistence to the principles formulated earlier.[73]

At the Asian Relations Conference at Bandung, when a rift arose between US allies who opposed communist expansionism and upheld the right of collective self-defence, and the advocates of peaceful coexistence and *Panchsheel*, Nehru abandoned thoughts of Asian unity. He had participated because India could not stay away while aspiring to a leadership role, despite his disclaimers: 'It is entirely wrong . . . to talk in terms of India being the leader . . . or to discuss the formation of any Asian bloc.[74] I do not mean to say that we in Asia are in any way superior ethically or morally'.[75] At the conference, Zhou's humility and moderation made an impact on delegates, including Western allies such as Thailand and the Philippines, at the expense of Nehru, who was seen as patronizing.

China War 1962 and After

The China war socialized India into the international order when Indian leaders realized the limits to their self-professed exceptional status. Southeast Asian nations neglected by Nehru like the Philippines, Thailand, Malaya and South Vietnam were among those that offered support, while countries like Burma (now Myanmar) and Ceylon (now Sri Lanka) no longer deferred to Nehru's advice as they did previously. Now it was Nehru who received advice from the six-nation Colombo group,[76] and the conflict had an enduring impact on India's psyche and foreign policy. For instance, the Indian delegation in the International Control Commission on Vietnam, after favouring Hanoi from 1954 to 1957, changed course to accuse Hanoi of aggression, and took a benign view of US military missions in the South. In 1972, the Commission shifted from Saigon to Hanoi, when India was excluded.[77]

Indian actions increasingly showed an Indo-centric, rather than global, character. Though the Nehruvian declaratory features remained, his successors Lal Bahadur Shastri sent Indian troops into Pakistan in 1965, Indira Gandhi into East Pakistan in 1971 and Rajiv Gandhi authorized open and covert interventions in Sri Lanka and Maldives and an economic blockade of Nepal. Overtures made in 1967 to India by the Association of Southeast Asian Nations were rebuffed, and India failed to get membership of the Organization of Islamic Conference in 1969. In 1975, Pakistan's Prime Minister Zulfiqar Bhutto taunted India not to 'aspire to control the destiny of the region and pretend to be the Mother India feeding her children'.[78] Nehru had attracted ridicule because he would not condemn the Union of Soviet Socialist Republics for its intervention in Hungary; Indira Gandhi repeated the same arguments on Soviet intervention in Czechoslovakia and later Afghanistan, holding that condemnations of superpowers were futile exercises that could exacerbate tensions. Indira Gandhi's principal aide, Parmeshwar Narain Haksar, wrote in 1969, 'Diplomacy is a function of power operating in a concrete place and time. Ideological considerations are meant for the neophytes'.[79]

Nuclear Weapons

The biggest discrepancy between rhetoric and practice was in the nuclear field. Until 1990, even after the so-called peaceful nuclear explosion of 1974, Indian prime ministers repeatedly disavowed the fabrication and use of nuclear weapons. Nehru in 1954 declared, 'India does not have the bomb, for we have neither the capacity nor the desire to produce one. . . .[80] India will in no event use atomic energy for destructive purposes . . . I am confident that this would be the policy of all future governments'.[81] Shastri in 1964 said, 'India's nuclear establishment is under firm orders not to make a single experiment, not to perfect a single device[82] . . . the possession of nuclear weapons would be directly opposed to the policy of peace and non-violence'.[83] After Chinese tests from 1965 to 1967 and its satellite launch in 1970, Indira Gandhi rejected the Non-Proliferation Treaty (NPT) of 1970 and undertook the 1974 test despite Pakistan lacking any similar capacity and the 'no first use' declaration by Beijing. But the solemn assurances continued: Indira Gandhi in 1982 said, 'India had no intention of embarking on the nuclear weapons programme',[84] and Rajiv Gandhi in 1985 said, 'We have not exploded any more devices. We have no stockpile. We do not have a nuclear weapon[85] . . . we would not like to develop a weapon and we are not developing a weapon'.[86]

The indefinite extension of the NPT, closer Sino-Pakistan ties, pressure to accede to the Comprehensive Test Ban Treaty and the Chinese test of 1995 provided the rationale for testing under Prime Minister Atal Behari Vajpayee in 1998. The non-aligned theory and ideas of Afro-Asian solidarity were attempts to project moral soft power, but India eventually joined the nuclear weapons club of hard power; nuclear weapon capacity was now portrayed as virtuous consolidation of self-esteem. In 2017, India, along with eight other nuclear weapon holders, refused to accept the UN Treaty on the Prohibition of Nuclear Weapons, which banned the use, development, testing or storing of nuclear weapons in any circumstances.

VALUES IN CONTEMPORARY INDIAN FOREIGN POLICY

Modern Foreign Policy

Judging from the debates in the Constituent Assembly, it is remarkable how domestic themes have remained constant for seventy years – communalism, corruption, caste, unemployment, inclusive development and gender equality. But in foreign policy there is no such continuity: The core value of morality has been long abandoned. As Nehru warned, 'It is not enough to have principles and ideals. The application of them, the implementation of them, depends on other circumstances. And these circumstances are hardly ever in our control. . . . Ultimately the foreign policy of every country is limited by the strength which that country possesses. Strength may be military or financial and may be also . . . moral'.[87] Hardly had Nehru died before morality was considered an attribute for individuals, but not nations.

Indian policy had been to reduce great power involvement in Asia and prevent global domination by any one power, its preference being for a security system that guaranteed national sovereignty and territorial integrity, and allowed India maximum manoeuvrability. Some later rare interludes recalled the days of high idealism; the Janata government hoped its moral stance, in scaling back its intelligence services and deporting foreign dissidents, would provoke a positive response, but there was no reciprocity. Prime Minister Gujral was also committed to idealism, seeking the high ground and addressing asymmetry with neighbours through non-reciprocal concessions in benign bilateralism. His influence was brief, and he was accused of lack of realism.

The government under Vajpayee comprised persons affiliated to the Rashtriya Swayamsevak Sangh (RSS), the ideological parent of the Bharatiya Janata Party (BJP), and described as Hindu nationalists in the tradition of Savarkar, but their influence on foreign policy was negligible due to Vajpayee's political skills and, more importantly, his fragile parliamentary majority. This handicap was removed during the premiership of Narendra Modi, who, supported by the Hindu right wing, secured an unambiguous mandate in 2014. Mohan Bhagwat said the RSS believed in 'no discrimination, and oneness of our nation and oneness of the world',[88] but his followers are less emollient, believing that Hindus today must confront any colonial-style denigration of weakness and effeminacy. They claim *Hindutva* represented the national consciousness, distinct from competitive faiths like Islam and Christianity. This approach, where the theological and social value of the religious 'other' is belittled, contrasts with traditional Indian respect for all faiths. In foreign affairs, *Hindutva* hankers for the Chanakya concept of *Akhand Bharat* or the imprecise frontiers of Chandragupta Maurya's third-century B.C. empire, or of the British Raj whose strategic vision was based on logical territorial limits for defence and the exercise of sovereignty. Modi evokes this in his appeal for freedom and human rights in Pakistan-occupied Kashmir, the Northern Areas and Baluchistan.

The centre of gravity in Indian politics has shifted rightwards: A new assertiveness is reflected in symbols of patriotism and respect for the military. In foreign affairs there is no reference to philosophical values other than *Hindutva*, nor to Nehru and non-alignment as points of reference. But universality and exceptionalism, which are hard-wired in the Indian psyche, continue to be promulgated. President Ram Nath Kovind declared:

> But our endeavours are not for ourselves alone. Down the ages, India has believed in the philosophy of *Vasudhaiva Kutumbakam* – the World is My Family. It is appropriate that the land of Lord Buddha should lead the world in its search for peace, tranquillity and ecological balance. India's voice counts in today's world. The entire planet is drawn to Indian culture and soft power. The global community looks to us for solutions to international problems. . . . In a globalized world, our responsibilities are also global.[89]

There is respect for Gandhi as father of the nation, but without the invocation of non-violence. Robust resistance to threats from China and its alliance with Pakistan is advocated, with concomitant emphasis on ties with the United States. In 2001 Vajpayee offered the United States the use of airports and ports; in 2016 Modi concluded agreements with Washington that included access to military facilities. Israel, praised by Savarkar before its statehood, is in favour. While India was first known for projection of soft power, under Modi there is an assumed virility, though this approach lacks credibility without the backing of comprehensive national strength. There is open support for the Indian Diaspora, and legislation is being considered to facilitate citizenship for Hindu, Sikh, Buddhist and Christian refugees from neighbouring Muslim countries. There is greater national pride and official prickliness; Indian diplomats are reluctant to be seen as petitioners – 'Staking out a moral position moves much of the discussion onto a plane that is considered non-negotiable [and] compromise tends to be equated with weakness'.[90] This has adversely affected India's world trade policy and the work of international civil society on issues like freedom of expression and religion, indigenous peoples, violence against women, human trafficking and Dalits. In asserting Westphalian principles, an Indian tradition has been established wherein any need to be accountable abroad on matters pertaining to its internal jurisdiction is stoutly rejected.

CONCLUSION

The contrast between Nehruvian and current foreign policy lies in the values-based idealism of the pre-independence leadership and the realist, non-ideological attitudes that emerged soon after Nehru's death and in a more pronounced manner after the end of the Cold War. In the early period, internationalism comprised non-alignment, self-reliance, non-violence and nuclear disarmament, when *Ahimsa* was linked to ideas of an alternative world order in which force was minimal, and all countries emancipated from imperialism would be treated equally, regardless of status. After 1990, India's policies implicitly call upon the world to recognize it as an emerging great power; India had to be one of the poles in any multipolar world. Its objectives continue to be ostensibly peaceful, with Modi stating, 'we contribute to the world and do not take anything from the world. For India, the land of Buddha and Gandhi, peace is not just a word, peace is in our veins'.[91] Modi is a modern man heading the BJP, a party that looks to a putative Vedic past before the Muslim invasions when there was within safe and extended borders of an *Akhand Bharat* a coherent cultural *Hindutva* connect of peace and harmony.

However, Indian core values comprise an unique exceptionalism grounded in India's 'soft power' – the power of ideas, spirituality, literature, music, cinema, arts, pluralist democracy, the power of culture and civilization – along with the firm conviction that the world looks towards India for moral leadership. The home minister said, 'We want to keep the country's integrity intact, not just for the welfare of the people of India but for the welfare of the entire world . . . the government wants to make India a world guru',[92] and Modi returned to this theme: 'The present era, being considered as an era of knowledge, our role and responsibility have increased. We have to emerge the universal leader not only to give new direction to the world but also to protect our own heritage . . . the whole world is looking up to India with expectations. The world is ready but we are not ready'.[93] This goes hand in hand with the desire for decision-making autonomy. India will engage in strategic and transactional partnerships where its political and economic gains are evident, but the nature of its aspirations remains potentially adverse to its greater integration with the global system. These two aspects will remain the dominant values in Indian foreign policy irrespective of whichever party is elected to form the government in New Delhi.

NOTES

1. Ramesh Thakur, 'India's Vietnam Policy', *Asian Survey* 19, no. 10 (October 1979): 965.

2. Jawaharlal Nehru, *Selected Works*, Series 2, Vol. 8 (3 November 1948): 290–91.

3. Ton That Thien, *India and Southeast Asia 1947–60* (Geneva: Librarie Droz, 1967), 47.

4. Dipti Patel, 'Religious Foundations of Human Rights': 8. https://www.nottingham.ac.uk/hrlc/documents/publications/hrlcommentary2005/religiousfoundationshumanrights.pdf.

5. *Hindustan Times* (11 September 2017).

6. Nehru, *Selected Works*, Vol. 14 Part 2 (2 May 1950): 503.

7. Saka Era attributed to the Buddhist Kushan king Kanishka (AD 127–150) was chosen as the calendar in 1957. It commences on 22 March with the zero year as AD 78.

8. Nehru, *Selected Works*, Vol. 13 (3 November 1949): 447.

9. Ibid., Vol. 26 (21 June 1954): 612.

10. Ibid., Vol. 39 (24 October 1957): 42.

11. Ibid., Vol. 13 (24 August 1949): 287. Letter to sister Vijayalakshmi Pandit.

12. Charles Allen, *Ashoka* (London: Little Brown, 2012), 406. Ashokan Rock Edict 1.

13. T. A. Keenleyside, 'Diplomatic Apprenticeship: Pre-Independence Origins of Indian Diplomacy', *India Quarterly: A Journal of International Affairs* (1987): 112. journals.sagepub.com/doi/abs/10.1177/097492848704300202.

14. Jawaharlal Nehru, Foreword to Rammanohar Lohia's 'Foreign Policies of the Indian National Congress and the British Labour Party' (AICC 1938).

15. Bimal Prasad, *The Origins of Indian Foreign Policy* (Calcutta: Bookland, 1962), 198.

16. Nehru, *Selected Works*, Vol. 10 (8 March 1949): 447–48.

17. Ibid., Vol. 6 (24 April 1948): 163.

18. Sitakant Mishra, *Parmanu Politics* (New Delhi: Gyan Books, 2015), 98.

19. Nehru, *Selected Works*, Vol. 12 (13 August 1949): 437.

20. Ibid., Vol. 25 (11 April 1954): 34.

21. Ibid., Vol. 28 (23 April 1955): 114.

22. Atharava Veda-Samjnana Sukta quoted in P. K. Yadav 'Concept of Human Rights in Hinduism' (2015). shodhganga.inflibnet.ac.in/bitstream/10603/ . . . /10%20 chapter%205%20hinduism.pdf.

23. Arvind Sharma, *Hinduism and Human Rights* (New Delhi: Oxford University Press, Law in India Series, 2003), 52.

24. Keenleyside, 'Diplomatic Apprenticeship', 111.

25. Ibid.

26. Ibid.

27. Rammanohar Lohia quoted in Keenleyside, 'Diplomatic Apprenticeship', 112.

28. Theresita Schaffer and Howard Schaffer, *India and the Global High Table* (Noida, India: HarperCollins, 2016), 17.

29. Nehru, *Selected Works*, Vol. 1 (5 September 1946): 439.

30. Ibid., Vol. 5 (19 March 1948): 597.

31. Ibid., Vol. 8 (16 December 1948): 333.

32. Ibid., Vol. 10 (22 March 1949): 459.

33. Ibid., Vol. 18 (21 May 1952): 439.

34. Ibid., Vol. 23 (18 July 1953): 56.

35. T. C. A. Raghavan, *The People Next Door: The Curious History of India's Relations with Pakistan* (New Delhi: HarperCollins, 2017), 196.

36. *The Telegraph*, Calcutta (3 May 2017).

37. Rityusa Tiwari, 'Regional Leadership in South and East Asia', Pavate unpublished paper, Karnataka University (2013): 52.

38. Nehru, *Selected Works*, Vol. 15 Part 1 (3 August 1950): 346.

39. Jawaharlal Nehru, 18 March 1946 at Singapore, quoted in Iqbal Singh, *Between Two Fires* (New Delhi: Orient Longmans, 1992), 153.

40. Nehru, *Selected Works*, Vol. 1 (7 September 1946): 404.

41. Radio Broadcast 7 September 1946 quoted in Singh, *Between Two Fires*, 169.

42. Nehru, *Selected Works*, Vol. 1 (5 December 1946): 417.

43. Ibid., Vol. 8 (12 February 1948): 325.

44. Ibid., Vol. 1 (4 September 1946): 437.

45. Ibid., Vol. 15, Part 1 (3 October 1950): 500.

46. Keenleyside, 'Diplomatic Apprenticeship', 110.

47. Nehru, *Selected Works*, Vol. 8 (3 November 1948): 291.

48. Michael Brecher quoted in Thien, *India and Southeast Asia 1947–60*, 33.

49. Sushanta Dattagupta, *A Random Walk in Shantiniketan Ashram* (New Delhi: Niyogi, 2016), 119

50. Willard Range, *Jawaharlal Nehru's World View* (Athens: University of Georgia, 1961), 120.

51. Bimal Prasad, *India's Foreign Policy* (New Delhi: Vikas 1979), 485.

52. Ibid., 481.

53. Nehru, *Selected Works*, Vol. 16, Part 1 (28 March 1951): 508.

54. Ibid., Vol. 37 (23 March 1957): 485.

55. Jawaharlal Nehru, Independence Day Address, 14 August 1947. http://nehrumemorial.nic.in/en/gift-gallery.html?id=214&tmpl=component.

56. Koenraad Elst, *Who Is a Hindu?* (New Delhi: Voice of India, 2002), 324.

57. Sarvepalli Radhakrishnan, *The Hindu View of Life* (London: Unwin, 1960), 20.

58. Girija Shankar Bajpai, 'Quarterly Report October-December 1945', *IOR/L/ P&S/12/4627* Agent General for India in Washington.

59. Nehru, *Selected Works*, Vol. 1 (7 September 1946): 404.

60. Yezdi D. Gundevia, *Outside the Archives* (Hyderabad: Sangam Books, 1984), vi.

61. Nehru, *Selected Works*, Vol. 4 (4 December 1947): 597–600.

62. Ibid., Vol. 7 (12 September 1948): 612.

63. Ibid., Vol. 25 (24 March 1954): 385.

64. Theresita Schaffer and Howard Schaffer, *India and the Global High Table* (Noida, India: HarperCollins, 2016), 24.

65. Nehru, *Selected Works*, Vol. 21 (16 February 1953): 30.

66. Girija Shankar Bajpai, 'The International Yearbook of International Affairs' (1952): 7.

67. Nehru, 'Diplomatic Apprenticeship', Vol. 15, Part 1 (4 August 1950): 350.

68. Ibid., Vol. 39 (2 September 1957): 530.

69. Ibid., Vol. 13 (3 November 1949): 377.

70. Ibid., Vol. 8 (19 December 1948): 427.

71. Ibid., Vol. 25 (24 March 1954): 390.

72. Ibid., Vol. 29 (15 August 1955): 45.

73. A full treatment is found in Chandrasekhar Dasgupta, 'A Brief History of Panchsheel', *Economic and Political Review* LI, no. 1 (2 January 2016): 26–31.

74. Nehru, *Selected Works*, Vol. 7 (12 September 1948): 611.

75. Ibid., Vol. 10 (8 March 1949): 446.
76. Burma, Cambodia, Ceylon, Egypt, Ghana, Indonesia.
77. A full treatment is found in Thien, *India and Southeast Asia 1947–60*, 145 seq.
78. Raghavan, *The People Next Door,* 129.
79. P. N. Haksar, quoted in Jairam Ramesh, *Intertwined Lives*, 136.
80. Nehru, *Selected Works*, Vol. 25 (11 April 1954): 31.
81. Jawaharlal Nehru, 24 July 1957, quoted in Mishra, *Parmanu Politics*, 93.
82. Mishra, *Parmanu Politics*, 107.
83. Ibid., 111.
84. Ibid., 129.
85. Ibid., 134.
86. Ibid., 136.
87. Nehru, *Selected Works*, Vol. 21 (16 February 1953): 25–29.
88. ' "Sangh Does Not Run the BJP, BJP Does Not Run the Sangh", Says RSS Chief Mohan Bhagwat,' *Scroll.in* (13 September 2017). https://scroll.in/latest/850458/sangh-does-not-run-the-bjp-bjp-does-not-run-the-sangh-says-rss-chief-mohan-bhagwat.
89. *The Indian Express* (25 July 2017).
90. Teresita Schaffer and Howard Schaffer, *India and the Global High Table* (Noida, India: HarperCollins, 2016), 116.
91. Kallol Bhattacherjee, 'For India, Peace Is Not a Word; It Is in Our Veins: Modi', *The Hindu* (14 November 2017). www.thehindu.com/todays-paper/for-india . . . is-not . . . modi/article20418068.ece.
92. Home Minister Rajnath Singh, quoted in *The Telegraph*, New Delhi (15 February 2018), 1.
93. *The Pioneer* (16 February 2018), 1.

BIBLIOGRAPHY

Allen, Charles. *Ashoka.* London: Little Brown, 2012.
Bajpai, Girija Shankar. 'The International Yearbook of International Affairs' Madras (1952). https://archive.org/stream/in.ernet.dli.2015.101545/2015.101545.The-Indian-Year-Book-Of-International-Affairs-1952_djvu.txt.
Dasgupta, Chandrasekhar. 'A Brief History of Panchsheel'. *Economic and Political Review* LI, no. 1 (2 January 2016): 26–31.
Dattagupta, Sushanta. *A Random Walk in Shantiniketan Ashram.* New Delhi: Niyogi, 2016.
Elst, Koenraad. *Who Is a Hindu?* New Delhi: Voice of India, 2002.
Gundevia, Yezdi D. *Outside the Archives.* Hyderabad: Sangam Books, 1984.
Keenleyside, T. A. 'Diplomatic Apprenticeship: Pre-Independence Origins of Indian Diplomacy'. *India Quarterly: A Journal of International Affairs,* (1987). journals.sagepub.com/doi/abs/10.1177/097492848704300202.
Lohia, Rammanohar. 'Foreign Policies of the Indian National Congress and the British Labour Party' (AICC 1938).

Mishra, Sitakanta. *Parmanu Politics.* New Delhi: Gyan Books, 2015.

Nehru, Jawaharlal. *Selected Works, Series 2*, Volumes 1–39.

Patel, Dipti. 'Religious Foundations of Human Rights'. https://www.nottingham. ac.uk/hrlc/documents/publications/hrlcommentary2005/religiousfoundationshumanrights.pdf.

Prasad, Bimal. *India's Foreign Policy.* New Delhi: Vikas, 1979.

Prasad, Bimal. *The Origins of Indian Foreign Policy.* Calcutta: Bookland, 1962.

Radhakrishnan, Sarvepalli. *The Hindu View of Life.* London: Unwin, 1960.

Raghavan, T. C. A. *The People Next Door: The Curious History of India's Relations with Pakistan.* New Delhi: HarperCollins, 2017.

Ramesh, Jairam. *Intertwined Lives.* New Delhi: Simon & Schuster, 2018.

Range, Willard. *Jawaharlal Nehru's World View.* Athens: University of Georgia, 1961.

Schaffer, Teresita and Howard Schaffer. *India and the Global High Table.* Noida, India: HarperCollins, 2016.

Sharma, Arvind. *Hinduism and Human Rights.* New Delhi: Oxford University Press, Law in India Series, 2003.

Singh, Iqbal. *Between Two Fires.* New Delhi: Orient Longmans, 1992.

Thakur, Ramesh. 'India's Vietnam Policy'. *Asian Survey* 19, no. 10 (October 1979).

Thien, Ton That. *India and Southeast Asia 1947–60.* Geneva: Librarie: Droz, 1967.

Yadav, P. K. 'Concept of Human Rights in Hinduism' (2015). shodhganga.inflibnet.ac.in/bitstream/10603/ . . . /10%20chapter%205%20hinduism. pdf.

Chapter 9

Values in Myanmar's Foreign Policy

Neutralism, Isolationism and Multi-Engagement

Sanjay Pulipaka and Chaw Chaw Sein

In 2016, addressing a press conference in China, State Counsellor Aung San Suu Kyi stated, 'Non-aligned foreign policy is something that we adopted from the moment we became independent in 1948. . . . I think different governments in my country have always tried to follow a non-aligned foreign policy. . . . Now we hope that we'll be able to follow our traditional non-aligned foreign policy successfully'.[1] It is interesting that more than one and a half decades after the end of the Cold War, Suu Kyi, in spite of her intense opposition to the previous military governments, found it important to endorse the policy of neutrality. Though there continues to be numerous faultlines such as ethnic conflicts, divergent views on devolution of power and disagreements on the 2008 Constitution, on foreign policy there is almost a rare unanimity on the need to pursue a non-aligned policy among various political actors in Myanmar. This unanimity has a long history dating back to independence. This chapter, therefore, seeks to identify factors that may have triggered neutralist policy and will map as to how it was implemented since independence.

ORIGINS OF NEUTRALISM – DOMESTIC FACTORS

Buddhism and Neutralism

The majority of the population in Myanmar practises Theravāda Buddhism, which has an impact on politics and society in the country. In institutional terms, the Buddhist Sangha may not have a clearly defined administrative structure like that of the military, but it is probably the only institution that is similar to the military in size, influence and national presence.[2] On the other hand, the precise impact of Buddhist values on politics and more specifically on foreign policy is difficult to quantify. Nonetheless, some tentative linkages between Theravāda Buddhism and the country's non-alignment policy can be attempted.

Theravāda Buddhism is centred on the individual's quest for enlightenment. While Buddha's teachings show the way, each being has to define his or her path to enlightenment.[3] Since each being has to define his or her own path, each needs to have a clear understanding of human nature. Theravāda Buddhism holds that humans are fundamentally driven by desire and simultaneously keeps open the possibility of attaining enlightenment.[4] The enunciation of the *Atthangika-magga* (Eightfold Path)[5] suggests the process through which a being can attain enlightenment. This dual dynamic of humans as inherently weak but also capable of attaining a higher moral status tends to define the political discourse in Myanmar. The advocates of an expansive state base their arguments on negative conceptions of human nature, and advocates of a more liberal state cite the inherent ability of human nature to take higher moral actions.[6]

In addition to the emphasis on enlightenment and the eightfold path, there are four principal virtues in Buddhism, which are called *brahmaviharas* (*byama-so taya* in Burmese), and they include *metta* (loving-kindness), *karuna* (compassion), *mudita* (sympathetic joy) and *upekkha* (equanimity).[7] *Upekkha* constitutes an important concept in Buddhism, which roughly translates into 'equanimity' or 'neutrality'. Equanimity is a quality of maintaining calmness even in the face of adversity. This also means that *upekkha* is behaviour devoid of excesses or deficiencies. U Silananda notes that since *upekkha* 'prevents deficiency or excess, it is not partial to any of the concomitants. Therefore, its function is also to inhibit partiality; it manifests as neutrality'.[8] However, it should be noted that neutrality is 'based on the vigilant presence of mind, not on indifferent dullness and it is often the result of rigorous training'.[9] Therefore, *upekkha* is not any neutrality but constitutes positive neutrality. The principle of positive neutrality is critical to ensure that the other principles are adhered to in a healthy manner, as Nyanaponika Thera notes: 'Isolated virtues, if unsupported by other qualities which give them either the needed firmness or pliancy, often deteriorate into their own characteristic defects'.[10] Given the centrality of the *upekkha* in Buddhist thought, it may have also translated into Myanmar's policy of positive neutrality in international relations.

Socialism, Domestic Unrest and Neutralism

Like various nationalist movements in many colonies, socialist ideas had a strong influence on the nationalist movement in Myanmar. While socialist ideas strongly influenced the Thakin movement, there was considerable discussion on the development path that Myanmar should adopt. Aung San, the main leader of the liberation struggle, noted that given the country's backward economy it would be imprudent to adopt a communist path to development. As he noted, 'Deeply touched as we are by the planned economy to be practised under communism, still we are still very strongly opposed to it'.[11] He was more interested in a middle path to 'socialism based on the gradual restriction of the private sector while at the same time encouraging the state and cooperative sectors'.[12]

In early years after independence, Myanmar had a robust presence of communists inside parliament as well as outside, constantly critiquing the government's foreign policy as leaning towards the American-led bloc. A fairly large number of administrators and educated persons were trained in the West, and as a consequence, there was concern that the government should not lean towards the communist bloc. And the insurgency of the Communist Party of Burma, which received support from China, ensured that any possibility of joining the communist bloc was limited. This diametrically opposed political current ensured that a policy of neutralism was followed.

Immediately after independence, Myanmar plunged into civil war. Various armed ethnic groups rebelled against the authority of the Rangoon government. These armed insurgent groups had sympathies from varied international actors; for instance, the communists received occasional support from China. Some of the armed ethnic groups elicited sympathy from Western countries and neighbours such as Thailand. As a consequence of the activities of these armed groups, the writ of the government often ended at the outskirts of Rangoon city. Given such fragility, it was difficult for the government to enter alliance frameworks. Prime Minister U Nu noted an alliance with one particular bloc might encourage others/outsiders to get involved in domestic affairs and thereby give a fillip to insurgent violence.[13] Neutralism was therefore also seen as a policy aimed at dissuading others from getting involved in domestic affairs. On the other hand, the policy of neutralism allowed Myanmar to access military hardware from countries such as India and Yugoslavia without generating anxiety in either of the blocs.[14]

Economic Imperatives

Myanmar's economy immediately after independence was characterized by low investment and considerable poverty. This meant that the route of private-sector-led development was not feasible as the domestic capitalist class was not robust. For a recently independent country, inviting the private sector from other countries was not a feasible option. All this obliged the country to move forward with the state-led development model when government launched an eight-year national economic development plan in 1952 called the Pyidawtha Plan. The plan was conceptualized by a private firm of the United States – Knappen Tippetts Abbett – and was financed by the US Technical Cooperation Administration.[15] It is interesting to note that a private sector company from the United States was hired to conceptualize planned economic development, essentially a Soviet approach. The policy of neutralism enabled the young nation state to adapt many such innovative ways to the challenges of global politics. Further, the non-alignment policy allowed Myanmar to access aid from diverse sources. For instance, from 1955 onwards Japan provided annual aid of $20 million as part of reparations, which also facilitated greater economic interactions between the two countries.[16] The United States also provided some modest development assistance.[17]

The policy of neutralism enabled Myanmar to respond to structural challenges confronting its external economic engagement. In the 1950s, rice exports accounted for almost 70 to 80 percent of export earnings.[18] However, during the same period, others such as the United States, Australia and other Asian countries also exported considerable amounts of rice and other cereals, and thereby created severe competition in the international market. To overcome these challenges, Myanmar entered into rice purchase agreements with China, USSR, Czechoslovakia, Hungary, East Germany, Poland and Romania.[19] Quite often these agreements involved barter arrangements, wherein in lieu of rice purchase, Myanmar would receive goods and not cash. The necessity to dispose of its excess rice and the need to diversify terms of trade had an impact on Myanmar's foreign policy in terms of pushing it towards a policy of neutrality in international affairs.[20]

NEUTRALISM – FORMATIVE YEARS

The role of Sangha as an important institution in mediating state-society relations witnessed a decline during the colonial period but did not entirely disappear from the social space. Monks such as U Ottama, and groups such as Young Men's Buddhist Association and the General Council of Buddhist Associations, played an important role in the anti-colonial struggle.[21] Subsequently, after independence, the Constitution of the Union of Burma that came into force in 1948[22] stated that the 'state recognizes the special position of Buddhism as the faith professed by the great majority of the citizens of the Union'.[23] There was also a revival of Buddhist organizations, and important events such as the Sixth Buddhist Council were held between 1954 and 1956. In 1961, under Prime Minister U Nu, the law declaring Buddhism as an official religion was approved by the parliament.[24] There was an instrumentalist dimension to promoting Buddhist identity immediately after independence.

Michael W. Charney notes that U Nu and other leaders 'believed that bolstering Buddhism among the general population would help to create an obstacle to communist victory' in the country.[25] However, the geopolitical location of the country ensured that domestic contest against communism did not get translated into a pro-Western posture in Myanmar's foreign policy.

As with many other countries, geography tended to define Myanmar's foreign policy. Located between two major powers, India and China, it became imperative that a neutral position was maintained in foreign policy. As U Nu noted: 'Take a glance at our geographical position – Thailand in the East, China in the North, India in the West, and stretching southward, Malaya, Singapore and so on. We are hemmed in like a tender gourd among the cactus. We cannot move in an inch'.[26] The political leadership during the early years of independence was acutely aware of its geographic context and the vulnerabilities it entailed. Given the diversity of countries surrounding Myanmar, there was very little space to pursue Cold War alliance politics.

In the early years of independence, Myanmar's territorial boundary with China was not well demarcated. There was anxiety that China might indulge in territorial aggression, which prompted the leaders to avoid foreign policy postures that would invite an aggressive Chinese response. Kyaw Nyein, a minister in the U Nu government, articulated this concern when he stated:

We don't consider China a menace, but we accept a possibility of China one day invading us. We are not alone in this concern. Our neighbours will also be perturbed as our fate may likely be theirs. We are entering into closer relations with India, Pakistan, Indonesia, and are trying to find a formula for peaceful co-existence in this part of our world. We don't want to do anything that will provoke China, but if she does invade, I am confident that the national spirit of our people will stand firm against her. We don't want Communist Russia or Communist China, but being a small nation, we must find ways and means of avoiding embroilment in power blocs.[27]

In addition to staying away from power blocs, the leadership made well-calibrated efforts to convey its friendly intentions to China. The Indian government was approached with the request to delay the recognition of the People's Republic of China (PRC) so that Myanmar would be the first to recognize the PRC,[28] being one of the first non-communist countries to do so. Subsequently, on 29 June 1954, China and Myanmar 'affirmed the Five Principles of Peaceful Coexistence as guiding principles in their bilateral relations'.[29] In 1955, Myanmar played an important role in preventing an invitation being sent to Taiwan to participate in the Afro-Asian conference.[30]

With the Communist Party of China under Mao Zedong emerging victorious in 1949, the nationalist Kuomintang (KMT) forces fled to Shan State in northern Myanmar. By 1951, approximately 15,000 KMT troops were operating out of Myanmar with the covert assistance of the United States.[31] Their presence deep inside Shan State was a source of concern not only for China but also for Rangoon. To compound the challenges, the KMT forces regularly carried out attacks on PRC from bases in Shan State. The government was helpless in disarming the KMT troops, as its forces were already stretched in fighting numerous insurgencies. Therefore, the U Nu government approached the United Nations (UN) to ensure the withdrawal of KMT forces. The possibility that the conflict could spiral out of control resulting in war with China prompted Myanmar's leaders to make persistent efforts to distance themselves from the actions of the KMT by often expressing disappointment with the UN in dealing effectively with the issue. While the KMT forces were expatriated to Taiwan/Formosa in 1955, the experience brought home the challenges confronting a nation with the presence of foreign troops on its soil. The KMT experience increased the Myanmar leaders' scepticism of military alliances.

In 1956, the border dispute between China and Myanmar escalated, and reports suggested that Chinese troops moved into Burmese territory.[32] In spite of the threat from a much bigger neighbour, Rangoon refrained from diluting its neutralist foreign policy and engaged China in prolonged negotiations which resulted in the 1960 Burma-China Boundary Treaty.[33] There was a strong opinion among Myanmar's leaders that their neutral foreign policy facilitated this boundary settlement agreement. As U Nu noted,

> As you perhaps know, Great Britain, at the height of her power, when the sun never set upon her empire, failed to get the entire border between Burma and China properly delimited. It required many months of patient negotiation to have the border clearly defined, and largely because of our policy of active neutrality between the world power blocs, we were able to get a large slice of Chinese territory in exchange for three villages.[34]

During the early years of independence, U Nu and subsequently Prime Minister Ba Swe often stated that since Burma was a small country, it should refrain from taking part in power politics. For instance, U Nu in 1954 observed that 'as you all know, our Union is a small country . . . with the internal situation unsettled, economy unstable and military strength poor'.[35] Ba Swe, at the peak of border tensions with China in 1956, called for restraint by stating 'it behooves a small country to lessen tension. Our foreign policy is based on the necessity to reduce tensions and avoid causes of tensions which are inherent in military alliances like SEATO'.[36] This approach of positioning itself as a small country was in contrast to the approach of Indian leaders who often referred to India as a great power which due to its past genius had a special role to play in global politics. Nonetheless, if the country's economic and military strength was factored in, the neutralist policy allowed its leadership to play a disproportionately larger role on the global stage. U Nu was recognized as a global statesman, and Myanmar's strict adherence to neutralism in the early years of independence helped U Thant to be elected UN secretary-general. Leading American newspapers noted that U Thant was respected for his tough neutralism: 'U Thant's . . . appointment reflected non-aligned Burma's good standing with both the US and USSR'.[37] In spite of the disclaimer of being a small country, Myanmar's impact in the 1950s and the 1960s on global politics was considerable.

ISOLATIONISM OR NEUTRALISM?

After General Ne Win's military coup in 1962, Myanmar witnessed significant changes in domestic policy, and there was a relative decline in the importance accorded to the Buddhist organizations. The military leadership sought control of the Sangha by either direct state intervention or influencing the Buddhist organization to initiate reform measures. These measures included stressing the need for promoting 'correct' religious practices/principles, awarding honorific titles to some of the revered monks and developing organization structures for Sangha by calling for the creation of proper membership/registration mechanisms.[38] The approach of according greater primacy to the State in its relationship with society was also extended to the economic sphere.

Ne Win ushered in the 'Burmese Way to Socialism', with the state playing a predominant role in the economy by taking over 'almost all foreign trade, monopolized distribution and instituted tax rate that virtually drove out the private sector'.[39] This meant that important sections of economic activity were nationalized, including the properties of large numbers of the Chinese and Indian Diaspora. Myanmar's bilateral relationship with India and China experienced some stress, and more so in the case of China, because anti-Chinese riots took place in 1967. The Chinese government scaled up its pro-Communist Party of Burma propaganda and was sharply critical of the Myanmar government.[40] In spite of the downturn in the relations with China, there was no dilution in Myanmar's neutral foreign policy posture.

While on the domestic front there were significant changes in government policy, on the external front, Ne Win ensured continuity by adhering to the policy of neutralism. Immediately after the military coup, the Revolutionary Council declared that it would adhere by the policy of 'positive neutrality', and addressing Burmese ambassadors, Ne Win stated:

What is well defined and clear-cut in our international relations is our policy of strict neutrality of non-alignment. It is extremely important for our ambassadors to adhere to this policy in the discharge of their duties. . . . Especially at this juncture when international politics is overshadowed by the split between the East and the West, the split doesn't stop with these two power blocs but at times has repercussions on us. Only if we can live up to our policy of neutrality, can we hope to meet the situation.[41]

A few years later, in 1968 he repeated, 'I wish again to declare that Burma will not discard her policy of strict neutrality under any circumstances'.[42]

Ne Win's neutralism moved closer to isolationism, and economic engagement with the rest of the world started declining. While earlier prime ministers such as U Nu engaged with the international community with vigour, Myanmar under Ne Win had constrained interactions. On the other hand, some reports suggest that the description of isolationism to define external engagement is somewhat exaggerated. For instance,

> Though the doors of Burma may seem closed to most British tourists and journalists, it is not closed to the world. Indeed, it has contact with more countries than ever before in its history . . . representatives of eastern European countries and West Germany, apart from Asian neighbours, solicit invitations [from Burma]. . . . A stroll through the bookshops show that the Burmese are encouraged to read foreign books.[43]

It is possible that in the first few years after Ne Win took over, the country was relatively open, but there is no denying that over time Myanmar's external engagement declined considerably. US official correspondence in the mid-1960s indicated that Myanmar discouraged foreign contacts and diplomatic relations were kept to the minimum.[44] Ne Win sought to ensure that the presence of the West in society was reduced considerably and the Ford Foundation, Asia Foundation, Fulbright, British Council and foreign information outlets were asked to leave the country.[45] While Ne Win's foreign policy appeared isolationist, he ensured a strict neutralist policy. On the Partial Nuclear Test Ban Treaty and the Sino-Indian border dispute, he moved away from Chinese positions.[46]

The Sino-Soviet rift and the Sino-US rapprochement had a significant impact on Myanmar's non-aligned policy. The Sino-US rapprochement meant that Myanmar had greater strategic space to engage the United States without being subjected to accusations from China of dilution in the policy of neutralism. The Sino-Soviet rift implied that three powers were competing for influence in Asia and Southeast Asia in particular. Myanmar's policy of neutralism had to balance the relationship between three powers – China, the Soviet Union and the United States. As a consequence, in spite of Ne Win's deep suspicion about the US attitude, Myanmar's relationship with the United States witnessed some improvement. Cooperation was growing between the two countries in combating narcotics. Myanmar even received equipment such as military helicopters from the United States, and its military officials were sent to the United States to receive training in anti-narcotics operations.[47] The Sino-Soviet rift also enabled Myanmar to received aid from multiple pro-Western institutional and governmental frameworks; for instance, in 1979 it received assistance from the Asian Development Bank (ADB); World Bank; and countries such as Britain, Italy, Japan and Germany.[48]

The Sino-Soviet rift also had an impact on Myanmar's attitude towards the non-alignment movement. The election of Cuba as chair of the Non-Aligned Summit in 1979 in Havana was seen by many as growing Soviet influence within the movement,[49] and Myanmar increasingly felt uncomfortable with this alleged pro-Soviet stance. By the late 1970s, China and Myanmar were concerned about a close Soviet-Vietnam partnership, and it became important for Myanmar to demonstrate it would not be part of any explicit or covert grouping to promote the interests of the Soviet Union. Foreign Minister Myint Maung launched a scathing critique of the Non-Aligned Movement (NAM), stating:

> The principles of the Movement are not recognisable anymore; they are not merely dim, they are dying. Differences of views and outlooks are only to be expected, but deliberate deviations from the basic principles can only be fatal to the Movement. And it is not enough for the Movement just to exist in name. There are among us those who wish to uphold the principles and preserve their own and the Movement's integrity. But obviously, there are also those who do not, and who deliberately exploit the Movement to gain their own grand designs. We cannot allow ourselves to be so exploited . . . the delegation of Burma, therefore, puts this motion . . . that we do resolve to begin anew, dissolving the Movement as it stands torn and divided today; that we do appoint a committee of members to draft a charter . . . may the delegation of Burma also add that should the Summit reach no decision and let things drift, the delegation will withdraw from the conference, and Burma will end her participation in the Movement.[50]

Subsequently, Ne Win called the ambassadors of India, Pakistan, Sri Lanka, Nepal and Bangladesh to reiterate the views expressed by his foreign minister.[51] The withdrawal from the NAM was an act guided by the isolationist mindset, guided by the Sino-Soviet rift and the need to factor in the concerns of China, which started withdrawing support to communist guerrillas in Myanmar from 1979 onwards. In addition to regional geopolitics, there was genuine disappointment with the trajectory of the NAM not just in the ruling dispensation but also among the dissidents and opposition leaders. Reflecting on Cuba's chairmanship and the movement's future, even the deposed U Nu in 1981 noted, 'hope has disappeared – not only the hope but the non-aligned movement itself. I was rather optimistic once upon a time, but now many things have changed'.[52]

Ne Win made continued attempts to have balanced engagement with countries on either side of the ideological divide. For instance, while North Korea assisted Myanmar in the construction of a ceramic industrial plant, South Korean firms received contracts to build hydroelectric projects.[53] This strict neutralist stance between the two Koreas was suspended only after a bomb blast in Rangoon killed more than two dozen people, including the members of the visiting South Korean prime minister's entourage in 1983.[54] After it was credibly proved that North Korean military officials were involved in the planning of the attack, Myanmar suspended diplomatic relations with North Korea.

THE END OF THE COLD WAR AND NEUTRALISM

The real test for the neutralist policy came after the end of the Cold War when the Myanmar government faced severe domestic unrest. Despite the structural changes in Sangha to ensure greater state control on the monkhood, the protests on 8 August 1988 received considerable monastic support in the form of public protests as well as a 'ritual boycott' of armed forces and their families.[55] The tilting of the Buddhist monkhood towards the pro-democracy movement as well as severe economic sanctions constrained space for political action by the military leadership. Internally, the military leadership sought to build bridges with monkhood by giving special privileges to monks, by visiting temples and by offering donations.[56] In the external realm, the response to student agitations in 1988 and the failure to move forward with the electoral experiment prompted sanctions from Western countries. The military government sought to respond to this challenge by seeking admission to various international platforms. In 1992, it sought re-admission to NAM, which was granted despite considerable criticism that NAM, instead of penalizing it, allowed an alleged human rights offender to rejoin. But Malaysian Prime Minister Mahathir Mohamad argued that enhanced engagement was the path for reforming Myanmar.[57] A few years later, a similar argument was used to facilitate Myanmar's entry into the Association of Southeast Asian Nations (ASEAN). The military leadership's attempts to join regional and global frameworks enabled it to circumvent the sanctions regime imposed by Western countries.

In response to pressures from the Western governments, particularly from the United States, on various international platforms and economic sanctions, Myanmar started scaling up its relationship with China, which was growing much faster than other neighbours, including India. Since Myanmar was under international sanctions, China emerged as the largest supplier of defence equipment. According to Stockholm International Peace Research

Institute databases, China's arms transfer to Myanmar which was negligible in 1990 reached a peak of approximately \$3.5 billion in 2005.[58] In the economic realm, China emerged as the largest trade partner as well as a significant investor. China operationalized oil and gas pipelines from Kyauk Phyu port to Kunming, and Myanmar became increasingly dependent on China to fend off international pressure. For instance, during the 2007 monks' protest, called the Saffron Revolution, in Yangon and other cities, China played an instrumental role in diluting a UN Security Council resolution against Myanmar.[59] However, there was a growing concern even among military leaders that the country was getting too close to China contrary to its neutralist impulse, and some members of the government opined that the decision to open up was also guided by an interest to restore neutrality by improving relations with Western countries and others.[60]

The elections of 2010 and the formation of a government under the leadership of President Thein Sein brought about significant changes in Myanmar's interaction with the outside world. Thein Sein reiterated the need for pursuing a 'non-aligned, independent and active foreign affairs policy'. Reflecting on the foreign policy goals at his inauguration, he stated:

> Our country will stand firm as a respected member of the global community while actively participating in the international organizations, including the UN, ASEAN, BIMSTEC and other regional organizations. This is why I invite and urge some nations wishing to see democracy flourish and the people's socio-economy grow in Myanmar to cooperate with our new government that emerged in line with the constitution by accepting and recognizing Myanmar's objective conditions and ending their various forms of pressure, assistance and encouragement to the anti-government groups and economic manipulations.

A few aspects emerge from this address. In the post–Cold War world for Myanmar to maintain a non-aligned posture it had to achieve two important objectives: first, breaking free from international isolation caused by the sanctions imposed by the West; and second, increasing the density of diplomatic interactions by engaging in regional and international frameworks.

Myanmar's attempts at engaging the global community met with favour. After Barack Obama took over the US presidency, he reassessed its sanctions policy, and Secretary of State Hillary Clinton noted in 2009, 'Sanctions remain important . . . they have not produced the results we would like, but that does not mean they don't have value'.[61] The United States also initiated its 'Pivot to Asia' policy wherein it decided to deploy 60 percent of its defence assets in the Asia-Pacific region in response to the rise of China.[62] To ensure the success of the Pivot policy, the United States recognized the need to recalibrate its policy towards countries in the region. Myanmar, on the continental landmass of Asia, with its significant resource base and location between India and China, required a policy shift. As elections were conducted in 2010 which ushered in a semi-civilian government, and in subsequent by-elections the Suu Kyi-led National League for Democracy (NLD) demonstrated an impressive electoral performance, many countries including the United States started either lifting or relaxing economic sanctions. In 2011 Hillary Clinton became the first secretary of state to visit Myanmar after John Foster Dulles in 1955, and a year later, the US government restored diplomatic relations between the two countries.[63]

These developments gave a strategic space for Myanmar to strike an independent foreign policy posture and address concerns on engagement with China. Thein Sein's administration took bold policy measures such as suspension of construction of the Myitsone Dam financed and constructed by a state-run Chinese company, China Power Investment.[64] There was considerable public discontent with the terms of the agreement governing the construction of the project as substantial power from the project was to be supplied to China.[65] Similarly, in 2012, there were protests against the activities at the Letpadaung copper mine, being operated jointly by the Wanbao Mining Company from China and the Myanmar Economic Holdings Limited. The protests stemmed from the perception that local people were adversely affected by the mining operation and allegations of lack of transparency.[66] The government constituted a committee which suggested a review of profit-sharing mechanisms, enhanced environmental protection efforts and proactive corporate social responsibility activities.[67] In the realm of diplomacy, in 2014 the government successfully organized an ASEAN summit in Nay Pyi Taw and deftly manoeuvred the regional organization on South China Sea issues. On the security front, Thein Sein adopted a tough policy and in 2015 declared a state of emergency in parts of the Northeast region dominated by ethnic Kokang Chinese.[68] The clashes between the military and Kokang forces resulted in an influx of refugees much to China's discomfiture. Thein Sein ensured fair general elections in 2015, a neutralist stance in foreign policy and a transition to a new government headed by Suu Kyi.

It is rare that a Nobel Laureate becomes a foreign minister as well as prime minister (in this instance, called the state counsellor). As a consequence, there was an expectation that democracy promotion, human rights and other values would come to define Myanmar's foreign policy under the state counsellor's leadership. There was also apprehension that Myanmar's foreign policy would have a westward tilt, specifically towards the United States. Contrary to such expectations, foreign policy retained its neutralist posture for two reasons: first, Myanmar was a semi-democracy with a significant military presence in the governance framework, and a sudden discontinuity in foreign policy would be a difficult enterprise. Second, Suu Kyi turned out to be an extremely pragmatic foreign minister. As she once noted: 'I am just a politician. I am not quite like Margaret Thatcher, no. But on the other hand, I am no Mother Teresa either'.[69] Even before the 2015 election campaign, she was guarded in her comments on big infrastructure projects being implemented by China, in spite of public discontent on some of them. After assuming office as foreign minister, she stated that she was keen on pursuing people-centred diplomacy.[70] The statement may appear equivocal, but probably the intent was to remain ambiguous.

Suu Kyi's first visit, along with President Htin Kyaw, was to Laos,[71] a small neighbour and chairman of the ASEAN forum in 2016. Subsequently, her first visit as state counsellor was to Thailand[72] – again a neighbour and a country that hosts considerable numbers of migrant labourers, refugees and expatriates from Myanmar. By visiting Thailand, she addressed, a major concern among the regional countries that she would neglect the relationship with ASEAN because of its 'constructive engagement' policy' towards Myanmar's military during the days of dictatorship.

Contrary to expectations, Suu Kyi demonstrated a purposive engagement with China. Before the 2015 elections, she visited China to develop party-to-party relations between her NLD and the Chinese Communist Party.[73] After her taking over as state counsellor, there was no significant change in policy towards China. She, like her predecessors, recognized that Chinese cooperation would be required to end ethnic conflicts in the country. Hence, she endorsed important Chinese projects, such as the Belt and Road Initiative (BRI). Even before this endorsement, Chinese presence in the infrastructure domain was considerable; by endorsing the BRI, Suu Kyi has not agreed to any new infrastructure project which could alter the balance of power in the region. The suspension on the Myitsone Dam continues, and Chinese attempts to have a more prominent presence in Dawei Special Economic Zone are yet to make progress. The railway line from Kunming to Kyaukpyu is still yet to take off.

The NLD government headed by Suu Kyi has maintained friendly relations with India. All three leaders, Suu Kyi, Htin Kyaw and Senior General Min Aung Hlaing, have visited India, and it appears that both the countries are on the same page on counter-insurgency operations along the India-Myanmar border.

Myanmar's relations with Japan do not receive the same publicity as its relations with the northern neighbours though Japan has played an important role in reviving its economy. In 2013, the Japan Bank for International Cooperation provided a bridge loan of approximately $950 million to the government to clear arrears of past loans from the ADB and World Bank.[74] During his visit in 2016, Japanese Prime Minister Shinzo Abe wrote off nearly $2 billion of Myanmar debt,[75] and promised to provide approximately $7.73 billion to support developmental activities.[76] Japan has been playing a role in developing railway infrastructure as well as in developing urban infrastructure in cities such as Yangon. The Thilawa Special Economic Zone, being developed by Japan, is emerging as an important hub of economic activity.

Myanmar's foreign policy, especially in the past five years, demonstrated an attempt to maintain a neutral posture by increasing the density of interactions with multiple players. A significant challenge to this multi-engagement approach has been the rise of Buddhist nationalism in the past few years. There are four reasons for the growth of Buddhist nationalism. First, given Myanmar's history of sustained ethnic conflict spread over decades, there is constant fear that the Union is always under threat. The opening-up of democratic space has resulted in an unhindered articulation of deep-seated anxieties. Second, Myanmar's political opening-up also coincided with the rapid growth of social media, which facilitated the spread of political angst with higher velocity. Third, in addition to Myanmar, the concern that Buddhism is under threat can be observed in Thailand as well as in Sri Lanka, and the religious exchanges with these countries have also resulted in the transmission of similar narratives of anxieties from those countries.[77] And finally, rapid socio-economic-political changes resulted in the concerns that Buddhism is under attack. It is broadly in that context that Myanmar has witnessed the rise of MaBaTha (Association for Protection of Race and Religion) claiming to be the protector of the religion. However, it should be noted that a fairly large section of the population may not be in consonance with all the views of the MaBaTha. The leaders of the MaBaTha often refer to the possibility of the country being overwhelmed by the outsiders through migration and inter-religious marriages.[78] Because of its shrill rhetoric, the MaBaTha has often been at loggerheads with the government as well as the Sangha Maha Nayaka (government-appointed council of monks).[79] The twin dynamic of violent rhetoric of some Buddhist organizations and the anti-Muslim sectarian violence in different parts of the country, particularly in the Rakhine State, has generated new foreign policy challenges.

As a consequence, again there was a reliance on China to fend off international pressure. It is too early to say if continued violence in the Rakhine State will prompt Myanmar to give up its neutralist foreign policy and move closer to China. Some suggest that this movement towards China is already happening.[80] However, the fact that India and ASEAN have adopted a restrained and nuanced stand towards sectarian violence in Myanmar is a validation of its current neutralist stance.

CONCLUSION

The preceding discussion demonstrates that Myanmar's neutralist policy was defined by its independence movement, economic imperatives and geopolitical context. The non-aligned foreign policy can be broadly divided into three phases: the first phase from independence to 1962, characterized as a formative phase of neutralism; in the second phase under Ne Win, neutralism portrayed isolationist tendencies. However, this isolationism was a consequence of an attempt to mediate the Sino-Soviet rift as well as the Sino-US rapprochement. In the third phase, a significant challenge to Myanmar's neutralist stance came after the end of the Cold War. Domestic political turmoil coupled with international sanctions pushed Myanmar towards China. However, it was the desire to maintain a neutral policy which was an important factor in ushering in political reforms. The gradual political and economic opening-up of the country enabled it to diversify and enhance its international engagement, and gave a new lease of life to the non-aligned foreign policy. The challenge to the foreign policy is not coming from the international domain. It is the domestic ethnic and sectarian conflict which will define Myanmar's foreign policy in the near future.

NOTES

1. 'Myanmar Will Stick to Non Alignment Foreign Policy: Aung San Suu Kyi', *CCTV* (21 August 2016). https://www.youtube.com/watch?v=yBIJ7ugDn6Y.

2. David I. Steinberg. *Burma/Myanmar: What Everyone Needs to Know* (Oxford: Oxford University Press, 2010), 25.

3. 'Theravada Buddhism', *BBC* (2 October 2012). http://www.bbc.co.uk/religion/religions/buddhism/subdivisions/theravada_1.shtml.

4. Matthew J. Walton, *Buddhism, Politics, and Political Thought in Myanmar* (Cambridge: Cambridge University Press, 2017), 65–96.

5. For details see Donald S. Lopez, 'Eightfold Path', *Encyclopedia Britannica* (9 January 2018). https://www.britannica.com/topic/Eightfold-Path.

6. Matthew J. Walton, *Buddhism, Politics, and Political Thought in Myanmar* (Cambridge: Cambridge University Press, 2017): 65–96.

7. Matthew J. Walton and Susan Hayward, 'Contesting Buddhist Narratives: Democratization, Nationalism, and Communal Violence in Myanmar', *East-West Center Policy Studies* 71 (2014): 36. https://www.eastwestcenter.org/publications/contesting-buddhist-narratives-democratization-nationalism-and-communal-violence-in-mya.

8. Sayadaw U Silananda, *The Four Foundations of Mindfulness* (Somerville: Wisdom Publications, 2002).

9. Nyanaponika Thera, *The Four Sublime States* (Penang: Inward Path, 1999), 20.

10. Ibid.

11. Li Chenyang, 'The Burmese Nationalist Elite's Pre-Independence Exploration of a National Development Road', *Kyoto Review of Southeast Asia*, Issue 10 (August 2008): Southeast Asian Studies in China. https://kyotoreview.org/issue-10/the-burmese-nationalist-elites-pre-independence-exploration-of-a-national-development-road/.

12. As cited in Tin Maung Maung Than, *State Dominance in Myanmar: The Political Economy of Industrialization* (Singapore: ISEAS, 2007), 34.

13. Chaw Chaw Sein, 'Myanmar Foreign Policy under New Government: Changes and Prospects', in Li Chenyang, Chaw Chaw Sein and Zhu Xianghui (eds.). *Myanmar: Reintegrating into the International Community* (Singapore: World Scientific Publishing, 2016): 28.

14. Jovan Čavoški, 'Arming Nonalignment: Yugoslavia's Relations with Burma and the Cold War in Asia (1950–1955)', *The Cold War International History Project Working Paper* 61 (April 2010).

15. Anne Winslow, 'The Burma Road to Pyidawtha', *International Conciliation* 518 (May 1958): 394.

16. Bert Edström, 'Japan and the Myanmar Conundrum', *Institute for Security and Development Policy – Asia Paper* (October 2009): 18.

17. Warren Unna, 'Neutralism and U Nu', *Institute for Current World Affairs* (January 1959): 4.

18. 'Asian Rice Problems and the Cold War', *Department of State Intelligence Report* 7087 (January 1956): 6–8.

19. Ibid.

20. Frank N. Trager, 'Burma's Foreign Policy, 1948–56: Neutralism, Third Force, and Rice', *The Journal of Asian Studies* 16 (November 1956): 89–102.

21. 'Country Profiles – Myanmar: The Colonial Era (1885–1948)', *Harvard Divinity School* (2018). https://rlp.hds.harvard.edu/myanmar/colonial-era-1885-1948.

22. Myanmar achieved independence in 1948, but constitution was drafted in 1947.

23. 'Constitution of 1947', *International Labour Organisation* (June 2008). https://www.ilo.org/dyn/natlex/docs/ELECTRONIC/79573/85699/F1436085708/MMR79573.pdf.

24. 'Nationalists Mark Anniversary of Divisive State Religion Bill', *The Myanmar Times* (1 September 2015). https://www.mmtimes.com/national-news/16243-nationalists-mark-anniversary-of-divisive-state-religion-bill.html.

25. Michael W. Charney, 'Ludu Aung Than: Nu's Burma and the Cold War', in Christopher Goscha and Christian Ostermann (eds.). *Imperial Retreat and the Cold War in South and Southeast Asia, 1945–1962* (Stanford: Stanford University Press, 2009): 333–355.

26. Fan Hongwei, 'China–Burma Geopolitical Relations in the Cold War', *Journal of Current Southeast Asian Affairs* 31 (2012): 10.

27. Frank N. Trager, 'Burma's Foreign Policy, 1948–56: Neutralism, Third Force, and Rice', *The Journal of Asian Studies* 16 (November 1956): 93.

28. Fan Hongwei, 'China–Burma Geopolitical Relations in the Cold War', *Journal of Current Southeast Asian Affairs* 1 (2012): 9.

29. China's Initiation of the Five Principles of Peaceful Co-Existence, *Ministry of Foreign Affairs, The People's Republic of China*. http://www.fmprc.gov.cn/mfa_eng/ziliao_665539/3602_665543/3604_665547/t18053.shtml.

30. 'Cable from Peng Di, "Third Intelligence Report on the Insider Situation of the Bogor Conference"', *History and Public Policy Program Digital Archive* (January 1955). http://digitalarchive.wilsoncenter.org/document/115504.

31. Kenton Clymer, 'The United States and the Guomindang (KMT) Forces in Burma, 1949–1954: A Diplomatic Disaster', *The Chinese Historical Review* 21 (2014): 24–44.

32. E. G, 'The Burma–China Frontier Dispute', *The World Today* 13 (February 1957): 88.

33. For details on the events leading to the 1960 Burma–China Boundary Treaty, see Maung Maung, 'The Burma–China Boundary Settlement', *Asian Survey* 1 (March 1961): 38–43.

34. Speech by U Nu, *Journal of Contemporary Asia* 1 (1970): 89.

35. John Seabury Thomson, 'Burmese Neutralism', *Political Science Quarterly* 72 (June 1957): 264.

36. Ibid., 263.

37. 'U Thant', *United Nations Information Centre*. https://unic.un.org/aroundworld/unics/uthant/common/documents/UThant.pdf.

38. Tin Maung Maung Than, 'The Sangha and Sasana in Socialist Burma', *Sojourn: Journal of Social Issues in Southeast Asia* 1 (February 1988): 26–61.

39. 'Burma under Ne Win', *Intelligence Weekly of Central Intelligence Agency* (2 September 1966): 2.

40. 'Peking and the Burmese Communists: The Perils and Profits of Insurgency', *Intelligence Report of Central Intelligence Agency* (May 2007).

41. Maung Aung Myoe, *In the Name of Pauk-Phaw: Myanmar's China Policy since 1948* (Singapore: Institute of Southeast Asian Studies, 2011): 57.

42. Dorothy Woodman, 'Burma's Socialist Road', *The New Statesman* (May 1968). https://www.newstatesman.com/society/2008/05/burma-burmese-china-british.

43. Ibid.

44. For details see 'Burma under Ne Win', *Intelligence Weekly of Central Intelligence Agency* (2 September 1966).

45. Ralph Pettman, *China in Burma's Foreign Policy* (Canberra: ANU Press, 1973).

46. Ibid.

47. Edwin W. Martin, 'Burma in 1975: New Dimensions to Non-Alignment', *Asian Survey* 16 (February 1976): 176.

48. William L. Scully and Frank N. Trager, 'Burma 1979: Reversing the Trend', *Asian Survey* 20 (February 1980): 170–171.

49. 'Non-Aligned Movement: Dynamics and Prospects', *Central Intelligence Agency – An Intelligence Assessment* (March 1979): 3.

50. U Pe Kin, 'Twilight of the Nonaligned Movement', *Asian Affairs* 7 (May 1980): 337.

51. Robert Taylor, *General Ne Win: A Political Biography* (Singapore: Institute of Southeast Asian Studies, 2015): 460.

52. Henry Kamm, 'Ousted Burmese Chief Forgives His Usurper', *New York Times* (11 October 1981). http://www.nytimes.com/1981/10/11/world/ousted-burmese-chief-forgives-his-usurper.html.

53. David I Steinberg, 'Burma in 1983: The Dilemmas of Neutralism and Succession', *Asian Survey* 24 (February 1984): 196–97.

54. Clyde Haberman, 'Bomb Kills 19, Including 6 Key Koreans', *New York Times* (10 October 1983). http://www.nytimes.com/1983/10/10/world/bomb-kills-19-including-6-key-koreans.html.

55. Bruce Matthews, 'Buddhism under a Military Regime: The Iron Heel in Burma', *Asian Survey* 4 (April 1993): 416–417.

56. Simrin Singh, 'Burma-Religion: Isolated Military Regime Woos Buddhist Monks', *Inter Press Service* (6 December 1996). http://www.ipsnews.net/1996/12/burma-religion-isolated-military-regime-woos-buddhist-monks/.

57. As cited in 'Burma', *Burma Rights Movement for Action*, 2 (September 1992), https://www.scribd.com/document/108039028/BI1992-09-V02-09-red (accessed 17 November 2017).

58. Importer/Exporter TIV Tables, *Stockholm International Peace Research Institute (SIPRI)*. http://armstrade.sipri.org/armstrade/page/values.php.

59. Justin McCurry, Jonathan Watts and Alex Duval Smith, 'How Junta Stemmed a Saffron Tide', *The Guardian* (30 September 2007). https://www.theguardian.com/world/2007/sep/30/burma.justinmccurry.

60. Based on personal interactions with the senior members of Myanmar's diplomatic community.

61. Ewen MacAskill, 'US Signals Major Policy Shift towards Burma', *The Guardian* (24 September 2009). https://www.theguardian.com/world/2009/sep/24/burma-obama-foreign-policy.

62. 'Leon Panetta: US to Deploy 60 Percent of Navy Fleet to Pacific', *BBC* (2 June 2012). http://www.bbc.com/news/world-us-canada-18305750.

63. Steven Lee Myers, 'Clinton's Visit to Myanmar Raises Hopes and Concerns', *New York Times* (29 November 2011). http://www.nytimes.com/2011/11/30/world/asia/clintons-visit-to-myanmar-raises-hopes-and-concerns.html.

64. Thomas Fuller, 'Myanmar Backs Down, Suspending Dam Project', *New York Times* (30 September 2011). http://www.nytimes.com/2011/10/01/world/asia/myanmar-suspends-construction-of-controversial-dam.html.

65. 'Irrawaddy/N'Mai/Mali Dams', *Burma Rivers Network*. http://www.burmariversnetwork.org/dam-projects/irrawaddynmaimali.html.

66. Andrew R. C. Marshall, 'Special Report: Myanmar's Deep Mine of Old Troubles', *Reuters* (28 December 2012). https://www.reuters.com/article/us-myanmar-reforms/special-report-myanmars-deep-mine-of-old-troubles-idUSBRE8BR02P20121228.

67. Yun Sun, 'Chinese Investment in Myanmar: What Lies Ahead?' *Stimson Centre Issue Brief* (September 2013). https://www.stimson.org/sites/default/files/file-attachments/Yun_Issue_Brief1_1.pdf.

68. Zeya Tun, 'Myanmar Declares Martial Law in Troubled Kokang Region', *Reuters* (17 February 2015). https://www.reuters.com/article/us-myanmar-clashes/myanmar-declares-martial-law-in-troubled-kokang-region-idUSKBN0LL11S20150217.

69. Guy Faulconbridge, 'Myanmar leader says no ethnic cleansing of Rohingya Muslims', *Reuters* (8 April 2017). https://www.reuters.com/article/myanmar-rohingya-suukyi-int/myanmar-leader-says-no-ethnic-cleansing-of-rohingya-muslims-bbc-idUSKBN1772XN.

70. 'Myanmar FM Stresses Adopting People-Centered Foreign Policy', *Xinhua* (22 April 2016). http://news.xinhuanet.com/english/2016-04/22/c_135304169.htm.

71. 'Suu Kyi, Htin Kyaw on Official Visit to Laos', *Mizzima* (7 May 2016). http://www.mizzima.com/news-regional/suu-kyi-htin-kyaw-official-visit-laos.

72. 'Official Visit of H.E. Daw Aung San Suu Kyi, State Counsellor of Myanmar to Thailand', *Ministry of Foreign Affairs, Kingdom of Thailand* (25 June 2016). http://

www.mfa.go.th/main/en/media-center/28/67964-Official-Visit-of-H.E.-Daw-Aung-San-Suu-Kyi,-State.html.

73. Jurgen Haacke, 'Why Did Myanmar's Opposition Leader Just Visit China?' *The Diplomat* (15 June 2015). https://thediplomat.com/2015/06/why-did-myanmars-opposition-leader-just-visit-china/.

74. 'Bridge Loans to the Republic of Union of Myanmar', *Japan Bank for International Cooperation (JBIC) – Press Release* (28 January 2013). https://www.jbic.go.jp/en/information/press/press-2012/0128-7371.

75. 'Shinzo Abe Ends Myanmar Visit with Aid, Debt Write Off', *Livemint* (26 May 2016). http://www.livemint.com/Politics/39JXmCDd7frnK3VbnpiVTJ/Shinzo-Abe-ends-Myanmar-visit-with-aid-debt-writeoff.html.

76. Kiyoshi Takenaka, 'Japan to Provide 7.73 Billion Dollars in Aid PM Abe Says', *Reuters* (2 November 2016). http://www.reuters.com/article/us-myanmar-japan-idUSKBN12X16I.

77. 'Buddhism and State Power in Myanmar', *International Crisis Group* (5 September 2017). https://d2071andvip0wj.cloudfront.net/290-buddhism-and-state-power-in-myanmar.pdf.

78. Poppy McPherson, 'We Must Protect Our Country: Extremist Buddhists Target Mandalay's Muslims', *The Guardian* (9 May 2017). https://www.theguardian.com/cities/2017/may/08/buddhist-extremists-anti-muslim-mandalay-ma-ba-tha.

79. Kyaw Phyo Tha and San Yamin Aung, 'State-Backed Monks' Council Decries Ma Ba Tha as Unlawful', *The Irrawaddy* (13 July 2016).

80. Nicholas Bequelin, 'Behind China's Attempt to Ease the Rohingya Crisis', *New York Times* (5 December 2017). https://www.nytimes.com/2017/12/05/opinion/china-rohingya-crisis.html?mtrref=www.google.co.in&gwh=705A82FF0A05E43FE E469651A4FF1796&gwt=pay&assetType=opinion.

BIBLIOGRAPHY

Bhatia, Rajiv. *India–Myanmar Relations: Changing Contours*. New York: Routledge, 2016.

Chenyang, Li, et al. *Myanmar: Reintegrating into the International Community*. Singapore: World Scientific Publishing, 2016.

E. G. 'The Burma-China Frontier Dispute'. *The World Today* 13, no. 2 (February 1957).

Egreteau, Renaud. *The Military and Political Change in Myanmar*. Oxford: Oxford University Press, 2016.

Egreteau, Renaud and Larry Jagan. *Soldiers and Diplomacy in Burma: The Foreign Policies of the Burmese Praetorian State*. Singapore: NUS Press, 2013.

Haacke, Jurgen. *Myanmar's Foreign Policy: Domestic Influences and International Implications*. London: The International Institute for Strategic Studies, 2006.

Hongwei, Fan. 'China–Burma Geopolitical Relations in the Cold War'. *Journal of Current Southeast Asian Affairs* 1 (2012).

Kin, U Pe. 'Twilight of the Nonaligned Movement'. *Asian Affairs* 7, no. 5 (May 1980).

King, Winston L. *In the Hope of Nibbana: The Ethics of Theravada Buddhism*. Seattle: Pariyatti Press, 2001.

Martin, Edwin W. 'Burma in 1975: New Dimensions to Non-Alignment'. *Asian Survey* 16, no. 2 (February 1976).

Maung Maung. 'The Burma–China Boundary Settlement'. *Asian Survey* 1, no. 1 (March 1961).

Myint-U, Thant. *Where China Meets India*. London: Faber, 2011.

Myoe, Maung Aung. *In the Name of Pauk-Phaw: Myanmar's China Policy since 1948*. Singapore: Institute of Southeast Asian Studies, 2011.

Pettman, Ralph. *China in Burma's Foreign Policy*. Canberra: ANU Press, 1973.

Popham, Peter. *The Lady and the Peacock: The Life of Aung San Suu Kyi of Burma*. London: Rider, 2011.

Scully, William L. and Frank N. Trager. 'Burma 1979: Reversing the Trend'. *Asian Survey* 20, no. 2 (February 1980).

Silananda, Sayadaw U. *The Four Foundations of Mindfulness*. Somerville: Wisdom Publications, 2002.

Steinberg, David I. 'Burma in 1983: The Dilemmas of Neutralism and Succession'. *Asian Survey* 24, no. 2 (February 1984).

Steinberg, David I. *Burma/Myanmar: What Everyone Needs to Know*. Oxford: Oxford University Press, 2010.

Taylor, Robert. *General Ne Win: A Political Biography*. Singapore: Institute of Southeast Asian Studies, 2015.

Than, Tin Maung Maung. *State Dominance in Myanmar: The Political Economy of Industrialization*. Singapore: ISEAS, 2007.

Thera, Nyanaponika. *The Four Sublime States*. Penang: Inward Path, 1999.

Thomson, John Seabury. 'Burmese Neutralism'. *Political Science Quarterly* 72, no. 2 (June 1957).

Trager, Frank N. 'Burma's Foreign Policy, 1948–56: Neutralism, Third Force, and Rice'. *The Journal of Asian Studies* 16, no. 1 (November 1956).

Walton, Matthew J. *Buddhism, Politics, and Political Thought in Myanmar*. Cambridge: Cambridge University Press, 2017.

Chapter 10

Values in Indonesian Foreign Policy

Independent and Active Doctrine

Dewi Fortuna Anwar

A country's political system and the world views of its dominant élites naturally affect its values in conducting foreign policy. Indonesia has undergone four major changes in its political system. These were the multiparty parliamentary democracy during 1950–1959 in which several different political ideologies competed for power marked by frequent changes of government; Sukarno's authoritarian 'Guided Democracy' with its revolutionary and Left-leaning anti-imperialist outlook during 1959–1965; the military-dominated 'New Order' regime under Suharto with its *Pancasila* democracy and strong opposition to communism and political Islam during 1966–1998; and the current *Reformasi* or reform era with its transition to a genuinely pluralistic and competitive democracy after 1998. While there has been continuity in the formal adherence to certain core foreign policy values, there have also been changes in how they have been interpreted and applied during the different periods. At the same time, fundamental changes in values have also taken place in line with the changes in the political system, which also directly influence Indonesia's foreign policy outlooks and priorities.

The Preamble to the 1945 Constitution contains the primary values, foundation and goals of the independent Republic of Indonesia that also guide the conduct of its foreign policy. The first sentence of the Preamble proclaims that 'independence is the inalienable right of all nations and thus all colonialism must be abolished in this world as it is not in conformity with humanity and justice'.[1] The fourth and final paragraph lays out the goals and the foundation of the Indonesian state. The government is obligated to protect all the people and territory of Indonesia, 'to improve public welfare, to educate the people and to participate in the establishment of a world order based on freedom, perpetual peace and social justice'. The five principles of the foundation of the state, known as *Pancasila*, are also enumerated here. These are belief in the One and Only God, just and civilized humanity, the unity of Indonesia, democracy and social justice. *Pancasila*, formulated by Sukarno during the preparation for independence, was a compromise between those who wanted a state based on Islamic sharia and those who wanted a secular state. At independence Indonesia also adopted a national motto of *Bhinneka Tunggal Ika* or Unity in Diversity, signifying the national commitment to be united despite the country's great diversity in terms of race, ethnicity, religion and culture, while continuing to respect the differences even as national unity is strengthened. Although nearly 90 percent of the Indonesian population were and are Muslims, and from the beginning there have been small groups who wanted to establish an Islamic state, the overwhelming majority of Muslims in Indonesia are moderate and adhere to the *Pancasila* ideals of national unity that respect diversity, including religious differences.

The Preamble to the 1945 Constitution contains at least two core values that inform Indonesian foreign policy. The first core value is independence as enunciated in the opening sentence. The strong emphasis on independence, whether in opposing all forms of colonialism and imperialism, or in refusing to take part in military alliances led by great powers, has characterized Indonesian foreign policy through the different phases in its political development, which will be discussed in some detail. The second core value is peace activism, for the Preamble mandates that the Indonesian government shall play an active role towards the development of a truly just and peaceful world order. Besides these two core values, the chapter will look at the transformation of values that have taken place in Indonesia in recent years, from being a strong proponent of cultural relativism to a full embrace of democracy and human rights as universal values, and their respective impacts on Indonesian foreign policy. As Indonesia is the world's largest Muslim-majority country, the chapter will also look at the evolving role of Islam in Indonesian foreign policy.

PRESERVING INDEPENDENCE
AS A CORE FOREIGN POLICY VALUE

Indonesia's national consciousness is built upon the shared experiences of the highly heterogeneous peoples of the archipelago living together under oppressive foreign rule, first under the long period of the Dutch East India Company and its replacement, the Dutch colonial administration, which lasted for three and a half centuries, and later under Japanese military occupation (1942–1945) which ousted the Dutch during World War II. These shared experiences provided the primary impetus for the development of Indonesian nationalism that transcended primordial identities, and the nationalist struggle for independence in the early twentieth century.[2] The most important defining moment in Indonesian history, during which the fundamental values and goals of the republic were forged, was the period between the declaration of independence on 17 August 1945 and the transfer of sovereignty from the Netherlands on 27 December 1949, when Indonesia engaged in a revolutionary war against the returning Dutch forces bent on reclaiming the former colony after Japan surrendered to the Allied powers in August 1945. Indonesia's revolutionary struggle to secure its independence coincided with the onset of the Cold War between the Western bloc led by the United States and the communist bloc led by the Soviet Union. The intensifying competition between these two opposing blocs divided Indonesian political forces along similar ideological lines. It was against this background that Vice President Mohammad Hatta, regarded as the father of Indonesian foreign policy, introduced the 'Independent/Free and Active' foreign policy doctrine in 1948 that has weathered several political changes and remained in force until today.[3]

Independent and Active Foreign Policy Doctrine

In late 1948, with nationalist forces fighting to keep the new republic alive and seeking support from the international community, there were those, especially the communists, who favoured that Indonesia sided with the Soviet bloc which shared the same outlook of opposing Western colonialism and imperialism. The majority of Indonesian political forces, led by President Sukarno and Vice President Hatta, were nationalists opposed to communism and had hoped that the United States, which had also fought for its independence, would support Indonesia's independence struggle against the Dutch, notwithstanding the Netherlands being a US ally. With different political factions looking to different sources of international support, foreign policy was in danger of being as divided as domestic politics. To overcome this division Hatta made a proposal approved in September 1948 by Indonesia's provisional parliament that Indonesia should not take sides between the contending superpower blocs, but instead should chart its own course, becoming a subject and not an object in international relations, able to pursue its own national objectives. Hatta's speech, titled *Mendayungantara Dua Karang* (Rowing between Two Reefs), gave birth to Indonesia's independent and active foreign policy doctrine which all subsequent Indonesian governments must adhere to, at least in principle. Hatta's historic speech is worth quoting here:

> But must we the Indonesian nation, who are fighting for our independence, only choose between being pro-Russia or pro-America? Is there not another stance that we can take to achieve our aspirations? The government is of the opinion

that the stance we must adopt is not to become an object in international political competition, but rather to remain a subject with the right to determine our own position, the right to pursue our own objective, namely Indonesia that is wholly independent.[4]

Hatta explained that being independent and active did not mean neutrality in international relations. While Indonesia must not join either superpower camp so that it could remain free to pursue the course that could serve its national aspirations and interests, the country must also play an active role in mitigating international tensions and promoting peace in accordance with the stipulation of the Preamble to the Constitution. In an article published in *Foreign Affairs* in 1953 Hatta explained that:

> the policy of the Republic of Indonesia is not one of neutrality – it is not constructed in reference to belligerent states but for the purpose of strengthening and upholding peace. Indonesia plays no favourites between the two opposed blocs and follows its own path through the various international problems. . . . Indonesia's independent policy keeps her from enmity with either party, preserves her from the damage to her own interests that would follow from taking sides, and permits her to be friends with all nations on a basis of mutual respect.[5]

In the 1950s and early 1960s, when many countries in Asia and Africa were still fighting for independence against European colonial powers while at the same time confronted with the Cold War divide, the independent and active foreign policy doctrine simultaneously pursued the twin objectives of supporting decolonization and autonomy in international relations. Indonesia organized the first-ever conference of Asian and African nations in 1955 in Bandung which produced the Ten Bandung Principles and the so-called Bandung Spirit, which made an important normative contribution to the development of a code of conduct in international relations.[6] The Bandung Conference is well known, among others, for its espousal of peaceful coexistence amid Cold War divisions, promotion of Asian-African solidarity, emphasis on the equality of all races and nations, non-interference in each other's internal affairs and peaceful settlement of disputes. In fact, the Ten Bandung Principles highlighted principles contained in the United Nations (UN) Charter but with the additional exhortation that countries inter alia abstain 'from the use of arrangements of collective defence to serve any particular interests of big powers'.[7] The Bandung Conference was the forerunner of the Non-Aligned Movement (NAM), established in Belgrade in 1961, of which Indonesia was one of the co-founders. Being a member of the NAM was and has continued to be regarded as part of Indonesia's foreign policy identity even after the Cold War.

Varying Implementation of Independent and Active Foreign Policy Doctrine

Notwithstanding formal adherence to the independent and active foreign policy doctrine, successive Indonesian governments throughout the Cold War period often deviated from its ideal. While Indonesia consistently avoided joining any military alliance, and never allowed foreign military bases within its territory, the political inclinations and priorities of different leaders pushed them closer to one camp or other. Simultaneously pursuing national goals of maintaining independence and economic development during the Cold War was often difficult, as each required different strategies and external support, but overt violation of the foreign policy doctrine had political consequences. In 1952 the Sukiman Cabinet was forced to resign after it was disclosed that Foreign Minister Subardjo had secretly signed an agreement with the United States for Indonesia to receive economic aid under the terms of the 1951 Mutual Security Act, which would make Indonesia a US ally.[8]

For Sukarno, the most important foreign policy theme for Indonesia and other Asian-African countries was the continuing struggle against colonialism and imperialism. Throughout the 1950s Indonesia's foreign policy was dominated by efforts to negotiate with the Netherlands to complete the transfer of the remaining territory still under its control, the province of West Irian/West Papua. When negotiations failed, which contributed to the collapse of Indonesia's first democratic experiment, Indonesia under Sukarno's 'Guided Democracy' launched a military campaign to liberate West Irian in the early 1960s. Once the West Irian campaign was successfully concluded, Sukarno initiated a confrontation against the newly established Malaysian Federation in 1963, seeing it as a British plot to retain influence in Malaysia which he regarded as a direct threat to Indonesia.[9]

Unlike Hatta, who as an economist believed that Indonesia should focus on developing its economy and improving the welfare of the people, which would necessitate cooperating with countries that could assist Indonesia, mostly Western industrialized countries, Sukarno wanted to keep revolutionary fervour alive by pursuing the complete independence of Indonesia from all forms of imperialism. In a 1965 speech titled 'Storming the Last Bulwarks of Imperialism' Sukarno stated that 'national instability is a thousand times better than colonial stability'.[10] He called on Asian-African countries to stand united against imperialism and build their economies through their own efforts. He argued that:

> economic independence is the prerequisite for real independence in political and cultural affairs. Let us build anti-imperialist economies, genuinely national economies that stand on their own feet, mutually assisting each other and not

relying upon the so-called aid of the imperialists. . . . We today stand firmly
upright in the mighty ranks of the neo-emerging forces, and we are now storming the last bulwarks of imperialism.[11]

Sukarno frequently emphasized the importance of achieving the 'Tri Sakti'
or three sacred missions of political sovereignty, economic self-reliance and
cultural distinctiveness. However, in pursuing his objective of complete independence by pitting the 'New Emerging Forces' against what he called the
'Old Established Forces', Sukarno's foreign policy increasingly veered left,
culminating in the forming of the Jakarta-Phnom Penh-Hanoi-Pyongyang-
Peking Axis, a major departure from Hatta's conception of Indonesia's
independent and active foreign policy doctrine – a factor which contributed
to Sukarno's fall. The growing influence of the Indonesian Communist Party
(PKI) and its close ties with China was strongly opposed by the anti-communist army and Islamic groups. After the murders of several army generals
in September 1965, which was blamed on the PKI, Sukarno was removed
from power and Indonesia came under the rule of the army-dominated 'New
Order' government led by President Suharto for the next three decades.[12]

Unlike Sukarno who viewed Western imperialism as the greatest threat to
Indonesia's existence, Suharto's New Order government regarded communist subversion and China as primary threats to Indonesian national security
and political stability. The New Order government banned the PKI, killed or
imprisoned PKI members and sympathizers and froze diplomatic relations
with China until the end of the Cold War. With its security outlook and focus
on ensuring internal political stability, economic development and social welfare, the Suharto regime moved further right, developing close relations with
the United States and its allies who could assist Indonesia in its economic
development. Indonesia also ended the confrontation with Malaysia and
co-founded in 1967 the Association of Southeast Asian Nations (ASEAN)
with four other non-communist countries, Malaysia, the Philippines, Singapore and Thailand. ASEAN was regarded as a bulwark against communist
expansion.

Despite this rightward tilt the New Order government was at pains to
reassure the public that Indonesia was not deviating from the independent
and active foreign policy principle, but was trying to correct the Old Order's
leftist deviation. Rather than compromising its foreign policy by associating
with countries openly allied with Western powers, the New Order leaders
argued that Indonesia was introducing the independent and active principle
into ASEAN. There was some truth to this, for Indonesia did indeed introduce
the concept of national and regional resilience into ASEAN as well as the
insistence that regional countries bear the primary responsibility for regional
security. During a visit to Malaysia in 1970 Suharto stated that countries like

Indonesia and Malaysia should not be dependent on the generosity or might of other powers, arguing that governments must be instilled with the belief that their people could achieve much for themselves, and that they were not helpless pawns in the international power game. Indonesia's independent and active stance was increasingly seen to be tied to the promotion of ASEAN's regional resilience and strategic autonomy.[13] These efforts were, however, insufficient to ward off criticisms from nationalist groups that Indonesia was no longer truly independent and active in its foreign policy.

After the Cold War questions arose of whether the foreign policy doctrine formulated during the bipolar global order was still relevant in the more complex post–Cold War international system which was becoming more multipolar and marked by both competition and cooperation. In fact, successive Indonesian governments reaffirmed the continuing importance of the independent and active foreign policy doctrine as the guideline of Indonesian foreign policy. President B. J. Habibie, who replaced Suharto and ushered in Indonesia's transition to democracy during 1998–1999, signed Law Number 37 of 1999 on Foreign Relations which stipulated that all conduct of foreign relations must adhere to the independent and active foreign policy principle. In his first speech on foreign policy in May 2005, President Susilo Bambang Yudhoyono (2004–2014), the first-ever directly elected president, remarked that 'over the years, governments have come and gone, Indonesia has had six presidents, and our political system has undergone major changes, but "independent and active" remains the primary foreign policy principle for Indonesia'.[14] He added that instead of 'rowing between two reefs' as in the past, Indonesian foreign policy in the vastly changed international environment with its myriad challenges was more like 'navigating a turbulent ocean'.

Yudhoyono elaborated on the conceptual properties of the independent and active foreign policy. Firstly, it entails independence of judgement and freedom of action, but it must also be constructive. According to him:

There is no sense for us to be different just for the sake of being different, or to be active just for its own sake. Our independence and activism must therefore be combined with a constructive mind-set so that we can attain our national objectives . . . having the ability to turn adversary into friend and friend into partner . . . putting to rest a siege mentality, wild conspiracy theories, excessive suspicion, an overly defensive attitude, or fear that the world is out to get us. [Yudhoyono reiterated that] independent and active means that we will NOT enter into any military alliances. Indonesia has never engaged in a military pact with a foreign country, and there will be no change in this policy. This also means that we will continue our policy of not allowing any foreign military bases on Indonesian territory. [He argued that] an independent and active foreign policy is all about connectivity . . . our ability to connect with the wider world is critical to the performance of our independent and active foreign policy.

Yudhoyono cited Indonesia's hosting the Bandung Conference and its role in the founding of ASEAN, which had made significant international and regional contributions, as proofs that 'connectivity is a source of diplomatic empowerment'.

President Joko Widodo, who won the presidential election in 2014, stressed the role of Indonesia's independent and active foreign policy in serving its national interests and focusing on the protection of the people. During the presidential campaign, Widodo pledged 'to make the presence of the state felt in order to protect the nation and giving a sense of security to all citizens, through an independent and active foreign policy' as the top of his nine priority programmes or 'Nawa Cita'.[15] Unlike Yudhoyono who emphasized the importance of Indonesia connecting with the world, Widodo expressed a more Sukarnoist nationalism, as he is a member of the Indonesian Democratic Party of Struggle, the successor of Sukarno's Indonesian Nationalist Party and chaired by former President Megawati Sukarnoputri, Sukarno's eldest daughter. Widodo expressed support for Sukarno's 'Tri Sakti' concept of ensuring Indonesia's complete independence: to be politically sovereign, economically self-reliant and culturally distinctive. Current realities, however, are very different from those of the Sukarno era as Indonesia has become fully integrated with the world economy, a member of various free trade arrangements including the ASEAN Economic Community and depends on large-scale foreign investment for its continuing economic development.

A constant theme in Indonesian foreign policy throughout the years is support for the Palestinian struggle for an independent state, which was included in the list of issues discussed in the 1955 Bandung Conference. Indonesia has refused to establish diplomatic relations with Israel until a satisfactory solution is reached on the Palestinian question, and during his campaign Widodo reiterated that support for the Palestinians to gain an independent homeland was at the heart of Indonesian foreign policy.

PEACE ACTIVISM AS A CORE
FOREIGN POLICY VALUE

The Preamble to the Constitution stipulates that one of the tasks of the Indonesian government is 'to participate in the establishment of a world order based on freedom, perpetual peace and social justice'.[16] Indonesia has tried to play an active role in promoting peace at the global and regional levels through different phases of its political development. There have, however, been important exceptions. To Sukarno true peace could not be realized as long as imperialism in all its manifestations remained, resulting in Indonesia's confrontational foreign policy during the 'Guided Democracy' period, which caused regional instability. Concerns about communist expansion led to the Suharto government's annexation of the former Portuguese colony, East Timor, under the pretext of decolonization in December 1974, which received international condemnation. East Timor was given independence from Indonesian rule only during the Habibie presidency in 1999. Notwithstanding these two exceptions, successive Indonesian governments since independence have tried to carry out the constitutionally mandated foreign policy obligation according to the varying circumstances, of being part of the solutions, not part of the problems in international affairs. Here will be traced five different forms of Indonesian foreign policy activity that can be categorized as its peace-promotion portfolio. These are first, Indonesia's consistent efforts to promote peaceful coexistence between contending forces; second, its commitment to ASEAN regional harmony; third, its proactive role in mediating regional conflicts; fourth, its support for UN Peacekeeping Operations (UNPKO); and fifth, its efforts to promote interfaith dialogue and moderate Islam.

Promotion of Peaceful Coexistence

The tenet of Indonesian independent and active foreign policy principle was not to take sides in the Cold War bipolar divide but to chart the country's own course while trying to develop friendly relations with all. By organizing the Bandung Conference, Indonesia together with India, Pakistan, Sri Lanka and Burma, the so-called Colombo Powers, tried to bring countries with different ideological backgrounds together as an effort to promote mutual understanding and reduce tension. A number of participants at Bandung were members of US military alliances, some belonged to the Soviet-led camp and others were uncommitted. The conference was the first international event to which China was invited in an effort to bring Beijing into the international fold after the communist victory in 1949. The conference has had a lasting legacy in its support for peaceful coexistence, international cooperation and solidarity among developing countries.

For Indonesia, the holding of the Bandung Conference is considered a high ideal in its foreign policy conduct, and the 'Bandung Spirit' has continued to inform Indonesian foreign policy thinking. The end of the Cold War has not led to an end of conflicts between major countries. In the spirit of supporting peaceful existence, Indonesia has consistently refused to take part in conflicts, tried to engage all parties and pushed for the development of more inclusive regionalism in the wider East Asia and Indo-Pacific regions. While from a realist perspective this behaviour can simply be described as hedging when confronted by great powers' competition, such as the growing competition between the United States and China in the Indo-Pacific region, Indonesia's comfort of living with differences may be due to the national values of tolerance embodied in *Pancasila* and the motto of 'Unity in Diversity'. Within the Islamic world, Indonesia, as the largest Muslim-majority country that is predominantly Sunni, has maintained friendly ties with both Saudi Arabia and Iran. Yudhoyono throughout his presidency emphasized Indonesia's role as a bridge-builder and its foreign policy of having 'a million friends and zero enemies'.

Ensuring ASEAN Regional Harmony

After ending Indonesia's confrontation against Malaysia in 1966 and the establishment of ASEAN in 1967, Indonesia's foreign policy in Southeast Asia has been marked by a commitment to maintaining regional harmony. Indonesia's 'free and active' foreign policy has increasingly been tied to its support for the development of regional resilience and ASEAN's strategic autonomy, which naturally depends on ASEAN's cohesiveness. Unlike in many other regional organizations where the largest member often tries to assert dominance, Indonesia in ASEAN has consciously adopted a non-assertive role. As the largest member, and with the damaging impact of its past confrontational policy never forgotten, Indonesia has mostly practised the Javanese concept of *Tut Wuri Handayani* or 'leading from behind' within ASEAN.[17] Despite the differences in outlook within ASEAN and amid rising criticisms in certain domestic quarters of ASEAN's slow progress, the government has been steadfast in regarding ASEAN as the cornerstone of foreign policy. It was Indonesia who first introduced the principle of *musyawarah-mufakat* or deliberations to reach consensus that has become one of the key features of the ASEAN Way, credited with maintaining regional harmony – though lately also blamed for the association's slow decision-making process and inability to make fundamental changes towards reform.

ASEAN's success has been attributed to a certain extent to Indonesia's 'big-heartedness' towards ASEAN. Kishore Mahbubani, diplomat and writer from Singapore, writes that Southeast Asian regional stability has mostly been due to the presence of ASEAN

> for which we shouldn't just thank God. We should also thank Indonesia. Why?
>   Just look around the world and ask yourselves why many regional organizations, including the Organization of American States, Gulf Cooperation Council and South Asian Association of Regional Cooperation, are struggling. One answer is that the largest member of these organizations exercizes too much dominance. Indonesia is, by far, the largest member of ASEAN. Of the 650 million people in Southeast Asia, 40 percent, or 260 million, live in Indonesia. Why then has the country not tried to dominate ASEAN? Quite honestly, this is a big mystery. This is abnormal behaviour.[18]

Mediating Regional Conflicts

Playing an active role in mediating or easing regional conflicts is another significant form of Indonesia's peace activism. Indonesia's efforts in trying to bring the warring Cambodian factions together through the Jakarta Informal Meetings in the 1980s are well documented. Indonesia and France co-chaired the Paris meeting which produced the Paris Peace Agreement of 1991, ending the Cambodian civil war. Before the issue was formally taken up by ASEAN, Indonesia had tried to ease tensions in the South China Sea by hosting a series of workshops on managing potential conflicts in the South China Sea throughout the 1990s and early 2000s. Indonesia has also been one of the prime movers in ASEAN in getting the Declaration of Conduct of Parties in the South China Sea operationalized, as well as in pushing for a more binding Code of Conduct. When border skirmishes broke out between Cambodia and Thailand over the Temple of Preah Vihear in 2011, Indonesia, as chair of ASEAN, brokered talks between the two countries to end the first open clashes between ASEAN member states since the founding of the regional body. Indonesia also assisted in the peace negotiations between the Philippines government and Muslim rebels in Mindanao. Recently, Indonesia has tried to widen its peace activism beyond the Southeast Asian region. When the bilateral relations between Saudi Arabia and Iran took a turn for the worse in early 2016, Widodo sent Foreign Minister Retno Marsudi to deliver letters to both Tehran and Riyadh, calling for restraint and Islamic solidarity, despite little expectation of success.

Contributing to International Peacekeeping Operations

Regularly contributing to UNPKO is a manifestation of Indonesia's peace activism. Indonesia has been an active troop-contributing country to UN peacekeeping missions since 1957, when it first sent a sizeable military contingent to Egypt. Indonesia's support for the UNPKO is seen as important in fulfilling its constitutional mandate to contribute to the maintenance of world order. Indonesia's participation has mostly been in the form of military contingents for non-combat missions under Chapter VI of the UN Charter, though lately police personnel have been deployed to assist in law enforcement duties. Indonesia has not taken part in any peace-enforcement operations as provided under Chapter VII of the UN Charter since the country so far does not allow its military to fight on foreign soil. Recognizing the increasingly complex regional and global security challenges, Indonesia is working towards increasing its national, as well as supporting the development of an ASEAN, peacekeeping capacity.[19] Indonesia aims to be among the top ten troop-contributing countries with the ability to deploy 4,000 peacekeepers, and has made increasing the number of female peacekeepers a priority agenda.

Promoting Interfaith Dialogue and Moderate Islam

Although the majority of Indonesians are Muslims, until recently Islam as a value has not played a significant role in informing Indonesian foreign policy, except in Indonesia's strong support for the Palestinian struggle for an independent state and opposition to Zionism. The rise in religious tensions globally, however, and particularly the emergence of Islamic extremism and terrorism misusing the name of Islam, which have led to rising Islamophobia in the West, have been of particular concern to Indonesia. Conflicts within the Islamic world as well as between Muslims and people of other faiths directly affect religious harmony in Indonesia's multi-religious and multi-ethnic society. Indonesia has, therefore, taken a lead in promoting interfaith dialogue internationally to enhance mutual understanding and respect between peoples of different religions.

Of equal importance is Indonesia's increasingly active role in trying to promote moderate Islam within the Islamic world. Indonesia has suffered from terrorist attacks by home-grown Islamic extremist groups linked to, or inspired by, transnational extremist movements such as Al Qaeda and the Islamic State of Iraq and Syria. Its much-lauded social harmony attributed to the inclusive national ideology *Pancasila* has been threatened by rising religious intolerance. While in earlier times Indonesia had tended to defer to the Middle East as the natural centre of the Islamic world, the endless conflicts and crises in the Middle East has pushed Indonesia to call for the true implementation of Islam as a religion of peace, as its name implies, highlighting the Indonesian experience. Since its transition to democracy, Indonesia has tried to promote its international image as a country where Islam, democracy, modernity and female empowerment can walk hand in hand.

Among the activities undertaken by Indonesia to share its experience include efforts to make Indonesia into a new international centre of Islamic learning, providing assistance to other Muslim countries when requested and revitalizing understandings about Wasatiyyat Islam. Indonesia is establishing the Indonesian International Islamic University near Jakarta, envisaged as a modern centre of learning on Islamic civilization in the age of globalization. At the request of the Afghan government, Indonesia is building an Indonesian Islamic Centre in Kabul, while Nahdlatul Ulama, the largest Muslim mass organization in Indonesia known for its tolerance, has also established branches in Afghanistan. In May 2018 Indonesia hosted a high-level consultation of World Muslim Scholars on Wasatiyyat Islam and presented a proposal on the conception and implementation of Wasatiyyat Islam, defined as Islam of the middle path that avoids extreme positions, that seeks a balance between the afterlife and the worldly life, and as a method 'to contextualize Islam in the midst of global civilizations'.[20]

FROM CULTURAL RELATIVISM
TO UNIVERSAL VALUES

Indonesian nationalist leaders mostly agreed that the new republic would be democratic, with sovereignty in the hands of the people. The national ideology, *Pancasila*, contains the principles of a just and civilized humanity and representative government. The founding fathers, however, disagreed on the form of democracy that should be developed. In 1945, Supomo, in a speech at the Indonesian Independence Preparatory Task Force debating the foundation and constitution of the new Indonesian state, rejected the stress on individualism found in Western Europe and the United States influenced by thinkers such as John Locke and Jean Jacques Rousseau, or the class theory put forward by Marx, Engels and Lenin. Instead, he proposed that Indonesia adopt the concept of the 'integralistic state' as proposed by Spinoza, Adam Muller and Hegel, which he argued was more suitable to Indonesian cultural traditions. According to the ideal of this integralistic state, there is a complete unity between the leaders and the people as had been the case in traditional Indonesian villages, and the state must be dedicated to serve the interests of the community as a whole, instead of focusing on the individuals or groups.[21] Supomo's view, shared by Sukarno, was highly influential in the formulation of the original 1945 Constitution.

Proponents of liberal democracy had the upper hand in the 1950s, and the 1945 Constitution was put aside, but political divisions and instability during the parliamentary period led to Sukarno's 1959 Decree restoring the constitution. The original fairly brief constitution contained no system of checks and balances, thus allowing the executive to dominate all branches of government, legitimized the military's involvement in politics as functional groups and had no articles guaranteeing human rights, thus paving the way for authoritarian rule in Indonesia which lasted till the forced resignation of Suharto in 1998. Imbued by the idealism of the nationalist struggle for independence against foreign colonial rule, Supomo did not foresee the need to protect the people from the possible abuses of power by their own native government.

The failure of the parliamentary era gave liberal democracy, derisively referred to as '50 percent + 1 democracy' by Sukarno, a tainted image in Indonesia for the next four decades. The Suharto regime was a strong proponent of the integralistic state with its emphasis on harmony which forbade any forms of dissent towards the government. Like Sukarno, Suharto and the New Order power-holders viewed liberal democracy as an alien Western concept unsuitable to Indonesian culture. With the establishment of ASEAN, the New Order government was in good company as many ASEAN member states shared similar views. Made confident by their countries' remarkable economic progress Suharto, together with Prime Ministers Mahathir of Malaysia and Lee Kuan Yew of Singapore, became champions of 'Asian Values' which were seen to be distinct from Western values. ASEAN sanctified the principle of non-interference in each other's internal affairs, taken from the UN Charter, to a much higher level to insulate member states from external criticism of their respective domestic policies that might be regarded as violating civil and political rights. ASEAN countries also studiously avoided criticizing each other.

For Indonesia, these aspects changed after the fall of Suharto amid the Asian financial crisis of 1998. The Suharto government had relied on its economic performance as the primary basis of its legitimacy, and when the financial crisis quickly spread to become a multidimensional crisis, the New Order political structure lost its political legitimacy and collapsed. Indonesia embarked on political reform or *Reformasi* to institutionalize a truly open and competitive democratic system of governance that would be more resilient and a mechanism for self-renewal. The constitution was amended four times in line with democratic principles and other universal values, such as instituting a strong system of checks and balances between the different branches of government, ending the social-political role of the military, limiting the presidential terms and guaranteeing basic human rights. Notwithstanding the substantive constitutional amendments that had taken place in 1999, 2000, 2001 and 2002, there is a national consensus to leave the Preamble to the Constitution untouched, since it contains the fundamental values that Indonesia holds dear and are regarded as critical to keeping the nation united, in particular the ideology of *Pancasila*. Talks about Asian Values in Indonesia have receded since the country began to embrace democracy and human rights as universal values.

Indonesia's domestic political changes have also had an impact on foreign policy, both in decision making and in the foreign policy agenda. Since the onset of democratization there have been more actors involved in foreign policymaking, including parliament and civil society, resulting in more varied viewpoints. One of these is the increasing pressure on the Indonesian government to be more active in promoting democracy within ASEAN and to take a firmer stance against human rights abuses committed by another ASEAN member. Indonesia took the lead in instituting the adoption of the principles of democracy, human rights and good governance in the ASEAN Charter in 2007.[22] Abandoning its formerly rigid stance on the principle of non-interference in each other's internal affairs, the Indonesian government since the beginning of the *Reformasi* has played an active role in pushing the

Myanmar military government to open its political system, and in offering technical assistance to Myanmar in its transition to democracy. Indonesia has also been particularly active in responding to the Rohingya humanitarian crisis which has sparked large-scale anti-Myanmar demonstrations in Indonesia fuelled by a feeling of solidarity towards the persecuted Rohingya Muslim minority. Both the Indonesian government and civil society organizations have mobilized humanitarian assistance to provide relief to the Rohingya refugees who fled to Bangladesh. There have been attempts to demonstrate that Buddhists and Muslims can live together in harmony. Indonesian Muslim and Buddhist civil society organizations, with support from the government, are building a hospital in Rakhine State to serve patients from all religious and ethnic backgrounds, with groundbreaking in November 2017, while in 2014 Indonesia provided financial assistance to build inclusive schools in the same area. Foreign Minister Marsudi has carried out shuttle diplomacy between Myanmar and Bangladesh to help find a solution to the Rohingya crisis, even though this irked the government in Naypyidaw.

CONCLUSION

Values play an important part in Indonesian foreign policy. Despite the many major political changes that have occurred, adherence to certain core values has characterized the formulation and conduct of Indonesian foreign policy. Maintaining independence and playing an active role in promoting peace have remained dominant themes in the implementation of the independent and active Indonesian foreign policy doctrine. Since the onset of the *Reformasi* era, Indonesian foreign policy has also been informed by the acceptance of democracy and human rights as universal values, and efforts to have them recognized within ASEAN. Nevertheless, the application of these latter values has been more selective, for while Indonesia has not hesitated to criticize Myanmar, a new member of ASEAN, Jakarta has been silent over the democratic and human rights regression in older ASEAN member states, such as the military coup in Thailand and the extrajudicial killings in the Philippines. Adherence to the principle of non-interference in each other's internal affairs, regarded as critical to maintaining regional harmony, still weighs more than any principled stance on universal values within ASEAN.

NOTES

1. 'The Constitution of the Republic of Indonesia of 1945', *The United Nations Educational, Scientific and Cultural Organization*, http://www.unesco.org/education/edurights/media/docs/b1ba8608010ce0c48966911957392ea8cda405d8.pdf.

2. For a good introduction to Indonesian history see M. C. Ricklefs, *A History of Modern Indonesia since C. 1200* (Stanford: Stanford University Press, 2008).

3. George McTurnan Kahin, *Nationalism and Revolution in Indonesia* (Ithaca, NY: Cornell University Press, 2003).

4. This historic speech has been published in a book by Mohammad Hatta under the same title *Mendayungantara Dua Karang – Rowing between Two Reefs* (Jakarta: BulanBintang, 1988). See also Ide Anak Agung Gde Agung, *Twenty Years Indonesian Foreign Policy, 1945–1965* (The Hague: Mouton, 1972), 27.

5. Mohammad Hatta, 'Indonesia's Foreign Policy', *Foreign Affairs* 31, no. 3 (April 1953): 441–52.

6. Amitav Acharya and See Seng Tan, 'The Normative Relevance of the Bandung Conference for Contemporary Asian and International Order', in See Seng Tan and Amitav Acharya (eds.). *Bandung Revisited. The Legacy of the 1955 Asia-African Conference for International Order* (Singapore: NUS Press, 2008).

7. 'The Ten Principles of Bandung', *China Daily* (23 April 2005). http://www.chinadaily.com.cn/english/doc/2005-04/23/content_436882.htm.

8. The best study about Indonesian politics in the 1950s is Herbert Feith's *Decline of Constitutional Democracy in Indonesia* (Ithaca, NY; London: Cornell University Press, 1962).

9. J. A. C. Mackie, *Konfrontasi: The Indonesia Malaysia Dispute, 1963–1966* (Kuala Lumpur: Oxford University Press, 1974).

10. Sukarno, 'Storming the Last Bulwarks of Imperialism', in Herbert Feith and Lance Castles (eds.). *Indonesian Political Thinking, 1945–1965* (Ithaca, NY: Cornell University Press, 1970), 466–70.

11. Ibid.

12. Questions of who were really behind the so-called 30 September Affairs have continued to engender political controversy and intense academic debates till today. The official explanation throughout the New Order period puts the blame squarely on the PKI with backing from the People's Republic of China, while a number of academics have argued that the abortive coup was an internal army affair.

13. Dewi Fortuna Anwar, *Indonesia and the Security of Southeast Asia* (Jakarta: CSIS, 1992), 12–14.

14. Speech by Susilo Bambang Yudhoyono, President of the Republic of Indonesia before the Indonesian Council of World Affairs, Jakarta, 20 May 2005.

15. '"Nawa Cita", 9 Agenda Prioritas Jokowi-JK'. *Kompas.com*, (21 May 2014).

16. 'The Constitution of the Republic of Indonesia of 1945', *The United Nations Educational, Scientific and Cultural Organization*, http://www.unesco.org/education/edurights/media/docs/b1ba8608010ce0c48966911957392ea8cda405d8.pdf.

17. Dewi Fortuna Anwar, *Indonesia in ASEAN. Foreign Policy and Regionalism* (Singapore: ISEAS, 1994).

18. Kishore Mahbubani, 'Indonesia's Big-Hearted Spirit in ASEAN', *The Straits Times* (16 August 2018).

19. Dewi Fortuna Anwar, 'Indonesia's Peacekeeping Operations: History, Practice, and Future Trend', in Chiyuki Aoi and Yee-KuangHeng (eds.). *Asia Pacific Nations in International Peace Support and Stability Operations* (New York: Palgrave Macmillan, 2014).

20. Office of the Special Envoy of the President of the Republic of Indonesia for Interfaith and Inter-civilization Dialogue and Cooperation, 'Wastiyyat Islam for Global Civilization: Conception and Implementation'. Indonesian Proposal presented before the High-Level Consultation of World Muslim Scholars on Wasatiyyat Islam. Bogor, 1–3 May 2018.

21. Supomo's 'Integralistic State Concept' speech in front of the Indonesian Independence Preparatory Task Force (BPUPKI), 31 May 1945, in Floriberta Aning, *Lahirnya Pancasila, Kumpulan Pidato BPUPKI* (Yogyakarta: Media Presindo, 2006), 56–80.

22. Jurgen Ruland, *The Indonesian Way: ASEAN, Europeanization, and Foreign Policy Debates in a New Democracy* (Stanford: Stanford University Press, 2017).

BIBLIOGRAPHY

Acharya, Amitav and See Seng Tan. 'The Normative Relevance of the Bandung Conference for Contemporary Asian and International Order', in See Seng Tan and Amitav Acharya (eds.). *Bandung Revisited. The Legacy of the 1955 Asia-African Conference for International Order*. Singapore: NUS Press, 2008.

Agung, Ide Anak Agung Gde. *Twenty Years Indonesian Foreign Policy, 1945–1965*. The Hague: Mouton, 1972.

Anwar, Dewi Fortuna. *Indonesia and the Security of Southeast Asia*. Jakarta: CSIS, 1992: 12–14.

Anwar, Dewi Fortuna. *Indonesia in ASEAN. Foreign Policy and Regionalism*. Singapore: ISEAS, 1994.

Anwar, Dewi Fortuna. 'Indonesia's Peacekeeping Operations: History, Practice, and Future Trend', in Chiyuki Aoi and Yee-Kuang Heng (eds.). *Asia Pacific Nations in International Peace Support and Stability Operations*. New York: Palgrave Macmillan, 2014.

Feith, Herbert. *Decline of Constitutional Democracy in Indonesia*. Ithaca, NY; London: Cornell University Press, 1962.

Hatta, Mohammad. 'Indonesia's Foreign Policy'. *Foreign Affairs* 31, no. 3 (April 1953): 441–52.

Hatta, Mohammad. *MendayungantaraDuaKarang – Rowing between Two Reefs*. Jakarta: Bulan Bintang, 1988.

Kahin, George McTurnan. *Nationalism and Revolution in Indonesia*. Ithaca, NY: Cornell University Press, 2003.

Mackie, J.A.C. *Konfrontasi: The Indonesia Malaysia Dispute, 1963–1966*. Kuala Lumpur: Oxford University Press, 1974.

Mahbubani, Kishore. 'Indonesia's Big-Hearted Spirit in ASEAN'. *The Straits Times,* 16 August 2018.

Office of the Special Envoy of the President of the Republic of Indonesia for Interfaith and Inter-civilization Dialogue and Cooperation, 'Wastiyyat Islam for Global Civilization: Conception and Implementation'. Indonesian Proposal presented before the High-Level Consultation of World Muslim Scholars on Wasatiyyat Islam. Bogor, 1–3 May 2018.

Ricklefs, M. C. *A History of Modern Indonesia since C. 1200*. Stanford, CA: Stanford University Press, 2008.

Ruland, Jurgen. *The Indonesian Way: ASEAN, Europeanization, and Foreign Policy Debates in a New Democracy*. Stanford, CA: Stanford University Press, 2017.

Sukarno. 'Storming the Last Bulwarks of Imperialism', in Herbert Feith and Lance Castles (eds.). *Indonesian Political Thinking, 1945–1965*. Ithaca, NY: Cornell University Press, 1970: 466–70.

Supomo's 'Integralistic State Concept', in Floriberta Aning, *Lahirnya Pancasila, Kumpulan Pidato BPUPKI*. Yogyakarta: Media Presindo, 2006: 56–80.

Yudhoyono, Susilo Bambang, Speech at the Indonesian Council of World Affairs, Jakarta, 20 May 2005.

Chapter 11

Values in Chinese Foreign Policy

Culture, Leadership and Diplomacy

Zhang Lihua

China's reform and opening-up has been carried out over forty years. China's economy has developed rapidly over the past four decades. Since 2000, the cultural revival movement has reappeared in mainland China – discovering and understanding traditional Chinese culture, essence and values – to construct a Chinese value and ethical system.

The values of traditional Chinese culture are the foundation of the Chinese people's identity. Once one understands the values of traditional Chinese culture, one can truly understand Chinese diplomacy because the political system and foreign policy of a country is rooted in its history and culture. The core of culture is the values that imperceptibly influence national psychology and national identity and directly affect the choice of strategic and foreign policies.

Chinese foreign policy and diplomacy have puzzled many Western politicians and political elites. For example, the ideas of 'China will never seek hegemony', 'building a harmonious world', 'building a new model of major power relationship', 'build a community of human destiny' and so on are considered nonsensical by some Western people. According to the theory of offensive realism, emerging powers will necessarily challenge existing powers; so a rising China will definitely challenge America, the only superpower of the world, for hegemony. As the saying goes, China and the United States will inevitably fight a war. The so-called China Threat is widely believed in the Western world. However, will China really contend for hegemony with America? After China's rise, will it really threaten the world?

We can get some answers if we analyse how traditional cultural values influence China's foreign policy and diplomacy. It provides a new perspective to foreigners to understand China's diplomacy.

WHAT ARE CHINESE
TRADITIONAL CULTURAL VALUES?

Cultural values are the values believed and worshipped by a majority of the people in a country, and function as criteria for judgement by people. Historically, values would be recognized by the majority and gain common recognition. Traditional Chinese cultural values came from the harmony of thought in ancient China. The harmony of thought was a complete system that included three aspects: first, a world outlook and methodology – Tai Chi Philosophy and harmonious dialectics (Yin-Yang dialectics). Second, a system of values: harmony, benevolence, righteousness, etiquette, wisdom, faithfulness. And third, an ideal goal, comprising:

Harmony between humans and nature
Harmony between humans and society
Harmony between persons

Harmony between the human body and mind

Traditional Chinese cultural values refer to the values jointly advocated by Taoism (道德经), the Book of Changes (易经), Confucianism (论语)and Huangdi Neijing (黄帝内经), with harmony as the core. Harmony means 'things fitting each other in an appropriate and well-balanced way'.[1] It indicates rationality, appropriateness and striking the right note. Rationality suggests doing things following objective laws and rules, and appropriateness means doing things properly and striking the right note. Harmony means that people who do things should be following the law of nature and society. Different things coexist in harmony and will produce new things, so harmony creates everything; it will promote the growth and abundance of materials by integrating different things. Based on the objective laws of 'harmony creates everything', the value of harmony advocates the coexistence of different things, integrating them through rational and appropriate combination, and attaining coordination and balance.

The Tai Chi Philosophy and Yin-Yang dialects advocate harmony between people and nature, people and society, people and people and body and mind. The idea of harmony was embodied in every aspect of life in ancient times, including music, dance, calligraphy, painting (landscape painting), garden, architecture, Tai Chi Quan (ancient Chinese martial art form), Qigong (ancient Chinese exercise), Chinese medicine, health systems, tea culture and so on.

According to the harmony thought, the universe and nature not only have violent motion but also have a state of balance and harmony. The state of balance and harmony prevails over the most part of time and space in the natural world. The universe instinctively strikes a balance. Although movement and changes in human society are more complex than those in nature because of the greed and selfishness of people, they cannot be beyond the laws of nature. Harmony is not equivalent to peace and does not mean there are no contradictions, struggles or conflict. It also does not mean neutrality and unprincipled compromise. For example, when a country is invaded by a foreign country, it must fight against the aggressor. This kind of struggle for self-protection to maintain own survival and security is in line with the laws of nature and society. So, the values of harmony tell people not only that countries should respect each other, achieve equality and mutual benefit, seek common ground while reserving differences and cooperate for win-win result, but also what is a reasonable and just fight.

Benevolence was proposed 2,000 years ago by the Chinese philosopher Confucius. It is the core value of Confucianism as well as the value commonly recognized and respected by Chinese people. Benevolence means to love others and know the difference between good and evil. There is an old saying in China, 'Family harmony leads to prosperity'. The idea of the benevolence expands kinship and family ties.

Righteousness refers to appropriateness and justice. It emphasizes that people should do things based on objective Tao laws; when people pursue their interests, they should be guided by morality and a sense of justice, and should safeguard personal dignity and protect the family and motherland from encroachment.

Confucius once said, 'Any one only doing things for personal interests would attract great resentment from others'.[2] Confucius advocated that the methods to further self-interest should be reasonable and legal, should not harm others and should not deceive others. In addition to personal interests, people living in society have collective and social interests, and should combine personal interests with social interests. For example, when the motherland is invaded by foreigners, everyone should realize that the rise and fall of the nation concerns everyone, realize the need to banish foreign invaders and restore the sovereignty of the nation and be willing to undergo the tribulations needed to safeguard the sovereignty of the motherland and the dignity of the nation.[3]

Benevolence and righteousness constitute indispensable values. Benevolence necessarily requires righteousness. People consider not only their own interests but also those of others in society.

Etiquette emphasizes that man should be modest and prudent and should not do what one wishes without restraint. According to Confucius, 'It is benevolent to control oneself to follow the etiquette'.[4] The etiquette recommended by Chinese traditional culture includes the customs and civil law. As Confucius said, 'When the rulers at higher ranks follow etiquette and obey laws, it becomes easier to govern people'.[5] Etiquette also means that man should be modest, respect others, be polite and avoid being arrogant and avoid bullying others.

Wisdom means that people should distinguish between right and wrong and have wisdom and strategic thinking. According to Confucius, the benevolent love people and treat others well, can distinguish between right and wrong, correctly judge people and solve problems through strategic thinking. This means that, in addition to benevolence, people should have a sense of what is right and wrong, as well as the wisdom and strategic thinking to reward virtue and punish vice.

Faithfulness refers to keeping one's words and being honest. According to Confucius in his *Analects*, 'Only when promise meets righteousness can words be realized' and could improve morals by focusing on loyalty and faithfulness and following righteousness. In daily life, Confucius advocates that people should rationally and appropriately acquire wealth through labour and not by cheating or dishonesty. Everyone should keep his or her promises. Faithfulness is a moral quality to which Chinese traditional culture attaches special importance.

TRADITIONAL CULTURAL VALUES AND DIPLOMACY

Although the Communist Party of China and the Chinese government officials claim to believe in Marxism and take Marxism as the guiding ideology, their lives have been steeped in Chinese culture and are or were deeply affected by traditional Chinese culture, values and method of thinking. When they give speeches, they often quote from classics and express their ideas through the classic words of ancient Confucianism and Taoism.

In addition, certain common perspectives of popular sentiment on issues, such as national identity, have been conveyed to state leaders through media, public opinion and information channels, exerting an influence on diplomatic decision making and the conduct of leaders. Traditional Chinese cultural values also present the following manifestations in China's current diplomatic practices.

Influence of the Concept of Harmony on Chinese Diplomacy

China adopted the Five Principles of Peaceful Coexistence in 1950, as the guidelines for China's foreign relations. In the era of Mao Zedong, however, too much emphasis was placed on class struggle and proletarian dictatorship, while imperialism and revisionism were opposed and proletarian internationalism was pursued in the field of foreign relations. The Eastern group, consisting of China and the Soviet Union, fought against the US-led Western group during the years of Mao Zedong. It was called 'two fists to fight against others' at that time. Also, the relationship between China and some Southeast Asian countries had been in a state of struggle and opposition.

Since the reform and opening-up in 1978, Chinese leaders Deng Xiaoping, Jiang Zemin, Hu Jintao and Xi Jinping have absorbed the Chinese traditional cultural values of harmony and solved the domestic problems with the harmonious dialectics. China has no longer focused on class struggle or launched mass political movements but implemented the policy of internal reform and opened up to the outside world, vigorously developing the economy and improving the people's livelihood. As for China's foreign relations, the concepts of harmony in diversity, seeking common ground while shelving differences and win-win cooperation, including the values of harmony, have also been applied and reflected. China has improved the relations with the European and American countries, Russia, Central Asian countries and neighbouring countries, and further developed friendly relations with the African, Latin American and Oceania countries.

Today, China continues to adhere to the Five Principles of Peaceful Coexistence in its foreign policy. The harmony value is embodied by the Five Principles of Peaceful Coexistence, namely 'mutual respect for territorial integrity and sovereignty, mutual non-aggression, non-interference in each other's internal affairs, equality and mutual benefit, and peaceful coexistence'. In half a century, the Five Principles of Peaceful Coexistence have been accepted by most countries of the world and have become important guidelines for international relations.

According to these principles, it would be a violation of righteousness if a country wages a war and kills innocent people for its own interests or interferes with the internal affairs of other countries and creates civil strife or secession in foreign countries for its own interests. Such actions should be condemned and opposed. Former Chinese premier Wen Jiabao said,

The reason why China chose the road of peaceful rise was because we have our own culture with a long history. The core of this culture is harmony, and this core focuses on the ideas of harmony and diversity. We should seek to learn from each other, rather than see our differences as a source of conflict.[6]

Since the beginning of the twenty-first century, the Chinese government has proposed a new security concept featuring mutual trust, mutual benefit, equality and cooperation and the principle of cooperation and common interest.[7]

The Confucian classic *Book of Rites* says, 'The future world will be open and in universal harmony'.[8] The ideal society is a harmonious society. In order to realize this ideal, the values of harmony propose that all countries should respect each other, cooperate for mutual benefit and exist and prosper together. On 11 October 2005, then Chinese President Hu Jintao proposed building a world of harmony at the summit meeting for the sixtieth anniversary of the United Nations (UN). In the twenty-first century, 'peaceful development', 'harmonious world' and 'mutual benefit' and 'win-win result' have become China's foreign strategies.[9] On 29 November 2012, then Vice President Xi Jinping proposed to realize the Chinese dream for the first time. The Chinese dream refers to the realization of great rejuvenation of the Chinese nation. As Xi said, 'The Chinese dream is a dream of pursuing peace. The Chinese dream needs peace and can be realized only in peace'. Peace and harmony are the ideals of the Chinese nation for thousands of years'.[10]

The Communist Party of China stressed in the 18th National Congress that China would

> continue to hold high the banner of peace, development, co-operation and mutual benefit and strive to uphold world peace and promote common development. We will continue to promote friendship and partnership with our neighbours, consolidate friendly relations and deepen mutually beneficial co-operation with them, and ensure that China's development will bring more benefits to our neighbours.[11]

Xi Jinping proposed at the 19th Congress of the Communist Party of China, that

> Adhering to the path of peaceful development and building a community of shared future for mankind, China will actively develop global partnership, expand converging interests with other countries, promote the coordination and cooperation with powers, construct a framework for major-country relations of overall stability and balanced development, deepen the relations with neighbouring countries in accordance with the diplomacy of amity, sincerity, mutual benefit and inclusiveness and also the neighboring diplomacy of being a good neighbour and partner, and strengthen solidarity and cooperation with developing countries by upholding the correct concept of justice and interests and the true concept of amity.[12]

The value of harmony is based on the Tai Chi philosophy and Yin-Yang dialectics that are cultural heritages of ancient China. The harmony value emphasizes that analyses of issues should be comprehensive and dialectical and should be based on recognition of diversity. When a country is growing stronger, it should not be self-righteous, arrogant, and should not seek to dominate the world. The major powers should avoid taking extreme positions in international relations, and a strong country will not seek world hegemony. In the Chinese context, hegemony is a negative word. Chinese leaders from Mao Zedong, Deng Xiaoping, Jiang Zemin, Hu Jintao to Xi Jinping today have repeatedly stressed that China will never seek hegemony. This announcement embodied the value of harmony, and the President Xi Jinping's proposed 'community of common destiny'[13] also embodied it.

Influence of the Concept of Benevolence on Chinese Diplomacy

China has pursued benevolent diplomacy and has wanted to be a peaceful power in the international community since 1979. On 7 October 2003, then Chinese premier Wen Jiabao attended the first Association of Southeast Asian Nations (ASEAN) Business and Investment Summit in Bali, Indonesia, and delivered a speech entitled 'Development of China and Revitalization of Asia'. In his speech, he proposed the concept of bringing harmony, security and prosperity to neighbours.[14] In 2013, the first symposium on peripheral diplomatic work in neighbouring countries since the founding of People's Republic of China was held in Beijing. At the meeting, Xi Jinping proposed a diplomatic concept of 'Amity, Sincerity, Mutual Benefit and Inclusiveness' to neighbours.[15] The relations between China and ASEAN and Central Asian countries fully reflect these ideas. The Shanghai Cooperation Organization (SCO) is exactly a good example. Since the twenty-first century, China's economic and trade relations with the ASEAN and SCO have become closer.

Xi Jinping proposed the building of a new type of international relations based on cooperation. China emphasizes that a big and strong country should not bully the small and weak; should not judge other countries using the social system, ideology and values of the big as the correct standard and rule; and should not attack, destroy or eliminate opposing countries. He put forward the Belt and Road Initiative based on the principles of shared and mutual benefit, reciprocity, cooperation and win-win situation.[16] China put the Asian Infrastructure Investment Bank and Brazil-Russia-India-China-South Africa New Development Bank into operation as soon as possible to contribute to the economic growth and improvement of people's lives in developing countries.

Since the 1960s, China has provided significant aid to African countries. Chinese aid to, and construction and investment in, African countries is free from political conditions or conditionalities. In recent decades, China has written off debts of renminbi (RMB) 30 billion due from now exempted fifty heavily indebted poor nations.[17] For over sixty years, China has been actively involved in international development and cooperation and has provided aid of approximately RMB 400 billion to a total of 166 national and international organizations and dispatched more than 600,000 aid workers. More than 700 Chinese people sacrificed their lives in the development of other countries.[18]

In September 2015, Xi Jinping made a speech at the UN Sustainable Development Summit and announced that China would set up the South-South Cooperation Fund, which would provide US$2 billion for the first instalment to help developing countries fulfil the development agenda after 2015. China will continue to increase investment in least developed countries (LDCs) and will try to touch the US$12 billion mark by 2030. President Xi Jinping has announced that China will 'exempt the debt of the outstanding intergovernmental interest-free loans due by the end of 2015 owed by the relevant LDCs, landlocked developing countries and small island developing countries'.[19]

China will establish an international development knowledge centre to jointly research and disseminate development models and practices that are tailored to the needs of individual countries. China proposes to discuss and build global energy networks and promote the development of clean and green energy to meet global power demands. These facts show China's benevolent diplomacy.

Influence of the Concept of Righteousness on Chinese Diplomacy

The value of righteousness implies that it is justified for a country to safeguard its sovereignty, territory and dignity, and for a country suffering foreign invasion, to attack and drive out invaders. In other words, when invaded by a foreign country, a country must defend itself and counterattack. It is in line with the laws of nature and society that a person or a country defends self and protects own safety, survival and development.

Chinese people believe in sentiments passed down from ancient China that we will not attack unless we are attacked; if we are attacked, we will certainly counterattack. These have informed Chinese preparations to handle foreign invasions. The Sun Zi's *Art of War* and Sun Bin's *Art of War* in ancient China provide the wisdom, tactics and strategies for struggle against invaders and intruders.

Therefore, traditional Chinese cultural values incorporate both moral norms including benevolence, righteousness, etiquette, wisdom and faithfulness, and the tactics and wisdom of the *Art of War* to resist foreign aggression and safeguard the motherland. Therefore, China does not take any initiative to get into trouble, provoke others, interfere with the internal affairs of other countries or contend for hegemony, but stands firmly committed to safeguarding its own sovereignty, territorial land, territorial sea and other core interests.

China is a country with nuclear weapons. After the explosion of China's first atomic bomb in 1964, China announced to the world that China would not first use nuclear weapons, or threaten to use nuclear weapons against non-nuclear-weapon states. On 29 July 1996, China successfully conducted an underground nuclear test in Lop Nor, Xinjiang. On the evening of the same day, the Chinese government issued a statement solemnly declaring that China would suspend nuclear tests from 30 July 1996 and reiterating that 'China develops nuclear weapons to safeguard world peace, break nuclear blackmail and threat, prevent nuclear war, and ultimately eliminate nuclear weapons. . . . Since mankind can produce nuclear weapons in the 20th century, it is also fully capable of eradicating them in the twenty-first century. The Chinese government and people are ready to work with the governments and people of other countries to realize this lofty goal'.[20] The Chinese government's statement and commitment indicate that China's limited nuclear arsenal is only for self-defence and maintaining peace.

In November 2013 China announced the establishment of an air defence identification zone, covering most of the East China Sea. In recent years, China's actions in the South China Sea have aimed to defend Chinese islands and territorial waters. China has taken some defensive actions to counter the provocations from the United States, Japan and the Philippines. These actions are purely based on principles of self-defence and safeguarding sovereignty. According to the Five Principles of Peaceful Coexistence, the settlement of the South China Sea issue should depend on the peaceful negotiation between China and the involved countries in the future.

In the Syrian crisis, the Chinese government opposed the United States and Western countries interfering in the internal affairs of, and supporting the anti-government armed forces in, Syria. This demonstrates China's principles of the big and strong country respecting the small and weak, and opposing interference by the big and strong powers in the internal affairs of other countries.

After becoming the US president, Donald Trump regarded China as the biggest competitor and imposed trade sanctions against China, forcing the Chinese government to take corresponding countermeasures. This also reflects the characteristics and manners of the Chinese culture, that is, I will neither trouble or antagonize you, nor accept your bullying and oppression. Facing the US provocation, China has to counterattack with rationality, in order to defend its own national interests. The fundamental motivation of China's reaction to the US-launched trade war is to bring two countries back to normal trade relations.

Influence of the Concept of Etiquette on Chinese Diplomacy

Traditional Chinese culture concepts of etiquette have also impacted its foreign policy. As a consequence, the values of courtesy, obeying the system of law of the UN in international society, respect for other countries and decorous and friendly relations with neighbours have come to figure in foreign policy. China's 'global government concept' is the concept of building business together, building together and sharing.

Lao Tzu said that the sea can hold thousands of rivers due to its low position. Because of this, the sea becomes the king of the rivers. Therefore, a great power should gain the dependence of small countries by being modest, while the small countries should win cooperation with the great power by being modest. In this way, the great power and small countries can attain their own will. In particular, the great power should be modest.[21] 'A man stretching on tiptoes to stand high may easily fall; a man leaping forward to move fast may easily be slow'.[22] These statements of truth emphasize the need to be modest and to be respectful of others. All countries should respect each other, treat people courteously, and work together for common prosperity.

Confucius said, 'It is a delight to have friends come from afar'. Although China is a big country, it does not domineer, but respects all small and poor countries in the world. Leaders of many small countries and especially African countries can receive respect and courtesy from Chinese leaders when they visit China. The fact that China has been maintained long-term friendly relations with most African countries proves this point.

Influence of the Concept of Wisdom on Chinese Diplomacy

Yin-Yang dialects, the basis of the value of harmony, advocate looking at things comprehensively and dialectically and generally oppose carrying things to extremes. A warning in the *Book of Changes* says 'in prosperity think of adversity'.[23] For instance, a dragon that is flying too high will find it hard to breathe due to thin air and coldness, and may therefore fall down and die, which demonstrates that high status may never last long. There is an old saying in China, 'The highest place is not the safest roost'. According to *Tao Te Ching* of Lao Tzu, 'A too strong thing could easily become old'.[24]

Tao Te Ching of Lao Tzu had explained many laws of softness conquering hardness. He said, 'The softest things can move freely within the hardest things of the world, while the intangible strength can penetrate tangible things without spaces'.[25] This idea is also reflected in Chinese diplomacy. For example, since reform and opening-up, China has maintained over four decades of rapid economic development and become increasingly powerful. However, for Sino-US relations, China does not challenge America's status as the elder brother but attaches special importance to building a relation of mutual trust, cooperation and common interest with the United States. The idea of building a new model of major power relationship was expressly proposed by Xi Jinping.

In September 2015, when Xi Jinping visited America and talked to President Obama, he again emphasized the need to enhance strategic mutual trust between America and China and to promote the constant development of a new model of major power relationship between America and China. He believes that there will be no 'Thucydides trap' in the relations between the two major powers.

The 'China Threat' has never died down in the United States and Western countries for many years past, and some people have expressed the opinion that China will definitely contend for world hegemony with America, which will inevitably lead to a war. Some hawks in the United States have urged the American government to regard China as the biggest threat and enemy. How does China defuse this situation? China vigorously develops Sino-US trade to soften America's hostility against China to ensure greater economic integration between the two countries, facilitate understanding between the two countries through cultural exchanges and people-to-people communication and reduces the antagonism of the United States by building a new model of major power relationship between America and China.

Influence of the Concept of Faithfulness on Chinese Diplomacy

Faithfulness refers to keeping one's word and being honest. Since the reforms and opening-up, China has made infrastructure construction, and many loans have been offered to China by the World Bank. China has always repaid its debts on time and is rated the best borrowing country by the World Bank.[26] China has kept the promises made at the Climate Conference of the UN to ensure a reduction in carbon emissions, to vigorously develop new energy and to implement environment protection projects. However, at present, there are still many problems in terms of environmental protection and pollution reduction in China. It needs to continue to govern the environment in the future.

China actively participates in the peacekeeping of the UN and abides by its commitment to assume the responsibility of a big country. In September 1988 China formally applied to join the Special Committee on Peacekeeping of the UN. In 1989, China sent experts to participate in the UN Transition Assistance Mission to Namibia to help Namibia gain independence from South Africa. In April 1990, China dispatched military observers to the Middle East and participated in the UN-led peacekeeping operations for the first time. In April 1992, China dispatched a military engineering brigade to Cambodia for the first time to participate in the UN peacekeeping operations. By now, China is the largest contributor of peacekeeping troops among the permanent members of the UN Security Council. There have, however, been occasions when China has fallen short. For example, in 2012, the World Trade Organization (WTO) ruled that the tariffs on China's high-end technology steel products do not meet the WTO requirements. In 2015, the WTO ruled that the export control of raw materials such as minerals in China is not in line with China's commitment to the WTO. Lack of integrity exists in some Chinese companies as they produce imitative and low-quality goods. In addition, China does have problems in protection of intellectual property rights. China needs to strengthen the rule of law to solve these problems.

CONCLUSION

Culture is the face as well as the soul of a nation. Chinese culture based on human relations pays attention to self-cultivation, concerns for family, love of country, cares about the world and benefits for the people. Chinese people not only practise these principles over themselves but also extend far beyond, showing the broad and deep feelings of brotherhood and compassion. Based on this character of national culture, China has chosen the road of peaceful development, internal harmonious society and an external harmonious world. We hope people all over the world would live under the same sky with freedom, equality, harmony and happiness and share the results of peace and development.[27]

> China does not agree with the idea of strengthening the state and hegemony over the state, and there is no gene in the blood of the Chinese people who call themselves hegemon and militarily. China will unswervingly follow the path of peaceful development. This will be beneficial to China, beneficial to Asia and beneficial to the world. No force can shake the belief that China will develop peacefully.[28]

Chinese traditional cultural values constitute the essence and treasure of Chinese traditional culture. Harmony, benevolence, righteousness, etiquette, wisdom and faithfulness – these values still exist and are the values recognized by most Chinese to judge right and wrong. Traditional Chinese cultural values are completely different from the law of the jungle and power politics; also different from the Cold War mentality and the 'zero-sum game' mentality. The law of the jungle will not lead to peaceful coexistence, and the arbitrary use of force cannot make the world a better place. In today's world, the principles of harmony in diversity, seeking common ground and resolving differences and peaceful coexistence provide new ideas for settling international disputes. The Chinese cultural values of harmony will contribute to world peace.

The principles and policies of peace diplomacy with Chinese characteristics are based on the integration between socialism's concepts and harmonious value system of traditional culture of China. The Chinese traditional cultural values of harmony, such as benevolence, righteousness, courtesy, wisdom and faith, have positive significance for world peace.

NOTES

1. *Modern Chinese Dictionary Revision* (Beijing: Chinese Academy of Social Sciences, 1996), 510.

2. Cheng Changming, *Analects of Confucius* (Liaoning: National Publishing House, 1996), 37.

3. Ibid., 173.

4. Ibid., 129.

5. Ibid., 168.

6. Lv Hong and He Hongze, 'Widely Initiating Civilization Dialogue and Cultural Exchange', *The People's Daily* (11 December 2003).

7. Statements by Ambassador Hu Xiaodi at Main Committees of the 2005 NPT Review Conference, *Ministry of Foreign Affairs of the People's Republic of China* (20 May 2005). http://www.nti.org/media/pdfs/35_4a.pdf?_=1316627913.

8. Xiufen Lu, 'The Confucian Ideal of Great Harmony (Datong 大同), the Daoist Account of Change, and the Theory of Socialism in the Work of Li Dazhao', *Asian Philosophy*: 171–192.

9. 'Build towards a Harmonious World of Lasting Peace and Common Prosperity', Statement by Hu Jintao, President of the People's Republic of China at the United Nations Summit, New York, 15 September 2005. http://www.un.org/webcast/summit2005/statements15/china050915eng.pdf.

10. Wang Long and Feng Dapeng, 'Xi Jinping's Description about the "Chinese Dream"', *xinhuanet.com* (29 November 2016). http://www.xinhuanet.com/2016-11/29/c_1120016588.htm.

11. Hu Jintao's Report at the 18th National Congress of the Communist Party of China: 'Firmly March on the Path of Socialism with Chinese Characteristics and Strive to Complete the Building of a Moderately Prosperous Society in All Respects', *China Daily Network* (19 November 2012). http://language.chinadaily.com.cn/news/2012-11/19/content_15941774.htm.

12. Xi Jinping's Report at the 19th National Congress of the Communist Party of China: 'Secure a Decisive Victory in Building a Moderately Prosperous Society in All Respects and Strive for the Great Success of Socialism with Chinese Characteristics for a New Era', *xinhuanet.com* (27 October 2017). http://jhsjk.people.cn/article/29613458.

13. Hu Jintao's Report at the 18th National Congress of the Communist Party of China: 'Firmly March on the Path of Socialism with Chinese Characteristics and Strive to Complete the Building of a Moderately Prosperous Society in All Respects', *China Daily Network* (19 November 2012). http://language.chinadaily.com.cn/news/2012-11/19/content_15941774.htm.

14. Wen Jiabao's Speech at the ASEAN Business and Investment Summit, *China.com.cn* (8 October 2003). http://www.china.com.cn/zhuanti2005/txt/2003-10/08/content_5417165.htm.

15. Liu Zhen, 'Xi Jinping's Diplomatic Concept in New Era Remains in Upholding These Four Aspects', *China.com.cn* (26 November 2017). http://www.china.com.cn/news/2017-11/26/content_41945566.htm.

16. Wang Yi's Statement on President Xi Jinping's visit to Kazakhstan to attend the 17th Meeting of SCO Council of Heads of State and Opening Ceremony of Astana Expo 2017: 'Carry Forward Silk Road Spirit and Write a New Chapter for Cooperation', *Ministry of Foreign Affairs, the People's Republic of China* (10 June 2017). http://www.fmprc.gov.cn/mfa_eng/zxxx_662805/t1469852.shtml.

17. 'China Has Exempted 50 Heavily Indebted Poor Nations of Debts of 30 Billion Yuan in Recent Decade', *The People's Daily* (4 November 2012).

18. Xi Jinping's Speech at UN Sustainable Development Summit, *Xinhua Net* (27 September 2015).

19. Xi Jinping's Speech at UN Sustainable Development Summit: 'Stressing to Realize Common Development of All Countries from New Starting Point of Post-2015 Development Agenda', *Ministry of Foreign Affairs, the People's Republic of China* (27 September 2015). http://www.fmprc.gov.cn/mfa_eng/topics_665678/xjp-dmgjxgsfwbcxlhgcl70znxlfh/t1302359.shtml.

20. Canghaiguanlan, 'We Will Suspend Nuclear Tests in the Face of the Vicissitudes of Time! China Shocked the World with Its Announcement 21 Years Ago Today!' *The First Military Website* (29 July 2017). http://www.sohu.com/a/160701824_600524.

21. Xu Shu and Liu Hao, *Tao Te Ching of Lao Zi* (Anhui: People's Publishing House China, 1990), 168–69.

22. Ibid., 68–69.

23. Xu Shu and Zhang Xinxu, *Book of Changes* (Anhui: People's Publishing House, 1992), 7.

24. Xu Shu and Liu Hao, *Tao Te Ching of Lao Zi* (Anhui: People's Publishing House China, 1990), 150.

25. Ibid., 121–122.

26. Vice President of World Bank: 'China Is One of the Best Clients for the World Bank', *people.com.cn* (25 November 2004). http://www.people.com.cn/BIG5/shizheng/1026/3011379.html.

27. Cai Wu, 'Chinese Culture and Peaceful Development of China', *China.com.cn* (28 September 2011). http://www.china.com.cn/policy/zhuanti/17jlzqh/2011-09/28/content_23596487.htm.

28. 'Xi Jinping's Speech at the 60th Anniversary of the Publication of the Five Principles of Peaceful Coexistence', *Xinhua* (28 June 2014). http://news.xinhuanet.com/politics/2014-06/28/c_1111364206_3.htm.

BIBLIOGRAPHY

Cai Wu. 'Chinese Culture and Peaceful Development of China'. *China.com.cn* (28 September 2011). http://www.china.com.cn/policy/zhuanti/17jlzqh/2011-09/28/content_23596487.htm.

Changming, Cheng. *Analects of Confucius*. Liaoning: National Publishing House, 1996.

'China Has Exempted 50 Heavily Indebted Poor Nations of Debts of 30 Billion Yuan in Recent Decade'. *The People's Daily*, 4 November 2012.

Hu Jintao. Report at the 18th National Congress of the Communist Party of China: 'Firmly March on the Path of Socialism with Chinese Characteristics and Strive to

Complete the Building of a Moderately Prosperous Society in All Respects'. *China Daily Network*, 19 November 2012. http://language.chinadaily.com.cn/news/2012-11/19/content_15941774.htm.

Hu Jintao. Statement at the United Nations Summit, New York, 15 September 2005. http://www.un.org/webcast/summit2005/statements15/china050915eng.pdf.

Hu Xiaodi. 'Statements at Main Committees of the 2005 NPT Review Conference'. *Ministry of Foreign Affairs, the People's Republic of China*, 20 May 2005. http://www.nti.org/media/pdfs/35_4a.pdf?_=1316627913.

Liu Zhen. 'Xi Jinping's Diplomatic Concept in New Era Remains in Upholding These Four Aspects'. *China.com.cn*, 26 November 2017. http://www.china.com.cn/news/2017-11/26/content_41945566.htm.

Lv Hong and He Hongze. 'Widely Initiating Civilization Dialogue and Cultural Exchange'. *The People's Daily*, 11 December 2003.

Modern Chinese Dictionary Revision. Beijing: Chinese Academy of Social Sciences, Commercial Press, 1996.

Tang Yong. 'China Is One of the Best Clients for the World Bank'. people.com.cn, 25 November 2004. http://www.people.com.cn/BIG5/shizheng/1026/3011379.html.

Wang Yi. Statement on President Xi Jinping's visit to Kazakhstan to attend the 17th Meeting of SCO Council of Heads of State and Opening Ceremony of Astana Expo 2017: 'Carry Forward Silk Road Spirit and Write a New Chapter for Cooperation'. *Ministry of Foreign Affairs, the People's Republic of China*, 10 June 2017. http://www.fmprc.gov.cn/mfa_eng/zxxx_662805/t1469852.shtml.

Wen Jiabao. Speech at the ASEAN Business and Investment Summit. *China.com.cn*, 8 October 2003. http://www.china.com.cn/zhuanti2005/txt/2003-10/08/content_5417165.htm.

Xi Jinping. 'Let the Sense of Community of Common Destiny Take Deep Root in Neighbouring Countries'. *Ministry of Foreign Affairs, the People's Republic of China*, 25 October 2013. http://www.fmprc.gov.cn/mfa_eng/wjb_663304/wjbz_663308/activities_663312/t1093870.shtml.

Xi Jinping. Speech at the 60th Anniversary of the Publication of the Five Principles of Peaceful Coexistence. *Xinhua*, 28 June 2014. http://news.xinhuanet.com/politics/2014-06/28/c_1111364206_3.htm.

Xi Jinping. Speech at UN Sustainable Development Summit: 'Stressing to Realize Common Development of All Countries from New Starting Point of Post-2015 Development Agenda'. *Ministry of Foreign Affairs, the People's Republic of China*, 27 September 2015. http://www.fmprc.gov.cn/mfa_eng/topics_665678/xjpdmgjxgsfwbcxlhgcl70znxlfh/t1302359.shtml.

Xi Jinping. Speech at UN Sustainable Development Summit. *Xinhua Net*, 27 September 2015.

Xiufen Lu. 'The Confucian Ideal of Great Harmony (Datong 大同), the Daoist Account of Change, and the Theory of Socialism in the Work of Li Dazhao'. *Asian Philosophy*.

Xu Shu and Liu Hao. *Tao Te Ching of Lao Zi*. Anhui: People's Publishing House China, 1990.

Chapter 12

Values in South Korean Foreign Policy
Search for New Identity as a 'Middle Power'

Lee Seong-hyon

South Korea's diplomatic footprints reveal that its foreign policy is less steered by certain values or philosophy, but more by its orientation towards a dominant power in the region. South Korea gravitates towards the country at full gallop, trying to emulate the nation as a 'role model' in an all-around way, including absorbing its world views and foreign policy: China in the past, the United States now. This may be the most pronounced feature of South Korea's foreign policy. It reflects a sense of desperation that has gripped the nation and its tumultuous history that sustained more than 900 foreign invasions. It also explains why there seem few indigenous Korean values that underlie Korea's modern foreign policy thinking. Korea was weak and did not have the ability to shape the regional order. Therefore, Korea's best strategy was to adjust well to the regional order. Koreans' dependency syndrome may lie in part in their thinking that resorting to the regional hegemon may best guarantee the nation's survival. Today, however, as the world's eleventh-largest economy and twelfth-biggest military power, South Korea is in search of a new identity.

FROM 'VALUE-ORIENTED' TO 'VALUE-NEUTRAL' IN AN UNCERTAIN WORLD

When South Korea's president Lee Myung-bak (February 2008–February 2013) said that he would promote a 'value-oriented' diplomacy during a meeting with President George W. Bush in 2008, the media response back home was as if he stepped into a minefield. For South Korea, emphasizing 'values' in its foreign policy is increasingly seen as a liability rather than an asset. Even some conservative media outlets with a pro-American leaning at that time expressed a concern that Lee's open emphasis on democratic values might antagonize some countries with different values, notably China. China is South Korea's largest trading partner, and Seoul has been careful not to offend its big neighbour. Lee underscoring values in such an open and public fashion therefore was seen as a self-limiting foreign policy posture in today's world where the United States is increasingly withdrawing its traditional leadership.

In history, Korea often became a battlefield for influence and power projection by powerful neighbours. Security experts have long regarded the Korean Peninsula as East Asia's Balkans, where powerful countries' interests converge and collide. Years ago, people were talking about Korea being squeezed between the two Asian rivals, China and Japan. In 1591, Toyotomi Hideyoshi, a Japanese warlord who rose to power, demanded Korea open the road for his invasion of China. Korea rejected this demand, and Japan invaded.

Today, observers say South Korea is again pinched between two major powers, this time the United States and China. The United States is South Korea's most important military ally, while China is South Korea's largest economic partner. There is a sense of entrapment among Koreans, fearing a major conflict between the United States and China amid deepening rivalry and competition between Washington and Beijing. When the two whales fight, they fear, it will be the shrimp, Korea, that will suffer. 'Those fears were very intense in Korea', said William Overholt, a long-time expert on Korea, who is a senior research fellow at Harvard Kennedy School.[1]

LEE MYUNG-BAK'S
VALUE-ORIENTED DIPLOMACY

In his speech at George Washington University in June 2009, Lee listed values such as freedom and peace as the key values of the twenty-first century.[2] The joint vision for the alliance of the Republic of Korea and the United States, issued a day earlier, stated: 'Our open societies, our commitment to free democracy and a market economy, and our sustained partnership provide a foundation for the enduring friendship, shared values, and mutual respect that tightly bind the Korean and American peoples'.[3]

Lee was unusual in that he was a president who often emphasized values in his various speeches. That perhaps may have to do with the fact that he is a devout Christian. When he was mayor of Seoul in 2004, he solemnly told the audience who packed an auditorium: 'I declare that the City of Seoul is a holy place governed by God; the citizens in Seoul are God's people; the churches and Christians in Seoul are spiritual guards that protect the city. I now dedicate Seoul to the Lord'.[4] When Lee ran for president later, a blogger remembered the statement and wrote: 'This is a very important piece of evidence that shows why Lee shouldn't become the president', questioning Lee's religious penchant. Many other bloggers also chimed in, quipping that Lee would try to dedicate the whole country to God if he became president. Some also jibed that God would be sued by Lee if he did not become president, given all the religious fervour Lee had publicly demonstrated. Some more analytic minds tried to give it more nuance, calling it as Lee's deliberate advance to appeal to the Christian voters. But that is a great understatement of Lee's faith.

Lee is a Christian and a real one for that matter. As a person born into a devout Christian family, Lee once said that the biggest blessing he had received from his mother was 'coming to know the love of God'. It is also well known that Lee – the ex-chief executive of the Hyundai conglomerate – had volunteered for more than three years as a church parking guide on Sunday mornings to get voted as an elder of his church. When this was later known to George W. Bush, a 'born-again' Christian himself, Bush personally complimented Lee on that. When Lee met Bush at Camp David in 2008, Lee also proposed a prayer to Bush, which was readily accepted. With the two leaders' personal bonding, as well as their devotion to Christian values, some see the Lee-Bush period as the heyday for the South Korea-US alliance. The great irony was that Lee, the former business tycoon, was elected president with a campaign promise that he would pursue pragmatism in diplomacy.

The Lee government's emphasis on values in foreign policy took on a more strategic sense when his foreign minister Kim Sung-hwan articulated it in 2012 thus: 'The alliance between South Korea and the US has gone beyond a security alliance and economic alliance. It is now in the age of an alliance based on values', adding that South Korea's growth to become a nation of vibrant capitalism and democracy had resulted in the two countries' 'shared values that are the sources as the most solid foundation uniting the two democracies'.[5] In fact, the leaders of South Korea and the United States have often referred to their relationship as 가치동맹 (value alliance). For instance, the first paragraph of the joint fact sheet on South Korea-US relations issued after an April 2014 summit between Presidents Park Geun-hye (February 2013–March 2017) and Barack Obama spelled out that 'our shared values of democracy, human rights, and the rule of law are the foundation of our relationship'.[6] When Park's Foreign Minister Yun Byung-se delivered a keynote speech at the Munich Security Conference in 2016, he also emphasized values: 'The ROK and NATO are like-minded partners who share the core values of democracy, human rights and the rule of law'.[7]

As mentioned, however, such a conscious act of publicly emphasizing values in South Korea's foreign policy was uncommonly conspicuous during Lee's term. Overall, it was taken more as a diplomatic decorum in the context of accentuating Seoul's robust alliance with Washington. In addition, as time passed, there was a nuanced shift in the very word 'value' as to what it would mean. In short, it came less to indicate democracy or human rights, and more about market economy and 'livelihood' – words that are also compatible with non-democratic countries such as China. This reflects an awareness also in South Korea that China, which has become the growth engine of the world economy, is to be reckoned as an economic magnet which allures, rather than one to shun.

SOUTH KOREA'S MODERN ERA INTERNATIONAL RELATIONS

South Korea as a modern nation began its statehood in 1948. For the past seven decades, its foreign policy has been predominantly anchored to its Cold War–era benefactor, the United States. The beginning of the modern South Korean-US relationship was, however, not an alliance partnership, but the United States as an occupying force in South Korea at the end of World War II. The asymmetrical nature of their relationship became a limiting factor when South Korea grew to be a middle power, seeking a more equal partnership with its former patron. In 1953, at the end of the Korean War, they became formal military allies, and until this day, the United States has been the sole nation with which South Korea has a signed military alliance pact. For South Koreans, America soon became more than just another nation. It soon became a socio-political black hole for South Korea for nearly everything that was touted as 'advanced', ranging from technology to culture, a role model for a political institution, as well as a beacon for moral leadership in Seoul's orientation in international relations.

South Korea's all-out gravitation towards the United States also has left a significant footprint in South Korea's world view and foreign policy. This partly explains why there seem very few indigenous Korean values that underlie South Korea's modern foreign policy thinking. *Hongik Ingan* (홍익인간 in Korean) is the original founding philosophy of Korea, referring to 'benefit broadly the human world'. Often it is regarded as the unofficial national motto of South Korea and also seen as a generic expression of South Korea's world view. Scholar Han Seung-jo argues that the *Hongik Ingan* spirit is the very source of South Korea's soft power and therefore should represent the values of South Korea's foreign policy.[8]

Even 150 years ago, very common Western normative values such as democracy were a very foreign concept to a nation such as Korea, which was then ruled over by a king and not a president. Korea was a kingdom until the second half of the nineteenth century, when East Asia's international system revolved around the Chinese tributary system.

In addition, Korea's transition to democracy in the past century was never smooth. As mentioned, Korea drifted into a colonial state from a traditional agriculture-based Joseon Dynasty (1392–1910), when Korea became a colony of Japan. It was a painful insult for Korean intellectuals to swallow because they used to think of Japan as a 'culturally downstream' island nation. Japan's early opening-up to the West through the Meiji Revolution (1868) made it quickly take over other regional powers that were slower in adopting modern technology as well as advanced weaponry. Koreans were also slow in realizing the change in times. Many historians and philosophers in Korea view the Joseon dynasty's adoption of Confucianism as a state ideology as the main contribution to military weakness and resultant external aggressions. According to this theory, Confucianism disdains science, technology and commerce.

After liberation from Japanese colonial rule, Korea was split into two along the 38th parallel by two American colonels who used a *National Geographic* magazine map. As a result, Korea became two Koreas. Conveniently, one came to be called North Korea; the other South Korea. It was, however, more than a physical divide. Socialism began to take root in Korea in the form of anti-colonial nationalism, dividing the nation between the pro-American Right and pro-communist Left camps. The two camps confronted each other, often militantly. Some members of political rivals were assassinated or kidnapped or brutally lynched. In 1950, the two Koreas entered into a full-scale war that ravaged the country for three years. After the war, political turmoil and unrest ensued. Powerful military generals took power and ruled the nation until 1987. In short, for South Koreans, the twentieth century was a period of trauma, filled with memories of wars, famines and political oppression.

South Koreans still carry this trauma. The overriding value South Korea had striven to secure in all this turbulent period, and throughout history, was not some political ideology such as democracy or freedom or human rights but more primordial: survival. By some estimates, Korea has been invaded by foreign forces 992 times in its history,[9] which makes survival all the more urgent. It is the 'life or death' value that has been embedded under the state's every behavioural disposition, including foreign policy.

Even though South Korea was one of the few post-colonial nations that achieved rapid economic development and democratization by the end of the twentieth century, as of 2018 South Korea is still a young and fledgling democracy, with a mere thirty years of democratic governance experience. In the meantime, the country has transformed from one of the poorest countries in the world, ravaged by the Korean War, to now the world's eleventh-largest economy and twelfth-greatest military power. It has retooled itself from an aid-dependent backwater to a modern, high-tech powerhouse. This changed status thrusts it towards searching for a new identity and new foreign policy values that can guide the nation forward in the world. In fact, in recent years South Korea's foreign policy has been experimenting with some new identity roles. For instance, it began to pose itself as a 'middle power'. In addition, the following words frequently appear in South Korean media, representing what the nation's new foreign policy platform should be, namely 'pragmatic diplomacy', 'niche diplomacy', 'balancer diplomacy' and 'strategic partnership diplomacy'. There is also a more descriptive expression, such as 'South Korea should take a diplomatic strategy that makes best use of both continental and maritime forces'. These are some of the publicly argued prescriptions. But before South Korea settles on any new diplomatic strategy for the future, it must first overcome the Sino-centric world order from the past.

OVERCOMING THE SINO-CENTRIC WORLD ORDER

Before the dawn of the modern era, Korea had been under the Sino-centric world order for centuries. The Sino-centric world order, which the Western academia commonly regards as a form of colonial system, was a de facto international norm in East Asia at that time. As in many parts of the world, it regulated war and peace between the strong and weak societies in East Asia. Scholars such as Lee Sam-sung of Hallym University, east of Seoul, argues that accepting the Sino-centric order, in which tributary countries made regular homage to China, offering tribute to the emperor of China and receiving titles and privileges in return, was about 'accepting the realities of existence of strong and weak' at that particular time and history in the region.[10] Korea was weak and did not have the ability to shape the regional order. Therefore, Korea's best strategy was to adjust to the regional order, which, at that time, was the Chinese order. It felt in doing so would be the best way to secure its survival. Importantly, Lee Sam-sung also argues that by doing so, smaller countries in China's vicinity were able to avoid falling into exploitative colonial order which could have been much worse. He then argues that we have to recognize the merits of the Sino-centric world order in that it operated as a kind of 'peace regime' in which the weak society maintained a relative autonomy as a tributary to the regional hegemon, which was China. It should be noted that Lee Sam-sung does not embrace the Chinese system as something wholly positive either, pointing out that Koreans' 'excessive immersion' in the Chinese system has diminished their sense of reality of the world. He writes:

> By expanding Sino-centrism to the metaphysical and cosmological level, Koreans were unable to recognize the forces that are outside the Chinese order and to create a logic or a behavioral model that would seek coexistence with them.[11]

Korea's history was heavily influenced by the China-centred world view. Some Korean scholars, deeply immersed in Chinese Confucianism, even called Korea 'Little China' to highlight its close preservation of the Chinese culture after the collapse of the Ming dynasty in China in 1644. Even after the Ming dynasty succumbed to the Manchus and was replaced by the Qing dynasty, Korea continued its alliance of loyalty to the Ming dynasty. As a result, Korea was invaded by Qing.[12]

Fast-forwarding to the present, as China has become more assertive and even aggressive, South Koreans have a conflicting image about China. South Korea feels great affinity with China economically while it feels threatened by China politically. This has made South Koreans confused. For instance, the two key phrases Koreans often have about China are 'a security threat', and 'poor quality products'. In a survey, 73.1 percent of South Korean respondents said China's military build-up poses a security threat to South Korea, reminding them of China's invasion and oppression, reflecting their fear over China's growing prowess.[13] This is the case despite the fact that South Koreans have positive cultural orientations towards China based on the same Confucian culture; many Koreans feel a natural affinity to Chinese culture and recognize China's spectacular economic expansion and China's hosting of the Six-Party Talks, a consortium of six nations to persuade North Korea to abandon its nuclear weapons ambition.[14] The South Korean perception of China is negatively tilted by the post–Cold War influence from the United States with which South Korea has been a major military ally. The Chinese bemoan that South Korea, a former tributary, looks at China through the American prism and thus has negative views on today's Communist China.

Relevant to this discussion are the concepts of *da guo* (big country) and *shangguo* (a country to look up to) – the two terms that were used in South Korea to refer to China. Namely, China as a 'big country' means that it is a country that has a big landmass and a huge population. In its extension, it also refers to China's growing sphere of influence in terms of economic might and in the international political and military realm. However, China is no longer a 'country to look up to'. China once was a powerful and highly civilized nation that smaller neighbour countries looked up to – this involves a historical mentality of respect that Koreans attached in revering a big and powerful country. The Chinese have a tendency to believe that the Koreans got away from the Sino-centric world view mainly due to the external factor, that is, the American influence in the post–World War II period, as well as due to South Korea's rising nationalism. Chinese researchers conclude: 'For South Koreans, today's *shangguo* is the United States, not China'.[15] After World War II, the United States replaced China as South Korea's new ideological centre too, effectively terminating the Sino-centric order.

However, today, with the rise of China and its conscious expansion of influence in the region using economic incentives, or withholding of them, there is an opinion that South Korea may be again inching closer towards China in its new geopolitical strategic calculus, gradually decoupling its relations with Washington. There are worries about South Korea in the United States that the Asian ally is drifting away from its orbit. Meanwhile, many Korean opinion makers today argue that Korea should shift from an ideology-driven diplomacy to practical diplomacy: that is, neither pro-American nor pro-Chinese. A case in point in this regard with the current President Moon Jae-in is a *Time* magazine report on him. On its cover, it described Moon as a 'negotiator'. A negotiator needs both flexibility and principle, an ability to shift positions when circumstances require, but then also a principled bottom line that it must adhere to. South Korea is then like a negotiator. People regard South Korea as flexible in many aspects. Previously, South Korea refused to engage in diplomatic ties with those countries that had maintained diplomatic relations with North Korea, in accordance with the Hallstein principle. But in the early 1990s, for instance, it broke the Hallstein principle by engaging former Cold War adversaries such as China, with which it elevated its relationship to a strategic level in 2008. Now South Korea pursues all-around diplomacy. There are 171 countries where South Koreans can go without a visa. This is the third-largest in the world, behind Canada and Germany.

DEBATES ON VALUES IN ALLIANCE

Like many other countries, South Korea also had to accommodate China that has been increasingly powerful in economy. Lee Jong-seok, a mentor for President Moon and former liberal President Roh Moo-hyun's security advisor, pointed out the importance of the South Korea-China relationship in the twenty-first century and said that the 'value alliance' advocated by the conservative and pro-American Lee Myung-bak administration was a misplaced idea, 'like a child who couldn't read the changes in the world'.[16] Moon Chung-in, another senior mentor to President Moon, also chimed in, saying such a 'diplomacy of the value-alliance reminds me of the Crusades of the Middle Age'. He added that 'we should ask whether that is in line with the national interests of South Korea'.[17]

Increasingly squeezed by the United States and China, South Korea has in recent years pursued a two-track policy in which it relies on China for economy and the United States for security. The problem is that China is also a rising military power, not just an economic power. China has displayed increasing annoyance with South Korea's military alliance with the United States, which China sees as a device engineered by the United States to contain China. Currently in Asia the United States has alliances with Japan and South Korea, and the three countries maintain security cooperation between them. However, there is no formal tripartite military alliance among them. What China fears most is the formation of an official trilateral military alliance among Washington, Seoul and Tokyo. The strategic cooperation between South Korea and Japan, however, is likely to remain fragmented due to two crucial factors – China and bilateral mistrust. Containing China through the alliance with the United States is not in the best interests of South Korea as its economic and political ties with China are deepening. On the other hand, Japan is increasing its military cooperation with the United States in the region to respond to China's manifest and potential aggression. Japan is less likely to receive the support of most Asian countries, considering the region's increasing economic interdependence with China and China's corresponding cheque book diplomacy.

Japan's value to Asian countries lies in its soft and normative power in uniting democracies in the region. In this regard, Japan should commit to a long-term strategy, as South Korea's short- and mid-term response would be of hesitance and misgivings due to the popular perception that Japan has failed to settle its historical and colonial wrongdoings. Koreans' mistrust of Japan may even intensify if Japan mounts a more serious challenge to South Korea's sovereignty over the Dokdo Islets (Takeshima), disputed by both countries.

Meanwhile, amid China's rise and resulting geopolitical shifts, China increasingly sees South Korea as a swing state that can be won over by Beijing, as the weak link among the trilateral Washington-Seoul-Tokyo structure. Taken together, China thinks it can work on Seoul to pull it away from Washington.

China has in recent years gained diplomatic currency in Seoul by more rigorously enforcing United Nations (UN) sanctions on Pyongyang. Seoul-Tokyo ties, a crucial element of Washington's Asia-Pacific web of alliances, have been troubled too by the neighbours' historical and territorial disputes. China, which has a similar problem with Japan, believes that Seoul is closer to China than to Japan. China also senses that the Korea-US alliance is facing challenges as Seoul tries to reposition itself in the global order in a manner commensurate with its rising global status. Today, South Korea is a major economy and spends the world's tenth military expenditure according to Stockholm International Peace Research Institute. In relations with Washington, that means that Seoul is trying to find its own voice. The dispute over the South Korea-US civilian nuclear agreement, and Seoul's desire to produce its own nuclear fuel, was one recent example. China did not miss Seoul's debate about the credibility of US deterrence against the threat posed by a nuclear-armed North Korea. It also noted Seoul and Washington's differing expectations regarding the US threshold for entering the inter-Korean conflict.

While US-ROK relations are often said to be at a historic high, the alliance is evolving at a time of geostrategic and economic shifts in the region. Seoul feels that its alliance with Washington must overcome a 'fairness' issue. Washington allowed Japan, a US ally, to produce its own nuclear fuel, but Seoul has been barred from doing so. Washington shares intelligence with Australia on China, but often does not do so with Seoul on North Korea. On several occasions, Washington even bypassed Seoul and struck a deal with North Korea, making Seoul nervous. Seoul's pursuit of the so-called middle power strategy and assertion of more independence in its foreign policy often put strains on the Washington-Seoul alliance.

VALUES IN MOON JAE-IN'S FOREIGN POLICY

The current Moon presidency began in May 2017 after an abrupt impeachment of former President Park Geun-hye, who stepped down amid corruption scandals and influence-peddling. Even though the people who have filled the Moon government are characterized as 'liberals', there are sufficient differences among them. The main conspicuous discord among Moon's advisors is less about their share of power, and more about ideological and philosophical values, regarding how to identify South Korea's position in the ROK-US alliance matrix, and also on the question of how to relate to North Korea, which is both an existential adversary and an estranged brother.

In South Korea's modern politics, having American support for one's side carries a significant domestic weight and a presidential candidate who has strained relations with the United States will likely suffer. Roh Moo-hyun (February 2003–February 2008) who said, 'I am not going to go to the US for the sake of a photo-op with a US president', paid the price in the court of public opinion in South Korea, particularly from the conservatives. Kim Dae-jung (February 1998–February 2003) botched his first summit with George W. Bush when he unsuccessfully tried to explain the merits of the Sunshine Policy to him. Even before his return to Seoul, South Korean media were up in arms, accusing him of missteps. That resulted in discord in the alliance. This is the ecology of public opinion in South Korea.

Moon is a more skilful politician, having learned from the mistakes of his predecessors. During the presidential campaign, he emphasized Seoul's relationship with Washington as the bedrock of his administration's foreign policy. For instance, immediately after the election, Moon said in his phone conversation with Trump that the US-ROK alliance was 'the basis of our diplomatic and security policy'.[18] In another case, during the inter-Korean dialogue in January 2018 in preparation for the PyeongChang Winter Olympics, Trump said he played an influential leadership role in helping brokering the talks.[19] When a question was raised by an American reporter to Moon during the New Year's press conference on whether Trump really contributed a big hand to the inter-Korean tension thaw, Moon deftly played along. With a smile, he said, 'I give President Trump huge credit for bringing about the inter-Korean talks, and I'd like to thank him for that'.[20] The press corps burst into laughter. They knew so well that that was not the case. But Moon was willing to stick to political correctness by publicly displaying the Seoul-Washington alliance solidarity.

TILTED PLAYING FIELD

Yet South Korea's liberal thinkers have long raised the issue of the so-called tilted playing field in the alliance relationship in which Washington always calls the shots. The alliance is seen as a partnership that is unfair from the perspective of the smaller partner, Seoul. The alliance was also seen as a political device to intervene in South Korea's foreign affairs. Whether it is Seoul's relationship with Pyongyang, or with Beijing, or with Tokyo, South Korean diplomats privately complain about Washington's interference and its tendency to 'coach' Seoul's diplomacy with other countries. Even when South Korea was planning about starting an economic project with Russia, Washington reportedly stepped in to tell Seoul to abandon it. These circles also do not appreciate US unilateralism, especially when it comes to dealing with North Korea, often bypassing South Korea.

After the Korean War, it was a period of anti-communism. The military dictators at that time used their enforcement of anti-communist policy as a justification to woo the US leadership. It was a political gimmick to send a signal that South Korea belonged to the American side which worked because it was the time of the Cold War. For South Korean intellectuals who looked to the United States as the beacon of freedom and democracy, the US tolerance of the military government was problematic. When there was a pro-democracy uprising in the southern city of Gwangju in 1980, they expected the US government to intervene to support the pro-democracy movement, which did not happen. Their idealistic view of America then transformed into a feeling of betrayal. They felt that they saw a two-faced America that openly preached democratic values, but in reality, looked the other way as student protesters were bled to death by airborne special forces sent by the military rulers. American diplomats such as David Straub, who served as the head of the Korea desk at the State Department, later wrote[21] about the 'mis-understanding' some South Koreans have about the matter, and the purported American role that he believes was distorted.

Over the years of accumulated experience of the unequal partnership, these liberal thinkers became very critical of America's role in the country and South Korean society was further polarized. On the one hand, there are conservatives who see America as the absolute guardian of South Korea and a staunch ally who safeguarded the nation from Communist North Korea, and they believe the nation's development would be possible only within the alliance with the United States. On the other hand, there are liberals who see America as an imperialist state that takes advantage of the division of the Korean Peninsula so as to politically maximize its own national interests. The former see themselves as the beneficiary from America; the latter see themselves as victims of American hegemony.

To liberals, the recent Terminal High Altitude Area Defence (THAAD) dispute – an advanced US missile defence system deployed in South Korea – also reflects US unilateralism because Washington hurriedly deployed the THAAD missile battery days before a presidential election. As a presidential candidate, Moon called for the delay of the THAAD deployment as it became a nationally controversial issue, arguing that the fate of THAAD should be better determined by the incoming government. His request, even though he was the number one candidate in the polls, was not honoured. A large portion of Moon's advisors inherit this thought tradition and the underdog sensitivity; they seek a breathing space in the relationship with the United States. As the alliance becomes mature, liberal thinkers argue that the two allies do not have to be on the same page on all issues at all times.

THE FUTURE OF SOUTH KOREAN DIPLOMACY

Korea has historically been driven by a sense of desperation for survival. This aspect manifested itself in diplomacy as well. Imagine a country surrounded by more powerful countries that ravaged the nation over and over again, as many as 922 times. In the latest Korean War, for instance, nearly 10 percent on the Korean Peninsula perished out of the then 25 million population. The war also resulted in separation of families that accounted for one out of every four families. South Korea therefore displays an uncommon preoccupation with sovereignty because of its experience of being pressured by big powers.

South Korea's sense of desperation made it align with a dominant power in the region to maximize its survival. Even South Korea's strong anti-communist diplomacy during the Cold War could be argued as its close mirroring of Washington's anti-communist foreign policy. This view can be controversial and can be put to debate. But it is introduced here as an interpretive prism to look at South Korea's foreign policy and explain the values that drive it.

Announcing 'Core Values' for the First Time

In 2012, for the first time in its history, South Korea's foreign ministry announced the so-called core values. They comprised four values.[22] Given that it was the first such case ever and the features were carefully chosen after interviewing as many as 600 foreign ministry officials, and also taking into account the opinions from retired diplomats, as well as surveying the cases of other countries, these four were surprisingly common words:

- Putting the national interest first
- Serving the public
- Contributing to humanity
- Aiming for the best

Kim Sung-hwan, foreign minister at that time, said the four values would 'play the role of pointing the directions for the ministry in proactively dealing with massive social change and rapid changes in the diplomatic environment'.[23] In other words, these values reflect both the domestic and international realities the nation faces today. Yet what is more important to note is that this is first-ever effort for South Korea to give serious thought to the values that its foreign policy embodies. That means South Korea realized it needed to have a set of foreign policy values, rather than adopting the values of others.

Entering into the incumbent government of Moon Jae-in, this trend continues. In addition, South Korea wants to stretch its diplomatic horizon. The current government announced that it would expand from its traditional diplomatic emphasis on 'Strong Four' (the usual four major powers, the United States, China, Japan and Russia) to other countries. Particularly, the Moon administration plans to strengthen ties with India, the Association of Southeast Asian Nations and Indonesia. Apparently, South Korea is gearing up to craft a more ambitious foreign policy that reflects the nation's middle power reality with a broader outlook for the world. On the North Korea issue, the Moon government also wants to take a primary role in handling the challenge by taking the driver's seat, as Moon himself put it. This is certainly an ambiguous goal and shows Seoul's desire to have more ownership of international affairs directly relevant to it.

CONCLUSION

Like his centre-left predecessors, Moon also wants to play a balancing role between the regional powers. So, this is a departure from Korea's traditional behaviour. Whether this indicates the opening of a new era in South Korea's foreign policy requires further observation. Political scientist Choi Young-jong, for instance, remains cautious as he argues that South Korea often displayed a poor reading of the outside world:

> After the world went into the full swing of globalization, South Korea still displayed a lack of ability to make best use of it and displayed a subjectivity in understanding the global order. South Korea placed priority for its nationality over the world, the past over the future, emotion over rationality. South Korea also showed uncritical hospitality toward North Korea, harboured wishful thinking on China. It went into conflict with the US, its most important ally, looking down on Japan – these have been manifested in its foreign policy.[24]

Choi, who is a former president of South Korea's Political Science Association, asserts that South Korea, which is not a powerful hegemon, should still be able to pursue its national interest based on multilateralism, an emphasis on negotiations to handle international conflicts, by finding its niche as a good citizen of the world, as well as by promoting universal values and a rules-based society.[25] Taken together, today, South Korea faces a set of strategic choices that will shape its economic prospects and national security, against the backdrop of China's mounting influence, North Korea's growing nuclear and missile capability, as well as the task of upgrading its alliance with the United States so as to steer its diplomacy in a modern, forward-looking and effective direction. South Korea's past was driven by the urge for survival, the primordial instinct that outstripped any other values. Even fairly recently, emphasizing values in its foreign policy was seen as a liability rather than an asset. Former Foreign Minister Han Seung-joo still emphasizes pragmatism in this regard, not values. 'Especially when it comes to safeguarding national security matters, we should put aside . . . our diplomatic notions. The most important criteria should be which course of actions will be most helpful to our survival', he said.[26] Apparently, South Korea is still haunted by the historical trauma and sense of desperation for survival. However, it is moving ahead too; it has been also testing new slogans for its diplomacy such as 'middle power diplomacy' and has made efforts to identify its own values that will guide the nation's diplomacy into the future. Today, South Korea's foreign policy is experimenting with a new identity with a new set of guiding values.

NOTES

1. Author's interview.

2. Lee's foreign policy slogan was 'Global Korea'. He envisaged a plan to expand South Korea's greater contribution to international society in such areas as overcoming the global economic crisis, providing more ODAs, dispatching PKOs, utilizing World Friends Korea (South Korean version of Peace Corps).

3. Barack Obama, 'Joint Vision for the Alliance of the United States of America and the Republic of Korea', *White House* (16 June 2009). https://obamawhitehouse.archives.gov/realitycheck/the-press-office/joint-vision-alliance-united-states-america-and-republic-korea.

4. Choe Sang-hun, 'Religious Peace under Threat in South Korea', *New York Times* (14 October 2008). http://www.nytimes.com/2008/10/14/world/asia/14iht-buddhist.1.16935374.html?pagewanted=all.

5. Lee Sun-young, 'South Korea, U.S. Partnership Has Become "Value Alliance": Foreign Minister', *The Korea Herald* (16 June 2012). http://www.koreaherald.com/view.php?ud=20120616000103.

6. 'US President Obama Visits ROK to Reaffirm ROK-U.S. Alliance: A Global Partnership', *Ministry of Foreign Affairs, ROK* (29 April 2014). http://news.mofa.go.kr/enewspaper/mainview.php?mvid=1803.

7. ROK Foreign Ministry, 'Foreign Minister Yun Byung-se Requests Active Cooperation from Europe at the Munich Security Conference to Respond to North Korea's Nuclear and Missile Tests', (12 February 2016). http://www.mofa.go.kr/eng/brd/m_5676/view.do?seq=316154&srchFr=&amp%3BsrchTo=&amp%3BsrchWord=Conference&amp%3BsrchTp=0&amp%3Bmulti_itm_seq=0&amp%3Bitm_seq_1=0&amp%3Bitm_seq_2=0&amp%3Bcompany_cd=&amp%3Bcompany_nm.

8. Han Seung-jo, *Asia-Pacific Community and Korea* (Seoul: Nanam Publishing, 2011), 168.

9. Wang Son-taek, '993 Times of Foreign Invasion. Is it true?' *YTN* (15 December 2005). http://www.ytn.co.kr/news/clmn_view.php?idx=292&s_hcd=01&s_mcd=0612.

10. Lee Sam-sung, *War and Peace in East Asia: Two Thousand Years of Chinese World Order and the Korean Peninsula* (Paju: Hangilsa Publishing, 2009), 11.

11. Ibid., back cover.

12. Choi Young-jong, *New Diplomatic Strategy for Global Korea* (Seoul: Oruem Publishing House, 2008), 47.

13. Dong Xiangrong, Wang Xiaoling and Li Yongchun, *Hanguorenxinmuzhong de zhongnguoxingxiang [South Korean images of China]* (Shehuikexuewenxianchubanshe, 2012), 177.

14. In addition to North and South Korea, the other participating countries are the United States, China, Russia, Japan – these six countries, thus the name, Six-Party Talks.

15. Dong Xiangrong, Wang Xiaoling and Li Yongchun, *Hanguorenxinmuzhong de zhognguoxingxiang [South Korean images of China]*, 179.

16. Lee Ha-won, 'The Debate on ROK-US Value Alliance [in Korea]', *Chosun Daily* (1 October 2012). http://news.chosun.com/site/data/html_dir/2012/10/01/2012100100900.html?Dep0=twitter&d=2012100100900.

17. To that, Kim Sung-hwan, former vice foreign minister, said, 'The value alliance does not mean a policy to expand our values to other countries'. http://news.chosun.com/site/data/html_dir/2012/10/01/2012100100900.html.

18. Lee Ha-na, 'Korea-US Alliance Based on Diplomacy, National Security: President', *Cheng Wa Dae* (22 June 2017). https://english1.president.go.kr/korea/korea.php?srh%5Bview_mode%5D=detail&srh%5Bseq%5D=472&srh%5Bdetail_no%5D=71&srh%5Bpage%5D.

19. Dan Merica, 'Trump Tells Seoul He's Open to Talks with North Korea', *CNN* (10 January 2018). https://www.cnn.com/2018/01/10/politics/donald-trump-north-korea-talks/index.html.

20. Anna Fifield, 'South Korean President Credits Trump with Bringing North Korea to the Table', *Washington Post* (10 January 2018). https://www.washingtonpost.com/world/asia_pacific/south-korean-president-credits-trump-with-bringing-north-korea-to-the-table/2018/01/10/ae0ee266-f606-11e7-91af-31ac729add94_story.html?utm_term=.2db0736560a2.

21. David Straub, *Anti-Americanism in Democratizing South Korea* (Stanford, CA: Shorenstein Asia-Pacific Research Center, 2015).

22. Ministry of Foreign Affairs ROK, 'Releasing Foreign Ministry's Core Values', (16 March 2012). http://www.mofat.go.kr/webmodule/htsboard/template/read/korboardread.jsp?typeID=6&boardid=235&seqno=341608.

23. Ibid.

24. Choi Young-jong, *New Diplomatic Strategy for Global Korea* (Seoul: Oruem Publishing House, 2008), 51.

25. Ibid., 285.

26. Suh Hwa-dong, 'Interview with Former Foreign Minister Han Seung-joo', *HankookKyungJe* (7 July 2017). http://newslabit.hankyung.com/news/app/newsview.php?aid=2017070732861.

BIBLIOGRAPHY

Choe, Sang-Hun. 'Religious Peace under Threat in South Korea'. *New York Times,* 14 October 2008. http://www.nytimes.com/2008/10/14/world/asia/14iht-buddhist.1.16935374.html?pagewanted=all.

Choi, Young-jong. *New Diplomatic Strategy for Global Korea*. Seoul: Oruem Publishing House, 2008.

Dong, Xiangrong, Xiaoling Wang and Yongchun Li. *Hanguoren xinmu zhong de zhongguo xingxiang [South Korean images of China]*. (Beijing: Shehuikexuewenxianchubanshe, 2012).

Fifield, Anna. 'South Korean President Credits Trump with Bringing North Korea to the Table'. *Washington Post*, 10 January 2018. https://www.washingtonpost.com/world/asia_pacific/south-korean-president-credits-trump-with-bringing-north-korea-to-the-table/2018/01/10/ae0ee266-f606–11e7–91af-31ac729add94_story. html?utm_term=.2db0736560a2.

'Foreign Minister Yun Byung-se Requests Active Cooperation from Europe at the Munich Security Conference to Respond to North Korea's Nuclear and Missile Tests'. *Ministry of Foreign Affairs ROK*, 12 February 2016. http:// www.mofa.go.kr/eng/brd/m_5676/view.do?seq=316154&srchFr=&amp%3Bsr chTo=&amp%3BsrchWord=Conference&amp%3BsrchTp=0&amp%3Bmulti_ itm_seq=0&amp%3Bitm_seq_1=0&amp%3Bitm_seq_2=0&amp%3Bcompany_ cd=&amp%3Bcompany_nm=.

Han, Seung-jo. *Asia-Pacific Community and Korea* (Seoul: Nanam Publishing Co., 2011).

Lee, Ha-na. 'Korea-US Alliance Based on Diplomacy, National Security: President'. *Cheng Wa Dae*, 22 June 2017. https://english1.president.go.kr/korea/ korea.php?srh%5Bview_mode%5D=detail&srh%5Bseq%5D=472&srh%5Bdet ail_no%5D=71&srh%5Bpage%5D=.

Lee, Ha-won. 'The Debate on ROK-US Value Alliance'. *Chosun Daily*, 1 October 2012. http://news.chosun.com/site/data/html_dir/2012/10/01/2012100100900.html ?Dep0=twitter&d=2012100100900.

Lee, Sam-sung. *War and Peace in East Asia: Two Thousand Years of Chinese World Order and the Korean Peninsula*. Paju: Hangilsa Publishing, 2009.

Lee, Sun-young. 'S. Korea, US Partnership Has Become 'Value Alliance': Foreign Minister'. *Korea Herald*, 16 June 2012. http://www.koreaherald.com/view. php?ud=20120616000103.

Merica, Dan. 'Trump Tells Seoul He's Open to Talks with North Korea'. *CNN*, 10 January 2018. https://www.cnn.com/2018/01/10/politics/donald-trump-north-korea-talks/index.html.

Obama, Barack. 'Joint Vision for the Alliance of the United States of America and the Republic Of Korea'. *White House*, 16 June 2009. https://obamawhitehouse. archives.gov/realitycheck/the-press-office/joint-vision-alliance-united-states-america-and-republic-korea.

'Releasing Foreign Ministry's Core Values'. *Ministry of Foreign Affairs ROK,* 16 March 2012. http://www.mofat.go.kr/webmodule/htsboard/template/read/kor-boardread.jsp?typeID=6&boardid=235&seqno=341608.

Straub, David. '*Anti-Americanism in Democratizing South Korea*'. Stanford, CA: Shorenstein Asia-Pacific Research Center, 2015.

Suh, Hwa-dong. 'Interview with Former Foreign Minister Han Seung-joo'. *Han-kook KyungJe*, 7 July 2017. http://newslabit.hankyung.com/news/app/newsview. php?aid=2017070732861.

'U.S. President Obama Visits ROK to Reaffirm ROK–U.S. Alliance: A Global Partnership'. *Ministry of Foreign Affairs ROK*, 29 April 2014. http://news.mofa.go.kr/enewspaper/ mainview.php?mvid=1803.

Wang, Son-taek. '993 Times of Foreign Invasion. Is It True?' *YTN*, 15 December 2005. http://www.ytn.co.kr/news/clmn_view.php?idx=292&s_hcd=01&s_mcd=0612.

Chapter 13

Values in Japanese Foreign Policy

Between 'Universal Values' and the Search for Cultural Pluralism

Tadashi Anno

The public espousal of values by a state is closely linked with its identity. For instance, US attempt to spread democracy worldwide is inseparable from its identity as a torchbearer of democracy. To publicly espouse a value is to open oneself the to evaluation based on that value. If we assume that states seek to enhance their self-esteem,[1] it follows that a state will seek to improve its self-evaluation measured by the value it espouses. Japan during the Meiji era (1868–1912), having accepted the Eurocentric standard of civilization, strove mightily to meet that standard and to join the 'family of civilized nations'.[2] We may also hypothesize that, *ceteris paribus*, states are likely to espouse those values according to which it is easiest to enhance their self-esteem. Soon after World War II, the notion emerged that post-war Japan had a 'mission' to spread pacifism around the world. Having lost out in the game of power politics, many Japanese found in pacifism a new value scale according to which Japan could attain self-esteem and international standing. In this manner, the advocacy of values in foreign policy is intertwined with the question of national identity.

Given the ineradicable human tendency towards self-justification, it is safe to assume that every country has at least a latent inclination to approve of itself, and to believe that it is somehow better than other countries. A state that is hegemonic on a global or a regional scale may have the capacity to project its own values and standards overseas through its foreign policies and to remake the international environment in its own image. But for secondary and smaller states, opportunities for external projection of domestic values are limited. For those states, espousal of values more often reflects an attempt to position themselves within an already-given international order. In such cases, the claim to espouse certain values may be driven less by domestic value orientations than by the country's foreign policy needs – by the need to take a certain stance in relation to dominant values of international society, and thereby to achieve security, welfare or self-esteem.

This chapter provides a historical survey on what sort of values post-war Japan has advocated in its foreign policy rhetoric and why.[3] Foreign policy rhetoric is a broad and amorphous category. This chapter's analysis focuses on the contents of speeches delivered by prime ministers and foreign ministers in and out of the Japanese National Diet, and on the contents of the *Diplomatic Bluebook* (*Gaikō seisho*) published annually by the Japanese Foreign Ministry since 1957.[4] Admittedly, these materials encompass only a small portion of what may be called Japan's diplomatic rhetoric. But they provide the most accessible, consistent and reliable indicators for Japan's public pronouncements on value-related questions.

JAPAN AND THE INTERNATIONAL SOCIETY: 1868–1945

To place Japan's foreign policy rhetoric in a proper perspective, I shall begin by summarily describing the values which have exerted major influence on the development of international relations. At the risk of oversimplification, these values may be classified into four successive 'layers'.

1) Layer I (sovereignty values): These are the values upon which the European states system of the seventeenth to nineteenth centuries was built, namely, the principle of state sovereignty and its corollaries, including non-intervention in domestic affairs, renunciation of distinction between just and unjust wars and so on. While sovereignty ensured equality among recognized members of international society, states and peoples regarded as not fulfilling the European standard of 'civilization' were subjected to less than equal treatment.[5] In other words, sovereignty values were compatible with the practice of imperialism.

2) Layer II (non-aggression values): These are values adopted as a result of the two world wars, having to do mostly with de-legitimation of colonialism and use of force except for self-defence or international policing action. They include injunctions against use of force, for instance, for the purpose of gaining new territory. These values began to spread after World War I and were codified in the United Nations (UN) Charter (and other relevant UN documents), which was in principle accepted by both sides of the Cold War.

3) Layer III ('Western' values): These include individual liberty, democracy, free market and basic human rights. These values go beyond traditional international law regulating relations among internally autonomous sovereign states. Some of these values are codified in documents such as the

Universal Declaration of Human Rights. These values are 'universal' in their potential reach, but they are often considered 'Western' because their lineage can be most directly traced to Western intellectual tradition, and because during the Cold War, states in the Western camp tended to adhere to these values more than the rest of the world.

4) Layer IV (postmodern values): These are values that have gained prominence on the international scene in the relatively recent past. They include environmental protection, as well as a host of new individual and group rights (lesbian-gay-bisexual-and-transgender [LGBT] rights, women's reproductive rights, etc.) some of which remain controversial even in Western states.

Since the Meiji period, Japan absorbed 'sovereignty values' and transformed itself into an empire. But to gain entry into the family of 'civilized nations', Japan had to Westernize culturally, in addition to strengthening military and economic power. The keynote of Japan's foreign policy in the Meiji era was therefore the effort to 'exit from Asia and enter Europe' (*datsu-a nyū-ō*), as a well-known slogan dating from the 1880s put it. Although Japan was successful in 'exiting from Asia' in that it avoided colonization and emerged as a great power in its own right, entry into Europe was difficult at a time when racial, religious and cultural differences constituted greater barriers in international affairs than they do today.[6] Faced with such difficulty, Japanese élite claimed that Japan is the 'leader of the Orient', and emphasized Japan's unique virtues embodied in its 'national polity' (*kokutai*), according to which Japan was a 'divine' country reigned over by an unbroken chain of Emperors descending from *Amaterasu*, the Sun Goddess.

After World War I, imperialist rivalry was delegitimized, and 'non-aggression values' gained in influence. Japan also adjusted to this shift by becoming a key player in the so-called Washington System. Yet, from the viewpoint of 'latecomer empires' such as Germany, Italy and Japan, the new, liberal international order appeared to be a thinly veiled attempt to freeze the territorial status quo advantageous to the established empires. In the 1930s, Japan sought to build a Japanocentric regional order in the Asia-Pacific region. In doing so, Japan claimed to be both acting as the 'leader of the Orient' and guided by the uniquely Japanese values embodied in the national polity.

Japan's defeat in World War II discredited the notion of the superiority of Japan's *kokutai*, and the country was to be reformed thoroughly under American occupation. The defeat also put an end to Japan's wartime bid to build a Japan-centred regional order in the 'Greater East Asia'. Thus post-war Japan became hesitant in asserting indigenous values even in its domestic affairs, not to speak of projecting them outward in the conduct of foreign policy. At the same time, the post-war world provided a rather favourable environment for Japan to assimilate into international society. With the onset of the Cold War, the distinction between East and West came to designate ideological rather than civilizational differences.[7] Also, the inclusion of an anti-racism clause in the Universal Declaration of Human Rights represented a major step in the direction of eradication of racial discrimination. Such changes lowered the barrier for Japan to join the West. The result was that post-war Japan's foreign policy rhetoric came to be more firmly based on the language of 'non-aggression values' and of 'Western values'.

PACIFISM AND 'PEACE DIPLOMACY'

The origins of post-war Japan's pacifism lie in military defeat. Going beyond the norm of non-aggression, Japan was required to accept general disarmament as a guarantee against the revival of military expansionism. Yet, pacifism was not accepted grudgingly. The anti-militarist sentiment festering during wartime and the desire to find some meaning in the country's total defeat led many Japanese to embrace pacifism as a new mission for the country.[8]

On 5 September 1945, less than three weeks after accepting the Potsdam Declaration, Emperor Hirohito issued a Rescript calling for the establishment of a peace-loving country (*heiwa kokka*).[9] The enactment of the 'Peace Constitution' in 1947 strengthened the claim that Japan has a unique mission to promote peace. In November 1949, Prime Minister Yoshida said that 'the very lack of armament is the guarantee for our own security and happiness, and the means for winning the trust of the world. It also provides the basis for Japan's pride as a peace-loving country'.[10] Part of this rhetoric may have derived from the occupation authorities' attempt to make defeat and disarmament more palatable to the Japanese populace, and part from the desire of the government to convince the occupation authorities of the genuineness of Japan's conversion and thereby to expedite the recovery of sovereignty. But there is no denying that pacifism was embraced by both the people and the government and became an important pillar of Japan's national identity in the early post-war era.[11]

The outbreak of the Korean War posed a serious challenge to Japanese pacifism. Article 9 of the Constitution stipulated the renunciation of 'land, sea, and air forces, as well as other war potential'. Initially, the government had interpreted this clause as prohibiting the possession of any coercive power going beyond police forces. After the outbreak of the war, however, the government was instructed by General MacArthur to establish a 'National Police Reserve', which later developed into the Self-Defence Forces (SDF). Article 9 was now reinterpreted as allowing for the use of force for ensuring national survival, and for the minimum level of armed force needed to exercise that right. Equally significant, the outbreak of the Korean War led to Japan's inclusion in the pro-American camp in the Cold War. Japan's pacifism was initially based on the assumption that cooperation among the Allied powers would ensure the security of Japan, which would no longer be a player in the balance of power. With cooperation among the Allies now broken, the United States moved quickly to incorporate Japan in the 'free world', and the Japanese government now sought to ensure Japan's security by joining it.[12]

While the government moved away from its original pacifist stance, progressive or leftist forces in Japan opposed both rearmament and Japan's inclusion in the pro-American camp. Since the government 'betrayed' the original ideals of the Constitution, pacifism in the sense of complete disarmament and transcendence of power politics became an ideal associated with left-wing politics. Yet pacifism did not disappear from the rhetoric of the ruling conservatives. After all, Japan's military capacity remained quite limited. Moreover, when the Japanese Diet approved the Self-Defence Forces Law in 1954, the Upper House passed a supplementary resolution confirming that 'the SDF shall not be dispatched overseas'. In this situation, Japanese policy could not be anything other than broadly pacifist, though no longer pacifist in the strict sense preferred by the leftists. Yoshida himself accepted this state of affairs, because it allowed Japan to concentrate on economic recovery. More generally, pacifism had struck deep roots in the Japanese populace; it was embraced not only by the leftists but also by many conservatives. Thus 'peace diplomacy' (*heiwa gaikō*) became an important part of Japan's foreign policy rhetoric from the 1950s through the 1980s.

The core policy components of post-war Japan's pacifism are well known.[13] Stringent restriction on offensive military capabilities, no dispatch of SDF troops overseas, the 'three non-nuclear principles' – observing which Japan shall not possess, produce or allow the introduction to its territory of nuclear weapons – use of force only in self-defence and the doctrine of exclusively defence-oriented policy (which requires that defensive force be used only in the event of an attack, and that the extent of use of defensive force be kept to the minimum necessary level) are some of the best known among them. Above and beyond these basic elements, the actual content of 'peace diplomacy' evolved over time.

When the term entered Japanese diplomatic rhetoric in the 1950s, 'peace diplomacy' connoted (a) emphasis on UN-centred multilateral diplomacy, as opposed to overdependence on the United States; (b) attempts to build normal relations with communist bloc states; and (c) emphasis on disarmament, and particularly nuclear disarmament. Of these, 'UN-centrism' was promoted as a central principle of Japanese foreign policy; it was mentioned as the first of the 'Three Principles of Japan's Foreign Policy' in the 1957 *Diplomatic*

Bluebook. However, judging from subsequent editions of the *Bluebook*, by the late 1960s, UN-centrism was downgraded from its original status as a key principle of foreign policy.[14] Attempts to develop normal relations with socialist states were also depicted as part of peace diplomacy. Such efforts reached a peak in the period of détente in the 1970s, but by the end of the 1970s, they receded as Cold War tensions mounted again. In the 1980s, when Japan's Official Development Assistance (ODA) increased rapidly, development assistance was characterized as a component of Japan's peace diplomacy. Regardless of varying content, pacifism and peace diplomacy remained an important part of Japan's foreign policy rhetoric throughout the Cold War era.

Japanese pacifism certainly contributed to international peace and security by removing an aggressive, expansionist state from the East Asian region. What was often lacking in Japanese pacifism of the Cold War era, however, was realistic thinking on how Japan might contribute to international peace and security beyond disarming itself. Left-leaning pacifists rejected the legitimacy of the SDF and adhered to the vision of 'peace by peaceful means only'. This made their thinking highly unrealistic. Spreading the spirit of Article 9 worldwide was sometimes mentioned as a strategy for making the world more peaceful, but such a plan hardly counted as a realistic policy proposal.[15] Japan's pacifist sentiments, articulated by the leftists in their purest form, failed to acknowledge any role for military force and focused on maintaining the moral purity of Japan by sticking to the idea of unarmed neutrality. Lurking behind this ethical purism was the notion that Japan was – and should be – a 'special' country. It is not far-fetched to see in post-war Japanese pacifism a reincarnation in a reversed form of the ideology of uniqueness and special mission characteristic of pre-war Japan.[16]

FREEDOM, DEMOCRACY AND SOLIDARITY WITH THE 'FREE WORLD'

If 'peace' served to emphasize Japan's unique identity in the post-war world, 'freedom' and 'democracy', or 'Western values', were used in Japan's foreign policy rhetoric during the Cold War era to emphasize Japan's belonging to the Western alliance. The principles of individual freedom and democracy are central to the constitution enacted in 1947. Its Preamble declared that democracy based on popular sovereignty is 'a universal principle of mankind'. Obviously, Japan in 1945 was not a democracy, and in the early postwar era, freedom and democracy were mentioned in official rhetoric as ideals that Japan should strive for. With the onset of the Cold War, however, freedom and democracy acquired a partisan connotation in international politics and began to serve as a symbol of solidarity among pro-American states, rather than real indicators of the nature of political regimes. This meant that democracies in the making, such as Japan, could be upgraded into the liberal democratic category ahead of time.[17]

Japan's foreign policy rhetoric was quick to exploit the Cold War division for advancement of Japan's security and political interests. Prime Minister Yoshida stated in his Diet speech of January 1951: 'Japan is now looked upon as a bridgehead of democracy, poised to check the influence of communist forces in the Far East . . . which raises the prospect of Japan being welcomed as a member of the community of liberal, democratic states'. The rhetoric of Japan's membership in the group of liberal democratic states achieved its initial peak in the 1950s. In this period, solidarity with liberal democratic states and with the 'free world' was repeatedly emphasized.

This Cold War political rhetoric receded significantly starting in the mid-1960s, giving way in part to the rhetoric of economic cooperation within the free world, and in part to that of 'peace diplomacy'. The escalation of the Vietnam War in the late 1960s made security ties with the United States less popular domestically, while the normalization of relations with People's Republic of China in 1972 blurred the boundaries between the 'free world' and the communist bloc. By the mid-1970s, references to the 'free world' had nearly disappeared from Japan's foreign policy rhetoric. Yet, in the late 1970s, the rhetoric of solidarity with the 'free world' was revived in a different form – through emphasis on the need for economic cooperation among 'advanced democracies'. With the Soviet invasion of Afghanistan in 1979, rhetorical emphasis shifted from economic to political solidarity. During the 1980s, Japan's foreign policy rhetoric placed more emphasis than before on solidarity with the Western alliance, and in that context, the sharing of values such as freedom and democracy was also underscored.

Both in the early Cold War era and in the 1980s, references to freedom and democracy in Japan's foreign policy rhetoric were associated with solidarity with other liberal democratic states. Although democracy and liberalism in the broad sense became nearly universally accepted norms in post-war Japan, Japan was a latecomer to the community of liberal democracies. There was nothing which allowed Japan to claim a privileged status within that community. It was perhaps for this reason that whereas peace diplomacy became an important part of Japan's foreign policy rhetoric, democracy promotion did not occupy a similar place in it. The values of freedom and democracy were invoked for show of political solidarity rather than serving as a basis for active promotion of such values overseas. This is evident in the government's reactions to suppression of human rights or of pro-democracy movements.[18]

THE SEARCH FOR
CULTURAL/CIVILIZATIONAL
IDENTITY

Post-war Japan's foreign policy rhetoric has been framed mostly in terms of appeals to 'universal' values, such as democracy, freedom and peace. But this does not mean that older indigenous values and ideas ceased to be important in Japanese national identity, or that post-war Japan became entirely assimilated into the West. Although differences of race and culture were no longer determinants of status in post-war international society, the consciousness of separateness from other Western states remained real.[19] Thus, the Japanese in the post-war era continued to ask questions about what constituted Japan's distinctiveness, and to search their country's place between Asia and the West.

The conditions of the Cold War era provided a favourable environment in which Japan could search for distinctive identity. During the Cold War era, solidarity among states in the free world was often regarded as more important than the degree to which pro-American states actually lived up to the standards of individual freedom, democracy or human rights.[20] As long as Japan remained loyal to the pro-American camp, some divergence from the Western model was not regarded as a problem, especially if it could be explained as cultural variations within the common theme of liberal democracy.

In the immediate post-war era, the Japanese tended to take a negative view of many aspects of indigenous Japanese traditions. Although the notion that Japan should strive to become a 'cultural state' (*bunka kokka*) was quite popular during that period, 'culture' in this context meant importation of 'universal' culture from advanced Western states. A 'cultural state' was democratic and peace-loving first and foremost. The emphasis was on the need for Japan to join the mainstream of world culture, not on the distinctiveness of the Japanese tradition.[21]

As Japan's economy grew rapidly, however, Japan's foreign policy rhetoric began to express the notion that Japan, though it was an advanced democracy belonging to the free world, was also a distinct civilization with its own unique culture. Already in the late 1950s, official rhetoric began to link the term 'culture' with Japanese traditions. The section on public diplomacy of the 1967 edition of the *Bluebook* stated that it was important 'to inform the world about today's Japan, which is achieving rapid development as a modern industrial state, while at the same time retaining a sophisticated culture and tradition of its own'. This passage indicates that the foreign policy rhetoric of the time sought to depict Japan not only as an economically advanced state but also as a country with a distinctive cultural tradition deserving the respect of the world.[22]

Emphasis on Japan belonging to Asia re-entered post-war Japan's foreign policy rhetoric somewhat earlier and with a slightly different momentum.

Though Japan re-joined the international society as a member of the Western camp, leftists preferred a neutral stance. US-Japan relations in the 1950s remained highly unequal, which stimulated anti-American sentiments, and increased support for neutralism – so that in 1959, 50 percent of the respondents to a Nippon Hōsō Kyōkai (NHK) poll preferred a neutralist stance against 26 percent who preferred a 'pro-free-world' stance.[23] In this context, the rise of the non-aligned group of Asian states such as India and Indonesia appeared to show the way for Japan. Thus, solidarity with Asia, coupled with autonomy from the United States and neutralist stance in the Cold War, became an important part of leftist rhetoric in the 1950s.

The theme of Japan's belonging to Asia also became part of the official rhetoric, though the meaning of 'belonging to Asia' was interpreted differently. In 1956, Foreign Minister Shigemitsu asserted in his UN General Assembly Speech – the first ever delivered by a Japanese representative – that Japan was 'a product of the fusion of western and Asian civilization over the past century' and, as such, could 'serve as a bridge between the East and the West'. The 1957 *Diplomatic Bluebook* listed 'taking the stance of an Asian country' as one of the 'Three Principles of Japan's Foreign Policy', and explained that this principle derived in part 'from strong psychological bond arising from racial and cultural affinity'. In official rhetoric, too, Japan was part of Asia, though belonging to Asia was not a matter of neutralism, but of cultural and racial affinity. Yet the rhetoric of racial and cultural affinity with Asia was toned down and replaced with an emphasis on 'universal' values a year later, when the *Bluebook* clarified that 'all three principles are permeated with a single fundamental spirit, which is to establish in international society a democratic order based on freedom and justice, and to seek our country's security and development within such an order'. Subsequently, Japan's foreign policy rhetoric preferred not to speak about cultural or racial affinity with Asia but focused more on supra-civilizational regional integration of the 'Asia-Pacific'.[24]

According to opinion survey data, Japan's national self-confidence reached its peak in the 1980s, based on Japan's economic successes.[25] During the 1970s and the 1980s, a number of books on the subject of *nihonjin-ron* (Japanese national character) were published, purporting to explain post-war Japan's 'success' by reference to various aspects of Japanese culture and society.[26] Japan's distinctive culture and traditions were now regarded more positively. By this time, economic success in Asia was no longer limited to Japan; Japan was the 'leading goose' in a flock of Asian economies demonstrating impressive growth. Some Asian leaders, including Lee Kuan Yew and Mahathir Mohamad, were advancing the argument that Asian countries shared 'Asian values' that were different from 'Western values', and that Western states should recognize the cultural relativity of their values and institutions. Due to growing economic friction and acrimony between Japan and the West during this period, the idea of Asian values resonated in some segments of society.[27]

Yet, overall, Japan's foreign policy rhetoric was reticent in making claims on the distinctive virtues of Japan or of Asia. There are a few instances in which Prime Minister Nakasone openly embraced 'Asian values', as when he stated in Kuala Lumpur in 1983:

> In a world where economic stagnation and political confusion is rampant, ASEAN countries have made dynamic strides in their development. . . . I believe that one key to this puzzle can be found in the spiritual and cultural tradition shared by East Asian states. . . . This tradition, which values unity over difference, cooperation over confrontation, and deference over self-assertion . . . is rare in a modern society, and its importance cannot be overemphasized.[28]

But such statements are exceptions rather than the rule. In speech after speech, prime ministers of this period (Ōhira, Suzuki, Nakasone and Takeshita) emphasized Japan's commitment to values such as freedom and democracy. The emphasis was clearly on how much Japan shared with other advanced democracies, not on how Japan was different.

What we do find in Japan's foreign policy rhetoric of this period instead, is a call for cultural pluralism in international society. Annual editions of the *Bluebook* from 1970 to 1988 contained a section concerning the promotion of mutual understanding between Japan and other states. Going beyond this, the government was making a modest plea for cultural and civilizational pluralism in international society. For instance, in a speech delivered at the UN General Assembly in 1985, Nakasone said:

> The starting point for a peaceful world must be found in the confirmation . . . of the cultural and civilizational diversity in the world, and in the humble attitude of mutual respect. Such mutual recognition and respect will . . . hopefully give rise to a new human civilization, built on the harmony of all cultures and civilizations.[29]

While the government clearly relished Japan's status as one of the advanced democracies, a world of many cultures and civilizations appeared more comfortable for Japan than a world where Japan was the odd man out. Promotion of cultural pluralism was an agenda that enjoyed broad support within the Japanese bureaucracy.[30] While the Japanese government (at least the Foreign Ministry) was careful to avoid being associated with the rhetoric of 'Asian values', it was quietly seeking to promote cultural pluralism in international society.

Advocacy for cultural pluralism in international society took a concrete form in Japan's support for conservation of cultural heritage, particularly in developing nations. This policy, launched by Prime Minister Takeshita in his London speech in May 1988, resulted in the establishment in 1989 of a United Nations Educational, Scientific and Cultural Organization/Japan Fund-in-Trust for the Preservation of the World Cultural Heritage.[31] While Takeshita's initiative may in part be explained as a policy designed to deflect international criticism on Japan for 'not doing enough' for the international community despite being an economic superpower, the fact that Japan directed part of its rapidly growing ODA to heritage conservation indicates that Japan took promotion of cultural pluralism seriously.[32]

ADAPTATION TO UNIVERSALISM IN THE POST–COLD WAR ERA

For many, the disintegration of the Soviet bloc signified the victory of liberal democracy and capitalism over communism. The end of the Cold War rivalry and the ideological victory of the Western camp seemed to open the way for the actual universalization of 'Western' values. Freedom and democracy were no longer just symbols of solidarity for the anti-communist camp; they were to become effective standards which all countries should live up to.

Further, the disappearance of the external enemy took away the rationale for tolerance of diversity in political regimes that characterized the Western alliance in the Cold War era. Pro-Western political orientation no longer guaranteed recognition as a respected member of the community of liberal democracies. Outwardly democratic states taking a pro-Western stance came under closer scrutiny. Despite its strong track record as a democracy, Japan also became a target of such scrutiny. By the end of the Cold War, the Japanese economy had grown to massive proportions, constituting close to 14 percent of the global economy, and its large trade surplus vis-à-vis the United States and European states had become a contentious issue. Japan came to be perceived by some in the West as a pseudo-democratic, pseudo-capitalist state, in which the façade of liberal democracy thinly covered the reality of bureaucratically manufactured consensus and unfair economic practices, legitimized by discourse of cultural uniqueness.[33]

Faced with this situation, Japan's foreign policy rhetoric began to de-emphasize the uniqueness of Japanese culture, and to put more emphasis on the universality of values such as liberty, democracy, and human rights. A good indication of this change is the way in which the *Bluebook* described Japan's participation in the UN's human rights efforts. Until 1988, successive editions of the *Bluebook* took a rather detached position, reporting on UN's efforts in a non-committal fashion. But the 1989 edition, in a sudden change of heart, stated that 'Japan's basic position emphasizes the importance of protection of human rights, which is a universal principle for the entire humanity. . . [R]especting human rights will ultimately contribute to peace and stability in the world'. The 1990 edition extended Japan's newfound emphasis on human rights retroactively to the past, stating that 'Japan has actively participated in the United Nations' efforts to protect and promote human rights around the world, taking the basic position that human rights is a universal value for the humanity, and that it is a foundation for peace and stability in the world'. The 1993 edition contained a passage symbolic of Japan's shift toward universalism: 'Liberty, democracy, and market economy are no longer an ideology poised against centrally-planned economy . . . they are universal values'.

In the early 1990s, themes of cultural relativism and plurality weakened noticeably in the speeches of Japan's prime ministers and foreign ministers. At the same time, the section on 'international understanding' in annual editions of the *Bluebook* emphasized the need to make more effort to live in harmony with the international community. According to the 1990 *Bluebook*, this meant that Japan must 'keep harmonious relationship with the international community by promoting internationalization of Japanese society. . . . It is incumbent on the Japanese to be open-minded and tolerant toward what is different, while maintaining Japan's distinctive traditions and values'.[34]

Japan's apparent conversion to universalism, however, was rather short-lived. After a big surge in the early 1990s, references to universal values and similar terms in the *Bluebook* dropped in the mid-1990s and stayed at a low level into the early 2000s. This may reflect the growing uncertainty of Japan's security environment since the mid-1990s. The North Korean nuclear crisis of 1993, the Taiwan Straits Crisis of 1996, ballistic missile launches by North Korea and increasing acrimony over 'history issues' with China may well have convinced Japanese policymakers that 'universal' values were not really becoming universal.

But despite the growing disillusionment with universalism, and despite the continuing atmosphere of acrimony between Japan and the United States over economic issues, the influence of 'Asian values' in the Japanese government remained limited. Apart from Nakasone's speech quoted earlier, we find only a few, indirect references to 'Asian values' in prime ministers' and foreign ministers' speeches, or in the *Bluebook*. In December 2003, the Tokyo Declaration adopted at a Japan – Association of Southeast Asian Nations (ASEAN) summit meeting called for 'an East Asian community which is . . . endowed . . . with the shared spirit of mutual understanding and upholding

Asian traditions and values'. But in June 2004, the Japanese Foreign Ministry informed partner governments in ASEAN that while Japan was open to functional cooperation and institutional arrangements with ASEAN, it found very difficult 'the creation of common identity based on shared values and principles'.[35] As before, the Japanese government took care to avoid being associated with 'Asian values', while it continued to push for 'an international order which . . . allows for coexistence and mutual respect among diverse cultures', as Prime Minister Koizumi put it in his February 2002 policy speech in the National Diet.

The end of the Cold War posed a challenge not only to the rhetoric of distinctive cultural/civilizational identity but also to Japanese pacifism, with its belief in Japan's uniqueness and national mission. Decisive in this respect was the impact of the Gulf War, and subsequent debate about sending the SDF on a peacekeeping mission in Cambodia. Having deeply internalized the negative lessons of expansionist wars, post-war Japan resolved not to send SDF troops overseas. But lacking from the purview of post-war Japanese pacifism was the possibility of military actions that cannot be categorized either as an aggressive war or as an act of self-defence. The Gulf War and the debate about the peacekeeping mission laid bare the inward-looking nature of the pacifist vision, which came to be criticized widely as 'pacifism in one country' (*ikkoku heiwa-shugi*). In this new environment, the left-wing conception of pacifism based on the idea of unarmed neutrality lost ground. The Japanese Socialist Party, the main supporter of unarmed neutrality during the Cold War era, recognized the legitimacy of both the SDF and the US–Japan Security Treaty, and formed a coalition government with the Liberal Democratic Party in 1994. This did not mean that Japanese pacifism as a whole was losing influence; only one interpretation of pacifism was declining. The core components of restraints on post-war Japan's security, including exclusively defence-oriented policy, the three non-nuclear principles and the ban on export of weapons, were preserved. A series of legislations passed in the 1990s and the early 2000s allowed the SDF troops to be sent overseas for UN-sanctioned peacekeeping missions, logistical support for foreign military forces engaged in military operations in Afghanistan and for reconstruction work in Iraq, but SDF's missions were non-combat missions of mostly logistical and humanitarian character. Moreover, ODA remained Japan's key contribution to the international community, with Japan being the top ODA donor in the world from 1992 through 2001. In 1998, under the leadership of Prime Minister Keizō Obuchi, Japan took up the banner of human security, seeking to demonstrate that Japan was not simply preaching peace, but actually laying the groundwork for peace through development assistance.[36]

VALUE-ORIENTED DIPLOMACY:
TOWARDS GREATER EMPHASIS
ON UNIVERSAL VALUES

The September 11 terrorist attacks on the United States threw cold water on any remnant of the euphoria that swept the Western world at the end of the Cold War. To many, the attacks demonstrated that the international community still faced mortal enemies. Meanwhile, the security environment in East Asia was becoming more complicated. Sino-Japanese political relations had deteriorated steadily from their peak in the 1980s. North Korea's attempt to develop nuclear weapons and ballistic missiles was another source of worry. The growing uncertainty in Japan's security environment gave Japanese leaders a strong incentive to deepen Japan's ties with the United States, partly by emphasizing the sharing of 'universal values'.

In the early 1990s, not much emphasis was placed on sharing of values with specific states. For one thing, when liberal universalism dominated, values such as freedom and democracy were considered truly universal; they were not to be shared only among selected states. For another, Japan's international environment at the time was perceived to be benign. But due to growing security worries and due to the re-emergence of friend–enemy distinctions in world politics, Japan's foreign policy rhetoric once again began to emphasize sharing of values with friendly states. This policy of emphasizing close relations with states that share common values has come to be known as 'value-oriented diplomacy' (*kachikan gaikō*) in Japanese diplomatic parlance.

The term 'value-oriented diplomacy' (VOD) was introduced during the first Abe cabinet, in a 2006 speech by Foreign Minister Asō. In the speech, Asō declared that henceforth, Japanese foreign policy would be putting more emphasis on universal values such as democracy, freedom, human rights, rule of law and market economy. His emphasis on the role of universal values took firm root in the thinking of the Japanese Foreign Ministry. Though the theme of VOD did not receive emphasis from prime ministers that followed Abe's first term (except Asō), upon his return to power Abe declared that emphasis on 'universal values' was one of the pillars of his foreign policy.

It is easy to regard Japan's VOD as a tactical move designed to check the influence of China. Some telling evidence points in this direction. First, the rhetorical emphasis in VOD is clearly on solidarity with states which already share 'universal' values, rather than on spreading them to countries that do not. Evidently, coalition-building is a central aspect of VOD. Second, the mention of Mongolia and particularly Taiwan as partners that share 'universal values' strengthens the impression that VOD is designed as an attempt at 'normative encirclement' of China, an impression further strengthened by the fact that the *Bluebook* describes Vietnam as 'a geopolitically important country with a long border with China'. Apparently, sharing of universal values is not a sine qua non for building close partnership.

Nevertheless, it would be erroneous to interpret the new emphasis on universal values only as a tactic of normative containment. One piece of evidence for this claim is the fact that universal values are emphasized not only in the context of relations with friendly states but also in describing an international order desirable for Japan. The *Bluebook* has since 2009 described efforts to strengthen the rule of law in international society as 'one of the pillars of our foreign policy'. Japan's National Security Strategy (NSS), adopted in 2013, states that 'the maintenance and protection of international order based on rules and universal values, such as freedom, democracy, respect for fundamental human rights, and the rule of law, are . . . in Japan's national interests'.[37] As the 2016 edition of the *Bluebook* explains, 'Since Japan is a maritime nation lacking in natural resources, the maintenance and development of an open, rule-based, and stable international economic order is of critical importance'. As long as the United States and the West collectively had the capacity and willingness to lead the international order, Japan could take the existence of an open, liberal international order for granted. On that basis, Japan could push for other, less central goals such as cultural diversity in international society. But this was decreasingly the case after the financial crisis of 2008. As the balance of power shifted, there was a growing concern about the durability of the liberal international order. Against this background, it becomes understandable why Japan's foreign policy rhetoric began to emphasize the theme of universal values.

PROACTIVE PACIFISM

Another major theme in the foreign policy rhetoric of the Abe Cabinet has been 'proactive contribution to peace' (*sekkyokuteki heiwa-shugi*, or PCP). The term *sekkyokuteki heiwa-shugi* has been used by other politicians since the 1990s, but it was under Abe that it was adopted as an official principle of Japanese foreign policy. The term became the central theme in the NSS, which was adopted in December 2013 as the basic guideline for national security policy. The NSS states:

> Under the evolving security environment, Japan will continue to adhere to the course that it has taken to date as a peace-loving nation. Japan . . . guided by the idea of proactive contribution to peace based on international cooperation, will do more to secure peace, stability, and prosperity of the international community, while achieving its own security as well as peace and stability in the

Asia-Pacific region. This is the fundamental principle of national security that Japan should uphold.[38]

It is easy to discern that one component of PCP is for Japan to 'do more to secure peace, stability, and prosperity of the international community'. Yet, it is important to note that 'achieving Japan's own security as well as peace and stability in the Asia-Pacific region' is also considered a part of PCP. As the NSS states:

> Enhancing Japan's resilience in national security . . . contributes to peace and stability in the Asia-Pacific region and the international community at large. This belief forms the core of the strategic approaches in the Strategy.

In fact, a key idea behind PCP is the notion that security in today's world is interdependent, and that a state can ensure its security only through international cooperation. More than half a century ago, Chief Justice Kōtarō Tanaka of Japan's Supreme Court had written in a concurring opinion to the ruling on the famous Sunagawa Case:[39]

> For a state to defend itself from aggression will help other states defend themselves. Conversely, to help other states defend themselves is to defend one's own state. In other words, in today's world, there is no 'self-defence' in the strict sense of the word: self-defence is defending others, while defending others is to defend oneself. Thus, every state may be said to have an obligation to defend oneself, and to help other states defend themselves.[40]

If self-defence and defence of other countries are one and the same, security can be provided only through international cooperation – through mechanisms such as collective security and collective self-defence. Tanaka went on to state:

> We must interpret the pacifism in our Constitution not just from the viewpoint of one country, but also from the viewpoint of world law, in such a way that agrees with the juristic convictions of democratic, peace-loving states. Not to be interested in the defence of other states would be an example of national self-absorption which the Preamble of our Constitution warns against. This is all the more true for the refusal to take one's own national defence seriously.

Building on Tanaka's opinion, the PCP concept suggested a radical rereading of the constitution. If conventional interpretations sought to ensure Japan's security by isolating it from troubles overseas, the PCP concept assumes that Japan can be secured only through international cooperation, using both non-military means and legitimate capacity for self-defence. Not surprisingly, more active participation in UN-sanctioned peacekeeping/peace-building missions and the exercise of the right of collective self-defence became key components of the PCP concept. The cabinet decided in July 2014 to reinterpret Article 9 of the constitution to allow for the adoption of the right of collective self-defence in some limited circumstances.

But this rereading of the constitution proved too radical for Japan's domestic political environment, especially because of its inconsistency with the long-standing official interpretation of Article 9. Thus, despite introducing the new concept of PCP, the Abe Cabinet retained many elements of established security policy, including the exclusively defence-oriented policy. The new security policy implemented so far by the Abe Cabinet stops short of the original vision of PCP. PCP emphasizes the need for an active contribution to peace through the UN, US-Japan alliance and through other frameworks for international cooperation. In making such contribution, PCP suggests that Japan be allowed a broader choice of instruments, including military means. But the policy adopted so far by the Abe Cabinet made only hesitant steps in this direction. In fact, the Cabinet Decision of July 2014 allowed for the exercise of the right of collective self-defence *only when exercising it is indispensable for Japan's own immediate security*. The paradox of allowing the exercise of the right of collective self-defence only for the sake of one's own immediate security is symptomatic of the halfway position in which Japanese security policy finds itself at present.

CONCLUSION

Post-war Japan in its foreign policy rhetoric has mostly espoused 'universal' values, such as peace, freedom, democracy, and human rights. While peace became deeply bound up with Japan's national identity and came to be seen as a value that Japan should propagate throughout the world, espousal of values such as freedom, democracy and human rights has more often served as tactical moves designed to strengthen Japan's ties with the United States and other friendly states, especially in times of international tension. This is not to say that post-war Japan's allegiance to freedom and democracy was only a diplomatic pose. These values have taken deep root in post-war Japan. Besides, Japan has made significant (though often indirect) contributions to spreading such values through its ODA policy, packaged under the slogan of human security since 1998. Yet it is impossible to deny that allegiance to freedom and democracy has been used instrumentally for achieving objectives that are extraneous to those values. Pacifism, by contrast, penetrated post-war Japanese society to such an extent that it almost has an indigenous value. Yet, from a broader perspective, pacifism was a price that Japan had to pay to regain acceptance into the international society after World War II. It is certainly true that the Japanese people in the post-war era embraced this ideal quite eagerly. But this does not change the fact that pacifism was a product of Japan's defeat. Espousal of values in post-war Japanese foreign policy could not simply be about projection of domestic values overseas. It was inevitably linked with Japan's attempt to ensure its own security, prosperity and international standing in a US-led, liberal international order.

Like other Asian states, Japan has had the desire to assert its own indigenous values. Such a desire has occasionally influenced Japan's foreign policy rhetoric in the post-war era. One way in which post-war Japan satisfied this desire was through appeals to pacifism. The idea that Japan, as the only nation to suffer from nuclear bombing, has a mission to call for world peace and the abolition of nuclear weapons was pacifist in its content but nationalist in form, for the notion presumed Japan's right to preach to the rest of the world from a moral high ground. Though post-war Japan's pacifism was based on the negation of pre-war Japanese history, in a paradoxical fashion it continued the idea of Japan's uniqueness and superiority. Another way by which post-war Japan satisfied its desire to assert a distinctive and positive identity was through a more straightforward assertion of Japan's native culture and traditions.

Characteristically, however, Japan's foreign policy rhetoric was stronger in asserting the existence of distinctive Japanese culture and traditions than in specifying what exactly those were. There are many value systems that are commonly associated with Japan's traditional culture. Japan's imperial myths, Shintoism, Buddhism (especially zen Buddhism), the spirit of *bushidō* (the way of the samurai) are some examples. But in the sources examined for this chapter, one hardly finds any references to them. One obvious reason is that some of these value systems (imperial myths, Shintoism and *bushidō*) were mobilized in support of Japan's war efforts and thereby became politically 'tainted'. But even when some other values which are less tainted (such as zen Buddhism) are mentioned, they are usually invoked as just *one element* in Japanese tradition, rather than as its defining feature.

Perhaps due to the long history of cultural borrowing and syncretism, the Japanese have found it difficult to identify the core element of their culture, and this may also explain their hesitance in articulating Japanese values in a concrete manner.[41] One theme that has repeatedly come up in Japan's rhetoric concerns precisely the hybrid, syncretic nature of Japanese culture. The claim has often been made that Japan has 'synthesized' Eastern and Western civilizations, or that Japan has a tradition of religious and cultural tolerance. Perhaps this may be regarded as an instance of concrete articulation of Japan's cultural distinctiveness. Japan's quest since the 1980s for a culturally pluralistic world, in which Western and non-Western cultures and civilizations could respect each other and peacefully coexist, has been very much in line with such self-understanding.

Since the end of the Cold War, Japan seems to have backpedalled on expressing a unique identity in its foreign policy rhetoric. In the early 1990s, the Japanese government felt it had to adapt to the growing trend of universalism, though the boom of universalism subsided rather quickly. Interestingly, Japan's commitment to universalism appears to have strengthened just when the global trend towards liberal universalism began to recede. Sensing the possibility that the changes in the global balance of power might lead to the erosion of the liberal international order, the Japanese government appears to have concluded that Japan's long-term national interest is in the maintenance of a liberal, open and rule-based international order.

This does not mean that the contest over Japan's national identity has been resolved with the complete victory of the Westernizers. Underneath the rhetoric of universal values and proactive pacifism, it is easy to see the stirrings of more traditionalist national identity. This is visible in the continuing debate within the country over history issues, immigration, demographic crisis and so on. Depending on the future course of international relations, it is not impossible that more openly nationalistic undercurrents may come to the fore in Japan's foreign policy rhetoric. However, for the foreseeable future, it is likely that Japan will continue to take its stand on the defence of a liberal international order with its 'universal' values, tempered by a modest plea for cultural pluralism.

NOTES

1. Tadashi Anno, *National Identity and Great-Power Status in Russia and Japan: Non-Western Challengers to the Liberal International Order* (London: Routledge, forthcoming), 16–21.

2. Shogo Suzuki, *Civilization and Empire: China and Japan's Encounter with European International Society* (London: Routledge, 2011).

3. This is to say that this chapter does not focus on what sort of underlying cultural values influenced Japanese foreign policy. It is impossible to deny that world views and values deriving from Shintoism, Buddhism, Confucianism and so on, or patterns of human relations influenced by such traditions, may have influenced Japan's perception of the international environment and actual conduct of policies. Kenneth Pyle's (on the whole convincing) argument concerning Japan's proclivity towards bandwagoning with the strong is one example of such an approach. I avoided this approach both because it is difficult to prove such an argument and because it results in broad generalizations which fail to account for shorter-term variations. See *Japan Rising: The Resurgence of Japanese Power and Purpose* (New York: Public Affairs, 2007), 33–65.

4. The *Diplomatic Bluebook* is edited and published by the Ministry of Foreign Affairs after obtaining an 'understanding' at a Cabinet Meeting. As such, it is a highly authoritative source on Japanese foreign policy.

5. Hedley Bull and Adam Watson (eds.), *The Expansion of International Society* (Oxford: Oxford University Press, 1984).

6. Naoko Shimazu, *Japan, Race and Equality: The Racial Equality Proposal of 1919* (London: Routledge, 1998).

7. Seizaburō Satō, 'Bakumatsu meiji shoki ni okeru taigai ishiki no shoruikei', in Satō Seizaburō and Roger Dingman (eds.). *Kindai nihon no taigai taido* (Tokyo: University of Tokyo Press, 1974), 30.

8. John Dower, *Embracing Defeat: Japan in the Wake of World War II* (New York: W.W. Norton, 1999).

9. Kunaichō (ed.). *Shōwa tennō jitsuroku* 9 (Tokyo: Tokyo Shoseki, 2016), 807.

10. All the speeches by prime ministers and foreign ministers quoted in this chapter have been translated from 'Japan and the World' database, maintained by Professor Akihiko Tanaka, http://worldjpn.grips.ac.jp/.

11. James Orr, *The Victim as Hero: Ideologies of Peace and National Identity in Postwar Japan* (Honolulu: University of Hawaii Press, 2001).

12. As Prime Minister Yoshida put it in his 24 July 1950 policy speech, 'To continue to call for a "comprehensive peace" or "permanent neutrality" in the face of [North Korean invasion] is . . . completely unrealistic. . . . The stability of our country will be ensured only by clarifying our people's commitment to the cause of international justice, and expressing our determination to contribute to world peace alongside those countries which stand for peace and order. This way, Japan will eventually be able to join the ranks of liberal states'.

13. Andrew Oros, *Normalizing Japan: Politics, Identity, and the Evolution of Security Practice* (Stanford, CA: Stanford University Press, 2008).

14. A clear indication of this is 'the Basic Guideline for Foreign Policy,' contained in the 1970 edition of the *Bluebook*, which mentioned the UN only in the third of the four agendas under the second of the two key objectives. Compared with the Three Basic Principles of 1957, the demotion of the UN in Japan's foreign policy priority was obvious.

15. Maeda Akira, a law professor and a peace activist who visited twenty-seven small states which abolished their own military, failed to identify tangible influence of the Japanese Constitution on any of those states. According to Maeda, Japanese pacifists failed to put into practice proactive pacifism as required by the Preamble of the Constitution (*Asahi Shimbun,* 18 June 2008).

16. Brian J. McVeigh, *Nationalisms of Japan: Managing and Mystifying Identity* (Lanham, MD: Rowman & Littlefield, 2004), 208; Yūichi Hosoya, *Ampo ronsō* (Tokyo: Chikuma shobō, 2016), 100.

17. Judging from the rhetoric used in the speeches of Japanese prime ministers, it was in the early 1960s when the Japanese government began to see the country as an established, stable democracy, but foreign policy rhetoric started emphasizing Japan's membership in the democratic community before that.

18. During the Hungarian Uprising, Foreign Minister Shigemitsu expressed sympathy towards the Hungarian people, but from the viewpoint of national

self-determination (Speech at the National Diet, 16 November 1956). Similarly, the Prague Spring was interpreted primarily as a challenge to world peace, and as violation of the UN Charter (*Yomiuri Shimbun*, 22 August 1968). Closer to home, Japan was consistently reluctant to denounce human rights violations in authoritarian South Korea. For instance, reacting to Carter's human rights diplomacy, Prime Minister Fukuda stated that while he 'fully supported' the cause of human rights, 'in concrete policy, Japan's approach was different from that of the US' (*Yomiuri Shimbun*, 11 March 1977). The Tiananmen Square incident of June 1989 did attract a critical remark from Prime Minister Uno, who stated that Chinese actions are 'incompatible with the democratic values which Japan professes'. But Japan's reaction to the incident was visibly more restrained compared with those of other advanced democracies.

19. Prime Minister Ōhira spoke for many other Japanese when he remarked in a conversation with an Italian-born academic in May 1980: 'So far the world has been led by people of European origin, and that is true even today. . . . We Japanese have been outsiders, so to speak. . . . We have felt that the international society is run by the Westerners, we are out of the loop'.

20. David F. Schmitz, *The United States and Right-Wing Dictatorships, 1965–1989* (Cambridge: Cambridge University Press, 2006).

21. Ken'ichirō Hirano, 'Sengo nihon gaikō ni okeru "bunka"', in Akio Watanabe (ed.). *Sengo nihon no taigai seisaku* (Tokyo: Yūhikaku, 1985), 343–45.

22. More or less identical passage appeared in the *Bluebook* continuously from 1967 to 1977.

23. NHK hōsō seron chōsajo (ed.). *Zusetsu sengo seronshi* (Tokyo: Nihon hōsō shuppan kyōkai, 1982), 166–67.

24. Mie Ōba, *Ajia taiheiyō chiiki keisei e no dōtei: Kyōkai kokka nichi gō no aidentiti to chiiki shugi* (Kyoto: Minerva shobō, 2004).

25. NHK hōsō bunka kenkyūjo (ed.), *Gendai nihonjin no ishiki kōzō* (Tokyo: NHK Books, 2015), 120.

26. Kosaku Yoshino, *Cultural Nationalism in Contemporary Japan: A Sociological Enquiry* (London: Routledge, 1992).

27. Mohamad Mahathir and Shintaro Ishihara, *No to ieru ajia* (Tokyo: Kōbunsha, 1994).

28. For another instance, see Nakasone's speech at the Parliament of India in May 1984.

29. Similar statements can be found in many of Nakasone's speeches, including his 1987 UN speech, and in his speeches at the University of Belgrade in January 1987 and at the Chulalongkorn University in September 1987.

30. In a May 1988 speech in London, Takeshita spoke of the need 'to enrich human culture by . . . preserving the cultural achievements of various peoples, and by promoting exchanges among different cultures of the world'. Not only did Takeshita repeat himself word for word in a speech in Xian in August; the same expression also appeared in the 1988 *Bluebook*, which suggests that Takeshita's speeches were written by Foreign Ministry officials.

31. Natsuko Akagawa, *Heritage Conservation and Japan's Cultural Diplomacy: Heritage, National Identity and National Interest* (London: Routledge, 2014).

32. There is considerable evidence suggesting that Japan's assistance in heritage conservation was undertaken for the preservation of the diversity of *national* cultures. In the London speech, Takeshita spoke of 'the preservation of the cultural heritage of mankind', implying that cultural heritages belonged to the mankind as a whole. Yet, later policy pronouncements suggest that, in helping countries preserve cultural heritages, Japan was assisting in those states' nation-building efforts. The 1991 to 1993 editions of the *Bluebook*, for instance, referred to 'promoting distinctive ethno-national cultures', while the 2001 edition spoke of 'assistance in the cultural aspect of nation-building'. The 2009–2011 editions, while acknowledging that cultural heritages are 'the common heritage of the mankind', also described them as 'sources of pride for the countries concerned', and as 'deeply implicated in their identities'.

33. Karel van Wolferen, *The Enigma of Japanese Power: People and Politics in a Stateless Nation* (New York: Vintage Books, 1990); James Fallows, 'Containing Japan', *The Atlantic Monthly* (May 1989): 40–50.

34. The 1990 to 1992 editions of the *Bluebook* included a section emphasizing the necessity of the internationalization of the Japanese society, and of a change in the consciousness of the Japanese people. After 1993, however, more emphasis was placed on the need to remove misunderstandings about Japan on the part of foreign countries.

35. Sumio Hatano, 'Nihon gaikō ni okeru ajia shugi no kinō: Sono hikari to kage', in Shindō Eiichi et al. (eds.). *Sengo nihon seiji to heiwa gaikō: 21-seiki ajia kyōsei jidai no shiza* (Tokyo: Hōritsu bunkasha, 2007), 117–118.

36. Bert Edström, *Japan and Human Security: The Derailing of a Foreign Policy Vision* (Stockholm: Institute for Security and Development Policy, 2011).

37. The English version of the NSS is available at https://www.cas.go.jp/jp/siryou/131217anzenhoshou/nss-e.pdf.

38. National Security Strategy (17 December 2013). https://www.cas.go.jp/jp/siryou/131217anzenhoshou/nss-e.pdf. (The translation has been changed to better reflect the Japanese original.)

39. The Sunagawa case is a 1959 case in which the constitutionality of stationing of US troops in Japan under the US–Japan Security Treaty was contested.

40. See Kōtarō Tanaka, 'Sunagawa Case', Supreme Court of Japan. http://www.courts.go.jp/app/files/hanrei_jp/816/055816_hanrei.pdf, 8.

41. Masao Maruyama, *Nihon no shisō* (Tokyo: Iwanami, 1961), 2–11.

BIBLIOGRAPHY

Bull, Hedley and Adam Watson (eds.). *The Expansion of International Society*. Oxford: Oxford University Press, 1984.

Dower, John. *Embracing Defeat: Japan in the Wake of World War II*. New York: W.W. Norton & Co, 1999.

Edström, Bert. *Japan and Human Security: The Derailing of a Foreign Policy Vision*. Stockholm: Institute for Security and Development Policy, 2011.

Fallows, James. 'Containing Japan'. *The Atlantic Monthly,* May 1989.

Hatano, Sumio. 'Nihon gaikō ni okeru ajia shugi no kinō: Sono hikari to kage', in Shindō Eiichi et al. (eds.). *Sengo nihon seiji to heiwa gaikō: 21-seiki ajia kyōsei jidai no shiza*. Tokyo: Hōritsu bunkasha, 2007.

Hosoya, Yūichi. *Ampo ronsō*. Tokyo: Chikuma shobō, 2016.

Mahathir, Mohamad and Shintaro Ishihara. *No to ieru ajia*. Tokyo: Kōbunsha, 1994.

Maruyama, Masao. 'Fukuzawa Yukichi no "Datsua-ron"' to sono shūhen', in Maruyama Masao techō no kai (ed.). *Maruyama Masao wabunshū* 4. Tokyo: Misuzu Shobō, 2009.

Miyagi, Taizō. *Bandon kaigi to nihon no ajia fukki: Amerika to ajia no hazama de*. Tokyo: Sōshisha, 2001.

NHK hōsō bunka kenkyūjo (ed.). *Gendai nihonjin no ishiki kōzō*. Tokyo: NHK Books, 2015.

NHK hōsō seron chōsajo (ed.). *Zusetsu sengo seronshi*. Tokyo: Nihon hōsō shuppan kyōkai, 1982.

Ōba, Mie. *Ajia taiheiyō chiiki keisei e no dōtei: Kyōkai kokka niche gō no aidentiti to chiiki shugi*. Kyoto: Minerva shobō, 2004.

Oros, Andrew. *Normalizing Japan: Politics, Identity, and the Evolution of Security Practice*. Stanford, CA: Stanford University Press, 2008.

Orr, James. *The Victim as Hero: Ideologies of Peace and National Identity in Postwar Japan*. Honolulu: University of Hawaii Press, 2001.

Satō, Seizaburō. 'Bakumatsu meiji shoki ni okeru taigai ishiki no shoruikei', in Satō Seizaburō and Roger Dingman (eds.). *Kindai nihon no taigai taido*. Tokyo: University of Tokyo Press, 1974.

Schmitz, David F. *The United States and Right-Wing Dictatorships, 1965–1989*. Cambridge: Cambridge University Press, 2006.

Shimazu, Naoko. *Japan, Race and Equality: The Racial Equality Proposal of 1919*. London: Routledge, 1998.

Suzuki, Shogo. *Civilization and Empire: China and Japan's Encounter with European International Society*. London: Routledge, 2011.

Wada, Haruki. *Heiwa kokka no tanjō: Sengo nihon no genten to hen'yō*. Tokyo: Iwanami 2015.

Wolferen, Karel van. *The Enigma of Japanese Power People and Politics in a Stateless Nation*. New York: Vintage Books, 1990.

Yoshino, Kosaku. *Cultural Nationalism in Contemporary Japan: A Sociological Enquiry*. London: Routledge, 1992.

Chapter 14

Reflections on Values in Asian Foreign Policy

ASEAN's Three Principles

Ravi Velloor

The Asian Civilizations Museum in Singapore has a section on ancient Asia's trade routes that reminds us that the continent was once dominated by two great powers, China under the Tang dynasty, and the Abbasid Caliphate with its capital at Baghdad. Srivijaya, established in Sumatra, Java and the Malay Peninsula, lay at the critical connection between East and West Asia, or in the parlance currently popular in Southeast Asia, enjoyed 'centrality'. India, midway between West and Southeast Asia, was connected equally in both directions. For the purposes of this chapter, however, the 'Asia' in focus is confined to three sub-regions: South Asia, or the Indian subcontinent, Southeast Asia, where the Sinic and Indic civilizations meet in the region grouped today under the Association of Southeast Asian Nations (ASEAN), and Northeast Asia, dominated by China, which has deeply influenced every nation in its periphery. While this by no means is a scientific way to divide a vast and varied region, it is a convenient guide to the examination of values in foreign policy, as seen through the actions of some key participants.

Given that India, China and Indonesia, which dominates Southeast Asia with its territory and size of economy, if not necessarily culture, all won independence within the space of four years after the end of World War II, an examination of values they bring to foreign policy is best done in the context of their records as free nations. That for the first time each of these three giant nations, and Japan, the continent's second-biggest economy and latent military power (now embarked on an activist foreign policy and in the process of revising its post–war Constitution), are all led by men born since freedom was achieved – in Japan's case, after the war ended – has a significant bearing on the perceptions they bring to office and consequently their actions.

This post-colonial, post-war leadership, in a sense, is free of the burdens of direct memory endured by their founding fathers who ploughed their furrows along popular movements against colonial rule and, in some cases, military campaigns – experiences that shaped their world views and the values on which their nationhood was moored, including in foreign policy. This shedding of the old garb allows the modern leaders, currently all men, significant room for improvisation as they navigate their nations along the world stage.

Asia's modern history is to a large extent about nations adapting their values to contemporaneous realities, often in contravention of guiding principles of state policy, and attempting to fit the narrative to the circumstances. While some of this apparent flexibility is borne of cynicism and triumphalism, brought on by the growing weight of their economies and contributions to world growth, the duty to defend this newfound prosperity and build on it for current and future generations also acts as an imperative for a measure of elasticity when it comes to principles, especially that of non-interference in another nation's affairs. Adherence and departure from this principle has brought about the biggest divergence among the major players, leading to the emergence of strategic constructs such as Japan's Shinzo Abe's 'Free and Open Indo-Pacific Strategy', a vision unveiled in 2016, and has since been embraced by other nations, notably India and the United States, and Australia to the extent that it has assiduously worked in the past four decades to draw closer to Asia.

The Free and Open Indo-Pacific, indeed the increasing use of the 'Indo-Pacific' coinage, is an optical counter to the narrative of Chinese expansionism and aggressive assertion of national interest. It has been fed by Beijing's claim to most of the South China Sea, its efforts to militarize islands it controlled or seized in those waters, nervousness that China may one day use its power to restrict freedom of navigation and overflight in the area and perceptions of the extractive nature of many of its investments across the world. Asia's current dynamics come into clearer focus when examined through the lenses of two values: ambition and insecurity.

In large tracts of post-colonial Asia the foreign policy chips initially tended to fall in three ways, reflecting contemporary history. There were countries allied to the Soviet Union, to the United States, and a third category that sought to tread a neutral path. This group would later come to represent the Non-Aligned Movement (NAM); its refusal to be part of either camp in the Cold War brought its own suspicions; and John Foster Dulles, US secretary of state, called non-alignment immoral. Soon enough, the United States dropped its initial hostility to NAM and attempted to court some members, particularly India.[1] In the 1980s and 1990s some countries yoked to the United States and Western Europe by the idea of free markets and welcoming of their capital, but resistant to the commitment of the West to democracy and human rights, would lay claim to 'Asian values' as justification for soft authoritarianism, intrusive social policies and a non-adversarial media and labour movement.

NEHRUVIAN VISION

No public figure had so broad or so optimistic a vision for Asia as India's first Prime Minister Jawaharlal Nehru. Krishnan Srinivasan writes that at independence in 1947 Indian foreign policy, directed by Nehru, was firmly anchored in values-based principles derived from religious traditions, the anti-colonial struggle against imperialism and racism, and the legacy of Mahatma Gandhi's non-violent struggle for freedom.[2] While ends mattered, the means mattered equally. Nehru was taken by Wendell Willkie's ideas of One World, and the inspiration of Gandhi, reflecting that: 'In those long years of struggle we were taught by our great leader never to forget not only the objectives we had but also the methods whereby we should achieve those objectives'.[3] Indian civilization, philosophy and nationality all contributed to the evolution of foreign policy as did the concept of non-violence, and Nehru's closeness to Gandhi meant that he tried to mould Gandhi's standards to foreign policy. Indian foreign policy in its initial years comprised anti-imperialism, anti-racialism and the creation of an area of peace between the worlds carved out by two opposing power blocs, later to be known as non-alignment but to which Nehru himself chose to refer to as an independent foreign policy.

Nehru's statesmanship and idealistic values confronted difficult challenges from the start of independence. In his recent book *The People Next Door: The Curious History of India's Relations with Pakistan*, Indian diplomat T.C.A. Raghavan describes the dilemma faced by Nehru in 1947, faced with having to keep a solemn commitment to release 550 million rupees due to Pakistan as part of the settlement over Indian Partition even as his troops were waging a war against Pakistani troops and irregulars in Kashmir. With his cabinet firmly against handing money to a neighbour who would doubtlessly deploy the funds for military operations, India was poised to renege on its commitment when Gandhi intervened on Pakistan's behalf, going on a fasting strike in mid-January 1948 that would end five days later when Nehru agreed to release the funds. Gandhi would be accused of taking his pro-Muslim bias too far, and he would pay with his life for his principles, an extremist Hindu assassinating him two weeks later.[4]

The very same year, 1948, Nehru would initiate India's external interventions when he sent a planeload of arms to save the embattled government of U Nu in Burma, whose regime was under threat from Karen rebels who had encircled the airport in Yangon, the Burmese capital at the time. While such examples of Indian intervention abroad were largely dormant for much of Nehru's time – his grant of asylum to a young Dalai Lama fleeing China's occupation of Tibet would be read differently by Beijing – subsequent prime ministers, most principally his daughter Indira Gandhi, who would become prime minister less than two years after his death, have a history of repeatedly intervening in India's neighbourhood, where India's critical interests were deemed to be involved.

Under Indira Gandhi's direction, Indian intelligence agencies aggravated the divide between West and East Pakistan before she sent in the Indian Army, leading to the creation of Bangladesh in December 1971 out of what was East Pakistan. India could explain the intervention by the massive violence perpetrated on the Bengali people by Punjab-dominated Pakistan and the consequent flood of refugees into India, which strained its then-meagre resources.[5] Harder to explain from the standpoint of a NAM member was the Indo-Soviet Treaty of Friendship and Cooperation signed earlier in 1971 that specified mutual strategic cooperation, in effect turning India, one of the NAM pillars, into a de facto Soviet ally. In 1975, it annexed Sikkim, ruled by a Chogyal, as an Indian state after orchestrating a rebellion in the Himalayan kingdom.

Uneasy about Sri Lanka's pro-West policies under Junius Jayewardene, Indira Gandhi tasked her intelligence services with arming and training separatists from Sri Lanka's Tamil minority, playing to long-standing grouses about domination by the majority Sinhala Buddhists. It would take a quarter century for Sri Lanka, once touted as a potential rival to Singapore because of its strategic location, to regain its balance and only after severe damage to its economy and tremendous loss of civilian life. In 2015, Indian intelligence agencies were thought to have orchestrated a cabinet revolt against then President Mahinda Rajapaksa – perceived to have drawn too close to China – that unseated the leader who had become a national hero for quelling the long-running Tamil insurgency.[6]

CHINA: PLOUGHSHARES INTO SWORDS

In 1922, the British philosopher Bertrand Russell, having spent a year in China, predicted the nation's resurgence and civilizational strengths. In the last chapter, he writes that 'China, by her resources and her population, is capable of being the greatest Power in the world after the United States'. Although his time in China was short, Russell quickly became aware of some cultural differences: 'The typical Westerner wishes to be the cause of as many changes as possible in his environment; the typical Chinaman wishes to enjoy as much and as delicately as possible'.[7] The 'homogenous mental life' of America and Western Europe he traced to three sources: Greek culture, Jewish religion and ethics and modern industrialism. On the other hand, he saw Chinese civilization as defined by codes of behaviour and the passivity of Taoism and Buddhism. The three worst qualities

of the Chinese, in his assessment, were avarice, callousness and coward-
ice, and his greatest fear was that a future China would merge its society's
worst qualities with the worst aspects of 'progress' – stripping itself of
its moral and cultural core in favour of a more efficient economy and an
assertive military.

Soon after Mao's forces drove the Kuomintang to Taiwan, China coined
the Five Principles of Peaceful Coexistence and Zhou Enlai presented them
to India in 1953 when they discussed their nettlesome border issue. These
five principles were the basis on which China approached its neighbours, and
adaptations of the theme have since appeared globally, including in India,
where Nehru soon announced India's own policy to be based on *Panchsheel* –
five principles.

The People's Republic of China's Ministry of Foreign Affairs[8] carries the
following passages, elaborating the birth of the Five Principles:

> China agreed to negotiations between China and India on their relations in
> the Tibet Region which were held in Beijing from 31 December 1953 to 29
> April 1954. Premier Zhou Enlai met with members of the Indian Govern-
> ment Delegation on 31 December 1953 where he put forward for the first
> time the Five Principles of Peaceful Co-Existence, namely, mutual respect
> for each other's territorial integrity and sovereignty, mutual non-aggression,
> non-interference in each other's internal affairs, equality and mutual benefit,
> and peaceful co-existence. In response, the Indian side agreed that the Five
> Principles of Peaceful Co-Existence advanced by Premier Zhou be taken as the
> guiding principles for the negotiations.
>
> The Five Principles of Peaceful Co-Existence have become the basic norms
> in developing state to state relations transcending social systems and ideologies.
> These principles have been accepted by the overwhelming majority of countries
> in the world.

Zhang Lihua[9] endorses the view that traditional Chinese concepts of etiquette have impacted its foreign policy and with it 'the values of courtesy,
obeying the system of the law in international society and respect for other
countries'. The Confucian saying 'When the rulers at higher ranks follow
etiquette and obey laws, it becomes easier to govern people' is cited as an
endorsement of such thinking. Such values are not unknown elsewhere in
Asia, particularly India, where the Sanskrit saying *yatha raja, tatha praja* –
as the king, so the people – turns on its head Western beliefs that a people get
the ruler they deserve. China's support for communist and other insurgents
in its near abroad continued until the 1980s. Jeffery Sng says in *Silenced
Revolutionaries: Challenging the Received View of Malaya's Revolutionary
Past* that Chin Peng, leader of the Communist Party of Malaya who operated

from Beijing for about three decades, had been advised by Deng Xiaoping to continue the fight, leading to the second armed struggle in Malaya being launched in 1968. It was only in 1980, after he returned to power and having received then-Singapore Prime Minister Lee Kuan Yew in Beijing, did Deng order Chin Peng to stop broadcasting hostile propaganda from Chinese soil.

The converse of Zhang's assessment of the Chinese approach was recently enunciated by the Indian analyst C. Raja Mohan in *The Indian Express*:[10]

> The . . . myth is that China, unlike India, believes in sovereign equality with countries big or small. Like all myths, this has no empirical basis. Mao's China intervened all across Asia to promote revolution. If Mao's successor, Deng Xiaoping, advocated a foreign policy that encouraged China to keep its head down and focus on economic development at home, Xi Jinping now sees the need to protect Beijing's growing economic and political interests beyond its borders with whatever means available, including interventions in the internal affairs of other states.

China and the Soviet Union started as ideological partners, and Beijing's classic buildings, such as the Great Hall of the People, have a distinctly Soviet look. However, while the Soviet Union became more and more inwardly drawn, post–revolution China dealt with the world with confidence. Although it fought significant wars in each of the first three decades of its independent existence – Korea (1950–1953), India (1962) and Vietnam (1979) – there has been no substantial breaking of its peace since. It is noteworthy that these clashes coincided with internal tumult: the mass executions at the start of the Mao era for the Korean War, the Great Leap Forward and the India war and the first full year of Deng Xiaoping's economic reforms in the same year as the conflict with Vietnam.

China's ties with the United States had been strained since China annexed Tibet in 1950 and entered the Korean War on the side of North Korea's Kim Il Sung the same year. Two decades later, it made a substantial breakthrough in diplomacy by receiving US President Richard Nixon, accentuating the widening fissures in its relations with the Soviet Union, the precise reason why Nixon's Secretary of State Henry Kissinger had pressed for the entente. However, it is clear that even at that high point of the US-China relationship, both sides were clear that competition was eventually inevitable. John Pomfret, author of *The Beautiful Country and the Middle Kingdom: America and China, 1776 to the Present*, had this to say:

> On February 14, 1972, President Richard Nixon and his national security adviser Henry Kissinger met to discuss Nixon's upcoming trip to China. Kissinger, who had already taken his secret trip to China to begin Nixon's historic opening to Beijing, expressed the view that compared with the Russians, the Chinese were

'just as dangerous. In fact, they're more dangerous over a historical period'. Kissinger then observed that 'in 20 years your successor, if he's as wise as you, will wind up leaning towards the Russians against the Chinese'. He argued that the United States, as it sought to profit from the enmity between Moscow and Beijing, needed 'to play this balance-of-power game totally unemotionally. Right now, we need the Chinese to correct the Russians and to discipline the Russians'. But in the future, it would be the other way around.[11]

China's focus after Mao has been the economic uplift of its people, and it recognized that border peace was essential. Of the fourteen countries with which it shares land borders and disputes, it settled twelve of them through negotiations in the 1980s and 1990s on generous terms offered by the Chinese. The unsettled borders were with India, where China did not recognize the British-drawn McMahon Line, and with Bhutan whose foreign policy was guided by India under a 1950 treaty.

China also has maritime borders with eight countries. Conflicting claims over territorial waters and exclusive economic zones have proved vexatious, particularly with Japan, the Philippines and Vietnam. There are also overlapping claims with South Korea, Brunei, Malaysia and Indonesia, aside from Taiwan which China regards as a renegade province. Seen from the maritime prism, it would appear that its five principles were observed more in the breach than observance and from early on. While the circumstances of the 1962 border clash between China and India come with varied interpretations of motives and provocations (China, having made its point, did withdraw swiftly), China's actions in the South China Sea starting from 1974 reflect the mainland's acute sensitivity to history, its perception of its own vulnerabilities and sense of timing.

China has always regarded the South China Sea as its peaceful backwater, a neighbourhood peopled with smaller and, possibly in its eyes, less civilized countries that fit its inherently hierarchical world view which has itself at the zenith. Kishore Mahbubani and Jeffery Sng point out that while Southeast Asia was part of the 'Sanskrit cultural cosmopolis', China's impact was greater in the political and economic realms. They observe

One feature remained constant in China-Southeast Asia relations. For centuries, the Indianized kingdoms of Southeast Asia paid tribute to the emperors of China. We do not know exactly how and when this tributary system started. But we do know that the Funan kingdom was sending tribute to China as early as AD500 . . . . Occasionally, Chinese rulers introduced sanctions to regulate or limit private trade in order to achieve foreign policy goals. . . . The mutual benefits of two-way trade, and the willingness of Southeast Asian rulers to submit at least symbolically, to China may also explain the lack of military conflict between China and Southeast Asia over the centuries.[12]

Mahbubani and Sng claim that while historically Chinese rulers thought of Southeast Asia as their backwater, they were generally comfortable allowing the region to flourish unhindered as long as it acknowledged Chinese over-lordship. Yet things on the ground have changed undeniably. The Paracels, called Xisha in Chinese and Hoang Sa in Vietnamese, were once a barren out-crop in the South China Sea with no settled population or habitation beyond a resting place for fishermen while they dried nets. During 1884–1885, France's efforts to incorporate them into French Indochina found objections from China. In 1933, France seized the Paracels and Spratlys and formally included them in French Indochina. In 1954 France ceased to be a factor when it accepted the independence of both South and North Vietnam and withdrew from Indochina.

In 1974, South Vietnamese soldiers came under fire from Chinese troops. Three Vietnamese soldiers were killed and more injured. A sea battle fol-lowed, and China bombed the islands and made an amphibious landing. A South Vietnamese request for assistance from the US Seventh Fleet was turned down by Washington. A total of fifty-three Vietnamese lost their lives, and the result was that China gained control over the Paracel Islands. Beijing's decisive action came at a time when the Nixon administration was preoccupied with the Watergate scandal. Also, the United States was quite evidently losing control over the Vietnam War, which would end with the fall of Saigon the following year. China's steady and well-timed steps to ring-fence its southern periphery would continue. In 1995, it occupied Mischief Reef in the Spratlys, an area of the South China Sea that the Philippines had always considered to be its territory. Three years earlier in 1992, the Ameri-cans had vacated Subic Bay and Clark Air Base. Without that reassuring cover, there was little that Philippine President Fidel Ramos could do. For a sense of Filipino, and eventually, Southeast Asian outrage at these develop-ments I reproduce my report, based partly on my conversations with former interior secretary Rafael Alunan and others, published in *The Straits Times* on 3 July 2015.

The Philippines had once defined its nationalism in anti-American terms. Today, the target is China. The sentiments in the archipelago underscore how Southeast Asia, which had begun to shed its old fears of the mainland, is feel-ing fresh unease about it. This is forcing government leaders to review defence budgets, seek new security alliances and ponder the future of a region that had not seen major conflict since the Indochina War ended nearly three decades ago. What now? Among maritime ASEAN states, the Philippines had one of the tighter relationships with China. It had been early to recognize the People's Republic. It established diplomatic ties in June 1975, following in the footsteps of the Malaysians, who were first off the mark. True, the year before, China had grabbed the Paracels after killing some 70 Vietnamese servicemen. But Vietnam was not in ASEAN then, so it was viewed as somebody else's problem, a fraternal dispute between two communist nations. Even the taking of Mischief Reef was seen as an aberration.

But just as that event began fading from Southeast Asian minds came the Scarborough Shoal confrontation in 2012, when the Philippine Navy sought to catch eight Chinese fishing vessels and was blocked by Chinese maritime surveillance ships. Suddenly, the issue took on a new dimension. The US intervened, getting both sides to agree to withdraw. Manila kept its word but the Chinese reneged, then used swarm tactics to prevent Filipino boats from re-entering the area. The following January the Philippines launched arbitral proceedings against China, taking the world by surprise with its action and the cultural affront it implied. ASEAN members privately used to look askance at Manila for its audacity. But attitudes are changing in some of the most unlikely places.[13]

Beijing cannot be unaware of the impact of its actions and perhaps that is the desired result. If, as Zhang Lihua says, 'obeying the system of the law in international society' is a Chinese core value, it is interesting to examine what leads China to circumvent it, as in 2016 when Beijing ignored The Hague tribunal's verdict on arbitration brought by the Philippines. China, having joined the World Trade Organization (WTO) in 2002, has considerable expertise in using the WTO's dispute settlement mechanism to good effect. What then could cause it to play by global rules where it suits it, and ignore them when it does not?

The values of insecurity and ambition are tools to assess the situation. First, strategic rivalry between an entrenched United States and a rising China was inevitable, as the conversation between Nixon and Kissinger reported by Pomfret makes clear. It is noted that they were discussing China even before Nixon's landmark visit. As a student of international dynamics China could not have been unaware of the magnitude and direction of this vector. After the collapse of the Soviet Union, China has been the only power to offer a substantial strategic challenge to the United States. It is little surprise that in the past two decades, China complained of intrusive surveillance by US warplanes of its coastline and attempts to penetrate its society.

In 2015, visiting China's National Institute for South China Sea Studies in Haikou, Hainan, I asked the institute's director, Wu Shicun, to explain China's security, or insecurity, policies in regard to the South China Sea. Wu listed the issues: The security dimension was that the United States and Japan were making it harder for China to enter the Western Pacific through the Yellow Sea and the East China Sea. The South China Sea, therefore, provided a natural shield against their possible intervention. The insecurity part was that Beijing felt the US rebalance was about containing China, and the South China Sea was merely a convenient vehicle. 'The US has already adjusted its position on the dispute', Wu told me. 'From limited intervention, it has moved to active intervention and it is taking sides'.[14]

Some analysts believe that the issue is about ballistic missile submarines, or SSBNs, which are considered the ultimate nuclear deterrent. The Soviets used to hide their SSBNs under the Arctic icecap to avoid detection. But the South China Sea is relatively shallow compared with the depths of the Indian Ocean and the Pacific, making Chinese submarines, which tend to be noisy, vulnerable to detection and attack. Thus some see a Chinese bastion policy at work – an attempt to turn the South China Sea into a private lake to give its submarines enough room to filter into bigger oceans.

It is undeniable that China is both attempting to secure its safety by taking preventive measures and preparing for a future when it will draw level with the United States in economic terms, even if not military parity. In the process, whether out of compulsion or the growing breadth of its ambitions, 'Asian values' – particularly respect for sovereignty and non-interference in another country's affairs – have become a casualty.

JAPAN REARRANGES ITS VALUES

At the war museum adjacent to Yasukuni Shrine in Tokyo, there is a short video of a battlefield ceremony held during World War II where an officer is seen distributing water in place of sake to young soldiers poised to say farewell to life. The look in the eyes of the young soldiers shows no fear. It is that look that Asia learned to fear and continues to do so to this day. Singapore's founding father, Lee Kuan Yew, was probably alluding to this in an interview to *Foreign Affairs* in 1994 when he spoke of the Japanese cultural trait of taking whatever they do to the 'nth degree'. He went on to say, presciently, that 'whether the Japanese go down the military path [again] will depend largely on America's strength and its willingness to be engaged in the Asia Pacific region'.[15]

The United States for now seems to be fully engaged, but it has been urging its allies to do more for themselves. This plays to the aspirations of Japanese revisionists who would welcome a more 'normal' Japan. Prime Minister Abe can be counted in this category. The deeper question is whether Japan, the only nation to have been attacked with atomic weapons, will one day build nuclear weapons. While the official position is stiffly anti-nuclear, Japan has the technology and the stockpile in place to build a nuclear arsenal. From the moment a decision is taken to have nuclear weapons to having actual bombs will probably take only a few weeks. But to cross that threshold will require considerable political courage and be influenced by the trajectory of its ties with the United States, China and North Korea. Abe, poised to be his country's longest serving post-war leader, has steadily pushed for a more 'normal' military, and Japan has changed the name of its Defence Agency to Ministry of Defence. He has implemented changes to allow Japanese troops to fight abroad, and, most importantly, attitudes towards the Self-Defence Forces (SDF) may be changing within Japan. The young, with no memories of the war, are far more positive towards the military than their seniors. In late 2017 some 26,000 people gathered at the foothills of Mount Fuji to watch live-fire exercises conducted by the SDF, often murmuring appreciatively.[16]

In his 2018 New Year message, Abe said,

> This is the year of putting our plans into execution. We will transition the poli-cies we pledged during the 2017 general election, one by one. Looking squarely ahead to 2020 and beyond, the Abe Cabinet is determined to press ahead vigorously with reforms towards building a new nation, hand in hand with the Japanese people.[17]

For Japan, the adjustments in its values to build a nuclear arsenal will need to move in tandem with steps to prepare its neighbourhood for the change. With or without its active participation, that is already happening. In nearby South Korea, for instance, polls show that more than two-thirds want the United States to bring back tactical nuclear weapons for battlefield use – weapons that had been withdrawn from the theatre in an earlier era.

Reuters reported in 2017 that the first of those steps for Japan to modify its nuclear stance could come as a tweaking of the Three Principles it adopted five decades ago, namely: not to possess, manufacture or allow nuclear weap-ons on its territory.[18] 'Perhaps it's time for our three principles to become two', a senior defence policymaker told the news service, suggesting that nuclear weapons be allowed into Japan, perhaps in the form of a US nuclear-armed submarine to operate from one of the bases in the country.[19]

The developments on the Korean Peninsula will influence Japanese behaviour greatly. Any wavering of the US commitment to maintain troops – Donald Trump has already signalled he is not averse to considering bring-ing US troops home – will prompt Japan to hedge against not only a China that dominates Northeast Asia but also a potentially hostile post-unification Korea. Japan has demonstrated that it can find creative solutions to bypass its values where strategic interests collide with values. Former Indian Foreign Secretary Shyam Saran recounts that when he travelled to Japan in 2008 to seek that country's endorsement of India-specific waivers from the Nuclear Suppliers Group he encountered Foreign Minister Taro Aso, who solemnly read out his ministry's brief on why Japan would find it difficult to support the waiver without India agreeing to sign the Nuclear Non-Proliferation Treaty and adhered to the Comprehensive Test Ban Treaty. Aso also referred to strong public opinion in Japan against nuclear weapons. The formal meeting over, Aso accompanied Saran to the elevator and conveyed that Japan may have to 'make a lot of noise' at the Nuclear Suppliers Group but would not oppose a consensus in favour of India. Aso said he was conveying this on behalf of Shinzo Abe.[20]

ASIAN VALUES

Across much of Asia, the period after World War II was the inkwell from which many nations scripted the values they wrote for themselves. Japan's defeat, the colonial retreat from Asia that saw the liberation of large nations such as India and Indonesia and the revolution in China that sent Chiang Kaishek fleeing to Taiwan were seminal events that contributed to the sense of Asian-ness as a cultural and intellectual construct. Thus, Nehru hosted the Asian Relations Conference before his country gained independence, its purpose being to 'bring together the leading men and women of Asia on a common platform to study the problems of common concern to the people of the continent . . . and to foster mutual contact and understanding'.[21] Nehru's intention in this conference was 'there are no leaders and no followers'.[22] Eight years later the Afro-Asian Conference was held in Bandung, partly because the organizing nations – Sri Lanka, Burma, Pakistan and India included – thought their experience and values were worth sharing with the African continent.

Are there anything like Asian values today? It would be a considerable stretch to identify Asian values beyond the obvious ones: stress on hard work, filial piety and love for family. In the 1990s Mahathir Mohamad, Malaysia's prime minister then as now and Singapore leader Lee Kuan Yew were seen as the most forceful voices that stressed that Asians, particularly in the regions influenced by Confucian thinking, were more comfortable with an ideology that emphasized the community over the individual and thus willing to countenance an abridgement of their individual and democratic freedoms in the collective desire to progress, particularly in economic development. It is noteworthy that Lee himself never appears to have used the term – 'I don't think there is an Asian model as such', Lee said in a 1994 interview with Fareed Zakaria for *Foreign Affairs*.[23] Nevertheless, he argued that there are marked dissimilarities between Eastern and Western cultures – 'But Asian societies are unlike Western ones', as he put it. Singapore diplomat and scholar Kishore Mahbubani has called the Asian values debate 'the most badly mistitled debate in the world',[24] tracing this to Asian reactions against Western triumphalism at the end of the Cold War and the certainty of the superiority of its model. In his view, it was not that Asians disagreed about the values of democracy or human rights, but their overhasty implementation, often with dysfunctional consequences as in Yugoslavia.[25]

The Asian values debate gained currency after the World Conference on Human Rights in 1993, which saw clashes between European and East Asian states over the latter's poor record on human rights and democratization.[26] The continued use of the death penalty is a continuing discord with states like Singapore seeing it as an important deterrent against crime, particularly drug trafficking, although it has recently scaled back its use and given judges more leeway in deciding the maximum penalty. Some observers suggest that East Asia's rising incomes and share of world trade also contributed to Western, particularly European, criticism of how East Asian states ordered their societies, especially given the relative stagnation in Europe.

Some key triggers for the debate were the Tiananmen Square shootings of 1989, called the June 4 Incident in China, the mild approach taken by Southeast Asian states to Indonesia's annexation of East Timor between 1975 and 1999 and the actions of the military junta in Myanmar. Malaysia led the soft approach on Myanmar in the cause of assimilating the state into Southeast Asia.

Unlike Malaysia, post-Sukarno Indonesia, ASEAN's biggest nation in terms of population and economy, has been deliberately punching below its weight in regional affairs to avoid intervening in the affairs of other nations. Sukarno, although he took Indonesia out of the United Nations (UN), had included 'internationalism or humanity' in the *Panca Sila* – the five principles of Indonesian identity – he expounded in 1945. While his successor Suharto brought Indonesia back into the UN, he chose to maintain a profile lower than his country could afford, prompted equally by his domestic agenda and embarrassment over the human rights record, particularly during its quarter-century annexation of East Timor.

The decade that Susilo Bambang Yudhoyono held power marked a more activist foreign policy, with efforts by Jakarta to use its influence in issues like the Rohingya Muslims of Myanmar's Rakhine State and to mediate the rift that exploded within ASEAN in 2012 when Cambodia used its chairman's privilege to block a reference to the South China Sea that was unflattering to China. However, under the current administration of Joko Widodo this activism subsided and where it has been tried – as with the Rohingya – there has been scant success.

Asian values as a foil to the West were deployed to ring-fence damage to China's reputation after Tiananmen when China suffered a period of international disapprobation. Japan, particularly Matsushita Corp., was one of the earliest to help China end its isolation by sending substantial investments. The company was acting upon a personal request from Deng Xiaoping to its founder. Because of this background, when Chinese protesters attacked a

Panasonic factory in Shandong – Panasonic is a Matsushita brand – in 2012, following Tokyo's nationalization of the Senkaku/Diaoyu islands, many Japanese felt a sense of betrayal that Chinese displayed such ingratitude and no longer cared for values like loyalty.

Less is heard about Asian values in the wake of the Asian Financial Crisis that erupted with the devaluation of Thai baht in 1997 which severely damaged the economies of South Korea, Indonesia and Malaysia. For a while it robbed the East Asian miracle economies of their sheen. To its credit East Asia showed little triumphalism against the West two decades later when it emerged relatively unscathed from the global financial crisis of 2008, although China's self-confidence in dealing with the United States increased significantly after that. Ruptures to the Asian fabric – China's refusal to acknowledge, much less heed, the verdict delivered at The Hague on its claims to the South China Sea, Myanmar's Rohingya issue that creates a chasm between Muslim and non-Muslim ASEAN and the Philippines decision to not press its victory at The Hague and instead build its economic links to China – have put paid to any Asian values in diplomacy. Currently, the Asian values of Southeast Asian states – ASEAN values, so to speak – can be summarized thus: (A) Mutual respect for the independence, sovereignty, equality, territorial integrity and national identity of all nations; (B) The right of every state, large or small, to lead its national existence free from external interference, subversion or coercion; and (C) Non-interference in the internal affairs of other states. In practice, these do not extend much beyond tact displayed while advising peers on matters that adversely impact the image of the region, as with Myanmar's treatment of its Muslim population in Rakhine that led to the exodus of hundreds of thousands of Rohingyas to Bangladesh. This was brought home to me in a conversation with Jose Ramos Horta, who won the Nobel Peace Prize for popularizing the cause of East Timor independence. Horta, standing firmly with Suu Kyi on the Rohingya issue, tended to take the long view of the antipathy the majority Buddhist Burmese feel towards Muslims, and advised the international community not to press Suu Kyi, Myanmar's de facto leader, as she searched for solutions.[27]

While Asian values have sometimes been used to fend off calls for democratization of authoritarian regimes, it is noteworthy that the ASEAN Charter that entered into force in 2008 includes a commitment to 'strengthen democracy, enhance good governance and the rule of law, and to promote and protect human rights and fundamental freedoms'. The charter also says ASEAN shall adopt a Human Rights Body and the association approved a human rights declaration in 2012. While the authors of the charter included the passage as an aspirational goal, once included, such things nevertheless take on a life of their own.[28]

CONCLUSION

Asia, and East Asian states particularly, continues to be wary of Europe's tendency to stress democracy, human rights, climate change, migration and other 'bleeding heart' issues. Regardless of what Asia might think or say, European commitment to stand up for these issues will never go away. In 2013, the European Union (EU) suspended free trade agreement talks with Thailand after the military coup there, underlining how strongly the EU feels. At the same time, few European nations complain about Chinese actions to restrict religious and other freedoms to its Muslim minority in Xinjiang Province or the Indian military's use of force in Jammu and Kashmir, scene of a long-running insurrection. In 2009, amid the swirling global financial crisis, the EU took the position that violence in Xinjiang 'is a Chinese issue, not a European issue'. Serge Abou, the EU's ambassador to China, said Europe also had its problems with minorities and 'we would not like other governments to tell us what is to be done'.[29] More recently, the EU hosted Uyghur-rights conferences, suggesting a certain flexibility of approach. However, in 2017 when the EU sought to draw renewed attention to human rights abuses in China with a statement at the UN Human Rights Council, it was blocked by a member nation – Greece, which is tipped to be a major beneficiary of China's Belt and Road Initiative. A Greek spokesman told the *New York Times* that 'when the stability of a country is at stake, we need to be more constructive in the way we express our criticism because if a country collapses there will be no human rights to protect'.[30] National interest trumps values, even in Europe.

In Asia's recent history, a rare flash of a Nehru-like idealism came from Singapore's George Yeo who, as foreign minister, worked assiduously to garner an international team to push the revival of Nalanda as a secular university to spread the message of peace to Asia and the world. A Buddhist institution set up in the early fifth century, ancient Nalanda was India's first residential university, attracting scholars from as far away as China, Persia and Turkey. Older than Oxford, in its heyday the university housed 10,000 students and faculty. It was burnt down by Arab invaders in 1193 after standing for 600 years. When the Nalanda revival was conceived, it got enthusiastic backing from Ban Ki-Moon, South Korea's foreign minister and later UN secretary-general. Other East Asian countries, China and Japan included, went along. In 2009, Nalanda was endorsed by the East Asia Summit, and a Mentor Group was formed, led by Nobel Prize–winning economist Amartya Sen, and including Yeo and others, mostly scholars from the United States, Japan, South Korea and Singapore. The Indian government adopted the university as a federal project, placing it, unlike other top institutions of higher learning, under the supervision of the Ministry of External Affairs (MEA).

From early on the project stuck in red tape and delay despite Sen's equation with then Prime Minister Manmohan Singh. The MEA, initially enthusiastic, developed reservations about Sen leading the project. In 2011, Yeo, the Mentor Group's other global star, lost his Aljunied constituency in Singapore and stepped down from the post of foreign minister. Although he continued on the board, the loss of a serving foreign minister affected the project's standing. The upshot was that Nalanda, which thrilled minds with connections to the Asian Renaissance, lost much of its lustre. Overseas interest dwindled, there was criticism that the Mentor Group was too overawed by Sen's reputation to check some of his decisions, and in 2015, Sen stepped down as chancellor. Yeo, his successor, also left after disagreements with the Indian government.[31] While some classes have started, it is clear the Nalanda project has lost its former appeal.

Beyond a deep stress on family values, education, a strong work ethic and stress on frugality and saving – values that may be changing in some parts of Asia lately, especially in advanced economies like South Korea and Singapore – it is not easy to identify what could be called Asian values. East Asians, particularly, see themselves as hard-working compared with Europeans, unaware perhaps of the Calvinist ethic that fired the spirit of capitalism. And while the incidence of divorce is less in Asia compared with Europe, Asian divorce rates are rising too. It is the rare nation that allows moral considerations to override the pragmatic pursuit of national interest. Certainly, no identifiable set of values permeate the foreign policy of Asian states compared with Europe, which has the most ideological foreign policy in the world, one that stands in contrast to the current US administration under President Trump, which has downplayed these elements.

The claim to universality in European values is ahistorical since the latter part of the twentieth century saw significant alterations in Western values, including on issues as varied as gender equality, homosexuality and democracy. Asia is undergoing a similar transition; the digital economy and social media are promoting new forms of self-expression and democratization of information and opinion with profound implications for Asian society. This, combined with the focus on sustainable development that has become a major issue with Asia's millennials, portends changes that in the not-too-distant future could bring Asian and European values more in alignment – intellectually, politically and economically – than they are at this point.

In every value system there are universal aspirations that could be given greater emphasis. Fraternity, however, is easier to nurture when the identity of the individual is respected. The essence of Asian values was the recognition that universality without respect for diversity comes across as a threat.

NOTES

1. R. Rob, 'Taking Nonalignment Seriously', *Foreign Policy* (27 August 2012). http://foreignpolicy.com/2012/08/27/taking-nonalignment-seriously/.

2. Krishnan Srinivasan's chapter: 'Values in Indian Foreign Policy'.

3. Verinder Grover (ed.), *UNO, NAM, NIEO, SAARC and India's Foreign Policy* (New Delhi: Deep & Deep Publications, 1992), 4.

4. T.C.A. Raghavan, *The People Next Door: The Curious History of India's Relations with Pakistan* (New Delhi: HarperCollins Publishers India, 2017), 7–9.

5. B. Raman, *The Kaoboys of R&AW*, Chapter 2 – 'Bangladesh and the Kaoboys'.

6. Ravi Velloor, *India Rising: Fresh Hope, New Fears*, Chapter 8 – 'Vengeance in Sri Lanka'.

7. Bertrand Russell, *The Problem of China* (London: George Allen & Unwin, 1922).

8. Ministry of Foreign Affairs, PRC: China's Initiation of the Five Principles of Co-Existence. http://www.fmprc.gov.cn/mfa_eng/ziliao_665539/3602_665543/3604_665547/t18053.shtml.

9. Zhang Lihua's chapter – 'Values in Chinese Foreign Policy'.

10. C. Raja Mohan, 'Turmoil in Maldives: What India Must Do', *The Indian Express* (6 February 2018).

11. John Pomfret, '45 Years Ago Kissinger Envisioned a Pivot to "Russia". Will Trump Make It Happen?' *Washington Post* (24 December 2016).

12. Kishore Mahbubani and Jeffery Sng, *The ASEAN Miracle: A Catalyst for Peace* (Singapore: NUS, 2017), 24–28.

13. Ravi Velloor, 'How China Is Losing the South-East Asia', *The Straits Times* (3 July 2015).

14. Conversation with the author.

15. Fareed Zakaria, 'Culture Is Destiny: A Conversation with Lee Kuan Yew', *Foreign Affairs* 73, no. 2 (March 1994).

16. Motoko Rich, 'A Pacifist Japan Starts to Embrace the Military', *New York Times* (29 August 2017).

17. 'New Year's Reflection by Prime Minister Shinzo Abe', *Prime Minister of Japan and His Cabinet* (1 January 2018). https://japan.kantei.go.jp/index.html.

18. 'Three Non-Nuclear Principles', *Ministry of Foreign Affairs, Japan* (11 December 1967). https://www.mofa.go.jp/policy/un/disarmament/nnp/index.html.

19. Tim Kelly and Nobuhiro Kubo, 'Allowing Nuclear Weapons in Japan Could Defuse North Korean Threat, Say Some Policy Makers', *Reuters* (6 September 2017). https://www.reuters.com/article/us-northkorea-missiles-japan/allowing-nuclear-weapons-in-japan-could-defuse-north-korean-threat-say-some-policy-makers-idUSKCN1BH1FO.

20. Shyam Saran, *How India Sees the World: Kautilya to the 21st Century* (New Delhi: Juggernaut Books, 2017), 229.

21. Nicholas Tarling, *Neutrality in Southeast Asia: Concepts and Contexts* (New York: Routledge, 2017).

22. Jawaharlal Nehru, '1st Asian Relations Conference', *Indian Council for World Affairs* (24 March 1947). http://icwadelhi.info/asianrelationsconference/images/stories/jawaharlalnehru.pdf.

23. Fareed Zakaria, 'Culture Is Destiny: A Conversation with Lee Kuan Yew', *Foreign Affairs* 73, no. 2 (March 1994).

24. Mahbubani on Youtube: http://bigthink.com/videos/kishore-mahbubani-what-are-asian-values.

25. Ibid.

26. See Seng Tan, 'The "Singapore School" of Asian Values: Down But Not Out', *Carnegie Council for Ethics in International Affairs* (26 January 2016).

27. 'It is unfortunate that the international community single out Ang San Suu Kyi for all the problems of Myanmar, ignoring that she inherited a situation that had been in the making for 40–50 years. I had never been to a country where there is such widespread fear and resentment towards a particular ethnic or religious group, in this case the vast majority of Burmese Buddhists towards Muslims, particularly Rohingya. So, Suu Kyi, as a responsible, wise leader has to handle a complex situation with prudence. Look at Indonesia, when Suharto fell in 1998, there was widespread ethnic violence. It took ten years for them to stabilize. Pushing Suu Kyi and demonizing her is not going to resolve a problem that is there in Burmese society'. – Jose Ramos Horta, conversation with the author, June 2018.

28. Professor Tommy Koh, conversation with the author, January 2018.

29. *Globe & Mail* (13 July 2009).

30. *New York Times* (20 June 2017).

31. *The Straits Times* (25 November 2016).

BIBLIOGRAPHY

'China's Initiation of the Five Principles of Co-Existence'. *Ministry of Foreign Affairs, The People's Republic of China.* http://www.fmprc.gov.cn/mfa_eng/ziliao_665539/3602_665543/3604_665547/t18053.shtml.

Mahbubani, Kishore and Jeffery Sng. *The ASEAN Miracle: A Catalyst for Peace.* Singapore: NUS, 2017.

Mohan, C. Raja. 'Turmoil in Maldives: What India Must Do'. *Indian Express,* 6 February 2018.

Pomfret, John. *The Beautiful Country and the Middle Kingdom: America and China, 1776 to the Present.* New York: Henry Holt 2017.

Pomfret, John. '45 Years Ago Kissinger Envisioned a Pivot to "Russia". Will Trump Make It Happen?' *Washington Post,* 24 December 2016.

Pomfret, John. *India Rising: Fresh Hope, New Fears.* Singapore: Straits Times Press, 2016.

Raghavan, T.C.A. *The People Next Door: The Curious History of India-Pakistan Relations.* New Delhi: HarperCollins, 2017.

Rakove, Rob. 'Taking Nonalignment Seriously'. *Foreign Policy,* 27 August 2012. http://foreignpolicy.com/2012/08/27/taking-nonalignment-seriously/.

Raman, B. *The Kaoboys of R&AW*. New Delhi: Lancer 2007.

Rich, Motoko. 'A Pacifist Japan Starts to Embrace the Military'. *New York Times*, 29 August 2017.

Russell, Bertrand. *The Problem of China*. London: George Allen & Unwin, 1922.

Saran. Shyam. *How India Sees the World: Kautilya to the 21st Century*. New Delhi: Juggernaut, 2017.

Velloor, Ravi. 'How China Is Losing the South-east Asia'. *The Straits Times*, 3 July 2015.

Zakaria, Fareed. 'Culture Is Destiny: A Conversation with Lee Kuan Yew'. *Foreign Affairs* 73, no. 2 (March 1994).

Index

About the Contributors

Tadashi Anno holds a PhD from the University of California, Berkeley. He is Associate Professor of Political Science and Director of the Institute of International Relations at Sophia University, Tokyo. His book *National Identity and Great-Power Status in Russia and Japan: Non-Western Challengers to the Liberal International Order* was published in 2018.

William J. Antholis is Director and Chief Executive Officer of the Miller Center, a non-partisan affiliate of the University of Virginia that specializes in presidential scholarship, public policy and political history. Before this, he was Managing Director and Senior Fellow at the Brookings Institution. He served at the White House and State Department during the administration of President Clinton from 1995 to 1999.

Dewi Fortuna Anwar holds a PhD from Monash University and MA and BA from SOAS, University of London. She is Professor at the Research Centre for Political Studies-Indonesian Institute of Sciences and has written widely on Indonesia's foreign policy and democratization, and on ASEAN.

Kingshuk Chatterjee is Associate Professor of history, University of Calcutta. He specializes in the Islamic language of politics in the Middle East, in particular Iran. He is the author of *Ali Shari'ati and the Shaping of Political Islam in Iran* and *A Split in the Middle: The Making of the Political Centre in Iran, 1987–2004.*

Fredrik Erixon is Director and co-founder of the European Centre for International Political Economy (ECIPE), one of Europe's leading think tanks on trade and global commercial policy. He is the author of several works on economic policy and has advised governments in Europe and Asia on trade and foreign economic policy. His latest book is *The Innovation Illusion: How So Little Is Created by So Many Working So Hard.*

Amit Das Gupta is Senior Researcher with the University of the Federal Army, Munich. After monographs about West Germany's South Asia Policy between 1949 and 1966 and a biography of former Indian Foreign Secretary Subimal Dutt, he is working on a book about the impact of the Indian Civil Service on Indian foreign policy.

Robert D. Kaplan is the author of eighteen books on foreign affairs, including *Monsoon, Asia's Cauldron,* and *The Return of Marco Polo's World.*

Zhang Lihua is Professor at the Institute of International Relations and Director of the Research Centre for China-EU Relations at Tsinghua University. She is a resident scholar at the Carnegie-Tsinghua Centre for Global Policy.

Bruno Maçães is a former Portugese minister and now Senior Advisor at Flint Global, London, advising on international political and regulatory issues. He is Senior Fellow at Renmin University and the Hudson Institute, Washington, and the author of *The Dawn of Eurasia,* and *Belt and Road.*

James Mayall is Professor Emeritus of International Relations at Cambridge University and Fellow of Sidney Sussex College and the British Academy. He has written widely on the impact of nationalism on international relations, the theory of international society and North–South relations.

Mehmet Ozkan completed his PhD in Spain and is Associate Professor at the Turkish National Police Academy, Ankara. He has extensive academic experience from South Africa, Sweden, Spain, Bosnia & Herzegovina, Colombia, India and Egypt. His studies focus on non-Western IR theory, religion and politics, the Middle East, Africa and Turkish foreign policy.

Sanjay Pulipaka is Senior Fellow at the Nehru Memorial Museum and Library, New Delhi and Adviser at the Indian Council for Research on International Economic Relations. He has been Fulbright Fellow and Visiting Fellow at Cambridge University.

Chaw Chaw Sein has a PhD from the University of Yangon, where she is head of the International Relations Department. She works as Adviser to the Union Civil Service Board and Advisory Group for establishing a Diplomatic Academy of the Ministry of Foreign Affairs.

Lee Seong-hyon is a graduate of Grinnell College, Harvard University and Tsinghua University. He is Director for the Centre for Chinese Studies and the Department of Unification Strategy at the Sejong Institute in Seoul.

Tatiana Shaumyan is head of the Centre for Indian Studies, Institute of Oriental Studies, Russian Academy of Sciences. Her interests range from India's foreign policy to international relations in South and Central Asia and the Far East in the twentieth and twenty-first centuries.

Krishnan Srinivasan is a former Indian Ambassador, Foreign Secretary and Commonwealth Deputy Secretary General. He has been Visiting Fellow at Cambridge, the Dutch Institute of Advanced Studies and the Swedish Collegium.

Hari Vasudevan is Professor Emeritus of History at Calcutta University and President of the Institute of Development Studies, Kolkata. He is a specialist on Russia and author of *Shadows of Substance, Indo-Russian Trade and Military Technical Cooperation* and *In the Footsteps of Afanasii Nikitin*.

Ravi Velloor is associate editor, leader writer and Asia columnist for the *Straits Times*, Singapore, Southeast Asia's influential newspaper. He previously worked with Bloomberg, Time-Warner and other publications. He is a regular speaker and moderator at the World Economic Forum, Jeju Forum, and the World Knowledge Forum.